Can the
Poor Save?

Can the Poor Save?

Saving & Asset Building in Individual Development Accounts

Mark Schreiner
& Michael Sherraden

Transaction Publishers
New Brunswick (U.S.A.) and London (U.K.)

Library of Congress Catalog Number: 2006048353
ISBN: 0-202-30836-7 (cloth); 0-202-30839-1 (paper)
ISBN 13: 978-0-202-30839-5
Printed in the United States of America

Library of Congress Cataloging-in-Publication Data

Schreiner, Mark, 1969-
    Can the poor save? : saving and asset building in individual development accounts / Mark Schreiner and Michael Sherraden.
        p. cm.
    Includes bibliographical references and index.
    Contents: Why saving and asset accumulation by the poor? — A theory of saving and asset building by the poor in IDAs — The American dream demonstration — Participants in ADD — Savings outcomes in ADD — IDA design, program structure, and savings outcomes — Participant char acteristics and savings outcomes — Toward inclusion in asset-based policy.
    ISBN 0-202-30836-7 (alk. paper) — ISBN 0-202-30839-1 (alk. paper)
    1. Individual development accounts. 2. Poor—Finance, Personal. 1. Sherraden, Michael W. (Michael Wayne), 1948- n. Title.

HG1660.A3S362006
332.0240086'942—dc22

                                                      2006048353

Contents

Preface and Acknowledgements

This book is a study of saving and asset accumulation in a demonstration of Individual Development Accounts (IDAs). IDAs are matched savings accounts that are, in this demonstration, targeted to low-income, low-wealth individuals. Savings in IDAs are used for home ownership, post-secondary education, microenterprise, and other developmental purposes. This study of IDAs is part of a growing body of theoretical and empirical work on assets and social policy.

An Environment of Policy Change

Fifteen years ago, almost no one in the United States or other industrialized countries was asking whether the poor can—or even should—save and accumulate assets. Asset building by the poor simply was not a point of discussion. Instead, the assumption was that the poor required income support whenever they were unable to earn income from the labor market. Income-support policies were designed to support industrial-era labor markets, characterized by relatively long-term, stable employment that required stable levels of human capital. Support included income transfers for the unemployed, single mothers with children, people with disabilities, and those who were retired. The dominant (almost exclusive) focus on income was the hallmark of the twentieth-century welfare state. Income served to support families and reduced severe hardship, and income also served to ease the social and political tensions of industrial capitalism.

During the 1990s, the discussion of social policy and well-being began to change. This was due in large part to the advent of the information age and changing labor markets. As long-term, stable, industrial employment became less common, it became increasingly apparent that traditional social policy based on income support was no longer sufficient. Information-age labor markets require higher levels of human capital. To adapt to rapidly changing demand for skills, people must continue developing their human capital across the life course. Asset holding provides greater opportunity and flexibility to do this. Also, as labor declines as a factor in production, it is more apparent that income from assets should complement income from labor to achieve greater well-being for the entire population.

Today, there is a rich and multifaceted discussion of alternatives in social policy around the globe. Indeed, it seems likely that we are in the midst of a major transformation in social policy, moving from a welfare state based almost exclusively on income support to something else. What that "something else" will turn out to be is not yet clear, and it may not become clear for several more decades. Nonetheless, a major pillar of the new social policy will probably be asset building in the form of individual accounts. This trend has already started in the United States and in other countries.

As new asset-based policy takes shape, a major issue will be: Does it include everyone? In our view, this is the most critical social policy question of our time. Accordingly, during the past decade we have undertaken a research program on inclusion in asset-based policy that has encompassed theoretical formulation, empirical research, and policy design. Our hope is that this work will help inform and promote more inclusive policies.

The Current Study

As mentioned, this book addresses saving by the poor in IDAs. The analysis is based on a unique data set with monthly bank statements for individual participants. Some of the measures of savings outcomes are new. For example, the measures highlight how saving happens through time (and define *saving* as moving resources through time). Also, the measures highlight how saving occurs in several stages and how problems and/or facilitation can occur in any of them.

Policy implications of this research may reach beyond IDAs and saving by the poor. For example, empirical associations between savings outcomes and match rates in IDAs may help inform the design of other subsidized savings policies such as Individual Retirement Accounts and 401(k) plans. Likewise, results on financial education for IDAs may help inform the design of adult financial-education courses. Such courses have become much more common during the past decade, in part due to the expansion of IDAs. The financial-education requirements in IDAs have not only generated greater awareness of financial education but have also helped create a stronger demand for high-quality financial-education curricula.

Academically, the study's detailed data and the analyses of the associations between institutional characteristics and savings outcomes for the poor may help inform theories of saving. Let us briefly place this is perspective.

Today, behavioral, institutional, development, and policy economists are leading a near-revolution in saving theory (for example, Choi, Laibson, and Madrian, 2004; Ashraf, et al., 2003; Mullainathan and Thaler, 2000; Rutherford, 2000; Owens and Wisniwiski, 1999). In this rapidly growing body of work, the intellectual focus is mostly on individuals, including their mental short cuts, limited horizons, misjudgments of the future, less-than-rational decisions, tendencies toward inertia, and so forth. All of this can be seen as a refinement on the extreme assumptions entailed in "rational choice" in neoclassical economics. In essence, this research agenda is bringing more of the complexity of humans onto the agenda for analysis (Thaler, 2000).

Our approach is consistent with this body of work, but might be viewed as the other side of the coin. Instead of focusing on individuals, we focus on the institutions themselves for policy design. This might be seen as an elaboration of the concept of "constraints" in neoclassical economics. Our aim is to bring more of the complexity of saving structures and incentives onto the agenda for analysis (Sherraden, 1991; Beverly and Sherraden, 1997; Schreiner, et al., 2001; Sherraden, Schreiner, and Beverly, 2003; Sherraden and Barr, 2004). We take this approach because we have reason to believe—and the current study bears out—that institutional features are associated with savings outcomes. In brief, we are less interested in the characteristics of individuals and more interested in the characteristics of policies and programs because we suspect that these are a central "story" in savings outcomes. To illustrate with a rhetorical question, how much retirement savings would there be in the absence of 401(k) plans?

Also, in our view, theory and evidence offer more direct policy implications when seen from an institutional perspective. If we test and find an association between savings outcomes and the use of automatic transfer, the level of the match rate, or the design of financial education, then it is a small step to get to implications for policy design. To illustrate, if there is an association between savings outcomes and the use of automatic transfer—and if this association is causal—then increasing access to automatic transfer (an inexpensive intervention) might lead to large improvements in savings outcomes. For example, some current proposals would allow taxpayers to choose to receive part of their tax refund (much of which for the poor comes from the Earned Income Tax Credit) as a check and part as an automatic transfer to a savings account. If higher match rates increase participation, then efforts to improve inclusion might include increases in match rates. Finally, if financial education improves savings outcomes, then financial education might be made more readily available in schools and community organizations.

Academic Context

No scholarship stands on its own. This book rests on theoretical, empirical, and policy studies done in the past two decades. Sen's writings on capabilities, such as *Development as Freedom* (1999), can be seen as framing a larger discussion within which asset-based theory and policy represent particular applications. In *Starting Even: An Equal Opportunity Program to Combat the Nation's New Poverty* (1988), Haveman proposes accounts for teenagers for welfare purposes. In *The Safety Net as Ladder: Transfer Payments and Economic Development* (1988), Friedman proposes that public assistance should provide not only consumption support (a "hand out") but also development support (a "hand up"). In *Assets and the Poor: A New American Welfare Policy*

(1991), Sherraden introduces "asset-based policy", sketches a theory of well-being based on assets, and proposes matched savings for the poor through Individual Development Accounts. Oliver and Shapiro, in *Black Wealth/White Wealth: A New Perspective on Racial Inequality* (1995), define racial inequality in terms of wealth, explain how such inequality came about, and show why it persists. Ackerman and Alstott offer in *The Stakeholder Society* (1999) a proposal for large "citizenship grants" to everyone at age 18. In *Being Black, Living in the Red: Race, Wealth, and Social Policy in America* (1999), Conley systematically argues that economic status, especially wealth, is more relevant today than race *per se*. Shapiro and Wolff, in *Assets for the Poor: The Benefits of Spreading Asset Ownership* (2001), provide an edited volume with studies of asset distribution and attention to policy. In *Top Heavy: The Increasing Inequality of Wealth in America and What Can Be Done About It* (2002), Wolff and Leone describe U.S. wealth inequality and offer policy proposals. In *The Hidden Cost of Being Black* (2004), Shapiro details the dynamics of asset accumulation by race and the potential role of "transformative assets" at particular junctures in the life course. In *Inclusion in the American Dream: Assets, Poverty, and Public Policy* (2005), Sherraden edits a group of essays that update research and policy in asset building.

Perhaps the key academic works are by Sen for reframing the meaning of well-being and development around the globe; Wolff for tracking the distribution of wealth in the United States over many years, long before it became a hot topic; Oliver, Shapiro, and Conley for illuminating the role of wealth in racial inequality in America with incisive theories and empirical investigation; and Sherraden for naming asset-based policy, offering theories on institutions for saving and the effects of asset holding, and suggesting a simple, politically feasible way to begin to include the poor in asset building.

Together, the above publications have put the idea of inclusion in asset building on the policy agenda. The question is no longer whether the poor should save and build assets; instead, the question is how to help them do it. In this book, we begin to answer this question. We analyze evidence from IDAs, a specific, concrete policy proposal that is already being implemented. We examine how savings outcomes are related both with the characteristics of participants and with the characteristics of programs and of IDA design. Attention centers on the institutional characteristics that comprise policy and program design. This book is an example of applied social science; we test theoretical constructs against data from a demonstration to find out how a saving policy is working and how it might be improved.

Support and Guidance

Support for this study came from the foundations that funded the American Dream Demonstration (ADD). They are the Ford Foundation, Charles Stewart Mott Foundation, Joyce Foundation, F.B. Heron Foundation, John D. and

Catherine T. MacArthur Foundation, Citigroup Foundation, Fannie Mae Foundation, Levi Strauss Foundation, Ewing Marion Kauffman Foundation, Rockefeller Foundation, Metropolitan Life Foundation, and the Moriah Fund. The Ford Foundation and the Charles Stewart Mott Foundation provided additional support for this book. These foundations are represented by talented leaders and program officers too numerous to mention, though we would like to acknowledge the particularly significant contributions to this research by Melvin Oliver, Ronald Mincy, Lisa Mensah, and Frank DeGiovanni at the Ford Foundation; Sharon King and Kate Starr at the F.B. Heron Foundation; Benita Melton at the Charles Stuart Mott Foundation; Andrés Dominguez at the Ewing Marion Kauffman Foundation; and Sibyl Jacobson at the Metropolitan Life Foundation. The Common Counsel Foundation provided a quiet place to write at Mesa Refuge; Michael Sherraden is grateful to Peter Barnes for making this possible. Philanthropy is one of the great strengths of America. We hope ADD reflects the very best in American philanthropy: supporting an innovative idea, testing it thoroughly, and—based on sound evidence—informing policy and program design.

Research in ADD was also guided by an expert Evaluation Advisory Committee. The members were Margaret Clark, Claudia Coulton, Kathryn Edin, John Else, Robert Friedman, Irving Garfinkel, Karen Holden, Laurence Kotlikoff, Robert Plotnick, Salome Raheim, Marguerite Robinson, Clemente Ruíz Durán, and Thomas Shapiro. We are grateful for their work on the research design and for their reviews and recommendations of analyses and reports.

Demonstration

We express our appreciation to Bob Friedman, who, as founder and chair of the Corporation for Enterprise Development, conceived of ADD. We also thank Brian Grossman, René Bryce-Laporte, and other staff at the Corporation for Enterprise Development for their work in the implementation of ADD and for their cooperation with the research. The productive working relationship between the Corporation for Enterprise Development and the Center for Social Development has played a major role in innovation and knowledge building for IDAs and for asset-based policy in general.

We are especially grateful to the host organizations in ADD and to the staff who ran the IDA programs. From the outset, they were committed to ADD research. For this study, program staff operated the Management Information System for Individual Development Accounts (MIS IDA) and spent considerable time with CSD staff to check and to correct data. Their time and effort made this part of the ADD research possible.

Software, Data Collection, Research Support

To our knowledge, this is the first time that software has been created to track all participants in a policy demonstration and also to serve as a management information system. This has required large investments to create and upgrade the MIS IDA software, provide support, facilitate data collection, make the data as accurate as possible, and undertake analysis. Over the past nine years, a large research team at CSD has made this possible, and every member of the team cannot be fully acknowledged here. We especially want to acknowledge Lissa Johnson, who managed the ADD research and led the creation and refinement of MIS IDA; Margaret Clancy, who created and implemented quality control in data collection in MIS IDA QC and who worked countless hours with program sites to ensure accurate data; and Dan Kelley, who wrote code for recent upgrades for MIS IDA and who manages the MIS IDA technical support line. Other key members of this research team have included Min Zhan, Jami Curley, and Michal Grinstein-Weiss. A much larger team at CSD, involved in other ADD research methods and administrative support, made invaluable contributions throughout the study.

We appreciate the administrative staff of the George Warren Brown School of Social Work at Washington University in Saint Louis. Especially, we are grateful to Dean Shanti Khinduka and Chancellor Mark Wrighton for their steady support of CSD's research on asset building.

Who May Find this Book Useful?

Can the Poor Save? Saving and Asset Accumulation in Individual Development Accounts may be useful for economists studying savings outcomes and the theory of the household; sociologists studying the mechanisms that transmit social class and economic inequality from parents to children; social workers and policy analysts studying the interaction between social policy and poverty; federal, state, and local policy makers looking for long-term development programs to complement short-term assistance programs; workers in community-development and social-service agencies designing savings programs targeted to the poor; home and consumer economists and extension agents searching for practical ways to help households save more; teachers and students in courses dealing with social policy and social issues; the U.S. general public debating individual accounts in Social Security and elsewhere; financial professionals looking for new markets for saving and investment services; and policymakers and scholars in other countries that are starting asset-building policies.

Contributions of this Research

Research on savings outcomes in ADD has informed developments in federal and state policy for IDAs and for other progressive savings strategies. Documentation of the simple fact that some poor people can save in IDAs has been remarkably important for policy purposes. For example, ADD data have directly influenced IDA policy in more than thirty states; the federal Assets for Independence Act; President Clinton's proposal for Universal Savings Accounts; President Bush's support for IDAs; Tony Blair's new Child Trust Fund (an asset-building account for every newborn in the United Kingdom); an IDA policy demonstration in Canada; Family Development Accounts in Taipei, Taiwan; a matched savings plan in Australia; and IDA projects in Uganda and elsewhere. Applied social research does not always have such extensive impacts.

Theory, empirical evidence, and policy models will gradually become more specified as the academic and applied discussion of asset-based policy grows. With good fortune, this book may be a contribution toward that larger effort. In this study, we have attempted to improve the measurement of savings, articulate a theory of saving and asset accumulation, pose questions derived from this theory, take these questions to the field in a demonstration, collect detailed data, and bring the data to bear on the questions. Though a great deal remains unanswered, we hope the book might contribute to a theory of saving, evidence on saving (especially among the poor), and asset-based policy design.

Mark Schreiner, Senior Scholar
Michael Sherraden, Director
Center for Social Development
Washington University in Saint Louis
June 2004

1

Why Saving and Asset Accumulation by the Poor?

Most Americans take as self-evident—and a good deal of research tends to support—Thomas Jefferson's idea that asset ownership is good for individuals, families, communities, and society as a whole. Indeed, the "pursuit of property" was almost enshrined as an inalienable right in the Declaration of Independence. Unfortunately, Jefferson's view of who should own assets was limited to white men. The twenty-first century requires a new vision of asset building, one that extends to all people. Asset building—both in the United States and elsewhere—should be inclusive.

We think that Individual Development Accounts (IDAs) can be a step toward greater inclusion in asset-building policy. IDAs are subsidized savings accounts. Unlike other subsidized savings accounts such as Individual Retirement Accounts or 401(k) plans, IDAs are targeted to the poor, provide subsidies through matches rather than through tax breaks, and require participants to attend financial education. Participants accrue matches as they save for assets that increase long-term well-being and financial self-sufficiency. Typical matched uses are home purchase, post-secondary education, and microenterprise. Accounts can be opened at birth and can remain open for a lifetime. Funds may come from public or private sources, and funding partnerships are common. IDAs are a conceptually simple community-development and public-policy tool that may be adapted to a wide range of applications and circumstances.

This book is a scientific attempt to ask whether evidence from the American Dream Demonstration on IDAs supports the view that asset-based policy should include everyone. The central question is whether the poor can save and build assets when they have access to structures and incentives to do so. We also ask how IDA design is associated with savings outcomes in IDAs. Our hope in this work is to help inform the design of an inclusive asset-building policy.

Assets, Development, and Public Policy

The best social policy aims to improve the well-being of the poor by moving beyond mere consumption toward what Sen (1985 and 1999) calls "capabilities." Improving capabilities usually requires saving and asset accumulation. This book focuses on saving and asset accumulation for homes, post-secondary education, microenterprise, and other developmental purposes. The goal is not to amass money for its own sake but rather to facilitate human, social, and economic development.

While saving is not easy for anyone, it is more difficult for the poor because they have less left over after they buy necessities and because scarce resources and the resulting limitations on their experiences may push thoughts of saving out of their worldview. As Lewis (1966) recognized, if the poor appear to have a short-term time horizon, it is largely due to the necessities of survival and to the circumstances of poverty.

Poverty itself, however, is not the only barrier to asset accumulation by the poor, nor is it necessarily even the most important barrier. Although the U.S. government helps the non-poor to save and build assets, it erects barriers for the poor, providing them with less access to asset-building subsidies and—when the poor do have access—smaller subsidies. The most prominent examples are retirement accounts, home ownership, and human capital, the three types of assets in which most Americans hold the bulk of their wealth. Tax breaks for retirement accounts are greater for high-income people in high tax brackets than for low-income people in low tax brackets, and the automatic mechanisms by which contributions are usually made are, for the most part, offered only to non-poor workers. Subsidies for home ownership increase with the size of the mortgage and with the level of appreciation, but the poor are less likely to own a home, more likely to have smaller mortgages if they do own a home, and are less likely to benefit from appreciation. (This holds in particular for poor African Americans; see Katz Reid, 2004, and Oliver and Shapiro, 1995). In terms of human capital, school-finance policy channels the largest subsidies to the non-poor, a structure reinforced by subtle, pervasive systems of ascribed privilege and social connections, the most obvious being residential segregation and racial discrimination. In the end, more than 90 percent of federal support for home ownership and retirement accounts (more than $200 billion per year) goes to households who earn more than $50,000 per year and who are disproportionately Caucasian. If the government is going to heavily subsidize asset-building, then it would seem fair to include all people equally.

Not only does policy fail to give the poor access to saving incentives, but it also places disincentives in their path; if their assets exceed certain limits, then they lose eligibility for means-tested public assistance such as Temporary Assistance to Needy Families ("welfare"), Food Stamps, and Medicaid. Overall, as public policy has become more asset-based over the past 30 years, it has become less inclusive of the poor (Sherraden, 1991 and 2001a). In effect, America has a dual asset-building policy with incentives for the non-poor and disincentives for the poor. Not only is this dual policy unjust, but it also fails to recognize that assets are the foundation of development, the only reliable road out of poverty. Greater equity generally improves the well-being of society as a whole, so if the goal is social well-being—and it is difficult to justify any other goal—then development is a central issue and, rather than a dual asset-building policy, it would make more sense to include all people. As a minimum standard, everyone should have the same level of subsidies. And, because of the likely positive pay-offs in development, it might even make sense to give higher asset-building subsidies to the poor.

Toward an Inclusive Asset-Based Policy

How can public policy promote saving and asset accumulation for all? Individual Development Accounts (IDAs) are a policy strategy designed to address existing constraints and improve poor people's access to institutions that promote saving and asset accumulation (Sherraden, 1988 and 1991). The short-term purpose of IDAs is to demonstrate that the poor might save and accumulate assets if provided an opportunity to do so. The long-term purpose of IDAs is to inform the creation of an asset-based policy that includes the whole population and provides equal or greater subsidies to the poor, whether this be a universal IDA (as originally proposed in Sherraden, 1991), a universal 401(k) plan, an expansion of the federal Thrift Savings Plan to include everyone, or some other policy design.

In the 1990s, IDAs were implemented in many community-based organizations, at first with funds from philanthropic foundations. At this writing, there are hundreds of IDA programs in the United States. Most states have some type of IDA-enabling policy, and federal legislation has provided a legal structure and a funding mechanism for IDAs. As a policy innovation, this is a good start. As a policy, however, IDAs are still insignificant in scope. Tens of millions of Americans are poor, but only tens of thousands have access to IDAs.

It is extraordinarily challenging in America to enact significant social policies for the poor. For the non-poor, the Congress readily enacts large asset-building programs such as 401(k) plans and Individual Retirement Accounts with little debate and strong bipartisan support. These asset-based policies distribute huge public subsidies through the tax system, though the poor benefit little. When these policies were enacted, the legislation did not call for a demonstration of their efficacy. Congress did not mandate research to ask if Americans could save in these policies nor to ask whether the savings would be "new" savings instead of "reshuffled" assets. Instead, the policies were enacted because they seemed to most legislators like a good idea. But when it comes to the poor, the assumptions in political debate and legislation are different. It is inevitably an uphill struggle to include the poor in existing policies, and more challenging still to enact a new, large-scale, and inclusive asset-based policy. Why is this? At best, policy makers have simply over-looked the fact that the poor—like everyone else—require assets for long-term development. At worst, there is suspicion that the poor are unworthy or incapable of acquiring assets and using them for development. For these reasons, IDAs so far have been limited to small programs and demonstrations.

To be clear, the point is not that the poor require special social policies but rather that social policy for the poor is held to a different political standard. Savings subsidies for the non-poor are more or less rubber-stamped, with in-stant, lasting consequences to the tune of hundreds of billions of dollars. In contrast, savings subsidies for the poor—with much smaller consequences for the budget and likely much larger consequences for social well-being—re-quire debate, demonstrations, experiments, and political wrangling. In our view, it is likely that policies for the non-poor are subjected to too little scru-tiny, not that policies for the poor are subjected to too much. In any case, the standards are not the same. Consequently, this book reports on a demonstra-tion rather than the first five years of a universal, permanent policy. This is the policy reality. It reminds us of a line in the novel *Plainsong* by Haruf (1999): when the young protagonist in a small town in eastern Colorado wishes she were somewhere else, she is told, "You are here now, honey; this is where you are." In policy terms with IDAs, we are here now; this is where we are. We study this demonstration in the hope that it will help to inform a more inclusive asset-based policy.

This study comes at a critical time, as debate intensifies on the merits of individual accounts in Social Security, health care, education, job training, and many other areas of social policy. The shift to asset-based policy is per-haps the greatest social-policy transformation of our time, yet it is little dis-cussed (Sherraden, 1997 and 2003). Asset accounts for various social purposes become more common with each passing year, and the poor are largely ex-cluded. IDAs are an attempt to give the poor the same level of access to asset-building policies as the non-poor. The research in this book offers policy lessons from the first major demonstration of IDAs.

Can the Poor Save in IDAs?

The key questions in this study are: Can the poor save in IDAs? If so, do all the poor save? Who among the poor can save? How much do they save? How is IDA design associated with savings outcomes? What have we learned with some degree of confidence, and what questions remain?

In this book, we analyze saving by IDA participants in the American Dream Demonstration (ADD). ADD was the first detailed, systematic study of IDAs or of matched savings by the poor of any kind. The data on savings outcomes are unusually detailed and accurate and permit a great range and depth of analysis. As far as we know, this is the first large study of saving by anyone—poor or non-poor—that uses monthly data from bank statements.

Toward a Theory of Saving and Asset Accumulation in IDAs

IDAs aim to do more than transfer resources to the poor. Of course, resources are good to have, if only because they can be converted into consumption. With IDAs, however, the institutional structure explicitly communicates the expectation that the resources transferred are to be saved rather than consumed. Of course, standard welfare transfers can also be saved. How are IDAs different? As the theory developed in this book suggests, the institutional features of IDAs are designed to promote saving and asset accumulation. IDA programs explicitly ask and expect participants to save their transfers and to accumulate assets in forms such as homes, human capital, or small businesses that are unlikely to be quickly consumed and that also promote long-term development.

The institutional package of IDAs matters because people are not the rational, omniscient beings assumed in economic theory. People are subject to suggestion, and they respond to patterns of "choices" that are required, facilitated, or worn smooth by public policy. Such choices take less effort than to imagine all possible choices and then to weigh the probabilities of various consequences. Institutional theory suggests that the structure of IDAs encourages the poor to see saving as an option that is easy to choose and will likely have positive consequences. The theory makes the following propositions:

- The existence of IDAs forges a social pattern because it sends the message that the poor can save.
- IDAs give poor people access to a way to commit to save.
- Matches increase the return on saving, increase the asset accumulation from a given level of savings, and attract people to IDAs.
- IDAs require participants to attend financial education that provides knowledge of how to save and information about the rewards of saving.
- In their minds, participants may turn the match cap—technically a limit—into a goal.
- Monthly statements give feedback and show progress toward goals.
- Program staff and peers provide informal encouragement. A focus on success makes saving easier.
- IDA programs ask for monthly deposits. This may help saving to become a habit.
- Through budgets, goals, and plans, IDAs help participants to focus on the future and increase future orientation.
- IDAs point out goals (such as home ownership or post-secondary education) that people might not see (or might not see as worthwhile) on their own.

- Mild informal discouragement of unmatched withdrawals helps to curb dis-saving.

This study analyzes associations—both theoretical and empirical—between the institutional features of IDAs and savings outcomes in ADD. The resulting policy implications are likely to be informative beyond IDAs. Institutional theory and evidence are probably the main contributions of the book, both intellectually and practically.

Toward a Theory of "Asset Effects"

Sherraden (1991) introduced the concept of *asset effects*, defined as the impacts of the ownership of assets as distinct from the impacts of the use of assets. Humans are forward-looking, and current well-being depends in part on expected future well-being. People with more assets in the present expect to have more resources in the future. Thus—for purely economic reasons—they expect to be happier. "Asset effects" occur when ownership improves expected future well-being and thus, for psychological reasons, improves current well-being. Not only do owners think differently, but others also treat them differently. It is possible that the social and political effects of ownership matter even more than the individual economic effects. Studies consistently find positive associations between ownership and a wide range of positive outcomes, but they fall short of proving causality, sometimes because the theory of asset effects is still incomplete but usually because of imperfect data and a lack of variation in asset ownership that does not depend on the actions of the owner. The most important work in this agenda still lies ahead.

Asset effects are critical as a primary rationale for an inclusive asset-based policy. If such effects exist, and if their benefits outweigh policy costs, then there would be a strong case for asset-building policy for all. Unfortunately, this study does not directly address these central questions.

The American Dream Demonstration

This book examines saving and asset accumulation in ADD, a demonstration of IDAs in fourteen programs across the United States. The first IDA in ADD was opened in September of 1997, and in all but one program, only deposits made through December 31, 2003, could be matched.

Data come from the Management Information System for Individual Development Accounts (MIS IDA), a software package that offers tools for program management and evaluation (Johnson, Hinterlong, and Sherraden, 2001). Data in MIS IDA were collected by program staff and may be the best ever assembled on high-frequency saving by the poor. In particular, records of cash flows in IDAs come from bank statements.

Given the unique data, we develop several new measures of savings outcomes that capture not only the final balance but also the frequency of deposits, the movement of resources through time, the occurrence of withdrawals (matched and unmatched), and the use of matched withdrawals for asset purchases. Together, these measures represent an unusually thorough view of savings outcomes.

Previous research reports relying on MIS IDA data from ADD have included the *Start-Up Evaluation Report* (Sherraden et al., 1999) which monitored ADD's start-up period through June 30, 1998; *Saving Patterns in IDA Programs* (Sherraden et al., 2000) which covered programs, participants, and saving patterns through June 30, 1999; *Savings and Asset Accumulation in Individual Development Accounts* (Schreiner et al., 2001) which analyzed savings outcomes in-depth through June 30, 2000; and *Saving Performance in the American Dream Demonstration* (Schreiner, Clancy, and Sherraden, 2002) which provided a concise summary of savings outcomes through December 31, 2001. This book builds on these previous reports, but with updated data, improved measures of savings outcomes, more detailed analyses, greater attention to institutional features, and more in-depth discussion of policy lessons.

Key Findings in ADD

The main statistical analyses use a two-step "Heckit" regression. For all participants, the first-step regression looks at associations between program and participant characteristics and the likelihood of being a "saver." For "savers," the second-step regression looks at associations between characteristics and the level of monthly net IDA savings.

Do IDAs work? Policy interest in MIS IDA data from ADD has focused almost exclusively on this question. In ADD, poor participants did indeed save and accumulate assets in IDAs. Savings outcomes included:

- Net IDA savings per month eligible for matchable deposits was $16.60.
- Participants saved about 42 cents for every dollar that could have been matched.
- Participants made a deposit in about one of every two months in which an IDA was open.
- With an average match rate of 1.88:1, the average participant accumulated $1,609 in IDAs, equivalent to $576 per year eligible for matchable deposits.
- About 52 percent of participants were "savers" with net IDA savings of $100 or more.
- The IDA saving rate as a share of income in ADD was about 1.1 percent.
- The average participant moved 1,090 dollar-years through time.
- Net deposits increased markedly in tax season. Apparently, IDA participants saved part of their tax refunds (much of which came from the Earned Income Tax Credit).

If poor people saved in ADD, what participant and program characteristics might have caused these outcomes? Social-science research can rarely claim to pinpoint causes and rule out all plausible competing explanations, usually because it cannot control for all relevant factors. Statistical associations, however, can be consistent (or not) with predicted patterns of causality, and as the analysis controls for more and more factors, the weight of the mix shifts more and more towards causality.

We turn first to participant characteristics. Controlling for a wide range of participant and program characteristics, the regression analysis in this study suggests that:

- Income was not strongly associated with being a "saver" nor with the level of net IDA savings among "savers."
- Poor participants with lower incomes saved more—relative to their income—than poor participants with higher incomes.
- Poor participants who owned homes, cars, land or property, financial investments, or small businesses were more likely to be "savers" than those who did not own these assets.
- Due to characteristics correlated with race/ethnicity that were omitted from the regression, there were differences in savings outcomes among groups.
- Women were more likely than men to be "savers." Among "savers," gender was not associated with the level of monthly net IDA savings.
- Participants who were married were more likely to be "savers" than never-married participants.
- Each additional year from the ages of 14 to 20 was associated with a decrease in the likelihood of being a "saver" and the level of monthly net IDA savings. Additional years after that were associated with increases in both savings outcomes.
- Participants with a college degree were more likely to be "savers," and they also saved more.
- IDA participants who enrolled planning for home purchase were the least likely to be "savers." Among "savers," however, this group had the highest monthly net IDA savings.
- Most measures of receipt of means-tested cash transfers ("welfare") were not associated with savings outcomes. (Receipt of Food Stamps was associated with less monthly net IDA savings for "savers.")
- The number of adults and children in the household was not associated with savings outcomes.
- Place of residence (urban versus rural) was not associated with savings outcomes.
- Employment status was not statistically associated with savings outcomes.

Especially noteworthy are the weak associations of savings outcomes with income, employment status, and most measures of welfare receipt. After controlling for other factors in the regression, even the very poor, unemployed, and past and current welfare recipients in ADD had about the same savings outcomes as others.

If many individual characteristics were only weakly associated with savings outcomes, what else might be considered? As noted above, the theoretical perspective in this book is that institutional characteristics might influence savings outcomes. We turn to these next:

- Higher match rates were associated with an increased likelihood of being a "saver." For "savers," however, a match rate of 2:1 was associated with less net IDA savings per month than a match rate of 1:1.
- A $1 increase in the match cap (eligibility for matchable deposits) was associated with a $0.57 increase in net IDA savings.
- Compared with lifetime match caps, annual match caps were associated with a greater likelihood of being a "saver" but with a lower monthly net IDA savings.
- The use of automatic transfer was associated with large increases in the likelihood of being a "saver," but—for "savers"—was not associated with monthly net IDA savings.
- The more time IDA participants had to make matchable deposits, the more likely they were to be "savers." For "savers," more time was associated with lower monthly net IDA savings.
- Attendance of general financial education (up to ten hours) was associated with large increases in monthly net IDA savings.

Overall, the structural characteristics of IDA programs were related to savings outcomes. This suggests that policy might be able to affect savings outcomes through institutional design.

Policy Implications

What lessons can we draw from these results? Some policy implications are related to the savings outcomes measured in ADD, and others are related to institutional characteristics.

- The poor can save in subsidized savings structures, and as such IDAs or similar programs could be a step toward inclusive asset-based policy.
- A broad range of poor people can save in IDAs. For example, the association between income and saving in ADD was weak. Indeed, the participants with the lowest incomes saved more, relative to income, than those who were not quite so poor. Also, welfare receipt—with the exception of Food Stamps—was not associated with savings outcomes. Employment status was also not associated with savings outcomes. Based on these results, there is no research basis for limiting IDA participation to only the working poor or only the poor with higher incomes.
- At the same time, people who started with more assets were more likely to end up being "savers." This may indicate that saving in IDAs is not

easy for the poor, and those who start in a better financial position were better able to stick with it.

- Most participants in ADD were women, and women were more likely to be "savers." We do not know if this has something to do with gender per se (for example, perhaps women are better long-term planners when it comes to family well-being) or with factors omitted from the regression that may have been both associated with gender and causes of savings outcomes. In any case, this bodes well for the possibility of asset-building for poor single mothers.

- All racial and ethnic groups saved in IDAs. Thus, there is no empirical reason to think that IDAs do not "work" for any group.

- Nonetheless, savings outcomes were associated with race/ethnicity. Of course, it was not race/ethnicity per se that caused differences in outcomes, but rather socially produced (not genetic) factors that were associated with race and were omitted from the regression. For example, people of one race may live farther from depository institutions, or they may have social networks that tend to deplete available resources. Still, differences in savings outcomes by race are discomfiting. More research on the causes of these outcomes is called for, and policy should be designed to reduce and eliminate such differences.

- Higher match rates were associated with a greater likelihood of being a "saver." For a given level of savings, higher matches increase asset accumulation. Higher match rates in ADD, however, were associated with lower levels of monthly net IDA savings among "savers," perhaps because they allowed participants to reach a fixed goal with less saving. This highlights a possible tension for match-rate policy and IDA's goals of inclusion, saving, and asset accumulation.

- Apparently, IDA participants in ADD turned match caps into goals, as higher match caps were associated with higher net IDA savings. At the same time, higher match caps were usually combined with lower match rates, so IDA policy might have to consider a trade-off between greater participation due to higher match rates and greater savings due to higher match caps.

- In ADD, longer time caps were associated with a greater likelihood of being a "saver" but, for "savers," with lower monthly net IDA savings. We speculate that in a permanent policy, lifetime effects on saving and asset accumulation per eligible person would likely be higher than in short-lived programs such as ADD.

- People who used automatic transfer to their IDAs were much more likely to be "savers." Like the non-poor, the poor apparently saved best when they took the monthly choice of whether to save out of their own hands.

- There was a sharp spike in IDA deposits in March and April, probably associated with income-tax refunds (augmented for many ADD participants by the Earned Income Tax Credit). The poor may have the most cash (and thus may be most able to save) in tax season. Facilitating the automatic transfer of tax refunds into IDAs might help build assets.

- Like the non-poor, the poor often save in fits and starts, and most IDA participants—even those who eventually made matched withdrawals—made some unmatched withdrawals. This suggests that short-term programs and rigid saving guidelines are not desirable. If the goal is to improve the well-being of the poor in the long term, IDAs should be universal and permanent, enroll everyone automatically, keep accounts open even with a zero balance, allow unmatched withdrawals, and not impose deadlines for deposits or matched withdrawals.
- Additional hours of financial education (up to ten) were associated with higher net IDA savings. At the same time, classes are costly (Schreiner, Clancy, and Sherraden, 2002; Schreiner, 2004a). More research is needed to know whether the long-term benefits justify the costs. Understanding exactly who benefits from financial education would also help to target resources.

Overall Results and Implications

The multiple findings and policy lessons summarized above can be boiled down into two observations. First, although many participant characteristics are associated with savings outcomes, the results of this study do not indicate that the very poor, the unemployed, or those on welfare cannot save and build assets in IDAs.

Second, institutional characteristics—that is, the structure, rules, and the implementation of the savings program—were associated with savings outcomes. For example, the match rate was associated with both the likelihood of being a "saver" and also—for "savers"—with the level of net IDA savings. Participants who were expected to save more—that is, who faced a less-restrictive match cap—did in fact save more, probably because they turned the limit into a target. Participants who used automatic transfer were more likely to be "savers." Financial education—up to a point—was also associated with greater savings outcomes.

These two observations—that some participant characteristics were less important than might be expected, and that several institutional characteristics were important—together suggest that attempts to include all Americans—even the poor—in asset-building would most fruitfully focus not on changing people but rather on changing policies.

Although this study offers a wealth of lessons about how poor people can save and accumulate assets in IDAs, there is of course much that remains to be learned. For example, the data cannot tell *how* or *why* the poor save in IDAs. Also, the data cannot tell whether the poor save more with IDAs than they would have saved otherwise. Still, this book is a significant step forward in knowledge of saving and asset accumulation by the poor. The general public and policymakers have generally assumed that the poor could not (or would not) save. ADD indicates that the poor very likely can save, in particular if they have access to saving incentives and structures similar to those available to the non-poor.

Plan for the Book

In this chapter, we have provided the motivation for this study and a brief summary of key savings outcomes and lessons for policy. In chapter 2, we specify the theoretical perspective that explains why we expect IDAs to encourage saving and asset accumulation by the poor. Chapter 3 describes the set-up of the American Dream Demonstration (ADD) and the design characteristics of IDAs in ADD.

Chapter 4 presents a portrait of participants in ADD. Overall, participants mostly came from the "working poor," probably because most ADD programs targeted this group. Among the "working poor," participants were disadvantaged in that they were disproportionately female, African American, and never married.

In chapter 5, we discuss savings outcomes in ADD. Savings in IDAs are built up from several elements. Deposits and interest increase balances; fees and withdrawals (matched or unmatched) decrease balances. Match rates affect total accumulation. The process of saving and asset accumulation can be seen in terms of three stages: "putting in," "keeping in," and "taking out." Because no previous research has used monthly data on cash flows from bank statements, this chapter develops several new summary measures of savings outcomes through time. The chapter also discusses the annual spike in deposits during tax season as well as matched and unmatched withdrawals from IDAs. We ask whether programs should allow unmatched withdrawals and how to permit them in emergencies while minimizing the effects on asset accumulation. We also discuss how ADD participants used matched withdrawals and the normative question of what types of assets IDAs "should" match. The aggregate savings outcomes reported in this chapter matter not only because they suggest how people save in IDAs but also because they inform efforts to expand access to IDAs. For example, financial intermediaries that hold IDAs want to know the likely number, frequency, and size of deposits and withdrawals. Likewise, new IDA programs can use the figures to plan and to set benchmarks.

In chapters 6 and 7, we turn to estimates from a two-step "Heckit" regression. Both steps control for a wide range of program and participant characteristics. The first step estimates the likelihood that a participant is a "saver" with net IDA savings of $100 or more. The second step estimates the level of net IDA savings for "savers." The two-step procedure controls for omitted characteristics associated both with the probability of being a "saver" and with the level of net IDA savings.

Chapter 6 examines associations between savings outcomes and key aspects of IDA design, including match rates, match caps, match-cap structure, use of automatic transfer, time caps, financial education, and restrictions on unmatched withdrawals. These associations matter for three reasons. First,

IDA design is under program control and is thus amenable to policy. Second, the empirical relationships between these potential policy levers and savings outcomes are largely unknown, whether for poor participants in IDAs or for non-poor participants in other subsidized savings structures such as Individual Retirement Accounts or 401(k) plans. Third, the "institutional theory of saving" of Sherraden (1991), Beverly and Sherraden (1999), and Schreiner et al. (2001) proposes that institutional characteristics—and not just participant characteristics—matter for savings outcomes.

In chapter 7, we examine the associations between savings outcomes and the characteristics of participants in ADD. Key results are summarized above. While policy usually can do little to affect individual characteristics, knowledge of how savings outcomes are associated with individual characteristics can nonetheless inform policy design. For example, if Latino immigrants saved less in IDAs (this study provides no evidence of this), then policy might explicitly include outreach in Spanish.

Chapter 8 summarizes and comments on the key lessons from the analysis of ADD for savings and asset accumulation by the poor in IDAs. The main conclusion is that the poor can save in IDAs and that the possibility of saving by the poor cannot be dismissed. This final chapter also reviews lessons for IDA policy design and discusses some of the broad questions about asset-based policy.

2

A Theory of Saving and Asset Building by the Poor in IDAs

The surest way to steadily improve long-term well-being is to accumulate assets. Without control over resources that last through time, people usually do not have the means to live the life that they want. This holds whether the assets are in the form of human capital (such as education or experience), physical capital (such as houses or cars), social capital (such as networks of friendships or rights of citizenship), or financial capital (such as balances in bank accounts).

The traditional view sees development and well-being more in terms of income than assets. This focus, however, mostly reflects valuation difficulties and a misguided emphasis on consumption rather than capabilities. In terms of valuation, assets are more difficult to measure than income. For example, while income must be measured each year for tax purposes, the non-financial assets (human capital and houses) that make up the bulk of most people's wealth are infrequently marked to market.

In addition, income is often mistakenly equated with well-being, for a couple of reasons. First, most people consume most of their current income, so consumption (at least in the short term) tends to go up and down as income rises and falls. Second, traditional economic models assume that well-being derives only from consumption and not also from production, contemplation, participation, existence through time, and the presence of a menu of life options.

The consumption-based view of well-being leads to an income-based view of development. In contrast, a capability-based view of well-being leads to an asset-based view of development. Compared with the paradigm of consumption, the paradigm of capabilities does a better job of capturing well-being in terms of how well people can do what they have reason to value (Sen, 1999).

Of course, assets are linked with income and therefore also with consumption. After all, most people earn most of their income by using assets (in particular, human capital in the labor market), and most people consume most of their current income. Consumption, income, and assets are at once both linked and distinct: although well-being is not the same as consumption, well-being does require some consumption; although income is not the same as consumption, income provides resources that may be consumed; and although assets are not income, the use of assets produces income.

These distinctions matter because, compared with an income-based or consumption-based view of well-being, an asset-based or capability-based view leads to different policy implications. For example, the consumption-based view leads to policies (such as Food Stamps for the poor or Social Security for the aged) that subsidize consumption. In contrast, the asset-based view leads to policies (such as tax deductions for interest paid on home mortgages or on student debt, or tax deductions for savings locked away in a retirement account) that subsidize asset accumulation.

Policies that support consumption are an essential part of the social safety net. But they stop too soon, providing only subsistence without going the next step to support development. In the United States, we do not want people merely to get by; we want them to thrive, to grow, to realize their dreams and to be participating citizens. While the United States has a wide array of asset-building policies, they tend to benefit mostly the non-poor who already own assets. Policies that support consumption, on the other hand, provide help for poor people only on the condition that they own few or no assets. In this way, public policy fails to help poor people build assets, and, in some cases, public policy may even make asset accumulation more difficult for the poor.

Because a lack of assets stunts development, Individual Development Accounts (IDAs) try to help poor people build assets. IDAs are subsidized savings accounts. Unlike other subsidized savings accounts such as Individual Retirement Accounts (IRAs) or 401(k) plans, IDAs are targeted to the poor, provide subsidies through matches rather than through tax breaks, and require participants to attend financial education. Participants accrue matches as they save for purposes that build assets that increase long-term well-being and financial self-sufficiency. The most common uses of IDAs are home purchase, post-secondary education, and small business. In principle, IDAs can be opened at birth and can remain open for a lifetime. Match funds may come from public or private sources, and funding partnerships are common. IDAs are a conceptually simple development and public policy tool that may be adapted to a wide range of applications and circumstances. Once an IDA is opened, almost anyone—government, employers, and development organizations—can plug into it by offering matches. In this sense, IDAs provide an institutional infrastructure for asset building, perhaps the most important aspect of an asset-building policy (Goldberg and Cohen, 2000).

Sherraden (1991) proposed IDAs as an attempt to shift policy toward assets and development. IDAs encourage participants to save, and, at the same time,

IDAs help participants to save. Through the match, IDAs transfer resources with the explicit message that the resources should be used to build assets (home ownership, post-secondary education, and small-business ownership) that are strongly associated with long-term development, improvement in well-being, and the American Dream.

This is a tall order. After all, asset accumulation—even in IDAs—requires saving, and if saving were easy, then few people would be poor. Even for the non-poor, saving is difficult because it means using fewer resources in the present—to save means to sacrifice. Of course, saving requires an even greater sacrifice from the poor because—compared with the non-poor—they have fewer resources available to be saved after they fulfill subsistence requirements. Furthermore, the poor lack access to some public policy mechanisms that, for the non-poor, increase the salience of the option of saving and also decrease the current cost of saving. Finally, the combination of scarce resources and attenuated access to policies that facilitate saving may partly obscure saving from the worldview of the poor; the idea that they might choose to save and build assets may not even enter their minds.

What is the nature of the roadblocks to asset accumulation by the poor, and how might IDAs address them? This chapter presents a theoretical framework—based largely on behavioral and institutional economics—in which low saving and low asset accumulation by the poor results not only from a low initial resource base and from individual choices but also from the constraints, opportunities, costs, and rewards defined by public policies and institutions. That is, the theory suggests that the poor own few assets not only because they have little to save and because they may choose to save little but also because institutions and public policy fail to facilitate their saving. It is not that choices do not matter. But policies and institutions also matter because they shape the costs and consequences of choices. In some cases—for example, automatic deposits from paychecks—institutions may be doing most of the "choosing" in saving behavior. Humans are not the all-knowing, confidently calculating, forward-looking, self-disciplined super-beings enshrined in traditional economic models (Mullainathan and Thaler, 2000; Kahneman and Tversky, 1979). People tend to follow the life paths worn smooth by policies and to take greater notice of options highlighted by institutions. In the end, this is a hopeful perspective; if institutions and policy are part of the problem, then better institutions and policies can help facilitate asset accumulation by the poor.

Assets and the Poor

Sawhill, in her 1988 classic "Poverty in the United States: Why Does It Persist?" concluded that "we still understand very little about the basic causes of poverty" (p. 1113). This lack of knowledge—and subsequent failure to make a dent in poverty—rests on "a fundamental problem in the research . . .

the lack of a basic structural model of the income-generating process" (p. 1112). This chapter lays out a theory—that is, a basic structural model—of the income-generating process in which the use of assets in production generates income and in which poverty persists because of a lack of assets. It also discusses how IDAs might be one way to help to break the vicious cycle.

The model is not new. Asset accumulation has always been a central theme of development research in non-industrialized countries (for example, Rutherford, 2000; Attanasio and Székely, 1999; Lipton and Ravaillon, 1995; Besley, 1992; Deaton, 1992a; Gersovitz, 1988). Likewise, much research on the non-poor in industrialized countries focuses on saving (Bernheim, 2002; Browning and Lusardi, 1996; Hubbard, Skinner, and Zeldes, 1995; Deaton 1992b), and the central choice facing decision-makers in almost all classical models of economic growth is how much to save. Asset accumulation for the poor in industrialized countries, however, has somehow been overlooked (Sherraden, 1991). Public assistance has aimed to fulfill short-term subsistence requirements, but it has stopped short of transfers whose amounts and forms could help people in the long term to break free of poverty.

The year 1988 saw the start of the birth of a movement in industrial countries to include the poor in policies that promote asset accumulation. Friedman's *The Safety Net as Ladder* proposed changes to the structure of public assistance so that it could encourage development beyond mere subsistence. Haveman's *Starting Even* declared that "transfer payments are necessary but not sufficient" (p. 149) and called for increased investments in human capital and for publicly funded, restricted-use accounts for youth. Sherraden's "Rethinking Social Welfare: Towards Assets" critiqued exclusive reliance on maintenance policies and proposed IDAs as a step toward development policies.

In the past decade, the movement has gained intellectual momentum (Shapiro and Wolff, 2001; Ackerman and Alstott, 1999; Conley, 1999; Stoesz and Saunders, 1999; Gates, 1998; Oliver and Shapiro, 1995). It has also attracted support from all points along the political spectrum. For example, Bill Clinton—who as governor of Arkansas wrote the foreword to Friedman's *The Safety Net as Ladder*—supported IDAs in his 1992 campaign and later proposed a large matched-savings program (Wayne, 1999; Clinton, 1999). Both George W. Bush (Bush, 2000) and Al Gore (Kessler, 2000) had billion-dollar IDA proposals in their platforms, and both proposed some form of individual asset accounts for retirement, with Bush proposing a regressive system of individual accounts within the Social Security system and Gore proposing a progressive system outside Social Security. About thirty-four states have IDA legislation (Edwards and Mason, 2003), and the Assets for Independence Act of 1998 authorized $250 million for IDAs in 1999–2009. Furthermore, the Savings for Working Families Act—if passed—would provide $450 million for 300,000 IDAs over ten years. Outside the United States, Taiwan has an IDA-like demonstration, and Canada has sponsored a randomized IDA experiment.

In the United Kingdom, the Savings Gateway resembles IDAs (Kempson, McKay, and Collard, 2003), and the new Child Trust Fund will give each newborn an account and a deposit, with larger deposits for children in poor families (H.M. Treasury, 2003).

Why Assets? A Model of Why Poverty Persists

Poverty is a trap of low assets. To develop a theoretical model to explain this more precisely, some definitions will be useful. *Income* is defined as inflows of resources in a period of time (excluding reimbursable inflows from loans), and *assets* are defined as resources kept through time. The use of assets—human, physical, social, or financial—produces income. Greater income requires greater production and thus greater assets.

Saving is defined as an increase in resources kept through time. That is, saving is an increase in assets. The act of saving produces savings (assets).

Consumption uses up resources. *Dissaving* is the consumption of assets. *Asset accumulation* occurs when, through time, saving exceeds dissaving. Because greater income requires greater production and thus greater assets, and because greater asset accumulation requires saving, greater income requires greater saving.

When people think of assets, they usually think of financial assets such as savings balances in bank accounts. In fact, however, assets are far more than just financial assets held as bank balances. The chief asset for most people—poor or non-poor—is their human capital, characterized by their particular combination of time, effort, and skill. Most people produce most of their income by selling the production of their human capital, that is, their labor. Just as the financial capital accumulated in a bank account is the result of saving, the human capital accumulated in a person is also the result of saving. To acquire skill, people allocate time away from leisure and towards study (education) or work (experience). The greater the skill accumulated in the past, the less time and effort required for a given task in the present. Thus, human capital results from saving a resource (time) by using it in work or study rather than consuming that time in leisure. Saving in the form of human capital increases productive capacity in the future.

Assets are inputs in the processes that produce income. This is true whether the assets are in the form of plant and equipment employed in factories or in the form of human capital employed in labor markets. Even financial assets are productive. Bonds, for example, produce a contracted interest rate; stocks produce dividends and price changes (production may be negative). Cash acts as a way to store resources through time; one dollar now produces one dollar tomorrow.

Non-financial assets also matter for many types of production, whether in the market or in the household. Homes produce housing services, with income equivalent to the resources that would be required to rent similar services.

Refrigerators, mops, and heirloom jewelry are assets that, when combined with human capital, produce household services such as cooked meals, cleaned floors, and cherished memories. Social capital—defined as networks, norms, and trust—produces information, reduces transaction costs, buffers shocks, and comforts psyches. In a racist and sexist society, race and gender are also resources that last through time and so act as if they were assets. Sherraden (1991, p. 100) presents a typology of assets and their returns.

At a point in time, people must allocate their assets (resources) between production (that is, saving) and consumption. The trade-off is that more consumption in the present means less saving, less production, and thus less income available to allocate between consumption and production in the future. The trade-off is sharpest for the poor because, once they meet subsistence requirements, they have fewer resources available to save. For the poor, the high cost of sacrificing current consumption tends to depress current saving and thus to depress future production, future income, and future consumption. Assets beget assets, so the poor, because they start with low assets, tend to stay poor. The question of how to escape from poverty is, in essence, the question of how to save and accumulate assets.

For example, suppose that someone has such low levels of human capital that he or she can earn just enough to pay for food and shelter. The person cannot attend classes to accumulate more human capital because school attendance brings with it ancillary expenses, for example for books and transportation to and from class. If the person could save and accumulate some financial assets, he or she could, with time, use these resources to cover the costs of study. With the additional education and with more human capital, the person's earnings might increase, and then the person could both save more (to further increase productive capacity and thus increase income in the future) as well as consume more in the present.

A Theory of Asset Effects

So far, this discussion of the role of assets in production and consumption has used a traditional "economic" framework that views people as consumers who save only because saving increases their future consumption and who benefit from saving only when they consume its fruits. Sherraden (1991) introduced the concept of *asset effects*, which he defined as the economic, social, and psychological effects of asset ownership that go beyond mere consumption. "Simply put, people think and behave differently when they are accumulating assets, and the world responds to them differently as well" (Sherraden, 1991, p. 148).

Because economic theory already explains most economic effects (changes in rational responses due to changes in constraints and opportunities), this chapter focuses on a theory of the "non-economic" (or social and psychological) effects of asset ownership. This is not to suggest that social and psychological effects are more (or less) important than economic effects. Rather, it simply recognizes that the economic theory of the effects of asset ownership is already well-developed. In contrast, no one has adequately explained *why* or *how* assets might have social and psychological effects.

It is important to develop a theory of social and psychological asset effects because much of the allure of IDAs comes from the claim that assets spark hope and change how people think and act. For example, an oft-quoted statement from Sherraden (1991) is that "while incomes feed people's stomachs, assets change their heads" (p. 6). Likewise, Sherraden (p. 155) says that assets "are hope in concrete form." Along the same lines, "IDA programs are aiming not merely to create savings but savers" (Sherraden, 2000, p. 6).

IDAs transfer resources; thus, for straightforward economic reasons, it would be no surprise to find that IDAs improve the well-being of the poor. The more radical claim, however, is that asset effects go beyond mere economic impacts.

The theory in this chapter describes how assets might affect not only pocketbooks but also hope, thought patterns, and social relationships. If IDAs spark hope (and if that hope is not to be false hope), then it must be the case that poor people—in the absence of IDAs—are too pessimistic. The theory attempts to explain how this pessimism might have come about and how assets might change pessimism into optimism.

Likewise, if IDAs improve worldviews—and if this improvement brings worldviews more in line with reality—then it must be that the poor had downwardly skewed worldviews. The theory in this chapter explains—without recourse to concepts of weakness or moral sloth—how the poor might come to believe that the world and their chances in it are worse than they really are. The theory also suggests how assets might help to align views more closely with the real world. Of course, the same theory suggests that the non-poor may have upwardly skewed worldviews (Mischel, 1977).

From the point of view of some IDA advocates who work in the policy arena, the presentation of this theory may appear risky. Because the theory suggests that the poor lack hope and/or lack accurate worldviews, these advocates may fear that some readers will see the theory as supportive of the idea that the poor are lazy or stupid. In fact, the theory explicitly derives the depressed hope and downwardly skewed worldviews that are hypothesized for the poor as a result of luck and normal limits on human rationality, two factors that the poor share in the same measure as the non-poor. The theory explains both how some of the poor may have room for improvement and how the existence of room for improvement resulted from forces beyond their control. Of course, some people are poor or have skewed worldviews because of their own mistakes. Still, poor children can hardly be blamed for their position and for what they have learned about the world, and of course many poor adults used to be poor children. In general, it is good to remember the advice that Nick Carraway, the narrator in *The Great Gatsby*, received from his father:

"Whenever you feel like criticizing anyone, just remember that all the people in the world haven't had all the advantages that you've had" (Fitzgerald, 1925, p. 1). To be perfectly clear, IDAs can help the poor, but, usually, the fact that the poor can use some help is not their fault.

There is also a risk that the presentation of a theory of social and psychological asset effects will be seen as suggesting that economic effects do not matter or that economic effects matter less than social and psychological effects. Such an interpretation would be mistaken. The theory encompasses both economic and socio-psychological effects, and the theory furthermore shows how the economic and the socio-psychologic reinforce each other. Although the theory here focuses on social and psychological effects, the presentation also shows the strength of economic effects and how they work.

Psychological Effects

Humans look to the future, and their current well-being depends in part on what they expect their future well-being to be (Frederick, Loewenstein, and O'Donoghue, 2002). For example, two people in otherwise-identical situations will feel different today if one plans to attend a party tomorrow and if the other plans to attend a funeral. Likewise, two otherwise-identical people will have different feelings—and thus different behavior going forward—if one has $10,000 in a savings account and the other has $10. Some evidence—as well as simple introspection—supports the idea that people enjoy thinking about future pleasure but dread thinking about future costs or difficulties (Prelec and Loewenstein, 1998).

All else constant, people with greater assets in the present quite sensibly expect to have greater resources in the future. Thus, for purely economic reasons, they expect to be happier and to have greater capability to do and to be what they have reason to value. For an individual, "asset effects" are when the economic effects of ownership improve expected future economic well-being and thus, for psychological reasons, improve current well-being. Asset effects are not about miserliness nor are they about the love of money per se; they flow from the improvement in current well-being that comes from contemplating the possible and reasonable future use of resources. When people have savings to savor, they fear less and hope more.

In traditional economic models that ignore social and psychological asset effects, savings serve no purpose until and unless they are consumed. For example, consider the lives of two people who are identical except in that the first wins the lottery at birth and deposits all $100,000 in a no-interest bank account while the second has no savings at all until winning $100,000 in the lottery the day before death. On their last day, both people consume their $100,000 throwing the "death party" that traditional economic models of saving and consumption so often assume. In their lifetimes, both people had the same consumption, but, given the social and psychological benefits of asset ownership, it seems likely that the person with $100,000 in the bank since birth had greater well-being in that she was happier, more confident about the future, better treated by peers, and so on.

In the psychological model of asset effects, the mere thought of the opportunities enabled by the ownership of savings provides benefits to the saver, even if none of these opportunities are ever realized. In the economic model, in contrast, assets matter only in use. In the psychological model, ownership itself, regardless of use, also matters, because people look ahead and enjoy contemplating the possible economic effects of the use of their savings.

Although the idea that asset ownership produces social and psychological effects seems like common sense, formal scientific evidence is scant. Almost all studies find that asset ownership is correlated with a wide range of positive outcomes. Asset ownership, however, is highly correlated with asset use, and few studies carefully distinguish between the economic effects of the *use of assets* and the non-economic effects of the *ownership of assets apart from use*. Of course, it is not surprising that the use of assets would have positive effects; mainstream economic theory predicts that. The challenge is to specify and test theories in which mere asset ownership—apart from asset use—leads to positive outcomes.

Likewise, few studies account for possible correlations between observed asset ownership and unobserved factors that might lead both to asset ownership as well as to greater positive outcomes independently of asset ownership. For example, homeownership may be linked with positive outcomes not only because thinking about the (quite likely) possibility of continuing ownership makes the owner happier and more optimistic about the future (a psychological effect) but also because—all else constant—homeowners enjoy better shelter than renters (an economic effect). Furthermore, those people who tend to have positive outcomes—regardless of whether they are homeowners—also tend to become homeowners, and this can thwart attempts to disentangle which positive outcomes are due to homeownership per se and which positive outcomes are due to the same factors that also caused home ownership in the first place. Most research, however, attributes all of the correlation between positive outcomes and assets to asset ownership even though much of the correlation could be attributed to asset use or to unobserved factors correlated both with assets and with positive outcomes.

A convincing test of the effects of asset ownership (as opposed to the effects of asset use) would require subjects who are given ownership of assets but who cannot—at least for a time—use the assets. Because the assets are not used, any changes in outcomes could be cleanly linked with ownership. Sherraden (1991, p. 152) describes one such experiment in which poor children in an inner-city grade school were promised full-ride college scholarships if they graduated high school. In effect, the promise of a college education was an asset that these children owned but could not yet use. The children ended up with unusually positive outcomes even in the years before they were able to "consume" the promised scholarships. These are purely socio-psychological effects of asset ownership, not economic effects of asset use.

In much the same way, IDAs provide matches on savings and thus increase asset ownership. Furthermore, IDA rules often require participants to wait for a time before making a matched withdrawal. Thus, during the time when the participant owns the match but cannot use it, there may be effects of ownership even though there cannot be effects of use.

Social and Political Effects

Asset effects may go beyond the psychology of individual owners because others may treat owners differently than they treat non-owners. These social and political effects of ownership are just as real as the individual economic and psychological effects, and they may be even more important.

As usual, some of the social and political effects of wealth are due to the use of resources; for example, the non-poor can buy friends and political allies. They may also enjoy disproportionate political influence and access to public services.

Some social and political effects, however, come from ownership and from the potential—as opposed to actual—use of resources. For example, the non-poor may get better treatment because they are more likely to be able to reciprocate, whether or not in fact they actually do reciprocate. Furthermore, since the time of the Puritans, some Americans have taken wealth as a sign of virtue (and poverty as a sign of vice), with the implicit or explicit social judgment that the poor deserve worse treatment.

Evidence for the social value of wealth as a signal can be seen in what might be called "conspicuous ownership." Some people (whether poor or non-poor) may invest in assets—such as clothes, cars, houses, or well-kept front yards—simply because, unlike balances in a bank account, these forms of resources are visible to the naked eye.

The social importance of the physical beauty of the human body offers additional evidence of the social value of ownership. On average, people tend to treat handsome or pretty people better than plain or ugly people. In the labor market, Hammermesh and Biddle (1993) find that good-looking people earn more. Of course, looks are an aspect of human capital that likely has no "use" value at all; its worth derives purely from how other people respond socially to its ownership. Furthermore, over time, a good-looking person who is consistently treated well may come to believe that he or she is a good and capable person. In turn, this increases the likelihood that the person will think and act in positive ways, creating a feedback loop between outcomes and asset ownership.

Feedback Effects

In broad terms, outcomes depend on three factors: choices, effort, and luck. People decide what to do, they work at their chosen activities, and they bear their luck, where "luck" is shorthand for all the factors beyond their control that influence outcomes and whose resolution is uncertain when choices are made and effort expended. The theory in this chapter argues that asset ownership improves the information available when making choices, reduces the psychological cost of making effort, and helps people to "make their own luck" by improving their social relationships.

People choose what to do and how much effort to expend based on their judgments of the chances (that is, the probability or likelihood) of the possible consequences. Of course, this is not to say that choices are unconstrained; all choices are limited by the resources available and by the policies and institutions in place. Unlike the idealized decision-maker in traditional economic models, real people often make three types of errors when they think about decisions. First, they may misjudge the chances of realizing the different possible consequences. That is, they may be too pessimistic or too optimistic. Second, they may be unaware of some possible consequences. For example, a potential saver might, when considering whether to open a bank account, fail to imagine that she might one day accumulate enough to make a down payment on a house. Third, people may misjudge the possible consequences—that is, costs and rewards—of the choices that they have thought about, for example, by underestimating or overestimating the joy of homeownership.

Sherraden (1991) argues that asset ownership reduces these mistakes and that this leads to better outcomes. That is, asset ownership makes people more optimistic, more realistic (in that they are aware of more alternative outcomes), and more knowledgeable of the true value of choices that entail some work and sacrifice in the short term but that promise large rewards in the long term. "Orientation toward the future begins in part with assets, which in turn shape opportunity structures, which in turn are quickly internalized" (p. 152). Assets affect choices not only through their effects on the chances of realizing different consequences but also through their effects on people's perceptions of choices, chances, and consequences.

This feedback theory of asset effects turns out to have much in common with the sociological theory of Alfred Schütz as described in Esser (1993). The "economic" rational-choice paradigm does not necessarily conflict with a "sociologic" paradigm in which people follow routines, act according to rules of thumb, and make choices that reinforce their existing notions about how the world works. What is required is to include subjective expectations, incomplete evaluations, imperfect information, risk, uncertainty, and costly decision-making. This is precisely what has been done here.

How do assets work these effects? The fundamental factor is that the use of assets improves the chances of positive outcomes. For example, a student with savings (or whose family has savings) and whose grades are on the rocks can buy better books, hire a tutor, or quit a part-time job to free up more time for study. Simply put, the use of assets increases the chances of academic success.

The chances of success also depend on effort; greater effort means greater chances for success. Effort, however, exacts a psychological cost. Moreover, the mental cost of effort decreases—that is, work is easier—if the person believes that the chances of success are good or that the rewards are large. For example, a student who knows that her savings can rescue her from an academic slump will have an easier time studying simply because she expects that the work will pay off in the end. Likewise, a student who knows people who have graduated and who have gone on to get good jobs will have a better idea of the rewards of academic success than a student who lacks such role models. A student with no savings knows that she is studying without a net and so will have less hope for success. This increases the mental cost of effort and, at some point, this cost may get so high that the poor student—sensibly, from her downwardly skewed point of view—opts to quit. In the same way, diplomas or degrees may be outside the worldview of a student with no successful role models. Of course, this makes studying all the more difficult. After all, why try if success is a long shot or if no one you know has succeeded? Clearly, effort and expected success form a feedback loop. Asset ownership can push the loop in a positive direction because, through the possibility of asset use, asset ownership makes success more likely and effort less costly. This is how assets can help turn vicious cycles into virtuous circles.

Finally, social effects imply that assets can "make their own luck." For example, imagine two students, one whose clothes, backpack, car, and housing reflect wealth, and another whose visible possessions reflect little wealth. All else constant, other students (and even teachers) will tend to gravitate toward the wealthy student, in part because drop-out is less likely to interrupt the relationship and in part because the student's resources make her more able to help to her friends. Classmates of the apparently poor student, however, may avoid associating with what they see as a ship which, if not already sinking, is less likely to weather a storm.

In the end, assets tend to reinforce a feedback loop that improves the chances for the success of a given choice, decreases the mental cost of the effort expended, and improves luck through strengthened social relationships. Importantly, this theory explains why the poor may make what seem to outsiders to be "bad" choices. For the poor, the choices make sense. They are not lazy or stupid; rather, they respond to the world as they know it as best they can (Lewis, 1966). Because IDAs help build assets, they have the potential to change the world as seen by the poor and thus can change choices, starting the feedback loop rolling in a positive direction. As Sherraden (1991, p. 152) observes, "Even the most poor and disadvantaged young people respond constructively to future possibilities when they *have* possibilities."

Bequests of Wealth and Worldviews

A few children inherit wealth when their parents die. More important for more children, however, are *inter vivos* bequests from living parents that facilitate investment in human capital. Born helpless and asset-less, children acquire human capital only if someone else provides for their subsistence and thus frees up time and effort for physical growth, education, training, and experience. Because shelter is the largest share of most family budgets, poor families tend to live in low-cost housing. Because local-school finance is based on property taxes, the children of poor parents tend to go to poorly funded, low-quality schools. Thus, the children of the poor tend to build less human capital. In adulthood, low human capital means low income. In turn, this stunts the chances of their children to acquire human capital and adds to a vicious cycle. This logic suggests that for the poor, saving may be out-of-mind because it is out-of-sight.

To some extent, children also inherit worldviews. A *worldview* is defined as a set of subjective judgments about which elements of life are subject to choice, about what consequences are possible, and about the chances (probabilities) of possible consequences. Choices, chances, and consequences have objective reality, but of necessity people must base their subjective worldviews on their imagination, on their own experience, and on the experience of people whom they know.

For example, people can choose whether to try to go to college. Some see going to college as a choice and, with full knowledge that they have a choice, make a decision. For others, going to college is not really a choice; they never pictured a world in which they did (or did not) go to college. Among people who believe that college is a choice, some perceive that the chances—given a level of effort—of getting a degree are low and that the rewards of a degree are small. Others are more optimistic. These beliefs affect the psychological cost of effort. In turn, the cost of effort affects the level of effort and thus affects the objective chances and consequences.

The theory in this section has attempted to show how and why assets have economic, social, and psychological effects. These effects result both from the use of assets and from mere asset ownership, quite apart from use. Social and psychological effects result not from mental or moral weakness but rather from the cost of effort and humanity's inevitably imperfect knowledge of choices, chances, and consequences. The theory applies just as well to the non-poor as to the poor. The theory matters inasmuch as it may explain why and how IDAs can spark hope or improve worldviews and thus improve outcomes and long-term well-being.

IDAs, Saving, and Asset Accumulation by the Poor

Three impediments stand between the poor and asset accumulation: low resources relative to subsistence requirements, lack of access to public polices that subsidize assets, and inaccurate views about saving. IDAs attempt to address all three.

Low Resources Relative to Subsistence

Most poor people have low incomes because of they have low human capital and thus earn low returns in the labor market. Thus, the best way to increase the amount of resources available to be saved by the poor is to improve public schools and so help the poor to build more human capital and thus earn more income. School reform, however, is slow, and, for many poor people, it is already too late. Furthermore, even if the poor attend good public grade schools and good public high schools, college is still expensive, even though college is also heavily subsidized.

The level and swings of the macroeconomy also affect income. Furthermore, when the economy sneezes, the poor catch a cold; shifts in unemployment tend to drive large changes in the income of the poor.

Of course, IDAs do not directly affect school quality, nor can IDAs influence the macroeconomy. They do address, however, some constraints that dampen income in the long term, and they do attempt to create institutions and incentives that can help the poor build enough savings to realize important improvements in their lives.

Among the matchable uses of IDAs are post-secondary education and job training. Thus, IDAs may be used to subsidize investments in human capital that may, in the long term, increase income and thus the ability to save. For these reasons, Curley and Sherraden (2000) suggest that IDAs might be most powerful for children and youth. Matches for small-business ownership might also raise incomes, and matches for home purchase might decrease shelter expenses and so increase resources available to be saved. Likewise, matches for computers or cars might also affect productive capacity in the market and in the household.

In broad terms, the match in an IDA increases asset accumulation from a given level of income or saving in three ways. First, the match attracts people to IDAs and thus may spark them to start to save or to save more. Second, the match increases the return on saving. In some sense, the match is akin to a very high interest rate or a very large tax credit. Third, the match increases the amount of resources accumulated so that a relatively small amount of saving can become a large asset—such as a house or a college education—that might be enough to transform a life-course. Given an asset-accumulation goal, the match substitutes to some extent for saving and thus indirectly substitutes for income from other sources.

Of course, IDAs do not—at least in the short term—increase the resources that the poor have available to be saved. Once the poor do save, however, IDAs increase the return on saving. Matched withdrawals for home ownership, post-secondary education, or microenterprise may also increase long-term productive capacity and thus increase both future income and future ability to save.

Access to Subsidies for Assets

Much asset accumulation in the United States is subsidized (Seidman, 2001; Howard, 1997; Sherraden, 1991). The largest, most widespread, and most important asset-subsidy policy is public education, from grade school through college. Interest deductions and below-market-rate student loans also subsidize college. Furthermore, deductions for mortgage interest act as subsidies for home ownership, the bedrock of the middle class and the second-most important asset of the poor. Finally, tax-advantaged retirement accounts such as IRAs or 401(k) plans form the core of most people's retirement nest eggs. In fact, the most-important forms of asset accumulation are highly subsidized. The effects of these pervasive asset-subsidy policies may resemble the effects of a consumption tax.

Compared to the non-poor, the poor benefit less from these asset subsidies because the policies directly or indirectly require participants to already own assets. For example, local-school finance based on property taxes places the best-funded public schools in wealthy neighborhoods. Tax-advantaged retirement accounts link subsidies to the prior accumulation of human capital because the tax breaks are worth the most to people whose high incomes (due to their high human capital) puts them in high tax brackets. The same holds for 529 College Savings Accounts (Clancy, 2003). Of course, there is no particular reason to tie asset subsidies to existing wealth, as shown in the pro-poor historical asset-building policies embodied in the Homestead Act (Williams, 2003) and the G.I. Bill.

Subsidized debt for home purchase or post-secondary education is indirectly linked to existing wealth because loans can finance only part of the total cost of acquiring a home or a degree and because lenders often take existing wealth as a signal of creditworthiness. For example, prospective home buyers must accumulate two types of assets: financial assets for a down payment, and enough human capital to establish that they can earn the income required to make mortgage payments through time. Likewise, student debtors must have savings (or wealthy parents, or time for a part-time job) to pay living expenses beyond college tuition and books. Finally, even if small-business owners could fund capital goods completely with subsidized debt, at least some savings are required to finance operating and living expenses until a firm gets off the ground (Berger and Udell, 1998; Bates, 1997). Without savings, most new, small ventures will fold before they fledge (Schreiner, 2004b).

Tax breaks for asset accumulation (such as tax deferments for IRAs, 401(k) plans, or 529 College Savings Accounts and tax deductions for interest on student loans or home mortgages) are weak incentives for the poor because the poor are in low (or zero) tax brackets. Furthermore, the poor save less for retirement and rely more on Social Security, so they get smaller subsidies on the retirement savings they accumulate. Likewise, bigger loans also mean bigger subsidies, so linking subsidies to debt means that the poor—who go to less-expensive colleges, and who buy less-expensive houses—get smaller subsidies. Of course, there are administrative, targeting, and incentive reasons to link asset subsidies to current wealth (and thus to previous saving), loans, and the tax system, but these linkages also mean that the current asset-subsidy system does much less for the poor than for the non-poor.

To increase access to asset subsidies for the poor, IDAs decouple the transfer mechanism from existing wealth, loans, and taxes. Participants deposit post-tax dollars in passbook savings accounts. Withdrawals are matched if used for homeownership, post-secondary education, or small-business ownership (and sometimes other asset-building uses are matched as well). IDA participants also receive financial education and encouragement from program staff. Overall, IDAs somewhat resemble Roth IRAs except that the subsidy is a cash match rather than a tax break.

Views about Saving

Even if the poor have resources available to save and even if they have access to asset subsidies, the poor must perceive saving as a choice that they might make and as a choice whose consequences are likely to be positive. The institutional structure of IDAs encourages such worldviews.

Institutions. Here, the term *institutions* refers to purposefully created policies, programs, products, and services that shape opportunities, constraints, and consequences. These purposeful institutions often lead to social patterns as well. For example, the institution of the income tax affects the return to time and effort in the labor market. Likewise, the institution of the interest rate on passbook savings accounts affects the trade-off of the current cost of saving against the future benefits of having saved. Laws against theft are also institutions that establish the consequences of crime. The institutional aspects of IDAs include eligibility requirements, financial-education requirements, match rates, match caps, time caps, waiting periods between enrollment and matched withdrawals, interest rates, account fees, and patterns of support from peers and program staff.

In the social sciences, the term *institutions* is often used much more broadly, but the focus here is narrowly on *conditions that are put in place on purpose*, as in a public policy. Although how policies and institutions arise is an interesting question, the focus here is only on their nature. This theoretical stance reflects an applied interest guided by the question: "What theoretical constructs and empirical evidence can inform efforts to improve social well-being through policies that subsidize saving?"

Institutions affect worldviews—and thus actions—because they shape constraints and consequences and expose people to knowledge of opportunities and choices. For example, laws against theft matter not only because people weigh the benefits and costs of theft but also because people—due to limited time, effort, knowledge, and cognition—often skip the benefit-cost calculus completely and instead assume from the mere existence of the law that the net benefits of theft are negative.

In standard economic theory, institutions do not affect worldviews. *Homo economicus* is rational, knows all the possible choices, knows all the possible consequences and the probabilities of realizing them, and—given this knowledge—has both the time and the energy to make the best choice. In fact, *Homo sapiens* is seldom rational, is not omniscient, and must work to make choices (Thaler, 2000). In the words of Thaler and Sunstein (2003, pp. 176–7), these decision-making costs often mean that "the existing arrangement, whether set out by private institutions or the government, tends to stick. . . . Any change from the status quo entails time and effort, and many people seem to prefer to avoid both of these." The potential effects of the institutional design of IDAs on saving will be discussed after the next section.

Institutional aspects of culture. Some aspects of culture—that is, shared patterns of beliefs and choices—can be seen as institutions that shape views of choices and beliefs about the probabilities of possible consequences. Standard economics ignores culture and pretends that each choice starts from scratch. But this takes too much time and effort, so people often infer choices, chances, and consequences from what they see others do around them (Mischel, 1977). Cultures differ from place to place because people can inexpensively observe only those near to them and because geographic variance in physical opportunities and constraints makes different choices optimal in different places.

Cultural institutions affect asset accumulation. For example, homeownership is part of the American Dream. On the one hand, people who grow up around homeowners may presume that this is the natural order; as adults, they are more likely to buy a home themselves, perhaps because they never even considered *not* buying a home. If they do see homeownership as a choice that they may or may not make, then, if they choose to rent, they may still feel inferior or that they are somehow unsuccessful as people. On the other hand, people who grow up around renters may not realize that they can choose to buy a home, or, if they were to consider such a choice, then they may underestimate the probability of positive consequences.

Culture shapes worldviews because human imagination is limited; people do not think much about what they might do but have not yet done nor seen done. Furthermore, choices that break with social patterns require extra mental effort to explain and to justify, both to the chooser and to others. It is difficult to take the road less traveled. Institutions shape rules of thumb and matter for behavior far beyond what economic theory predicts because the process of completely rational choice is too costly. Madrian and Shea (2001) present evidence that norms and suggestions influence saving choices.

Institutional aspects of IDAs. Institutions have both "economic" effects on opportunities, constraints, and consequences and "non-economic" (socio-psychological) effects on worldviews. Because economic theory already describes non-psychological effects, the term *institutional effects* is reserved here to describe socio-psychological effects beyond the realm of economic theory. Although policy often focuses on economic effects, non-economic effects are real. Policy almost always has non-economic effects, and they sometimes matter more than economic effects.

The design of the institutional structure of IDAs takes into consideration both economic effects and institutional effects. For example, the match is an institutional aspect of IDAs that provides an economic subsidy for asset accumulation by the poor; tax breaks would be weaker incentives. At the same time, other structural elements of IDAs aim to nudge worldviews toward saving and asset accumulation. Some of these insights come from socio-psychological and behavioral theories of saving (Sherraden, et al., 2000; Beverly and Sherraden, 1999; Bernheim, 1997; Caskey, 1997).

First and foremost, the mere existence of IDAs sends a message that the poor can (and perhaps should) save (Sherraden, et al., 2000). The presence of IDAs creates a social pattern; because IDAs exist, the poor do not have to work as much to see that they can gain from the choice to save. Current asset-subsidization policy already does much of this work for the non-poor (Sherraden, 1991, p. 127): "The middle class accumulates its wealth, not so much through superior individual investment, but through structured, institutionalized arrangements that are in many respects difficult to miss. . . . This is not a matter of making superior choices. Instead, *a priori* choices are made by social policy, and individuals walk into the pattern." Thaler and Sunstein (2003, p. 177) find this reflected among participants in 401(k) plans: "With respect to savings, the designated default plan apparently carries a certain legitimacy for many employees, perhaps because it seems to have resulted from some conscious thought about what makes sense for most people." Bernheim (1997, p. 30) expounds a similar idea: "When saving incentives are in place, boundedly rational individuals are more likely to learn that others regard the benefits of saving as important. The very existence of a pro-saving policy may indicate that 'authorities' perceive the need for greater thrift." In this sense, institutional theory suggests that if you build it, they will come.

Second, IDAs are linked to financial education. In standard economic theory, financial education is superfluous because people already know everything that they need to know. In real life, however, knowing how to save makes saving easier. For example, the act of drawing up a household budget makes people more aware of their financial choices and more aware of the consequences of those choices. In turn, this increases the likelihood that people will remember to consider saving (in contrast, people in economic models never forget to do what is best for themselves). The common exhortation to "pay yourself first" may boost accumulation if it encourages people not to set a consumption target and then save whatever is left over but rather to set a saving target and then consume whatever is left over.

Third, IDAs set targets. In technical terms, the match cap on an IDA is a limit and constrains the highest amount of savings that may be matched. In the minds of IDA participants, however, match caps may turn into goals. A key hypothesis of institutional theory as applied to IDAs is that people try to save up to the targets that have been set for them. The match cap implicitly sets a psychological norm, so higher caps may spark greater saving not only because higher caps allow greater savings to be matched but also because people feel better if they meet the norm, and higher norms lead them to try harder to meet the norm. For example, if two identical IDA participants both save $500, the one with an annual match cap of $500 will feel more successful than the one with an annual match cap of $750, and this may spur the participant with the higher match cap to make a greater effort to save more.

Fourth, IDAs give feedback. Monthly IDA statements show progress toward asset-accumulation goals. These constant reminders help to prevent IDAs from being "out of sight, out of mind" and in this sense resemble the efforts by the U.S. government to boost retirement saving by sending annual statements of projected Social Security pay-outs so that future retirees are less likely to forget that they should prepare to supplement Social Security with their own savings. Furthermore, program staff and peers in the IDA program may provide informal encouragement. Positive reinforcement helps people to focus their thoughts on positive consequences (Mischel, 1977). This decreases the cost of effort, increases the salience of possible positive outcomes, and thus tends to increase saving. In mainstream economics, feedback has no place because people are supposed to already know how well they are doing.

Fifth, some IDA programs explicitly ask that participants deposit something each month, even if it is just a pittance. The intent is that participants will then form a norm or a habit of making regular IDA deposits and that this habit will then decrease the mental cost of saving. In some sense, creating the expectation of monthly deposits also gives poor people access to a way to commit to save (Maital and Maital, 1994; Thaler, 1994; Maital, 1986). Such a commitment device is useful because the poor often lack access to other common ways to commit to save, for example direct deposit of paychecks, monthly payments on home mortgages, and automatic deduction from bank accounts. In a way, expectations of monthly deposits are a commitment device that allows participants, when they open an IDA, to tie their own hands in the future. Participants enroll knowing that they will be expected to make monthly deposits. Thus, they expect to feel unsuccessful or guilty if they fail to meet this norm. Although they may regret having accepted this expectation in months when making a deposit requires extra sacrifice or in months when they do not make a deposit and thus feel bad, they nonetheless agree to the arrangement because they recognize that such constraints on their short-term choices encourage asset accumulation and may thus improve their long-term well-being (Hoch and Loewenstein, 1991; Ainslie, 1984). The expectation to make a deposit in each month may also increase saving because—as in informal savings arrangements—it provides IDA participants with a socially accepted excuse to deny requests by members of their social networks for gifts of surplus cash (Ashraf, et al., 2003; Anderson and Baland, 2002; Rutherford, 2000; Owens and Wisniwiski, 1999).

Sixth, to budget, to save, and to plan to use savings may increase how often IDA participants think about the future consequences of current choices, and this increase in future orientation may increase saving. Likewise, classes in personal financial planning may expose people to the practice of setting long-term goals, further encouraging future orientation. Furthermore, doing something once—such as setting a budget—changes behavior because it decreases the cost of doing it again.

Seventh, financial education may offer more accurate views of the chances (probabilities) of realizing the various possible consequences of saving. For example, some poor people may believe that they cannot save up enough to make a difference, but classes can show how, through time, small-but-consistent deposits can add up. Classes may also provide information about how college degrees are associated with increases in lifetime income, about the likelihood of success in small-business ownership, and the costs and rewards of home ownership. In short, financial education can help to set straight downwardly skewed worldviews.

Eighth, limits on the use of matched withdrawals may highlight choices that people on their own might not otherwise have considered. For example, matches for home purchase may serve to point out the expectation that homeownership is both worthwhile and possible for the poor. Likewise, matches for small-business ownership and for post-secondary education suggest that the poor can (and perhaps should) attend college or run their own small businesses. By offering matches for the purchase of certain types of assets, IDAs make ownership of those assets more salient in the minds of participants.

Ninth, rules that limit matches to illiquid assets (homes, post-secondary education, and small businesses) may serve to curb temptations to consume (dissave) assets. In principle, a participant could make deposits into an IDA, take a matched withdrawal, sell the asset, and then pocket or squander the cash proceeds. In practice, the rules of IDAs send a message that match-eligible assets are worth keeping. Furthermore, IDAs convert resources in liquid forms (cash deposited in a passbook savings account) to resources in illiquid forms (matched withdrawals used for home purchase, post-secondary education, and small business) that are difficult to convert into consumption. With time, effort, and transaction costs (akin to friction), resources in any form can be converted into consumption or into resources in any other form. *Liquid* resources are easily converted; *illiquid* resources have high conversion costs. Cash is the most-liquid form because it may be converted into almost any other form (for example, a house). Houses and small businesses are illiquid because they are difficult to sell and convert to cash. Human capital (such as the skills developed through post-secondary education) is probably the most illiquid resource; it can be converted to other forms only through time and effort and cannot be completely converted all at once. Through cash wages, human capital can be converted into a house. In fact, different types of *resources* might be characterized by how easily they can be converted into desired forms. The defining characteristic of *waste* is the lack such convertibility.

Tenth, informal limits on unmatched withdrawals may curb temptations to dissave. IDA programs use exhortations, follow-up phone calls after an unmatched withdrawal, reminder notes after a month passes without an IDA deposit, and discussions in financial-education classes of how, if the match rate is 2:1, a dollar removed from an IDA in an unmatched withdrawal costs the participant two dollars in lost matches. Highlighting these costs increases their salience to participants and so decreases unmatched withdrawals. Of course, because the poor are subject to frequent unexpected shocks to income and expenses, unmatched withdrawals are often necessary, so formal restrictions on unmatched withdrawals are ill-advised. Informal limits, however, capture the essence of what Thaler and Sunstein (2003) call "libertarian paternalism": the informal limits attach small costs to choices that are tempting in the short term but that tend to have negative long-term consequences. Participants can still make unmatched withdrawals, but the slight difficulty of doing so helps to prevent frivolous decisions.

Eleventh, IDA programs ask for "new" saving. In principle, deposits in IDAs may come either from new saving (that is, saving that would not otherwise have taken place and that results from an increase in the difference between income and consumption) or from shifted resources (that is, assets already accumulated in another form such as balances in a checking account). For example, IDA classes may teach ways to save on grocery bills or how to find less-expensive lenders (to reduce consumption). Furthermore, staff may guide participants to sources of ads for jobs (to increase income). IDAs also require a waiting period between enrollment and matched withdrawals; this allows time for institutional effects to sink in, and it deters attempts to quickly make matched withdrawals based on assets that were shifted from already-saved forms (or even from saving made from borrowed resources). It is difficult to guarantee that IDA deposits come from new savings; because IDA staff do ask participants to save by earning more and/or consuming less, however, new savings are more likely than if no one asked in the first place.

In sum, institutional theory suggests that IDAs send the message that the poor can save. Furthermore, the institutional structure of IDAs helps to increase financial knowledge, set targets, provide feedback, create norms, boost future orientation, discourage dissaving, and highlight the choices, chances, and consequences of saving. In the stylized world of mainstream economic theory, institutions would not have these effects because people already have all that they need to make the best choices. In the real world, however, people do learn from education; people are tempted to do things in the short term that harm their well-being in the long term; people do forget or deviate from their plans; practice does help to make perfect; people are subject to suggestion; and norms do affect mental costs. By taking advantage of these realities, the information, expectations, and norms embedded in the institutional structure of IDAs tend to encourage saving and asset accumulation.

How Do IDAs Differ from Other Means-tested Transfer Programs?

In the preface to Sherraden's 1991 *Assets and the Poor*, Neil Gilbert (p. xiv) asks a classic question of IDAs and of the asset-based view of well-being: "If society were to increase social transfers to the poor, why do it in the form of welfare measures that stimulate the future accumulation of assets rather than through direct cash grants for immediate consumption?"

Sherraden (1991) says that IDAs transfer assets but that income-tested public transfer programs (such as Food Stamps or Temporary Assistance for Needy Families) transfer income. The income/asset distinction, however, hinges on the time frame of measurement, not on the resource transfer itself. Any resource may be consumed, and any resource may be saved. From the point of view of an IDA participant, matches are income when disbursed (that is, matches are inflows of resources in a given time frame). Likewise, the resources transferred in TANF checks, if saved, become assets (that is, resources kept through time). How then do IDAs differ from other transfer programs?

TANF transfers liquid cash; IDAs transfer illiquid home equity (through home purchase), illiquid human capital (through post-secondary education), and illiquid business assets (through small-business ownership). Of course, illiquid resources can still be consumed, but the conversion costs are greater than for cash. Thus, people are more likely to save resources transferred through IDAs than through TANF. Of course, even though IDA resources are more likely to be saved, IDAs need not increase overall asset accumulation because people might make IDA deposits by shifting already-saved assets or by going into debt. It is even possible—albeit unlikely—that IDAs could decrease overall asset accumulation. Still, on the whole, standard income-tested transfer programs encourage resource use, while IDAs encourage resource ownership. Rather than cash, IDAs attempt to transfer homes, post-secondary education, and strengthened microenterprises.

Furthermore, standard income-tested transfer programs are designed to just barely meet subsistence requirements, and their institutional structure sends the message that resource transfers are not to be saved but rather consumed. In particular, rules that disqualify people who own assets worth more a given limit discourage public-assistance recipients from saving part of their transfers. For example, Powers (1998) finds that asset limits reduce saving both by people who currently receive income-tested public transfers and by people who—if they suffered a setback such as an illness or job loss—are close to receiving income-tested public transfers. Likewise, Hubbard, Skinner, and Zeldes (1995) find that asset limits may explain why many poor U.S. households hold no financial assets (see also Orszag, 2001. Hurst and Ziliak, 2004, and Ziliak, 2003, argue that asset limits do not affect saving by the poor.) For the non-poor, Feldstein (1995) finds that asset limits on eligibility for college financial aid depress saving. Although asset limits on income-tested transfers were relaxed during the 1990s, it seems that few poor people realize this (Hogarth and Lee, 2000). Although consuming income-tested public transfers is at least partly a calculated response to rules that limit eligibility to those with few assets, the response may also have an important psychological component. For example, some people may infer from the mere presence of a limit on assets (or from hearing a story of someone who saved and then lost benefits) that saving is punished. Such people may then form a rule-of-thumb of not saving, even though they might find, if they worked out the details, that saving, even though it would make life more difficult in the short term, would improve their well-being in the long term.

In contrast to standard income-tested transfers, IDA transfers are packaged in an institutional structure that suggests that long-term well-being depends on asset accumulation. As discussed above, the financial education associated with IDAs serves to help to shift worldviews first that may fail to perceive the salience of the choice to save and second that may underestimate the likely rewards from saving. Furthermore, once resources are deposited into IDAs, participants may simply forget that the resources may be withdrawn and consumed, or participants may assign the resources to a "mental account" that is marked for long-term purposes (Sherraden, et al., 2004; Moore, et al., 2000; Thaler, 1992 and 1990; Shefrin and Thaler, 1988). Most of all, the existence of IDAs suggests that the poor can (and perhaps should) save.

In the end, the asset-based view of well-being matters for two reasons. First, transfers that are consumed can increase well-being only through consumption (and not through contemplation), only if they are very large, and only as long as they last. Small, temporary consumption-based transfers have tenuous political support; large, permanent consumption-based transfers would be infeasible, both politically and fiscally. Second, the well-being of the poor mat-ters not only in the present but also in the future. As explained in this chapter, income results from the use of assets in production, assets result from saving, and saving results from not consuming income. If all income is consumed (as encouraged by the structure of current income-tested public transfers), then the poor are less likely to build up the assets required to support increased future income, and the cycle repeats. For most poor people, only asset accumu-lation can improve well-being in the long term.

IDAs and the Political Economy of Asset Subsidies

The match in IDAs represents a huge subsidy. Is this fair? Does it have a precedent? As it turns out, nearly all types of assets are heavily subsidized. In any case, no one accumulates much wealth without a lot of unearned help. The large subsidies in IDAs are nothing new, other than that they accrue to the poor.

As already discussed, saving in the form of human capital increases future productivity. Seen in this way, children may save at a higher rate than any other group, as they spend large shares of their time building human capital. Of course, children can afford to invest their time in asset accumulation (rather than in work to produce income to be consumed) only if others (usually their parents and the taxpayers in the local school district) provide "subsidies" in the form of subsistence and schools. In fact, millions of children across the globe become trapped in poverty at a very young age because they fail to build human capital in school precisely because they must work because their parents cannot otherwise provide them with subsistence.

In general, subsidies are central for all types of asset building. The chief subsidy is that which flows from parents to children to help them to build human capital, but asset subsidies are pervasive far beyond the family. To see this, consider first that assets result from saving, that saving results from unconsumed income, and that income has four possible sources: private gifts, earnings, public transfers, and theft.

When thinking about private gifts and asset accumulation, most research has zeroed in on inheritances. In broad terms, this work concludes either that inheritances do not account for much of the differences in wealth that persist across generations (because few people receive more than token inheritances) or that inheritances do account for much of the differences in wealth that persist across generations (because the few inheritances that do take place tend to be huge) (Bowles and Gintis, 2002). In other words, inheritances matter a lot for the rich few, but, for most others (and in particular for the poor), inheritances matter very little. This whole debate, however, ignores the far more common (and probably far more valuable) *inter vivos* transfers that take place in all families across the wealth spectrum, that start long before a child is born, and usually last into adulthood. Without unearned gifts of time, goods, and services, babies would simply die (or at least never develop much human capital). In this sense, life itself is an unearned asset.

The second source of income that may be saved and converted into assets is *earnings*, defined as the returns from the use of assets in production. For the richest in the leisure class who do not need to work, earnings come from combining their financial and physical capital with the labor of others. For most people—and in particular for the poor—earnings come from employing their human capital in labor. For both the rich and the poor, however, earning assets are at least partly unearned and built with the aid of subsidies, either through inheritance or through constant, long-term, low-level *inter vivos* transfers. Work involves time, effort, and skill (that is, human capital), and—mountain men or Horatio Alger heroes aside—most people tend to ascribe their earnings only to their own contributions of time and effort while ignoring the subsidies that helped to build their human capital. Although rarely recognized, most earnings are produced at least in part with assets whose owners did not earn them solely by the sweat of their own brows.

Income from public transfers also subsidizes asset accumulation. Beyond consumption-based transfers such as Food Stamps or Social Security that help maintain life (and thus human capital), public transfers subsidize a wide range of assets, most famously retirement saving through tax-advantaged accounts such as 401(k) plans and home ownership through deductions for interest on mortgage debt. The most important asset-accumulation policy—especially for the poor for whom human capital is the main asset—is public education in grade school, high school, and college. Of course, residential segregation and local-school finance mean that, compared with the non-poor, the poor receive much smaller subsidies. In sum, public transfers heavily subsidize the three most important forms of assets: human capital, housing, and retirement savings.

The final source of income that might be saved is theft. While perhaps no longer so common, theft historically has been a major source of unearned assets for countries that ruled colonies or won wars. For example, much of the initial asset base of the United States came from land stolen from native peoples or from human capital stolen from slaves (Feagan, 2000). Even if no living people have driven others off the land or owned slaves, the importance of *inter vivos* "inheritances" in the development of human capital suggests that many Caucasians in the United States who are now non-poor have benefited from their forebears' access to cheap land (for example, through the Homestead Act, Williams, 2003) or from on-going unearned advantages in labor markets and other social arenas vis-à-vis Native Americans, African Americans, women, and other currently and historically oppressed groups.

The point of this discussion is simple: regardless of the source of the income that is saved, most asset accumulation is heavily subsidized. Few people can claim to have earned all of their wealth completely on their own.

What does this mean for IDAs? First, heavy asset subsidies such as those implied by the matches provided in IDAs are nothing new, except inasmuch as they have rarely reached the poor. Second, matches in IDAs targeted to the poor can hardly be seen as unfair, as even the hardest-working middle-class person has benefited from unearned assets. Third, it may not be a fluke that the United States has had both uncommon economic success and extensive asset subsidies; perhaps asset subsidies are sound economic policy. (Pervasive asset subsidies may act like a tax on consumption, a policy with healthy—albeit regressive in its current form—long-term effects, see Frank, 1999.) Fourth, given that the American public strongly supports existing asset subsidies, it may also support IDAs.

Why Not Assets?

Development and well-being in the long term depend on assets. All else constant, more resources are better than less, and few people would oppose asset accumulation. For public policy, however, not all else is constant, and the key question is not whether some assets are better than no assets. Rather, the question is how, if assets beget assets, policy might create institutions that help the poor to build assets, and how to pay for these institutions.

Saving requires current sacrifice through decreased consumption and/or increased work. Some people are so poor that, once they meet subsistence requirements, they have few resources available to save. This is why IDAs are voluntary and allow people to skip deposits in some months and, if they wish, to make unmatched withdrawals.

Although not always acknowledged, saving is risky. Future returns are uncertain. For some people, death comes too soon, and for others, the future will not turn out the way that they expected. Although the United States has been an uncommonly safe place to build assets, financial savings may be threatened by inflation, bank failures, or market declines. Human capital loses value in recessions, and most small businesses die before their third birthday. For their part, homes are highly leveraged, undiversified investments that may depreciate. Depreciation has always been a real threat in minority neighborhoods, and it is threatening to become a broad risk as the baby boom ages and starts to sell off their assets to pay for consumption in retirement (Bernheim, 1995). A theory of asset accumulation must recognize that saving has a dark side; all owners enjoy ownership effects, but some will also suffer losses.

For the non-poor, the debate on the merits of asset subsidies has centered on whether the policies attract new savings or merely allow participants to re-shuffle existing savings to take advantage of tax breaks (Attanasio and DeLeire, 2002; Engelhardt, 1996; Bernheim and Scholz, 1993). For IDAs, participants could, for example, transfer savings from existing savings accounts straight into IDAs, picking up the match without decreasing consumption nor increasing income. The poor, of course, have fewer assets to shift than the non-poor, and IDAs send a strong institutional message that savings should be new. The jury, however, is still out. Even if a large share of IDA deposits is shifted, IDAs may still be worthwhile, for example, if they create large net benefits in other ways such as helping people to think more about saving and asset accumulation and thus increasing home purchase, post-secondary education, and self-employment in microenterprise.

Some advocates for the poor worry that a development paradigm based on assets will squeeze out the subsistence paradigm based on consumption (Schwartz, 2001). This seems highly unlikely; support for asset building is a complement—not a substitute—for support for consumption. A related fear is that, for the poorest of the poor, saving would mean starving (Johnson, 2000). But no one plans to use the asset-building paradigm as a way to pull the safety net out from under the poor. Sherraden (1991, p. 215) states, "Clearly, income-based policy will always play a role in welfare in the United States, probably the principle role."

Others fear that the match in IDAs is so strong an incentive that poor IDA participants will save too much, neglecting to see the doctor or eating substandard food. It is true that IDAs increase the return to saving and that IDAs trust people to judge whether the reward is worth the sacrifice. The important point, however, is that IDAs are voluntary; no participant is forced to save, and most participants probably will not save too much. Furthermore, unmatched withdrawals are always possible.

On the other side, some commentators worry that IDAs do not go far enough. Here, the claim is either that even with matches for savings over many years, poor people are unlikely to accumulate enough to make a difference (Bernstein, 2003). A related concern is that most IDA programs so far have not provided matches for purchases of cars or computers (Iskander, 2003), assets that play key roles in participation in labor markets. But the question is not whether IDAs are a panacea; they are not, and nothing is. The question is whether IDAs help and whether they help more than alternatives would. So far, the evidence from the American Dream Demonstration of IDAs suggests that at least some poor people can use IDAs to buy homes, to go to college, and to invest in small businesses.

Subsidies for assets may have social benefits, but they definitely have social costs. One person's subsidy is another person's tax. Beyond the cost of the match, program operation incurs costs. In the absence of non-economic effects, subsidies distort markets. Of course, everything has costs; the question is whether costs exceed benefits. The experimental-design component of ADD will attempt to measure benefits (Schreiner, 2000a; Sherraden, et al., 1995). The fact that costs have already been measured and discussed extensively (Schreiner, 2004a, 2002a, and 2000b; Schreiner, Ng, and Sherraden, 2003; Sherraden, 2000; Ng, 2001) is unusual; the incentives for new policy proposals usually means that "it pays to be ignorant" (Pritchett, 2002), leading proponents preferring not to measure costs and benefits.

Like all anti-poverty policies, IDAs redistribute from the non-poor to the poor. The fact that these IDA transfers are explicit expose them to attack; asset subsidies hidden in tax breaks (such as the more than $300 billion that goes to the non-poor each year) encounter less flak. Also, some people view taxes as theft by the government and so see tax breaks not as subsidies but as a decrease in theft. In this view, subsidies for people who pay little taxes are unjust. Of course, this is an untenable viewpoint because it ignores that the non-poor use services and benefits provided by taxes to a much greater extent than do the poor. This viewpoint also assumes that everyone deserves their current position because they somehow earned it, which, as discussed above, is not the case. Furthermore, absent efficiency concerns, greater equality improves social well-being (Atkinson, 1992), and greater equality may well improve efficiency as well.

Means-tested subsidies for assets expand the welfare state and, like all means-tested transfers, decrease work incentives for people who anticipate that they may qualify to receive means-tested transfers (Moffitt, 1986). Furthermore, like all phased-out transfers, reductions in match rates or reductions in access to IDAs as income and/or wealth increases serves to decrease work incentives for people once they start to receive the means-tested transfers. In the time while people have IDAs, however, work incentives may increase if participants maintain consumption levels but increase saving at the same time.

Although IDAs have so far been free of scandals, fraud and abuse do happen, as in all public programs. Several aspects of the institutional design of IDAs—such as annual match caps, financial education, direct disbursement of match funds to vendors, and waiting periods between the time deposits are made and when matched withdrawals are possible—serve to deter abuse.

IDAs are not a panacea. They cannot replace cash transfers for subsistence; they are not costless; they do not attract only new savings; and they are not immune to abuse. They will not enable the poor to become rich very quickly. Rather, IDAs are one way to nudge some impoverished people toward a path that may, with time and effort, lead to development and improvement in their long-term well-being. The research on the American Dream Demonstration in this book is among the first attempts to assess how IDAs do this.

Summary

This chapter has detailed the theoretical background for economic, social, and psychological impacts of IDAs. IDAs aim to do more than just transfer resources to the poor. Of course, resources are good to have, if only because they can be converted into consumption. IDAs, however, expect that the resources that they transfer will be saved rather than consumed. But standard welfare transfers can also be saved. How are IDAs different?

Sherraden (1991) proposed an answer in terms of institutional theory. IDAs are packaged in an institutional structure that explicitly asks and expects participants to save their transfers in forms (such as homes, human capital, or small businesses) unlikely to be quickly consumed. In contrast, standard welfare comes with the message that welfare transfers are strictly for consumption.

The institutional package matters because people are not the rational, omniscient beings assumed in economic theory. People are subject to suggestion, and they respond to patterns of choices worn smooth by public policy because that takes less effort than to imagine new choices and then to weigh the possible consequences.

Sherraden (1991) introduced the concept of asset effects, defined here as the impacts of the ownership of assets as distinct from the impacts of the use of assets. Humans are forward-looking, and current well-being depends in part on expected future well-being. People with more assets in the present expect to have more resources in the future. Thus—for purely economic reasons—they expect to be happier. "Asset effects" occur when ownership improves expected future well-being and thus, for socio-psychological reasons, also improves current well-being. Not only do owners think differently than non-owners, but others also treat them differently. The social and political effects of ownership may matter even more than the economic effects.

Plan of this Book

The rest of this book proceeds as follows. The following chapter introduces IDAs in general, IDA programs in the American Dream Demonstration, and the institutional characteristics of IDAs. The next chapter describes the characteristics of participants in ADD and hypotheses about how these characteristics are linked with savings outcomes. The following chapter presents measures of savings in IDAs in ADD, accounting for "putting in" (deposits), "keeping in" (balances maintained through time), and "taking out" (matched and unmatched withdrawals). The chapter after that uses multivariate regressions to look at associations between the institutional characteristics of IDA programs in ADD and savings outcomes. The next chapter continues the regression analysis, now focusing on the characteristics of participants. The regressions associate the characteristics of programs and participants first with the likelihood of being a "saver" (having net IDA savings of $100 or more) and then—for "savers"—with the level of monthly net IDA savings. The final chapter summarizes the analysis and what it means for policy, programs, and research.

3

The American Dream Demonstration

The first large-scale demonstration of Individual Development Accounts was the Down Payments on the American Dream Policy Demonstration (the "American Dream Demonstration"). This chapter describes the research goals for ADD and the questions posed in this book. It also documents the characteristics of the host organizations in ADD and presents summary information on the institutional characteristics of the IDA programs. Later chapters analyze these data to learn about how institutional characteristics are linked with savings outcomes. From a policy perspective, the characteristics of IDA programs matter because—although it is hardly possible to modify the characteristics of IDA participants—policy has some leeway to adjust program characteristics.

The data that form of the basis of the empirical analysis in the rest of this book are derived from the Management Information System for Individual Development Accounts (MIS IDA). This chapter describes MIS IDA and the data that it collects on savings outcomes, program characteristics, and participant characteristics. This chapter sets the stage for the empirical analyses in the following chapters.

Research on ADD

The purposes of research on ADD are first to explore the outcomes of IDAs and second to see how these outcomes are associated with the institutional characteristics of programs and with the socio-economic characteristics of participants. IDAs are a new policy proposal, so there is much to learn. Research is central to ADD, and research goals shaped much of ADD's design.

The research on ADD is multi-faceted and may be one of the most comprehensive investigations of a social or economic policy demonstration. The research program uses multiple methods and was designed by the Center for Social Development with the advice of an expert Evaluation Advisory Committee (Sherraden et al., 1995). The multiple methods, implemented over the course of seven years (1997–2003), were designed to look at ADD from many perspectives and to gather timely data as the demonstration progressed in order to inform the on-going development of IDA policy and IDA programs outside of ADD. Indeed, research from ADD has influenced the start-up and design of asset-based saving policies in Canada, Taiwan (Cheng, 2003), and Great Britain (Kempson, McKay, and Collard, 2003; H.M. Treasury, 2003 and 2001). To the extent possible, the research design for ADD followed from theoretical statements, tested hypotheses that explicitly sought alternative explanations, and allowed for the emergence of unexpected findings. The research methods included: (1) an assessment of program start-up and implementation (Page-Adams, 2002); (2) monitoring of savings outcomes (Sherraden et al., 1999; Sherraden et al., 2000; Schreiner et al., 2001; and Schreiner, Clancy, and Sherraden, 2002); (3) case studies of participants (Sherraden, Moore, and Hong, 2000; Beverly, McBride, and Schreiner, 2003); (4) cross-sectional survey of participants (Moore, et al., 2001); (5) in-depth interviews with participants (Sherraden et al., 2003a and 2003b; McBride et al., 2003); (6) randomized assignment and longitudinal surveys for an experiment at one IDA program; (7) assessment of outcomes at the community level (Emshoff et al., 2002); and (8) cost analysis (Schreiner, 2004a, 2002a, and 2000b).

Overall, research on ADD seeks to learn lessons in four main areas: (1) an answer to the most fundamental question: do IDAs work? That is, can poor people save and accumulate assets through IDAs? (2) associations between savings outcomes and the institutional characteristics of IDAs; (3) program models that can be scaled up and used to guide state and federal IDA policy; and (4) knowledge about patterns of saving and asset accumulation by the poor.

ADD research seeks answers to the following questions (Sherraden, 1999a): (1) What impedes or facilitates the start-up and implementation of a successful IDA program? (2) What are the impacts of IDAs on asset accumulation and life goals (for example, home ownership, post-secondary education, and small-business ownership)? (3) What are the social, psychological, and financial impacts of asset ownership on IDA participants and their families? (4) What is the net financial return of IDAs to participants and to society? (5) What are the community-level effects of an IDA program? (6) What design features are useful for an IDA program? (7) What patterns of saving are observed of IDA participants? (8) How are institutional characteristics associated with savings outcomes in IDAs? (9) How are participant characteristics associated with savings outcomes in IDAs? (10) What types of assets do IDA participants accumulate with their savings? This book focuses mainly on questions six through ten.

Host Organizations, Programs, and Sites

ADD ran from September 1997, and, in general, deposits made through December 31, 2001 were eligible for matches. Through a competitive process, thirteen *host organizations* were selected from across the United States to design, implement, and run fourteen IDA *programs* (one host organization ran two programs). In addition, many of the IDA programs in ADD had more than one *site*, and each site within a program had different funders and/or different account designs. Details about each host organization and the specific features of each program and site appear at the end of this chapter.

All IDAs in ADD were interest-bearing accounts in regulated, insured depository institutions, either banks or credit unions. Match funds were kept in a separate account and were not commingled with participant savings. Match funds were disbursed either as checks made out to vendors (for example, a home seller or a college) or, in the case of matched withdrawals for use in small businesses or home repair, reimbursed to participants upon presentation of receipts or estimates from third-party contractors.

All programs received monthly account statements from depository institutions. Data on the cash flows in the account statements was then entered into the Management Information System for Individual Development Accounts. MIS IDA then produced a monthly statement that was mailed by the program to participants. (The depository institution mailed their own statements to participants monthly or quarterly.) The monthly statement from MIS IDA showed the balance in the IDA, the matchable balance, the corresponding match, and the sum of the matchable balance plus the match. (The IDA balance could exceed the matchable balance if there were savings in excess of the match cap.) Thus, participants could track their own progress toward their goals because they received regular monthly statements. These monthly statements helped to remind participants to keep saving and also reinforced in their minds the saliency and worthwhileness of saving in IDAs.

All the IDA programs in ADD provided matches for the three universal uses of home purchase, post-secondary education, and small business. Some programs also provided matches for job training/technical education, home repair or remodeling, or retirement saving in Roth IRAs (table 3.1). In addition, some IDA programs outside of ADD (not discussed here) provide matches for car purchase or computer purchase.

One program in ADD (CAPTC Large-scale in Tulsa) was an exception in many regards. First, with 456 participants, it was the largest program in ADD. Second, CAPTC Large-scale had a few participants who were eligible to make matchable deposits after December 31, 2001. Thus, whereas data for all other ADD programs were collected through December 31, 2001, data for CAPTC Large-scale were collected through October 31, 2003. Third, CAPTC served as the host organization for two programs in ADD (dubbed "Small-scale" and "Large-scale"). The CAPTC Small-scale came first, and, true its name, had fewer participants (163) than CAPTC Large-scale. Program staff at CAPTC believe that, on average, participants in CAPTC Small-scale were more motivated and able to save than participants in CAPTC Large-scale, perhaps be-

Table 3.1
Matchable Uses in ADD

Matchable Use	Number of Programs
Home Purchase	14
Post-Secondary Education	14
Small Business	14
Job Training/Technical Education	11
Home Repair or Remodeling	8
Retirement	4

cause the most willing-and-able people were more likely to be among the first to sign up when IDAs were first introduced in Tulsa. Fourth, CAPTC Large-scale had an experimental design; about half of the qualified applicants—selected at random—were allowed to open an IDA, while the other half were not allowed to open an IDA. Members of both the treatment group with access to IDAs and the control group without access to IDAs were interviewed before random assignment and then again eighteen months and forty-eight months after assignment. Other research will use this survey data to attempt to detect the impact of access to IDAs for qualified applicants on a range of social, political, and financial outcomes. CAPTC Large-scale was also the subject of a detailed cost study (Schreiner, 2004a).

Participants

Participants are defined as enrollees with at least one IDA account statement recorded in MIS IDA. ADD had 2,350 participants. Enrollment began in July 1997 and was scheduled to end on December 31, 1999 (some programs allowed a few participants to enroll after the deadline). This figure excludes people who enrolled in ADD but who never opened an account as well as those whose net deposits were constrained to be zero. These constrained people include those who were discovered to be ineligible, those who had IDAs in both of ADD's two IDA programs in Chicago, those who died without a matched withdrawal, and those who moved away and so were forced to close their IDA with an unmatched withdrawal of the entire balance.

For most participants, matches were possible only for deposits made through December 31, 2001, although a few participants had earlier or later time caps.

Data from ADD pertain only to participants, that is, people who had the option to participate and who exercised that option. In particular, the data from ADD do not cover *eligibles*, that is, people who had the option to participate but who did not exercise that option. Thus, the results described here pertain only to the self-selected people who enroll in an IDA program and who opened an account.

Most likely, the self-selected participants differed in key respects from eligible non-participants. In particular, participants were probably drawn more heavily from those who, compared with non-participants, expected greater net rewards from IDAs. Because of this self-selection, the average participant probably saved more and had more favorable outcomes than the average eligible person would have had, had the average eligible participated in ADD. For policy purposes, it is useful to have estimates of outcomes of interventions for participants, but it is even more useful to have such estimates for eligibles (Ravaillon, 2001; Plotnick and Deppman, 1999). Because ADD only collected data on participants, however, this research can look only at outcomes for participants.

Participants in ADD are unlikely to closely resemble the average eligible person not only because they were self-selected but also because they were program-selected. IDA programs in ADD usually targeted specific groups such as the working poor, women, and/or people of color. Furthermore, they often promoted IDA participation among people who were already clients of other services provided by the host organization. It is an open question whether program selection led to participant outcomes that were better or worse than what could be expected from the average eligible in the absence of program selection.

The American Dream Demonstration and the Assets for Independent Act

The Corporation for Enterprise Development administered ADD and channeled funds from eleven private foundations to the fourteen IDA programs in ADD. After ADD had started, some host organizations were awarded contracts through the Assets for Independence Act (AFIA) from the U.S. Department of Health and Human Services. As a result, some matches and administrative expenses in ADD were funded through AFIA.

Because AFIA specified account designs that differed from those already in place for ADD, IDA participants within a program that received funds from AFIA were grouped into sites, one site with the original account design and a second site with the new AFIA design. The data here include both types of sites. Some host organizations also ran IDA programs in sites outside of ADD, but these non-ADD sites are not included in the analysis here.

In general, account design in the original sites was less restrictive than in the new AFIA sites. For example, the original sites allowed account ownership to reside either solely with the participant or jointly between the participant and the program. Furthermore, the original sites placed no formal constraints on unmatched withdrawals. Finally, in addition to the three "cornerstone" uses of home ownership, post-secondary education, and small business permitted under AFIA, some of the original sites also allowed matched withdrawals for uses such as home repair, retirement saving, or job training.

In contrast, the new AFIA sites required joint ownership of accounts, so program staff had to sign off on all withdrawals (matched or unmatched). Unmatched withdrawals were ostensibly to be limited to "emergencies", although in practice it appears that program staff—to their credit—signed off on any and all requests for unmatched withdrawals. Also, the new AFIA sites allowed matched withdrawals only for the three "cornerstone" uses of home purchase, post-secondary education, and small business. Furthermore, eligibility for the new AFIA sites was limited to people with income at or below 150 percent of the poverty line, whereas the original sites sometimes set the cut-off as high as 200 percent of poverty. The new AFIA sites also required a six-month waiting period between enrollment and the first matched withdrawal; some of the original sites had shorter (or no) such waiting periods.

IDA Design

IDA design refers to the rules that govern an IDA. Among the most important design elements are the aspects of account structure: (1) time cap; (2) match cap; (3) monthly deposit target; (4) match rate; (5) financial education; (6) waiting periods; (7) automatic transfer; and (8) informal discouragement of unmatched withdrawals.

Time Cap

The time cap is the last month (the deadline) for making deposits that are eligible for matches. Although deposits made after the time cap are not matchable, participants can still make matched withdrawals after the time cap of matchable deposits made before the time cap, and of course participants can make unmatched withdrawals at any time before or after the time cap. In ADD, the number of months between enrollment and the time cap for the average participant was 33.6 months. The median was 36 months (3 years), with a low of 4 and a high of 54 (table 3.2).

Table 3.2
IDA Design in ADD

Aspect of IDA design	Mean	Median	Low	High
Time Cap (months)	33.6	36	4	54
Total Match Cap ($)	1,330	1,000	240	6,000
Annual Structure (%)	52	N/A	N/A	N/A
Lifetime Structure (%)	48	N/A	N/A	N/A
Monthly Deposit Target ($)	41.50	41.67	6.67	208.33
Average Match Rate	2.07:1	2:1	1:1	7:1
Use of Automatic Transfer (%)				
No	94	N/A	N/A	N/A
Yes	6	N/A	N/A	N/A
Waiting Period (weeks)	18	24	0	52

In general, the longer the time cap, the greater the opportunity to save in IDAs. Thus, the longer the time cap, the more likely it is that a participant will save something. (This reflects good-practice guidelines—Schreiner, Clancy, and Sherraden, 2002—in which participants are not kicked out of IDAs for making irregular deposits or for keeping low or zero balances.) Furthermore, given that something is saved, the longer the time cap—all else constant—the greater the savings.

In principle, IDAs would be permanent, and everyone would have an account from birth through death. Of course, the account might wait in the wings with low or zero balances for years or perhaps decades until the participant is willing and able to make deposits. There is nothing wrong with "empty" IDAs. From a developmental perspective, people should be able to use IDAs when they are ready. For example, the policy of subsidizing retirement savings for the non-poor is permanent and permits low or zero balances; no one is precluded from opening an IRA or 401(k) plan at age fifty just because he or she has not saved anything up to that point. In this sense, the poor should not be "on" or "off" IDAs any more than the non-poor are "on" or "off" IRAs or 401(k) plans (Sherraden, 1991, p. 201). At the moment, however, IDAs are in a "demonstration" phase. They are not a permanent policy with sustainable funding. Thus, programs in ADD had time caps, in part because funds would—in theory—revert to funders if they were not spent by a deadline.

Because time caps varied across and within programs in ADD, different participants had different opportunities to save. Thus, measures of savings outcomes in this book generally control for the length of participation. In particular, the central outcome measure—net IDA savings per month—divides net IDA savings by the number of months between enrollment and the time cap.

Total Match Cap

The total match cap is the limit on net IDA savings, that is, the maximum matchable deposits. Participants may make deposits in excess of the match cap, but withdrawals of these excess deposits are not eligible for matches. For participants in ADD, the average total match cap was $1,330 (table 3.2). The median was $1,000, with a low of $240 and a high of $6,000.

ADD had two types of match caps, annual and lifetime. Overall, 52 percent of participants in ADD had annual match caps, and the remaining 48 percent had lifetime match caps (table 3.2). Although most of the original sites had annual match caps, most of the new AFIA sites had lifetime match caps.

Annual match caps limit matchable deposits in each participation-year. The total match cap is the sum of the annual match caps. For example, suppose a participant's IDA in ADD had a two-year time cap and a $500 annual match cap. In the first twelve calendar months after enrollment, up to $500 of deposits were matchable, and in the second twelve calendar months, another $500 of deposits were matchable. The total match cap was then $1,000. (In ADD, sometimes time caps were reached before the end of a participation-year. In these cases, some programs pro-rated the annual match cap, while other programs allowed participants to make matchable deposits as if this final shortened year were twelve months long.)

With annual match caps, unused match eligibility is lost at the end of each year, much as unused contribution room in Individual Retirement Accounts and 401(k) plans are lost each year. For example, if someone with a two-year time cap and a $500 annual match cap in ADD made deposits of $200 in the first year and $900 in the second year, $200 would have been matchable in the first year, and $500 would have been matchable in the second year. The $300 of unused match eligibility in the first year would be lost forever.

Balances in excess of an annual match cap, however, could become matchable in following years of ADD. For example, if someone with a two-year time cap and a $500 annual match cap deposited $900 in the first year and $200 in the second year, then the $400 that was not matchable in the first year becomes matchable—if it was still in the IDA—on the first day of the second year. Only $100 of the $200 deposited in the second year would then have been matchable.

With *lifetime match caps*, all deposits made before the time cap in ADD were matchable, up to the total match cap. That is, the total match cap was equal to the lifetime match cap. For example, if someone with a two-year time cap and a $1,000 lifetime match cap made deposits of $200 in the first year and $900 in the second year, then $1,000 would have been matchable. In ADD, 48 percent of participants had lifetime match caps. A few programs had rules meant to discourage large last-minute deposits just before the time cap, but it is unknown how or whether they were enforced.

In theory, the type of match-cap structure—whether annual or lifetime—has two opposing effects on saving. First, the presence of a recurring deadline—as with an annual match cap—discourages procrastination and thus may help boost saving. With a lifetime match cap, participants may believe that they can "wait until next year," running the risk that, when next year comes around, they will again believe the same thing. In the short term, saving requires sacrifice, so recurrent deadlines can prompt participants to bite the bullet while they still have the chance.

Second, the presence of a recurring deadline can get in the way of large lump-sum deposits. The poor often receive much of their income in bunches, for example, from tax refunds or from the Earned Income Tax Credit. Saving is easier from such large lump sums, if only because the participant can go on an immediate "consumption binge" and still have something left over to save (Shefrin and Thaler, 1988). If the lump sum exceeds the annual match-cap, however, then an annual match cap might—compared with a lifetime match cap—lead to lower matchable deposits because, by the time the next year rolls around, the excess deposits may have been removed in unmatched withdrawals. Furthermore, lifetime match caps allow more "second chances". After all, participants with lifetime match caps do not lose any match eligibility until after the final deadline passes, but participants with annual match caps can lose match eligibility each year. Given the lump-or-trickle nature of flows of income and expenses for the poor, second chances can be worth a lot.

Milligan (2003) discusses the effects of the type of match cap (annual versus lifetime). While IRAs and 401(k) plans in the United States have annual match caps in which unused eligibility is lost each year, Registered Retirement Savings Plans in Canada and Personal Pensions in the United Kingdom allow unused eligibility to be carried-over to following years, creating what amounts to a lifetime match cap. Abstracting from institutional and psychological effects, Milligan's model predicts that a lifetime match cap will tend to decrease saving in early years but increase saving in later years such that total lifetime saving increases. Milligan acknowledges, however, that the procrastination-deterring effects of annual match caps could overwhelm this theoretical advantage of lifetime match caps.

ADD featured both annual and lifetime match caps, so the strength of the two opposing effects can be tested (see chapter 6). Regardless of the outcome of this test, however, it seems likely that any large-scale, permanent IDA policy in the United States will end up with annual match caps, for four reasons. First, an annual match cap is much simpler. People can grasp it, and it is easier to administer. Simplicity is a virtue in financial programs for the poor, or, for that matter, the non-poor (Sherraden, 1991). Second, IRAs and 401(k) plans for the non-poor have annual contribution limits, and it would be difficult for an IDA policy aimed at the poor to be different. Third, annual match-cap structures spread out fiscal costs. With lifetime match-cap structures, it is possible that most matches would be disbursed in the first years of the program, as people rush to save very large amounts and then make matched withdrawals quickly for fear of not being able to take advantage of the matches later, either because the policy is revoked or because the participant dies too soon. Fourth, lifetime structures would make reshuffling assets easier; participants could save outside IDAs (keeping their savings liquid if needed for a rainy day) until they were ready to buy a house, go to college, or start a small business. Then they could suddenly shift their existing assets into an IDA to get a match without the IDAs' having ever sparked "new savings" in the sense of increasing the difference between income and consumption more than would have occurred without IDAs.

Monthly Deposit Target

The monthly deposit target is the total match cap divided by the number of months between enrollment and the time cap. A participant who made the targeted deposit each month without any unmatched withdrawals would—in the last month before the time cap—accumulate net IDA savings equal to the total match cap. In ADD, the mean monthly deposit target was $41.50 (table 3.2). The median was $41.67 (corresponding to a match cap of $500 per year), with a low of $6.67 and a high of $208.33.

Although the match cap is technically a limit on matchable deposits, participants may mentally change it into a goal or target (Choi, Laibson, and Madrian, 2004; Bernheim, 1998; Sherraden, 1991). Indeed, most programs in ADD present this amount as a target, and some explicitly ask participants to try to meet this target each month. If participants do change the match cap into a deposit target, then higher match caps (and hence higher monthly deposit targets) should be associated with greater saving. Chapter 6 looks at evidence of this institutional effect in ADD.

Milligan (2003, p. 278) tests what he calls a "rule-of-thumb" behavioral hypothesis in which people set a goal for themselves to save some fixed percentage (perhaps 100 percent) of the match cap (equivalent to what is here called the monthly deposit target). That is, Milligan tests whether savers turn limits into goals. Controlling for censoring of desired savings at the match cap, a $1 increase in the match cap in Canada's Registered Retirement Savings Program was associated with a fifty-cent increase in saving. This is a huge institutional/psychological effect. Apparently, the savers in this Canadian program turned limits into goals, perhaps because they assumed that the limit resulted from careful thought by someone who knew better than them how much saving would be wise (Thaler and Sunstein, 2003).

Match Rate

The match rate is the number of dollars disbursed by the IDA program to a vendor for each dollar in a matched withdrawal. The mean (and median) match rate in ADD was about 2:1, with a low of 1:1 and a high of 7:1 (table 3.2). In ADD, the match rate sometimes varied among participants in a given program. Furthermore, the match rate received by a given participant varied in those cases where the program offered different match rates for different matched uses and where the participant made matched withdrawals for these different uses.

Higher match rates increase the pressure to save because they increase the reward for a given level of saving. In economic theory, this is known as the *substitution effect* because higher match rates lead participants to substitute out of other uses of resources and into IDAs (Smyth, 1993; Deaton, 1992b; King, 1985).

Higher match rates can also lead, however, to decreased saving through what might be called the *fixed-goal effect*. Suppose, for example, that a participant opens an IDA because he or she wishes to make a down payment of

$1,500 on a home. If the match rate is 1:1, the participant must save $750 to achieve a down payment of $1,500. If the match rate is 2:1, however, then the participant needs to save only $500 to accumulate $1,500. Of course, some participants with a 2:1 match rate may choose to save $750 (or more) anyway to make a larger down payment and to take advantage of the match, but others may prefer to save only the $500 minimum and to consume the $250 that they would have saved if the match rate had been 1:1.

Economic theory also describes an *income effect* in which higher match rates lead to lower saving. The income effect, however, is just the fixed-goal effect generalized to the case where the goal is not a specific purchase but rather a level of consumption, so no additional discussion is needed here.

Match rates vary in ADD—both across and within programs—so it is possible to test (see chapter 6) whether the substitution effects that increase saving are stronger than the fixed-goal effects which decrease saving.

Financial Education

Besides matches, a central feature of IDAs is required financial education. In ADD, general financial education aimed to increase awareness of saving as a wise choice, to increase knowledge of how to save (techniques to make income exceed consumption), and to strengthen future orientation. In addition, asset-specific financial education aimed to help participants prepare for complex asset purchases (such as buying a home) or for the on-going maintenance and asset management required of homeowners and small-business owners.

Topics in general financial-education classes included how to make a budget and how to manage money. Exercises attempted to show how small changes in habits (such as taking a sack lunch to work instead of buying lunch) could add up to big differences through time. The general financial-education classes also taught psychological and behavioral strategies to assist participants to find resources to save, to deposit the saved resources in an IDA, and then to maintain the resources untouched in the IDA. Other general financial-education topics included credit repair, borrowing and debt management, compound interest, and personal financial planning.

Asset-specific education in ADD dealt with the purchase and management of assets resulting from matched withdrawals. For example, asset-specific education for home purchase often involved one-on-one counseling with program staff to ensure that the participant could demonstrate sufficient creditworthiness to qualify for a mortgage loan and sufficient future income potential to make monthly mortgage payments for the life of the loan.

In economic theory, *homo economicus* already knows everything and so has no need for financial education. In the real world, however, many people need help when thinking about their finances. After all, finance is mathematical and abstract, the costs of saving are felt now, and the rewards of saving come only in the future. Therefore, it is not surprising that most evidence suggests that even the non-poor tend to save more when they are exposed to financial education (Bernheim, Garrett, and Maki, 2001; Bayer, Bernheim, and Scholz, 1996), when they know techniques that help keep spending in check (Bird, Hagstrom, and Wild, 1997), and when they have a stronger future orientation (Americks, Caplin, and Leahy, 2002; Lusardi, 2001). Requiring financial education as part of IDAs reflects the belief—right or wrong—that the poor lack assets at least in part because they do not know how to save and accumulate assets or are too short-sighted for their own good.

Whatever the rewards may be, there is no doubt that financial education is costly, both for the participant and for the program. Like everyone else, poor people are short on time, so if potential participants perceive required classes as useless hoops that they must jump through in order to qualify for the match, then they may choose not to spend the time and effort to open an IDA. Furthermore, financial education is extremely labor intensive and thus very expensive for the IDA program. By examining the link between financial education and savings outcomes, the empirical work in later chapters seeks to inform the debate about whether the rewards of required financial education are worth the costs.

Waiting Period

The waiting period is the number of weeks that must pass between enrollment and the first matched withdrawal. The purpose of the waiting period is to blunt incentives to reshuffle existing assets into IDAs without doing any new saving, that is, without having increased the difference between income and consumption relative to what it would have been in the absence of access to IDAs. Nine of the fourteen programs in ADD required waiting periods, with a mean across programs of 18.1 weeks (table 3.2). The median is 24 weeks (about 6 months), with a low of 0 weeks and high of 52 (1 year). These data are likely somewhat inaccurate, as some programs did not make a rule for a waiting period until after the program started, and enforcement may have been uneven.

Automatic Transfer

In ADD, 6 percent of participants reported that they had arranged for automatic transfer to their IDAs (table 3.2). Some programs in ADD promoted automatic transfer more than others. The data do not reveal which participants could have used automatic transfer—that is, who had "access" to this service—had they known about it and wanted to use it. Probably, all participants had access, as depository institutions are usually happy to have money deposited into their accounts via automatic transfer. For at least six reasons, participants are expected to save more if they arranged for automatic transfer into their IDA from another bank account.

First, automatic transfer reduces the recurrent transaction costs of physically putting money in the IDA. With automatic transfer, the participant need not make a trip to the bank each month. Especially for small deposits, the value of the time spent driving (or walking, or taking the bus) to get to a bank branch or to an automatic teller machine could easily swamp the value of the deposit itself (Adams, 1995).

Second, automatic transfer removes the need to remember to make a deposit. Contrary to traditional economic theory, people do sometimes forget. Remembering is costly because it takes effort. Eliminating this cost makes regular deposits more likely. For the example of 401(k) plans—possibly the largest single type of personal financial savings in the United States—nearly all deposits are made via automatic transfer. In this sense, the structure of 401(k) plans uses automatic transfer to do the saving for the participant.

Third, automatic transfer removes the need to make recurrent choices to save (Beverly, McBride, and Schreiner, 2003; Beverly and Sherraden, 1999; Bernheim, 1997; Caskey, 1997; Thaler, 1990). Even when people remember to think about saving, they may still choose to consume. Automatic transfer can act as a pre-commitment device; in a clear moment of foresightedness, the participant can use automatic transfer to tie his or her hands in future months when the will to save may be weaker or when the short-term costs of saving are higher. In short, automatic transfer decreases the cost of choosing to save and increases the costs of giving in to temptations to spend.

Fourth, automatic transfer may help people to place psychological importance on saving, to "pay themselves first," or to think of the monthly deposit as "just another bill" (Sherraden et al., 2003a). Making saving a foregone conclusion decreases the mental cost of saving, and it also curbs temptations to consume.

Fifth, automatic transfer may help to make saving a habit. In general, IDAs in the United States have focused less on helping the poor to develop a saving habit and more on including the poor in public policy structures that support and encourage asset accumulation. Thus, U.S. IDAs do not have monthly limits on matchable deposits that would force participants to spread large lump-sum deposits over several months. In contrast, the main goal of the IDA-like Saving Gateway in the United Kingdom is to inculcate the poor with a saving habit (Kempson, McKay, and Collard, 2003). These U.K. "IDAs" do place monthly limits on matchable deposits. Although the effort involved in the decision to save is costly, having done it once decreases the mental cost of doing it a second time (Becker, 1995). In addition, if the participant believes that saving is a wise and responsible thing to do, then breaking the habit—that is, stopping after having started—may lead to feelings of disappointment and guilt (Sherraden, et al., 2003a). Thus, automatic transfer makes developing a saving habit more likely because it decreases the mental costs of saving and because it increases the mental costs of not saving. The participant no longer must "remember" and then "choose" but rather merely follows a "wise" path that previous choices have worn smooth. Habits are especially important in months when saving requires greater sacrifice due to unusually low income and/or unusually high expenses.

Sixth, even if automatic transfer does not cause greater (or more regular) saving, its use may be correlated with other unobserved factors that do cause greater saving. For example, the use of automatic transfer requires that the participant own—in addition to an IDA—a passbook account or a checking account. (Participants could also arrange to have their employers deposit their paychecks directly into their IDAs, but this was uncommon, as it would have led to very frequent, large unmatched withdrawals as participants spent their pay for monthly living expenses.) Many of the poor are "unbanked" (including about 19 percent of ADD participants), so it cannot be taken for granted that participants own the passbook accounts or the checking accounts that are necessary to use automatic transfer (Caskey, 2002; Dunham, 2000; Hogarth and Lee, 2000; Hogarth and O'Donnell, 1999). Compared to poor people who do not own savings accounts, poor people who do own savings accounts are more likely to possess unobserved characteristics (such as a propensity towards planning or thrift) that may also cause greater saving in IDAs. Thus, even if automatic transfer itself does not cause greater saving, it may serve as a proxy for other, difficult-to-quantify factors that do cause greater saving. In particular, automatic transfer still requires the participant to ensure that the account from which the money is drawn has a sufficient balance on the right day each month. The non-trivial management required is more relevant for the poor than for the non-poor because their lower balances mean that careful management is more often required to avoid "bounced automatic transfers" and the attendant embarrassment and possible penalty fees.

This danger of "overdrafts" in the account from which automatic transfers are drawn may lead to automatic transfer's being associated with lower saving in IDAs (Schreiner, Clancy, and Sherraden, 2002). That is, participants who arrange for automatic transfer may elect to transfer small amounts each month to reduce the risk of being caught short of funds.

In much the same way, participants' desire to keep funds (mentally) liquid may mean that automatic transfer is associated with less saving in IDAs. To reserve some on-going control over their deposits, some participants may choose to make small automatic transfers. That way, they have more cash on-hand should they need it, and they can still make non-automatic deposits if they end up with "extra" cash.

Finally, some participants may prefer to take cash by hand to the bank because it helps them emotionally "feel" like they are actively saving and making progress toward a goal (Kempson, McKay, and Collard, 2003).

Penalties for Unmatched Withdrawals

Of the fourteen programs in ADD, nine reported rules stipulating penalties for unmatched withdrawals (Schreiner et al., 2001). Except for the three programs and in all the AFIA sites in which the IDA account was jointly owned by the program and participant and in which unmatched withdrawals required a program signature, however, it is not clear what these penalties were. Furthermore, it is likely in practice that—even in the cases of joint-account ownership—any "formal" penalties were enforced inconsistently or not at all. Most likely, the only "penalty" for unmatched withdrawals was the disappointment that participants might feel for having failed to meet a goal or a target and the bother or embarrassment of having to request a signature from program staff or of having to talk about an unmatched withdrawal if a staff member who noticed it on an account statement called to inquire how things were going.

Of course, all IDA programs enforce an implicit penalty on unmatched withdrawals simply by not matching them. The loss of potential match dollars seems like a reasonable way to deter unmatched withdrawals while still allowing participants unrestricted access to their own funds.

Unlike traditional IRAs or 401(k) plans, IDA deposits are not tax-deductible, and interest on IDAs does not accumulate tax-free. Furthermore, participants do not receive matches when they make unmatched withdrawals. In the end, there is no subsidy on IDA savings taken out as unmatched withdrawals, so there is no need for a formal penalty.

In theory, increasing the financial or psychological cost of making unmatched withdrawals could wind up serving to encourage or discourage saving in IDAs. On the one hand, the income and expenses of the poor tend to go up and down both frequently and unexpectedly. Faced with a high likelihood of having to cope with crisis, the poor value the ability to make unmatched withdrawals. Indeed, in non-industrialized countries, experts in savings services for the poor advise that, after safety, the feature that the poor most desire in a savings instrument is the ability to make quick, low-cost withdrawals (Robinson, 2001 and 1994; Rutherford, 2000; Adams, 1978). In this sense, penalizing unmatched withdrawals could deter poor participants from ever making deposits in the first place. If potential savers fear that withdrawals will be difficult, and if they believe that they may need to make such withdrawals to face emergencies, then they may decide to play it safe and not to make any deposits in the first place. In the case of subsidized savings through 401(k) plans, the ability to remove deposits via loans seems to be associated with higher levels of deposits (General Accounting Office, 1997; Holden and VanDerhei, 2001), as participants are more willing to put funds in if they feel confident that they can get them out if needed.

On the other hand, poor savers (just like non-poor savers) often express a wish to put their assets out of their own reach (Maital, 1986). In calm moments of rational insight, they may realize that saving and asset accumulation is in their own long-term best interests. At the same time, they realize that later, in less lucid moments, the prospect of the short-term costs of the sacrifices required to save may blind them to the rewards of saving or sap the will required to leave IDA balances untouched (Frederick, Loewenstein, and O'Donoghue, 2002; Angeletos, et al., 2001; Maital and Maital, 1994). In this sense, the "Dr. Jekyll" saver would prefer an IDA with mild short-term costs of making unmatched withdrawals because it would help constrain the ability of the "Mr. Hyde" consumer to make unmatched withdrawals.

According to Beverly, McBride, and Schreiner (2003), asset accumulation involves three stages: making income exceed consumption (saving), converting saved resources from liquid to illiquid forms (depositing), and then resisting the temptation to dissave and consume the assets (keeping). In some ways, this final stage is the most difficult because it presents a constant challenge. After all, it may take a month to save by making income exceed consumption, it may take an hour to deposit saved resources in an IDA, but it takes repeated effort to maintain assets in an IDA.

The non-poor enjoy access to many "commitment mechanisms" that assist in the stages of saving and depositing (Beverly, McBride, and Schreiner, 2003). IDAs can serve the same purpose for the poor. But what about mechanisms that assist in the "keeping" stage? Again, institutions that provide such assistance are more commonly available to the non-poor than to the poor. For example, these institutions include substantial penalties for early withdrawal from certificates of deposit, the illiquidity of human capital and housing, and the 10 percent penalty (and income tax) levied on pre-retirement cash-outs from IRAs or 401(k) plans. The poor would welcome similar help in the "keeping" stage. Mild costs on unmatched withdrawals from IDAs would fit well with the spirit of "libertarian paternalism" (Thaler and Sunstein, 2003); people are often glad to submit to small changes in arrangements that constrain their choices as long as it reduces the risk that they will make short-term choices that may harm their long-term well-being. Indeed, Moore, et al. (2001) and Kempson, McKay, and Collard (2003) report that some ADD participants—but not all—seem to appreciate the informal restrictions on unmatched withdrawals.

Still, recurrent emergencies are a fact of life for the poor, so one of the few ways that IDAs might do harm would be to put the poor's assets out of their reach. Therefore, the penalties on unmatched withdrawals (other than the loss of the match) should remain strictly informal. The costs should be psychological and derive mainly from the letdown from not meeting expectations or targets and from the bother of having to explain to an IDA staff person the reason for an unmatched withdrawal. In the extreme, an IDA program might "require" signed agreement from program staff before unmatched withdrawals. Even though this "requirement" would never be enforced and even though the agreement would always be signed, following the ritual would allow a "cooling down" period and would also force participants to discuss their choice. In this way, the poor could make unmatched withdrawals fairly easily, but not too easily.

In the end, policy must strike a delicate balance when designing the "silken handcuffs" that help participants commit themselves to a savings plan while keeping savings liquid (Ashraf et al., 2003; Benartzi and Thaler, 2004).

Caveats on Measures of Aspects of IDA Design

Tests for links between institutional characteristics and savings outcomes are most powerful when there are clean data on both characteristics and outcomes. In general, the design features reported by the staff of IDA programs in ADD are both relevant and accurate; they reflect both the rules communicated to participants at enrollment and the rules implemented in practice. Unfortunately, the data also hint that the rules were not always well understood by participants nor consistently implemented by staff. The rules' complexity, frequent staff turnover, and software limitations may have contributed to this. Furthermore, rules in the data may not match rules in the field because some programs did not think carefully about some aspects of IDA design (such as the time cap or waiting periods for matched withdrawals) until long after they started and/or because programs changed the structure of their IDAs in midstream but did not record the change in MIS IDA. Thus, the data on the institutional characteristics of IDAs in ADD are imperfect, but the exact issues are unknown. Although this weakens the usefulness of the results in other chapters that describe apparent links between institutional characteristics and savings outcomes, it probably does not invalidate them. While seldom recognized, these sorts of data issues likely pervade all large-scale demonstrations in which many different organizations implement a program and in which data are self-reported by program staff.

To make matters worse (from a research perspective), the administrators of ADD encouraged program staff to revise IDA rules as the demonstration progressed according to what staff believed was working or not working. Of course, this was intended to produce more effective designs and thus greater development and well-being for IDA participants in ADD. Furthermore, it facilitated qualitative research on the effects of program design because changes in design could be qualitatively linked to changes in outcomes through discussions with participants and program staff. Unfortunately, these design changes were not recorded in the ADD data, making quantitative research more difficult.

Furthermore, changing rules in response to outcomes leads to the possibility of two-way causation; in ADD, it is possible not only that rules affected outcomes but also that outcomes affected rules. Clearly, this hampers how well research can make statements about how outcomes are associated with aspects of institutional design.

For practical reasons, the administrators of ADD at the Corporation for Enterprise Development did not randomly assign design attributes to participants, nor did they assign (randomly or non-randomly) design attributes to programs. Instead, each IDA program came up with its own rules and account designs. In some cases, programs may have shaped institutional structures not only in response to observed outcomes after ADD started (as discussed just above) but also in response to *expectations* of outcomes for members of their intended target groups. Expected outcomes may have affected rules even if rules were set before actual outcomes were observed. This possible two-way causation may have biased estimates of associations between outcomes and aspects of institutional design.

For example, suppose that programs wanted to equalize asset accumulation across groups. To do this, they might have assigned lower match rates to groups that they believed would save more—regardless of the match rate—and higher match rates to groups that they believed would save less. If these expectations were even partially correct, then higher match rates could seem to be linked with lower saving (or to have no link at all) even if—all else constant—higher match rates would be associated with higher savings. Sherraden et al. (2000) argue that this may have happened in ADD and that it may explain why lower levels of net IDA savings per month were associated with higher match rates.

Caveats on the Time Frame

For policy, a relevant research question is how the poor would save if they had permanent access to IDAs. ADD had time limits, however, so its data cannot address this question.

ADD recorded savings outcomes only while participants had IDAs. The data do not include non-IDA saving in months after the start of ADD but before a participant opened an IDA nor non-IDA saving in months after the IDA was closed. For some policy purposes, it would be useful to know something about outcomes across all months of eligibility. This would capture, for example, the effects of the timing of enrollment, of the timing of breaks and restarts in saving, and of the timing of matched and unmatched withdrawals.

Unfortunately, the ADD data for a given participant span only the months from account opening through December 31, 2001 (or, in the case of CAPTC Large-scale, through October 31, 2003). This covers the vast majority (but not all) of the months in which matchable deposits could have been made, and it covers some (but not all) of the months in which matched withdrawals could have been made. If the ADD data had been collected over a longer time frame, then matched withdrawals (and unmatched withdrawals) would be higher than the figures reported here. In this sense, the results on withdrawals are somewhat incomplete and the reported figures for net IDA savings are somewhat overstated.

Finally, this book can address only questions about programs with designs similar to those in ADD and at similar points in the project life-cycle. Again, such limitations are the norm in policy demonstrations.

Data from the Management Information System for Individual Development Accounts

Data for research on ADD was collected by staff in IDA programs with the Management Information System for Individual Development Accounts. The purpose of MIS IDA—beyond gathering data for research—was to help programs to manage the logistics of IDAs, for example, tracking participants' IDA balances and managing matched withdrawals.

Program staff in ADD used MIS IDA to record five classes of data: (1) at the start of the program, aspects of IDA design; (2) at participant enrollment, socioeconomic characteristics; (3) at the end of each month, cash-flow data from depository-institution statements; (4) at the end of each month, program inputs and expenses; and (5) intermittently, events such as class attendance and account closing.

MIS IDA provided management tools such as account statements, mailings, and administrative reports. It also generated a comprehensive database on program characteristics, participant characteristics, and enrollments, deposits, and withdrawals. Moreover, with MIS IDA in place, IDA programs could track their own performance, and of course the resulting database also facilitated external research.

In practice, MIS IDA was invaluable to IDA programs; without it, ADD— and indeed, hundreds of IDA programs currently running throughout the United States—may have never left the drawing board. Unlike some social-service programs, IDAs require precise and accurate financial accounting; for IDAs as a policy proposal, little could be worse than the distrust bred by administrative mistakes that lead to lost savings, broken promises, and disappointed expectations. Good software makes a difference.

In consultation with the ADD Evaluation Advisory Committee, the Center for Social Development identified the need for a management-information system for IDAs in 1995. Researchers with experience in tracking demonstration projects advised that ADD could not take for granted that programs on their own would track even the most basic information on outcomes, program characteristics, and participant characteristics. Thus, a national team was assembled in 1996 to identify the types of data that should be collected. As a result, the Center for Social Development designed and wrote the MIS IDA software package and has distributed and supported it ever since (Johnson, Hinterlong, and Sherraden, 2001; Hinterlong and Johnson, 2000). Some of the fields in MIS IDA Version 4.0 for program characteristics, participant characteristics, IDA design, and monthly cash flows appear in tables 3.3, 3.4, and 3.5.

Table 3.3
Program Characteristics Collected in MIS IDA

Characteristics of Programs:

    Age of host organization

    Type of financial institution(s)

Funding Partners:

    Type of organization

    Allowed uses of match funds

    Starting and ending dates of partnership

    Amount and type of contribution

Account Structure:

    Frequency of account statements

    Number of signatures required for withdrawals

    Penalties for unmatched withdrawals

    Matchable uses

    Waiting period(s)

Inputs and Costs:

    Types of marketing activities

    Salary expenses (including fringe benefits)

    Non-salary expenses (consultants, rent, equipment, utilities, supplies, travel, other)

    Hours of salaried staff in the IDA program

    Hours of volunteer staff in the IDA program

    Hours of staff of partner organizations who provide IDA services to participants

Financial Education:

    Hours of general financial education offered

    Hours of general financial education required

    Hours of asset-specific education required

Table 3.4
Participant Characteristics Collected in MIS IDA

Identification:

    Social Security number

    Name and address

    Name and address of relative

    Previous relationship with host organization

    Referral from partner organization

Participant Status:

    Enrollment date

    Date of exit

    Reason for exit

Demographics:

    Gender

    Year of birth

    Marital status

    Adults in household

    Children in household

    Race/ethnicity

    Education status

    Employment status

    Urban/rural residence

Monthly Gross Income at Enrollment:

    Wages

    Government benefits

    Pensions

    Investments

    Self-employment

    Child support

    Gifts

    Other

Table 3.4 (cont.)
Participant Characteristics Collected in MIS IDA

Receipt of Public Assistance:

> Former receipt of TANF or AFDC
>
> Current receipt of TANF
>
> Current receipt of Food Stamps
>
> Current receipt of SSI/SSDI

Assets:

> Passbook savings account
>
> Checking account
>
> Home
>
> Car
>
> Small business
>
> Land or property
>
> Investments

Debts:

> Home
>
> Car
>
> Business
>
> Land or property
>
> Family or friends
>
> Overdue household bills
>
> Overdue medical bills
>
> Credit cards
>
> Student loans

Insurance:

> Health
>
> Life

Financial Education:

> Hours of general financial education attended
>
> Types of asset-specific education attended
>
> Hours of asset-specific education attended

Table 3.5
IDA-Design and Cash-Flow Data Collected in MIS IDA

IDA Design:

       Account number

       Financial institution

       Date account opened

       Date account closed

       Use of automatic transfer

       Annual/lifetime match cap

       Total match cap

       Match rate

       Time cap

Monthly Deposits and Withdrawals:

       Start balance

       Amount of deposits

       Number of deposits

       Amount of withdrawals

       Number of withdrawals

       Amount of interest

       Amount of service fees

       End balance

Matched Withdrawals:

       Date of withdrawal

       Amount withdrawn

       Amount of match

       Use of withdrawal

       Vendor name and address

Data Quality

The cash-flow data for ADD from MIS IDA are probably the best data (and perhaps the only data) that exist on high-frequency savings outcomes for the poor in a subsidized-savings program. The cash flows are known to be accurate and complete because they come directly from records from depository institutions and satisfy accounting identities. This cash-flow data is central in most of the empirical analyses in this book.

The rest of the ADD data—data not derived directly from account statements—is less clean. The dirty little secret of much empirical research in the social sciences is that data are often of low quality. Sometimes the problem is simple "dirt": random errors in response or recording. More insidious—and probably more important in ADD where non-researchers collected data in multiple programs—are fields that may be inconsistently defined and recorded by different programs and fields with many missing values.

The staff members of IDA programs are not full-time researchers, and, despite their consistent commitment to accurate data and their strong support for the ADD research overall, quality varies among programs and among types of data. Most time-constant demographic variables—such as gender and date of birth—are accurate. After ADD started, however, some questions were added to MIS IDA (for example, whether the participant carried health insurance or life insurance). Programs went back and asked most participants the new questions, but they did not ask for the answers as of the date of enrollment. Even if the questions had been asked retrospectively, it would still have been difficult for participants to give answers based on what they remembered as their at-enrollment status. Thus, for questions that were added to MIS IDA only after a program started, data are sometimes missing for early enrollees. Likewise, it was difficult to ask these new questions of former participants who had already closed their accounts before the questions appeared in MIS IDA.

As in all surveys, the data on income, assets, and debts are measured with error. To begin with, participants often do not know these values, especially for non-financial assets such as homes or cars. Informal income also tends to be both important and underreported (Edgcomb and Armington, 2003; Losby, Kingslow, and Else, 2003; Edin and Lein, 1997). Furthermore, measures of total income, total assets, and total debt were computed as the sum of many sub-items, and this compounds measurement error (Deaton, 1997). Also, if a sub-item was missing, then it bubbled through to make the total missing as well. In addition, MIS IDA asked for income at the household level but for assets at the individual level. It is unknown how participants reported assets (or debts) that they held jointly with other household members (such as the house itself), although it appears that most responded as if they were sole owners or sole debtors. Of course, eligibility for ADD was means-tested, so some participants may have understated the value of their income or assets in the belief that this would increase their chances of acceptance into the program.

Most data in MIS IDA were entered on a regular schedule. For example, cash-flow data were received each month, and participant characteristics were entered at enrollment. Some data, however, were entered only intermittently whenever a triggering event took place, and this left room for errors or omissions. For example, programs had to keep up on entering data from account statements so that they could send their own statements to participants and so that the program could calculate matches. Data on hours of financial education attended by participants, however, served no direct programmatic purpose and so, on average, did not receive as close of attention. Furthermore, data on attendance at financial-education classes was generated intermittently. Unfortunately, there was not always a way to detect when data simply was not entered into MIS IDA.

Data on the inputs and costs borne by the host organization to supply IDA services were measured with a good deal of error. Most IDA programs in ADD were not distinct cost centers within their host organizations, so breaking costs down and assigning them to the IDA program was likely viewed by program staff as extra work with little reward. Furthermore, few host organizations explicitly tracked the hours contributed to the IDA program by employees of referral organizations, by volunteers, or by partner organizations. Cross-checks on this data are difficult, if not impossible. In addition, two of the IDA programs in ADD were collaboratives whose member organizations provided the actual IDA services. Because the collaboratives had no practical way to track the costs incurred in all of their member organizations, their data on inputs and expenses were set to missing. Overall, cost data in MIS IDA were so unreliable that, after June 30, 2000, researchers stopped collecting it.

Low-quality data is a concern because it can lead to fragile or misleading results. Few researchers talk openly about data quality, in part because government policymakers and other funders tend to demand simple answers and apparently incontrovertible bullet-type results stripped of any messy caveats that might require them to carefully read and judge what might possibly turn out to be non-conclusive sources of evidence. Dirty data also survive in social science because replication is rare, both because researchers have few incentives to redo someone else's work and because uncooperative authors often thwart nascent replication efforts (McCullough and Vinod, 2003; Dewald, Thursby, and Anderson, 1986). Much empirical work, even that published in top academic journals, is little more than "sausage" about whose recipe and ingredients the producers and consumers seem to prefer a policy of "don't ask, don't tell".

Still, data quality matters much more than, for example, the sophistication of the statistical technique (Hand et al., 2000; Pyle, 1999). Research on ADD has paid extraordinary attention to data quality. For example, the Center for

Social Development created a complementary software program—MIS IDA QC—as a quality-control tool that researchers and IDA programs could use to check the reasonableness and consistency of the data recorded in MIS IDA. Researchers spent several person-months with program staff reviewing reports from MIS IDA QC and doing cross-checks for data-entry errors, missing values, and accounting inconsistencies. In some cases, program staff would telephone participants or dig out paper files to confirm or correct data. While tedious, this extensive process improved the quality of the data for ADD from MIS IDA and has paid rewards in terms of empirical results that more often square with theory and more often reach standard levels of statistical significance. Still, some types of errors cannot be detected or cross-checked, so this book (and Schreiner, 2002b) documents known or suspected issues and discusses how they may affect the accuracy and reliability of the empirical results. What is unusual is not that these data issues exist—they usually do, and often with greater severity and worse consequences than in ADD—but rather that the research has been careful to facilitate replication and interpretation by making these issues explicit. In this sense, the quality of the empirical work is well above average (Schreiner, 2002c).

Host Organizations and the Design of IDA Programs in ADD

The final part of this chapter documents the characteristics of the thirteen host organizations in ADD and the elements of account design in their fourteen IDA programs.

All the host organizations existed before ADD, and they all run other programs in addition to IDAs. As of the first year of ADD, the average age of the hosts was twenty years, with a low of two and a high of thirty-four (Schreiner et al., 2001). Many hosts had run IDA programs before, with the average host organization having run an IDA program for about two years before ADD. All the hosts were private non-profits, and the distribution of the specific organizational type appears in table 3.6.

Through the Corporation for Enterprise Development, all IDA programs in ADD received funds from eleven private foundations. Programs also supplemented this with funds from public, not-for-profit, for-profit, and/or individual sources (table 3.6). IDAs are unique among policy proposals in that they invite both public and private funders to participate. Indeed in principle, once an IDA account exists, anyone can contribute match funds for it (Goldberg and Cohen, 2000), much as anyone can contribute to a beneficiary via a 529 College Savings Account (Clancy, 2003).

ADVOCAP, Fond Du Lac, Wisconsin

ADVOCAP, Inc. is a community-action agency founded in 1966 whose mission is to create opportunities for people and communities to reduce pov-

Table 3.6
Organizational Types of Hosts

Organizational Type	Number of Hosts
Community Development Organization	6
Social-Service Agency	2
Bank or Credit Union	2
Housing-Development Organization	2
Collaborative	2

Types of Funding Partners

Type of Funding Partner	Number of Programs
Not-for-Profit	14
Public	12
For-Profit	9
Individual	2

Note: All programs in ADD had multiple funders.

erty. In 2000, operating revenues of $8.1 million supported 180 staff positions and agency services across twelve departments in rural areas and small towns in three counties. ADVOCAP provides emergency services as well as permanent solutions based on asset-development approaches. Its asset-development models include a business-development program (established 1985), a first-time home-ownership program (established 1991), and one of the first IDA programs anywhere. This pioneer IDA program was established 1995 and is described in Lazear (1999).

ADVOCAP ran four IDA sites, two of which were in ADD, the original site and a new site under AFIA rules. ADVOCAP's IDAs were targeted to the working poor and former AFDC/TANF recipients at or below 150 percent of the poverty line. The eighty-two participants had income that averaged 127 percent of the poverty line.

ADVOCAP required participants to take ten hours of general financial education before they could make a matched withdrawal. Although asset-specific education was offered, it was not required.

ADVOCAP offered a match rate of 2:1 on deposits of up to $1,000 in a twenty-four-month lifetime match-cap structure. (Participants who enrolled after December 31, 1999 could be matched only on deposits made through December 31, 2001.) Thus, maximum asset accumulation was $3,000. Participants had twenty-four months after the twenty-four-month time cap to make matched withdrawals. The matchable uses were home purchase, post-secondary education, small business, home repair, and job training.

Alternatives Federal Credit Union, Ithaca, New York

Alternatives FCU, founded in 1979, is a community-development credit union whose mission is to provide a full range of banking services and financial resources for small businesses, nonprofit organizations, and underserved segments of the small cities and rural areas of its local community. Alternatives FCU stresses customer service and provides alternative financial options including flexible mortgages, community-lending partnerships, and a youth credit union.

The credit union partnered with the Ithaca Housing Authority's Family Self-Sufficiency Program to develop and implement its IDA program. It targeted single parents and youth, and the first account was opened in February 1998. The eighty-six participants in ADD had income that averaged 98 percent of the poverty line.

Alternatives FCU required that participants take ten hours of general financial education before they could make a matched withdrawal. Asset-specific education was also required for matched withdrawals for home purchase (ten hours) and small business (thirty-three hours).

Alternatives FCU had a 3:1 match rate and a $500 annual match cap. Participants were encouraged to deposit the monthly target of $62.50 each month. The time cap for all ADD participants at Alternatives FCU was December 31, 2001. Matchable uses were home purchase, post-secondary education, small business, and home repair.

Bay Area IDA Collaborative, Oakland, California (EBALDC)

The Bay Area IDA Collaborative comprises twenty-eight community-based organizations which together serve a large share of the low-income population in the San Francisco Bay area. The lead organization in the Bay Area IDA Collaborative is the East Bay Asian Local Development Corporation, a Community Development Corporation founded in 1975 that has expanded its mission from serving the Asian-American and Pacific-Islander communities to building strong communities among diverse low-income populations. Services include affordable housing, community organizing and planning, and economic development.

The Bay Area IDA Collaborative runs four IDA sites; ADD included only the original site and a new site under AFIA rules. These two sites served low-income people of color referred by organizations in the collaborative. The 238 participants in ADD had income that averaged 112 percent of the poverty line.

Because the Bay Area IDA Collaborative collected data from many smaller IDA programs run by many organizations, its data quality suffered. In particular, it proved impossible to consolidate accurate data on program costs and inputs from all the collaborative members. Even in the other host organizations in ADD that were not made up of collaborative members, the data on inputs and costs are suspect because the organizations rarely tracked this information or, if they did track it, they accounted for it differently than the way in which it was recorded in MIS IDA.

The Bay Area IDA Collaborative required participants to take ten hours of general financial education before they could make a matched withdrawal. Asset-specific education was also required for home purchase (fourteen hours) and small business (thirty hours).

The Bay Area IDA Collaborative offered a match rate of 2:1 with lifetime match caps and a time cap of December 31, 2001. Participants who planned matched withdrawals for post-secondary education, small business, or job training had a match cap of $600 (maximum asset accumulation of $1,800). To accommodate the high cost of homes in the San Francisco Bay Area, the match cap was set at $1,920 for participants who planned matched withdrawals for home purchase (maximum asset accumulation of $5,760).

Capital Area Asset Building Corporation (CAAB), Washington, D.C.

CAAB is a nonprofit corporation comprised of eleven community-based organizations whose goal is to bring an asset-based economic-development system to scale in the disadvantaged neighborhoods of the District of Columbia. The collaborative was created in 1997 with a mission to build capacity through a centralized, systemic approach to the implementation of IDAs in the District, to craft a collaborative fundraising strategy to minimize competition among community-based organizations, and to join forces in advocacy activities to help pass legislation in support of asset accumulation for low-income residents. Member organizations in CAAB run IDA programs and provide services to participants.

CAAB ran two IDA sites, an original site and a new site under AFIA rules. The sites served urban youth and adults with a focus on TANF recipients, African Americans, Hispanics, and Asian Americans. The 142 participants had income that averaged 143 percent of the poverty line. As in the case of EBALDC (the other collaborative in ADD), CAAB collected data from many smaller IDA programs run by different organizations. Thus, data quality suffered, and cost data were not reliable.

Requirements for financial education varied among the member organizations in CAAB, but the average requirement was about twenty hours. Some members required that participants complete some general financial education before opening an IDA, while others required only that classes be completed before matched withdrawals. On average, CAAB reported that asset-specific requirements were thirty-two hours for home purchase, twenty hours for post-secondary education, and twenty-two hours for small business.

Depending on the member organization and on the planned use, CAAB offered match rates from 2:1 to 7:1. Match caps also varied across member organizations, but all participants had lifetime match caps. Time caps were thirty-six months for most participants and up to forty-eight months for youth. For CAAB as a whole, matchable uses included home purchase, post-secondary education, small business, and job training.

Foundation Communities, Austin, Texas

Foundation Communities (formerly the Central Texas Mutual Housing Association) is a community-based non-profit organization whose mission is to provide affordable housing to help families to improve their lives and to pursue their dreams. Founded in 1986, Foundation Communities has developed 1,655 units of affordable housing in ten Central and North Texas urban-rental communities. With a staff of twenty-seven, Foundation Communities has created several resident-service programs for low-income tenants, including after-school and summer-youth programs, classes in computers and English-as-a-Second-Language, and its IDA program. Counseling and training are offered in both English and Spanish.

Of the four IDA sites run by Foundation Communities, this report includes only the two ADD sites: the original site, and a new site under AFIA rules. The 125 ADD participants had income that averaged 139 percent of the poverty line.

Participants at Foundation Communities were required to complete ten hours of general financial education before they could make a matched withdrawal. Participants who planned matched withdrawals for home purchase or small business also had to take twelve hours of asset-specific education.

Foundation Communities offered a match rate of 2:1 and an annual match cap of $500. Participants had time caps of three years (a few who enrolled in December 1999 had two-year time caps). Thus, maximum asset accumulation in IDAs for most participants was $4,500. Deposits made after December 31, 2001 were not eligible for matches. At Foundation Communities, matchable uses were home purchase, post-secondary education, small business, and job training.

Unlike any other host organization in ADD, Foundation Communities allowed a given participant to have more than one IDA. These additional accounts were in the names of children or other family members. In effect, the multiple accounts increased the annual match cap for individuals. Thus, some participants had maximum asset accumulations of $9,000, $13,500, $18,000, or $22,500. The analysis here consolidates all IDAs owned by a given participant as if they were a single account.

Central Vermont Community Action Council, Inc. (CVCAC), Barre, Vermont

CVCAC, a community-action agency founded in 1965, focuses on community-economic development and developmental family services. Each year,

the 130 professionals in CVCAC provide advocacy and programmatic services to about 6,000 people from economically disadvantaged families in
fifty-six towns in rural north-central Vermont.

CVCAC partnered with several community agencies to implement its IDA
program, serving clients of CVCAC, TANF recipients, and young adults. CVCAC
ran two IDA sites, the original site and a new site under AFIA rules. The 150 ADD
participants had income that averaged 76 percent of the poverty line.

CVCAC required participants to take sixteen hours of general financial
education before they could make a matched withdrawal. Asset-specific education was also required for home purchase (eight hours), post-secondary education (two hours), and small business (two hours).

In the original ADD site, CVCAC offered a 1:1 match rate. If a participant
received TANF at any time during participation, then the match rate for that
participant was permanently changed to 2:1. In the new ADD site under AFIA,
CVCAC offered a 2:1 match rate. If a participant received TANF at any time
during participation, then the match rate for that participant was permanently
changed to 3:1.

The original ADD site at CVCAC had an annual match cap of $500. The
new ADD site had a 24-month time cap and annual match caps that ranged
from $250 to $1,000. In all cases, the deadline for matchable deposits was
December 31, 2001. Matchable uses were home purchase, post-secondary education, small business, and home repair.

Community Action Project of Tulsa County (CAPTC), Tulsa, Oklahoma

CAPTC, founded in 1973, is a community-based, comprehensive anti-poverty agency whose mission is to help individuals and families in economic
need to achieve self-sufficiency through emergency aid, medical care, housing, community development, education, and advocacy. Recent examples of
new programs that have grown in response to client demand include an affordable-housing program and an Earned Income Tax Credit program.

The IDA programs at CAPTC focused on people who were making the effort to
achieve self-sufficiency but who were not yet able to escape poverty. They targeted working-poor households with children who qualify for the maximum EITC
refund. Many of the IDA participants were also clients of other CAPTC services.

As a host organization in ADD, CAPTC was unique in that it had two IDA
programs and also the largest number of total participants (619).

The first IDA program—CAPTC Small-scale—enrolled its first participant
in February 1998. The Small-scale program targeted people at or below 200
percent of the poverty line. The income of its 162 participants averaged 134
percent of poverty.

The CAPTC Small-scale program required participants to take six hours of
financial education—general or asset-specific—each year. Asset-specific edu-

cation was required for matched withdrawals: five hours for home purchase, two hours for post-secondary education, sixteen hours for small business, and two hours for retirement.

CAPTC Small-scale offered a match rate of 2:1 for matched withdrawals for home purchase and a match rate of 1:1 for all other uses. The annual match cap was $750, and the time cap for all participants was December 31, 2001. Matchable uses were home purchase, post-secondary education, small business, home repair, and retirement.

The second program—CAPTC Large-scale—had an experimental design. Of 1,103 qualified applicants, 537 were randomly assigned to a treatment group with access to IDAs, and 566 were assigned to a control group without access to IDAs. (Of the 537 in the treatment group, 456 eventually opened accounts and did not die or move away and thus had a chance for positive savings outcomes.) All 1,103 qualified applicants were surveyed just before their randomized assignment and then again in follow-up surveys eighteen months and forty-eight months after assignment. The experiment and data collection were designed to facilitate estimates of the impact of access to IDAs. Future work will study these impacts.

The Large-scale program targeted people at or below 150 percent of the poverty line. Average income for the 441 participants was 130 percent of poverty.

CAPTC Large-scale required participants to take twelve hours of general financial education, four hours of which were required prior to opening an account. Asset-specific education was also required prior to making a matched withdrawal: five hours for home purchase, two hours for post-secondary education, sixteen hours for small business start-up, and two hours for retirement. No asset-specific education was required for matched withdrawals for existing small businesses, but these participants had to present a business plan.

Like CAPTC Small-scale, CAPTC Large-scale offered a match rate of 2:1 for matched withdrawals for home purchase and a match rate of 1:1 for all other uses. The time cap was thirty-six months from the date of account opening, and the annual match cap was $750. Thus, participants who did not buy a home had a maximum asset accumulation of $4,500, and participants who did buy a home had a maximum asset accumulation of $6,750. Matchable uses were home purchase, post-secondary education, small business, home repair, and retirement. The data for CAPTC Large-scale go through October 31, 2003, unlike the data for all the other IDAs programs in ADD, which go through December 31, 2001.

Heart of America Family Services (HAFS), Family Focus Center, Kansas City, Missouri

HAFS is a 120-year-old non-profit organization whose mission is to support and to strengthen families in need through information, education, and intervention. Its programs serve 60,000 people annually at more than 14 locations. One of HAFS' community-based programs, The Family Focus Center, provides neighborhood-based family support to a primarily Hispanic population on Kansas City's West Side. The Family Focus Center implemented the IDA program in partnership with other neighborhood organizations and with the University of Kansas School of Social Welfare. Counseling and training were offered in both English and Spanish. The IDA program served the neighborhood area and clients at the Family Focus Center. The Family Focus Center had one IDA site with eighty-five participants whose income averaged 108 percent of the poverty line.

HAFS claimed to require participants to take forty-five hours of general financial education before they could make a matched withdrawal. The data, however, suggest that this requirement was almost never met, suggesting that it was not really a requirement in the first place. All types of matched withdrawals required asset-specific education: twelve hours for home purchase, six hours for post-secondary education, twelve hours for small business, and fifteen hours for retirement.

HAFS offered a match rate of 2:1 and a lifetime match cap with a time cap of December 31, 2001. The match cap differed for each participant and was computed as $30 multiplied by the number of months between account opening and December 31, 2001, with an additional $45 for each year of participation. For example, someone who opened an account in December 1999 would have been eligible to participate for twenty-five months over three distinct participation-years with a total match cap of $30·25 + $45·3 = $885. At HAFS, matchable uses were home purchase, post-secondary education, small business, home repair, job training, and retirement.

Mercy Corps, Portland, Oregon

Mercy Corps (formerly Human Solutions) was founded in 1988 as a nonprofit community housing organization whose focus is to provide housing and related services to homeless and low-income families in East Portland and East Multnomah County. Since 1992, the organization has purchased and developed more than 222 units of low-income housing, and it manages market-rate housing owned by others for homeless families.

The IDA program at Mercy Corps served 118 residents of Multnomah County. Their income averaged 125 percent of the poverty line.

Participants were required to complete eight hours of general financial education within six months after they opened their IDA. Asset-specific education was required for all matched uses: eight hours for home purchase, three hours for post-secondary education, three hours for job training, and twelve hours for small business.

The match rate at Mercy Corps was 1:1, the annual match cap was $500, and the time cap was December 31, 2001. Matchable uses were home purchase, post-secondary education, small business, and job training.

Mountain Association for Community Economic Development (MACED),
Berea, Kentucky

In 1976, MACED was created by ten community-development organizations in Central Appalachia to provide technical assistance to community-based groups. Its core programs are business development, sustainable communities, and land and resources. The "Pathways to Prosperity" IDA program targets low-income residents of Owsley County, the poorest county in Kentucky, and in particular African Americans, rental-property residents, and the working poor.

Several local community organizations partnered with MACED to implement the IDA program, including the Owsley County Action Team (a citizens' group that participates in MACED's Sustainable Communities Initiative) and the Central Appalachian Peoples Federal Credit Union. MACED had three IDA sites, all in ADD. The sixty-three participants had income that averaged 86 percent of the poverty line.

MACED required participants to complete twelve hours of general financial education (one hour of financial education each month) before they could make a matched withdrawal. MACED did not require any asset-specific education. Unlike any other host organization in ADD, MACED did not allow matched withdrawals unless net deposits equaled the lifetime match cap of $360.

The time cap at MACED was twenty-four months. For the first group of participants to enroll, deposits were matched at the rate of 6:1; this group had a maximum asset accumulation of $2,520. A second group of participants who enrolled later were matched at a rate of 1:1; their maximum asset accumulation was $720. Matchable uses at MACED were home purchase, post-secondary education, small business, home repair, and job training.

Near Eastside IDA Program, Indianapolis, Indiana

The Near Eastside Community Federal Credit Union (NECFCU) and the John H. Boner Community Center together created the Near Eastside IDA Program. The NECFCU, founded in 1981, held the IDA accounts and is the only community-development credit union in Indiana. The Boner Center is a neighborhood community center that has provided a broad spectrum of social services since 1972. The Near Eastside IDA Program serves youth and adults who live in the Near Eastside of Indianapolis and who are in programs of the Boner Center or of NECFCU.

Near Eastside ran four IDA sites, two of which were in ADD. One was an original site, and the second was a new site under AFIA rules. The 190 ADD participants had income that averaged 87 percent of the poverty line.

Near Eastside required participants to complete nine hours of general financial education before they could make a matched withdrawal. Although asset-specific education was offered, it was not required.

In the original ADD site, Near Eastside offered most participants a match rate of 3:1, although some had match rates of 1:1, 2:1, or 6:1. The annual match cap was $250, $300, or $500, depending on the funding source. The time cap was April 30, 2001; deposits made after that were not matchable. Matchable uses were home purchase, post-secondary education, small business, and job training.

In the new ADD site, Near Eastside offered a match rate of 3:1. The new site had a lifetime match cap of $500 and a time cap of December 31, 2001. Thus, maximum asset accumulation at the new site was $2,000.

Shorebank, Chicago, Illinois

Shorebank, created in 1978, is a community-development financial institution whose mission is to increase opportunities in underserved communities by identifying and supporting investment in local assets. The IDA program is a joint effort between South Shore Bank and the Shorebank Neighborhood Institute, Shorebank's nonprofit affiliate. The primary focus of the Shorebank Neighborhood Institute is human and social-capital development, as well as targeted enterprise development. The program targets African Americans who live in the South and West Sides of Chicago, including families who live in subsidized rental properties owned by Shorebank.

Shorebank runs three IDA sites, two of which are in ADD. The 202 ADD participants had income that averaged 122 percent of the poverty line.

In the original ADD site, Shorebank required six hours of general financial education before a matched withdrawal. In the new ADD site, Shorebank required eight hours. No asset-specific education was required.

In the original site, Shorebank offered a match rate of 1:1 with an annual match cap of $500. The time cap was twenty-four months. Thus, maximum asset accumulation in the original site was $2,000. Matchable uses were home purchase, post-secondary education, small business, home repair, and job training.

In the new site, Shorebank offered a match rate of 2:1 and a lifetime match cap of $600 (a few participants had a match cap of $500). The time cap was thirty-six months. Thus, maximum asset accumulation in the new site was $1,800. As in the original site, matchable uses were home purchase, post-secondary education, small business, home repair, and job training.

Women's Self-Employment Project (WSEP), Chicago, Illinois

WSEP, started in 1986, is a microenterprise-development organization that provides entrepreneurial training, business-development services, and financial services to low- and moderate-income women. Its mission is to increase the income and the degree of economic self-sufficiency of women through a strategy of self-employment and to serve as a catalyst for the development of viable options to alleviate poverty.

In 1995, WSEP started an IDA program targeted to welfare recipients; it was one of the first IDA programs anywhere. The IDA program in ADD—consisting of an original site and a new site under AFIA rules—served participants from the Center for New Horizons, graduates of WSEP programs, and employees of the businesses of WSEP participants. The 227 ADD participants had income that averaged 100 percent of the poverty line.

WSEP required participants to take sixteen hours of general financial education before they could open an IDA. Some types of matched withdrawals also required asset-specific education: eight hours for home purchase, six hours for post-secondary education, and, depending on the experience of the participant, eight to thirty-five hours for small business.

Participants in the original ADD site at WSEP had match rates of 2:1, and a few had match rates of 5:1 or 6:1. In WSEP's new ADD site, the match rate was 2.5:1. Participants in the original site had lifetime match caps of $500 or $600, and participants in the new AFIA site had lifetime match caps of $600. At both sites, the time cap was twenty-four months. Matchable uses at WSEP were home purchase, post-secondary education, and small business.

4

Participants in ADD

This chapter paints a broad picture of the 2,350 participants in ADD. The discussion here of the characteristics of ADD participants and their hypothesized associations with savings outcomes serves as preparation for the empirical analysis in later chapters.

Why might participant characteristics matter? First, policymakers want to know who saves in IDAs. Can anyone—regardless of how poor they may be—save in IDAs? Or do IDAs work only for the "working poor" and those whose lives are reasonably stable? Second, even though policymakers control only program characteristics, program characteristics—and hence their design—may depend on participant characteristics. For example, the association between saving and match rates (or match caps, or financial education) may depend on the participant's marital status, gender, race/ethnicity, or existing asset ownership. Some initial evidence suggests that this may be the case, at least for rural/urban location (Curley and Grinstein-Weiss, 2003; Grinstein-Weiss and Curley, 2002), single mothers (Zhan, 2003), small-business owners (Ssewamala, 2003), and race/ethnicity (Grinstein-Weiss and Sherraden, 2004). If policy-makers knew which participant characteristics are linked with saving in IDAs, and if policymakers knew how these participant characteristics interact with program characteristics, then this knowledge could guide IDA design. In turn, this could lead to inclusion of broader segments of the poor, and it might also lead to IDA designs tailored to the situations of specific groups. In the end, the analysis in this book is intended to help increase saving and asset accumulation in IDAs as well as balance out differences in saving and asset accumulation across groups.

Overall, the people who were targeted by IDA programs in ADD and who self-selected into participation are probably best described as disadvantaged members of the "working poor." ADD participants were not generally among the "poorest of the poor" (those without jobs, education, or financial capital), nor were they among the "richest of the poor" (married Caucasian males). Rather, they tended to be unmarried, female, and non-Caucasian and to have jobs, some education, and existing bank accounts.

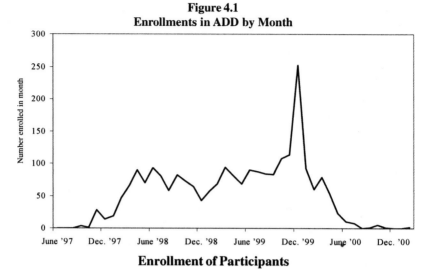

Figure 4.1
Enrollments in ADD by Month

Enrollment of Participants

In ADD, a *participant* is defined as someone who opened an IDA. People who opened an IDA but who later closed it without making a matched withdrawal are still counted as participants. This definition of *participant*, however, excludes people who opened an IDA but whose subsequent savings outcomes were completely determined by program rules or by other factors beyond their control, including, for example, people who died, people who moved to a place with no IDA program, or people who were never should have been eligible to enroll in the first place. In other words, people whose net IDA deposits were constrained to be zero were not counted as participants.

The pace of enrollment in the first twelve months of ADD was slow, but it picked up and became seventy to ninety enrollees per month (five to seven enrollees per program) in the eighteen months following June 1998 (figure 4.1). More than 250 people enrolled in December 1999 (the month planned for the enrollment deadline). Enrollment declined rapidly thereafter.

In cumulative terms, there were 831 enrollments in ADD as of December 31, 1998 (figure 4.2). By the planned deadline of December 31, 1999, ADD had 2,016 enrollees, sixteen more than its goal. By the end of the year 2000, enrollment reached its total of 2,350.

Participant Characteristics

In ADD, program staff recorded participant characteristics in MIS IDA at the time of enrollment. After that, they sometimes updated characteristics that could change through time, for example, marital status, number of children, employment status, or income. Some programs made these updates twice a year, some made them once a year, some made one or two rounds of updates and then stopped, and some programs never made any updates at all. Program

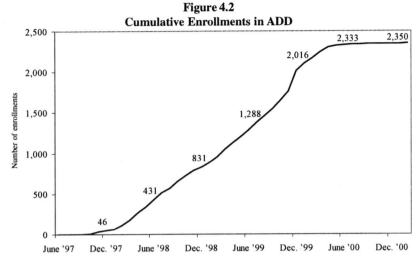

Figure 4.2
Cumulative Enrollments in ADD

staff also corrected problems detected during data cleaning. Both updates and corrections resulted in new, dated records for the participant in MIS IDA, and any old records remained in the database. Although there is no way to know whether the data in the most-recent record for a given participant is an update or a correction, the descriptive measures of participant characteristics in this chapter use the most-recent record because it received the most thorough cleaning. The regression analysis in later chapters uses the at-enrollment record because, even though the at-enrollment data has more noise, it is free of two-way causation. For example, income after enrollment could affect IDA saving and also be affected by IDA saving, but IDA saving could not affect income at enrollment.

The characteristics of participants in ADD are defined and summarized in the text and tables that follow in this chapter. Overall, participants mostly come from the "working poor." Among the "working poor," participants are relatively disadvantaged in that they are disproportionately female, African American, and never-married.

The descriptive statistics below do not relate participant characteristics with savings outcomes. Such bivariate analysis has a greater potential to mislead than does the regression analysis that is presented in later chapters because the regression analysis associates a given participant characteristic with savings outcomes while controlling for other characteristics in the regression.

Demographics

For ADD as a whole, the demographic characteristics of participants are in table 4.1. Appendix C of Schreiner, Clancy, and Sherraden (2002) breaks down the demographic information for participants in each of the fourteen programs in ADD.

Table 4.1
Demographics of Participants

Characteristic	%
Gender	
Female	80
Male	20
Age (mean 36 years)	
13 to 19	4
20s	25
30s	36
40s	25
50s	7
60 or older	2
Race/Ethnicity	
African-American	47
Asian-American or Pacific Islander	2
Caucasian	37
Latino or Hispanic	9
Native-American	3
Other	3
Residence	
Urban (population 2,500 or more)	86
Rural (population less than 2,500)	14

Gender. About 80 percent of participants were female, and 20 percent were male. Given the general oppression of women and their subsequent disadvantage in labor markets and other social arenas, women might be expected to save less than men. The experience in low-income countries, however, suggests that women often save more, perhaps precisely because their disadvantage confers a greater precautionary motive to save (Ardener and Burman, 1995; Morris and Meyer, 1993). Women's greater responsibility and concern for children may also increase their saving (Littlefield, Morduch, and Hashemi, 2003; Vonderlack and Schreiner, 2002).

Age. The average age of participants at enrollment was thirty-six years, with a low of thirteen and a high of seventy-two. About 86 percent of participants were between twenty and forty-nine years of age.

Age has several possible links with saving in IDAs. First, as people age, they may become "wiser" in that they know more about the saving choices that they might make and that they more accurately evaluate the costs and rewards of saving. If younger people undervalue saving and if people learn with time, then greater age would lead to increased saving.

Second, older people are more likely to already own a home or to have already finished their education (or to have ruled out going back to school). This tends to depress their IDA saving because it eliminates two of the three universal matched uses for IDAs. Of course, homeownership and post-secondary education are attractive possibilities to many younger participants (in fact, for the youngest participants, post-secondary education is likely the only possible matched use), and older participants may make matched withdrawals for the post-secondary education of other people such as their children or grandchildren. On the other hand, small-business ownership—the third universal use of IDA matches—is usually more viable for older people (Blanchflower and Oswald, 1998; Aronson, 1991; Evans and Leighton, 1989). Finally, some programs in ADD offered matches for withdrawals rolled into Roth IRAs, and these retirement accounts are probably most attractive to people close to retirement. All in all, age interacts with the matched uses of IDAs in several different ways.

Third, older people have had more time to accumulate assets. If they have more liquid assets available to shift or reshuffle into an IDA, then they may have higher IDA balances.

Fourth, income usually increases with age, so, all else constant, older people may have more resources available to be saved and thus may save more.

Fifth and finally, expenses vary over the life-cycle, often peaking in middle age as children go to school. All else constant, this would decrease saving for middle-aged participants.

Race/ethnicity. Participants self-identified their race/ethnicity (table 4.1) as African American (47 percent), Asian American or Pacific Islander (2 percent), Caucasian (37 percent), Latino or Hispanic (9 percent), Native American (3 percent) or as "Other" (3 percent).

Comparing Caucasians and African Americans, asset ownership is extremely unequal, much more unequal than income (Carney and Gale, 2001; Badu, Daniels, and Salandro, 1999; Conley, 1999; Oliver and Shapiro, 1995). At the same time, some research has found that African-Americans save a greater share of their income than do Caucasians (Olney, 1998; Blau and Graham, 1990).

How could a high saving rate accompany low asset accumulation? One possibility is that African Americans' lower income means that they accumulate fewer dollars in absolute terms even though they save a higher share of their income in relative terms. A second possibility is that although African Americans save at a high rate, they also are subject to greater and more frequent shocks to income and expenses and so are also more likely to dissave, leading to low asset accumulation. Along these lines, African Americans who own assets may face greater demands to provide assistance within their social networks (Chiteji and Hamilton, 2000 and 2002).

IDAs may be a way to improve asset accumulation for African Americans both because the mild costs of unmatched withdrawals may help to put resources beyond the reach of social networks and because the match increases the amount of asset accumulation that results from a given level of saving (see also Sherraden, 1999b).

Location of residence. Areas with a population of 2,500 or more were counted as "urban" (86 percent), and all other areas were classified as "rural" (14 percent).

Location of residence might affect IDA saving in several ways. First, the types of assets available for purchase may differ along rural/urban lines. For example, urbanites probably live closer to post-secondary schools, but rural dwellers may be able to buy a given home for a lower price. Furthermore, rural dwellers may be more likely to own land and/or a small business (such as a farm). Second, the transaction costs involved in IDA participation—mainly getting back and forth between home, the depository institution, and financial-education classes—are probably higher for rural dwellers, not only because rural distances are greater but also because of the absence of public transport. Third, many rural areas combine a strong sense of community with a growing realization that something must be done to strengthen the local economic base. Development efforts are often spearheaded by the local depository institution. Thus, social support for IDAs in the community may be greater in rural areas. Differences in IDA saving by location of residence are examined in Curley and Grinstein-Weiss (2003) and in Grinstein-Weiss and Curley (2002).

Household Composition

Household composition might matter for IDA saving because, although IDAs are *Individual* Development Accounts, saving and asset accumulation usually results from cooperative efforts among all household members. For example, household composition might affect saving through its effect on income (contributions by other adults) as well as expenses (consumption by children and other adults). It also matters how other household members provide social support for the IDA participant and his or her saving goals. Aspects of household composition for participants in ADD appear in table 4.2.

Marital status. Participants were never-married (48 percent), married (22 percent), divorced or separated (27 percent), or widowed (2 percent). (Marital status was missing for 1 percent of participants.) In total, three-fourths (75 percent) of participants in ADD were not married.

On average, marriage is associated with greater stability and greater income and so with greater savings. Furthermore, being married may serve as a proxy for difficult-to-quantify characteristics (such as persistence, future-orientation, and kindness) that influence both marital status and saving. In general, then, married people would be expected to save more than unmarried people, although unmarried people may have a greater precautionary motive to save.

Table 4.2
Composition of Participant Households

Characteristic	%
Marital Status	
Never-Married	48
Married	22
Divorced or separated	27
Widowed	2
Missing	1
Household Type	
One adult with children	44
One adult without children	15
Two or more adults with children	32
Two or more adults without children	9
Missing	1
Single mothers	
No	48
Yes	52
Missing	1
Adults in Household (mean 1.5)	
1	58
2	34
3	6
4	1
5 or more	1
Missing	1
Children in Household (mean 1.7)	
0	24
1	24
2	26
3	14
4	7
5 or more	4
Multiple Participants in Household	
Yes	6
No	94

Household type. Household types in ADD included one adult with children (44 percent, with 95 percent of these being single mothers with children), one adult without children (15 percent), two or more adults with children (32 percent), or two or more adults without children (9 percent). Thus, while three-fourths (75 percent) of participants in ADD were not married, only 58 percent of participant households had only one adult.

Single mothers. More than half (52 percent) of participants in ADD were unmarried women with children. Zhan (2003) compares savings outcomes for single mothers with other participants in ADD and, in general, finds no large differences. This is somewhat of a surprise, given that single mothers have two strikes against them (being female and being unmarried) and that IDAs are not particularly well suited for precautionary saving.

Adults. The average number of adults aged eighteen years or older in the household was 1.5, and 58 percent of households had only one adult. The number of adults was missing for the 1 percent of participants who reported being married but who reported only one adult in the household.

The number of adults in the household could influence IDA saving in a couple of ways. On the one hand, more adults could mean more income and thus greater resources available to be saved. On the other hand, the additional adults may not be sources of income (for example, they may be unemployed, or disabled, or retired) and so may serve to increase expenses and decrease the financial resources available to be saved.

Children. The average number of children aged seventeen years or younger in the household was 1.7. Most households (76 percent) had at least one child. All else constant, children generate expenses but not income, so more children means fewer resources available to be saved.

Multiple participants in a household. About 6 percent of the participants were in households that probably had at least one other IDA participant. This information was not recorded directly in the MIS IDA database, but the researchers identified likely cases of multiple participants in a single household by hand-matching a combination of last names, addresses, and phone numbers. Of course, IDAs are held by individuals, so there is nothing wrong with multiple accounts in a single household.

Although multiple participants in a household might reduce per-participant IDA saving by diluting it across two accounts, it seems unlikely that it would reduce total household saving in IDAs. In the first place, having multiple accounts effectively increases the household's match cap. This not only relaxes the limit on matched savings (for example, if the match cap is $500 but the household would like to save $750, they can do so if they have two IDAs but not if they have only one) but also may have a psychological effect in which the household turns the (higher) match cap into a goal and then makes a greater effort to save than if the limit were lower. In the second place, households may have multiple participants precisely they are unusually enthusiastic about saving. In these cases, the presence of multiple participants serves as a proxy for unobserved factors such as "eagerness to save." Furthermore, participants in multiple-IDA households can provide support and examples for each other. Finally, households with large amounts of existing assets available to shift or reshuffle into IDAs may be more likely to have both multiple participants and greater saving.

Education and Employment

Both education and employment status reflect human capital, that is, accumulated training and experience that is available to use for production in the market and in the household. All else constant, greater human capital decreases the effort required to make a given level of resources available to save. Education may also reflect future orientation, as people who place a greater value on future well-being are both more likely to invest in schooling and—whatever their schooling—more likely to save in financial forms. Employment also is linked with greater income (and thus greater saving) and with regular or recurrent (bi-weekly or monthly) income. These regular income flows may make it easier to form a saving habit.

Empirical analysis in later chapters suggests that students—and especially students who are also employed—are likely to have above-average savings outcomes in IDAs. The education and employment status of participants in ADD appear in table 4.3.

Education. The highest grade completed by a participant was either less than a high-school diploma (15 percent), a high-school diploma or GED (22 percent), some college but no degree (39 percent), a two-year college degree (6 percent), a college degree with two-year or four-year unspecified (8 percent), or a four-year college degree or more (10 percent). Most participants (61 percent) had at least attended some college.

Employment status. Participants were either employed full-time (58 percent), employed part-time (20 percent), unemployed (7 percent), not working (4 percent), a student but not working (5 percent), or a student and working (5 percent). *Not working* includes homemakers, retirees, and the disabled. *Unemployed* includes people who were laid-off and awaiting a call back or who were seeking employment. Almost 90 percent of participants were working or were students.

Small-business owners. Self-employed participants were identified as those who reported owning business assets or who reported receiving self-employment income (18 percent). Economic theory does not provide an unambiguous prediction about the saving of self-employed people in IDAs. On the one hand, the self-employed have greater investment opportunities than the wage-employed; they can invest in their businesses. After all, despite policy's overwhelming focus on loans to assist small business start-ups, most new enterprises

Table 4.3
Participant Education and Employment Status

Characteristic	%
Education	
Did not complete high school	15
Completed high school or GED	22
Attended college	39
Completed 2-year degree	6
Completed unspecified degree	8
Completed 4-year degree or more	10
Employment	
Employed full-time	58
Employed part-time	20
Unemployed	7
Not working	4
Student, not working	5
Student, also working	5
Small-Business Owners	
Yes	18
No	82

are financed mostly by owner's equity (Montgomery, Johnson, and Faisal, 2000; Bates, 1996; Holtz-Eakin, Joulfaian, and Rosen, 1994; Evans and Jovanovic, 1989). IDAs fit this investment motive well (Schreiner, 2004b; Schreiner and Woller, 2003; Schreiner and Morduch, 2002). Furthermore, owners almost always must use their assets to finance business operations and household consumption in the first months and years after start-up as the new venture gets off the ground (Schreiner, 1999a and 1999b; Taylor, 1999). On the other hand, the self-employed face volatile streams of income and expenses, leading to strong precautionary motives to save (Servon and Bates, 1998; Balkin, 1989). Because IDAs may impose mild costs on unmatched withdrawals, they may not fit this "rainy-day" motive very well, so the desire to avoid tying assets up in IDAs may decrease the saving of the self-employed. Ssewamala (2003) compares the saving of small-business owners with that of other participants in ADD.

Income/poverty level. Household income for the average participant in ADD was about 116 percent (median 106 percent) of the family-size adjusted federal poverty guideline. About 20 percent of participants were under 50 percent of the poverty line, and 12 percent were over 200 percent of

Figure 4.3
Distribution of Participant Income as a Percentage
of the Federal Family-Size Adjusted Poverty Guideline

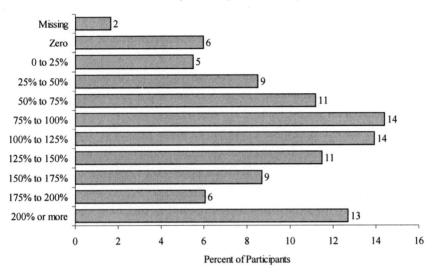

Percent of Participants

poverty (figure 4.3). Income data were missing for about 2 percent of participants, and about 6 percent reported zero income in the previous month.

In terms of monthly dollars, income for the average participant in ADD was $1,494 (table 4.4), or about $18,000 per year.

Economic theory proposes three basic links between income and saving. (Sherraden, Schreiner, and Beverly [2003] discuss the theory of income and saving extensively, and the institutional theory presented in chapter 2 suggests that income is not the only factor nor necessarily the most important factor.) First, because greater income makes it easier for income to exceed consumption, theory predicts that increased income will lead to an increased absolute level of saving. Indeed, Wolff (1998) shows a strong, positive correlation between income and asset accumulation.

Second, economic theory predicts that greater income may or may not lead to a greater saving rate. That is, as income increases, the share of income saved might increase, or it might decrease. Given a rate of saving, people with more income can also consume more. As they consume more, the reward from additional consumption may diminish faster than the diminishing reward from additional saving. If so, then the sacrifice required to save may be softened for people who already have high income and therefore high consumption, and this leads to a greater saving rate. On the other hand, if the additional rewards to saving are less than the additional rewards of consumption, then additional income could decrease the saving rate. Theory provides little guidance as to which case is more likely, and the relationship between income and the saving

Table 4.4
Participant Income per Month by Source

Income Source	N	Mean ($)	Median ($)	Min. ($)	Max. ($)	Cases Missing	Participants with an Income Source (%)	Distribution of Total Income by Source (%)
Wages	2,350	1,088	1,050	0	6,260	0	78	67
Government Benefits	2,350	136	0	0	3,400	0	27	14
Pensions	2,350	12	0	0	2,000	0	2	1
Investments	2,312	4	0	0	5,000	38	1	0
Recurrent Sources	2,312	1,243	1,200	0	6,760	38	90	82
Self-employment	2,350	138	0	0	5,000	0	16	9
Child Support	2,350	51	0	0	1,833	0	15	4
Gifts	2,350	16	0	0	2,000	0	5	1
Other Sources	2,349	55	0	0	3,514	1	9	4
Intermittent Sources	2,349	260	0	0	5,000	1	37	18
Total Income	2,311	1,494	1,360	0	6,760	39	99	100
Income/Poverty	2,311	1.16	1.06	0	7.21	39	N/A	N/A

rate may change directions more than once as the absolute level of income increases.

Third, economic theory suggests that the regularity of income affects saving (Carroll and Samwick, 1998 and 1997; Dercon, 1998 and 1996; Deaton, 1992a). All else constant, people are more likely to save a dollar received from an irregular or intermittent source than a dollar from a regular or recurrent source. Intermittent flows strengthen precautionary motives to save because they imply more "rainy days."

Recurrent income. Recurrent income comes from wages, government benefits, pensions, or investments. For participants in ADD, recurrent income represented about 82 percent of total income (table 4.4). About four-fifths (78 percent) of participants had income from wages, and these wages accounted for two-thirds (67 percent) of the value of total income. About one-fourth (27 percent) of participants received government benefits (14 percent of the value of total income).

Of the sixteen participants in ADD aged sixty-five or older, five reported income from pensions (1 percent of the average value of total income). Furthermore, only 1 percent of participants (twenty people) reported any income from investments. These figures fit with the ideas that most of the elderly poor did not have jobs with pension benefits and that the poor in general are unlikely to earn much income from investments.

Intermittent income. About one-fifth (18 percent) of total income ($260 per month) came from self-employment, child-support payments, gifts, or other sources (table 4.4). Gifts accounted for 1 percent of the average value of total income ($16 per month), and other sources accounted for 4 percent ($55 per month).

On average for all participants, child-support payments were about 4 percent of the value of total income. The average figure for those who received child support was $376, equivalent to 23 percent of their average total income of $1,640. Average total income for single mothers who did not receive child support was $1,361. Thus, the value of child support was equivalent to about three-fourths of the difference in total income for single mothers with versus without child support.

Income from self-employment was counted as "intermittent" because it is highly variable, even for the full-time self-employed. About 16 percent of participants in ADD reported income from self-employment (table 4.4). Furthermore, about 13 percent reported that they had business assets, and 2 percent reported business debts. Overall, 18 percent of participants in ADD had business assets, business debt, or business income.

Furthermore, 18 percent of participants had either made a matched withdrawal for small business or had stated at enrollment that they planned to make such a matched withdrawal. Of participants who had made a matched withdrawal for small business, 55 percent were apparently start-ups, given that they had not reported any self-employment income, assets, or debt. Among participants without a matched withdrawal but who stated at enrollment that they planned to make a matched withdrawal for small business, 70 percent were apparently planning start-ups. All in all, 12 percent of participants in ADD did not yet own a business but either used or planned to use their IDA to start one.

All this suggests that, compared with the U.S. population, ADD had a high concentration of small-business owners and of would-be small-business owners. For example, about 8 percent of all U.S. workers are self-employed (Blanchflower, 2000; Clark et al., 1999). Likewise, Spalter-Roth, Hartmann, and Shaw (1993) find that 6 percent of all U.S. working men and 2 percent of women were full-time self-employed. By way of comparison, 5 percent of men and 4 percent for women in ADD reported that all their income came from self-employment, and 9 percent of men and 9 percent of women in ADD reported that at least half of their income came from self-employment.

Why this high concentration in ADD of small-business owners and would-be owners? First, many host organizations in ADD also sponsored microenterprise programs, and they may have referred some of their existing clients to the IDA program. Second, IDAs may attract entrepreneurial people; after all, small business is one of the three universal matched uses. Third, small business is perhaps the least restricted of the three universal matched uses. Many low-income people already sometimes do odd jobs to earn extra cash (Losby et al., 2002; Edin and Lein, 1997). Rather than make an unmatched withdrawal, they may find it worthwhile to make a matched withdrawal to buy a kitchen utensil, a lawn mower, or a piece of playground equipment that they can use in their existing small business. Fourth and perhaps most importantly, the dream of small business ownership is apparently alive and well among poor people in American (or there is a dearth of good wage jobs).

Receipt of Public Assistance

In the United States, means-tested public assistance includes programs such as Aid for Families with Dependent Children (AFDC), Temporary Assistance for Needy Families (TANF), Supplemental Security Income (SSI), Supplemental Security Disability Income (SSDI), and Food Stamps. At the time of enrollment, about 45 percent of participants in ADD had received some form of means-tested public assistance. According to Hurst and Ziliak (2001), more than 90 percent of the recipients of means-tested public assistance report less than $500 of liquid financial assets. Carney and Gale (2001) found that receipt of means-tested public assistance was negatively correlated with assets. Receipt of public assistance could be associated with lower saving for at least four reasons.

First, public assistance is income-tested, so people who receive it have low incomes and thus, for the economic reasons outlined just above in the discussion of saving and income, would be predicted to save less.

Second, public assistance is also asset-tested, so people are ineligible if they own liquid assets in excess of a limit (Orszag, 2001; Greenberg, 1999). In general, the limits on assets were more stringent before the advent of TANF in 1996, but many recipients of public assistance may be unaware of the newer, more relaxed limits (Hogarth and O'Donnell, 1999; Caskey, 1997). In any case, if a poor person turned to public assistance but was disqualified for owning too many assets, then the asset limits would act like a 100 percent tax on wealth (Hubbard, Skinner, and Zeldes, 1995 and 1994). Because the poor are more likely to use public assistance, this potential tax matters much more to them than to the non-poor. A great deal of research finds that asset tests serve to depress saving by the poor, whether or not they currently or formerly receive public assistance (Ziliak, 2003; Hurst and Ziliak, 2001; Gruber and Yelowitz, 1999; Powers, 1998; Neumark and Powers, 1998; Moffitt, 1986).

Third, the prospect of the possibility of using public assistance in the future decreases precautionary saving in the present, both because of the asset tests just described and because—with or without asset tests—the public safety net reduces the need for precautionary saving. This effect is especially pronounced for the poor because receipts from public assistance are likely to be large relative to other sources of income and because uninsured risks (such as catastrophic illness) would represent a larger share of their normal income.

Fourth, current or former receipt of public assistance could be associated with unobserved characteristics that tend both to increase the likelihood of receipt of public assistance and to depress saving. For example, people are more likely to have low income, to own few assets, and to qualify for public assistance—all else constant—if they have visceral dislike of saving, if they are spendthrifts, if they suffer from mild disabilities, if they are victims of domestic violence, if they smoke, if they place a low value on future well-being, if they make careless choices, if they have low self-esteem, or if they live in a household in which someone is addicted to alcohol or drugs. None of these characteristics are recorded in the ADD data, but they may be correlated both with receipt of public assistance and with low saving. Thus, current or former receipt of public assistance may act as a proxy for unobserved characteristics that cause low saving.

Receipt of public assistance. About 38 percent of participants reported that they had received public assistance from Aid for Families with Dependent Children or from Temporary Assistance for Needy Families at some time before enrollment (table 4.5). At enrollment, 10 percent of participants reported receiving Temporary Assistance for Needy Families. All but two of these participants also reported having received Aid for Families with Dependent Children or Temporary Assistance for Needy Families before enrollment. Altogether, about 38 percent of participants had received Aid for Families with Dependent Children or Temporary Assistance for Needy Families at some point, whether at the time of enrollment or before.

Table 4.5
Participant Receipt of Public Assistance at Enrollment

Characteristic	%
Former receipt of AFDC/TANF	
No	62
Yes	38
Current receipt of TANF	
No	90
Yes	10
Current receipt of SSI/SSDI	
No	88
Yes	12
Current receipt of Food Stamps	
No	83
Yes	17
Receipt of any type of public assistance	
No	49
Yes	51

Note: About 1 percent of cases have missing data for receipt of AFDC or TANF, and about 6 percent of cases have missing data for receipt of SSI/SSDI or Food Stamps.

About 12 percent of the participants who answered this question reported receiving Supplemental Security Income or Supplemental Security Disability Insurance at the time of enrollment. About 6 percent of participants had missing data because this question was added to MIS IDA after the start of ADD.

About 17 percent of participants reported receiving Food Stamps at enrollment. Again, about 6 percent of participants had missing data.

Altogether, about 51 percent of participants with non-missing data had received some form of means-tested cash public assistance at enrollment or before. Zhan, Sherraden, and Schreiner (2004) examine IDAs and recipients of public assistance in ADD.

Asset Ownership

As discussed in the theoretical framework of chapter 2, assets beget assets, so it should come as no surprise that the ownership of non-IDA assets is generally hypothesized to be linked with greater IDA saving. This effect works along several pathways.

First, assets are required to produce income, and economic theory—in the absence of institutional and psychological considerations—suggests that more income will often translate into more saving. The most important income-producing asset—for almost everyone, but especially for the poor—is human capital. Small-business assets also matter, in particular among ADD participants. Furthermore, a car can be an income-producing asset in that it can facilitate the use of human capital in remunerative employment (Kim, 2002; Edin, 2001; Kasarda, 1995).

Second, assets not only produce income but also reduce expenses (Sherraden, 1991, pp. 157–159). With income held constant, fewer expenses translate into more resources available to be saved. Homeowners, for example, do not pay rent. Car owners save time as well as bus or taxi fares, and they bear lower transaction costs when they make a trip to a bank branch or to an automatic teller machine. Owners of passbook accounts and checking accounts economize on check-cashing fees (Caskey, 2002 and 1994). Of course, asset ownership also has maintenance costs, for example, to fix the roof on a house, change the oil on a car, or to pay monthly fees on a bank account.

Third, people own assets now only if they saved in the past. Those who saved in the past are more likely to possess difficult-to-quantify characteristics (such as thrift, future-orientation, or skill in mathematics) that probably influence current IDA saving. Thus, even if current asset ownership does not cause IDA saving, current asset ownership probably acts as a proxy for unobserved characteristics that do cause both past saving and current IDA saving.

Fourth, existing assets may be shifted or reshuffled into IDAs. For example, a participant could transfer $100 from a passbook savings account into an IDA. Sherraden (1991) argues that most IDA saving is probably new saving (that is, saving that results from an increase—compared to what would have happened in the absence of IDAs—in the difference between income and consumption). This is because, compared with the non-poor, the poor have fewer assets available to shift. Indeed, some evidence from IRAs and 401(k) plans suggests that the poor are more likely to make deposits from new saving (Engelhardt, 2001; Engen and Gale, 2000; Gale and Scholtz, 1994; Bernheim and Scholz, 1993; Joines and Manegold, 1991). Still, the promise of the IDA match provides a strong incentive to come up with resources for deposits, and in some cases for some people it may be easier to shift than to save.

It is easier to shift or reshuffle liquid assets than illiquid assets. Compared with illiquid assets, liquid assets have lower transaction costs when they are converted into other forms of resources. The ADD data do not record participants' holdings of cash (the most liquid asset), but the data did record the presence and value of passbook savings accounts and checking accounts. In terms of illiquid assets, the ADD data record the presence and value of homes, cars, small businesses, land or property, and other investments such as IRAs or 401(k) plans.

The mean and median of the different classes of liquid and illiquid assets for ADD participants appear in table 4.6. The table also shows the percentage of participants who own a given class of asset as well as the distribution of the value of total assets across classes (computed as the average of the shares at the participant level).

Table 4.6
Participant Assets by Class

Asset Class	N	Mean ($)	Median ($)	Min. ($)	Max. ($)	Cases Missing	Participants with an Asset Class (%)	Distribution of Total Asset Value by Class (%)
Passbook Account	2,332	270	2	0	11,000	18	50	12
Checking Account	2,302	281	50	0	32,000	48	66	14
Total Liquid Assets	2,294	555	125	0	32,005	56	78	26
Home	2,346	11,347	0	0	290,000	4	19	18
Car	2,323	3,481	1,300	0	32,000	27	67	46
Small Businesses	2,348	1,255	0	0	350,000	2	10	5
Land or Property	2,344	636	0	0	180,000	6	2	1
Investments	2,344	677	0	0	140,000	6	14	4
Total Illiquid Assets	2,311	17,459	2,500	0	426,000	39	72	74
Total Assets	2,262	18,081	2,982	0	427,000	88	88	100
Total Debts	2,300	13,654	2,900	0	272,700	50	N/A	N/A
Net Worth	2,231	4,087	360	−230,550	349,000	119	N/A	N/A

Like all data, the asset data from ADD are not perfect. For example, if participants thought that they were more likely to qualify to participate if they reported low wealth, then they may have understated the value of their assets. Missing values sometimes appear in the asset data, in part because illiquid assets such as homes or cars are difficult to "mark to market" and in part because participants often simply did not know what their assets were worth. Although the measure of the value of assets is noisy, the measure of the presence of a class of assets is probably quite accurate. After all, even if participants did not know the market value of their homes, they still knew whether they owned their homes.

Passbook savings accounts. Before they opened their IDA, half of participants in ADD had a passbook savings account. The mean balance for all participants was $270, but this average was pulled up by a few extremely large values. The median was $2. Three participants reported passbook balances of $10,000 or more, and 137 participants (6 percent) reported balances of $1,000 or more. For the average participant, passbook balances represented about 12 percent of the value of total assets.

For the 53 percent of participants who were "savers" (that is, participants who had net IDA savings of $100 or more), the average passbook balance was $367, and passbook balances were 23 percent of net deposits. For these "savers," at most 23 percent of net IDA deposits could have been shifted or reshuffled from passbook accounts. (For non-savers, the question of new saving versus asset shifts is moot, because their net deposits were zero or almost zero.)

Checking accounts. About two-thirds (66 percent) of participants had a checking account. The mean balance for all participants was $281, but this was once again skewed, as the median was $50. Two participants reported balances of $30,000 or more, and 7 percent of participants had $1,000 or more. For the average participant, checkbook balances were 14 percent of the value of total assets. Among "savers" who had net IDA savings of $100 or more, the average checking balance was $394, so checking balances were 29 percent of net deposits.

Total liquid assets. On average, participants in ADD had $555 of liquid assets in passbook and checking accounts (table 4.6), accounting for 26 percent of the value of total assets. Cash holdings were not recorded. About 78 percent of participants had some type of bank account, whether passbook and/or checking. Seven participants had bank balances of $10,000 or more, and 15 percent of participants had bank balances of $1,000 or more. All together, there was some scope for some participants to shift liquid assets from their existing bank accounts into IDAs, but most participants in ADD did not have large bank balances.

Bank-account ownership. Participants may be put in four groups according to their ownership of passbook and checking accounts: both passbook and checking, only checking, only passbook, or "unbanked" (neither passbook

Table 4.7
Account ownership ("Bankedness") of ADD Participants versus the Low-Income Population

	1995 SCF (%)	ADD (%)
No Account	24	21
Checking Account	72	66
Passbook Account	25	50
Both Passbook and Checking	22	39

Source: 1995 Survey of Consumer Finances as reported in Hogarth and O'Donnell (1999)."Low-income population" refers to households with income less than 80 percent of the median. This encompasses 45 percent of households and so likely represents a more-advantaged segment than that which was generally eligible for ADD.

nor checking). Compared with households at 80 percent of median income or lower in the 1995 Survey of Consumer Finances (Hogarth and O'Donnell, 1999), ADD participants were more "banked" in that they were less likely to have no account at all (21 percent for ADD versus 24 percent for SCF) and more likely to have a passbook account (table 4.7). Although ADD participants were less likely to have a checking account, they were more likely to have both passbook and checking accounts.

Account ownership and savings outcomes. For at least three reasons, participants who own passbook or checking accounts are expected to have greater savings outcomes in IDAs. First, account owners have more resources—all else constant—available to shift or reshuffle into IDAs. Second, account owners probably have more experience with saving and—all else constant—are probably more comfortable using banks. Third, account owners probably have other unobserved characteristics (such as the ability to manage a checkbook) that cause greater saving both in bank accounts and in IDAs.

Furthermore, because a passbook—unlike a checkbook—does not require active management, passbook ownership is a weaker proxy than checkbook ownership for unobserved characteristics positively associated with saving. In fact, evidence in Hogarth and Lee (2000) suggests that people who own only a passbook savings account resemble "unbanked" people more than they resemble people who own a checking account. Results from ADD were consistent with this view (table 4.8). Compared with those who owned only a passbook savings account or no account at all, savings outcomes were better for those who owned a checking account or both types of accounts.

Table 4.8
Saving Outcomes in IDAs in ADD by Ownership of Passbook Savings Accounts and Checkbook Accounts

	All ADD	Passbook and Checkbook	Only Checkbook	Only Passbook	"Unbanked"
Share of Participants (%)	100	39	28	12	21
For All Participants:					
Average balance in bank accounts ($)	555	986	449	401	0
Average net IDA savings per month ($)	18.14	23.42	19.89	12.31	9.38
Share (%) of "savers" (participants with net IDA savings of $100 or more)	53	65	58	38	32
For Participants with Net Deposits of $100 or More:					
Average balance in bank accounts ($)	764	1,144	578	471	0
Maximum share of net IDA savings that could have been shifted or reshuffled from an existing bank account (%)	44	61	39	40	0

About 39 percent of participants had both a passbook savings account and a checking account. In this group, average net IDA savings per month were about $23 (compared with about $16.60 for all of ADD). Furthermore, about 65 percent of members in this group were "savers" who ended up with net IDA savings of $100 or more (compared with 53 percent for all of ADD). For these "savers," non-IDA bank balances averaged $1,144, or about 61 percent of net IDA savings.

About 28 percent of participants had only a checking account but not a passbook savings account. Their average net IDA savings per month were about $20 (versus $16.60 for all of ADD). About 58 percent of this group were "savers" with net IDA deposits of $100 or more (versus 53 percent for all of ADD). For these "savers," non-IDA bank balances averaged $578, or about 39 percent of net IDA savings.

The 12 percent of participants with only a passbook savings account but not a checking account had average net IDA savings per month of about $12. The 38 percent of this group who were "savers" had average passbook balances of $471, or about 40 percent of their net IDA savings.

Finally, about one in five (21 percent) participants in ADD were "unbanked" in that they had no bank account before they opened their IDA. In this group, average net IDA savings per month was about $9, and 32 percent were "savers." Among the four groups defined by account ownership, the "unbanked"—unsurprisingly—saved the least in IDAs. Still, about one-third of previously "unbanked" participants did save and accumulate assets in their IDAs, so IDAs could be one way to help the "unbanked" to start to use formal saving services.

Homes. In dollar terms, homes were the most important asset owned by ADD participants. About one in five (19 percent) of participants owned their homes (table 4.6). The average value across all participants was $11,347, accounting for 18 percent of the value of total assets.

Among homeowners, the average home was worth about $53,000 (median $52,000). Four people owned homes worth $200,000 or more, and 10 percent of homeowners had homes worth $100,000 or more. About 17 percent of homes owned by ADD participants were worth $25,000 or less.

Homes are illiquid assets, so direct shifts into IDAs would seem less relevant than the possibility that homeownership serves as a proxy for unobserved characteristics (such as thrift or future-orientation) that cause greater saving, whether with or without IDAs. (Indirect shifts of assets out of homes, however, are certainly possible, for example if a participant who had been making extra payments on her mortgage stopped doing that to free up cash to save in an IDA.) Homeowners are likely to possess unobserved characteristics that increase saving; otherwise, they would be less likely to have saved enough to have bought their home in the first place. In a simple bivariate comparison that fails to control for other factors that could be both correlates of homeownership and causes of greater saving, these unobserved factors appear to matter a lot: average net IDA savings per month were $16.60 for all ADD participants, but about $29 for homeowners.

Cars. Like homes, cars are illiquid and so probably are linked with IDA saving mostly through their association with the unobserved characteristics that cause both IDA saving and the saving that led to the car purchase in the first place. Cars may also increase IDA saving by reducing the transaction costs of making deposits or of attending required financial-education classes.

As shown in table 4.6, two-thirds of ADD participants owned a car. For the average participant, the value of a car (mean $3,481, median $1,300) was almost half (46 percent) of the value of total assets. In this sense, cars were the most important assets for ADD participants. Among car owners, the average asset value of cars was $5,223 ($3,000 median). About 17 percent of cars were worth less than $1,000.

Small businesses. About 10 percent of ADD participants reported owning small-business assets, accounting for 5 percent of the value of total assets (table 4.6). The mean value was $1,255, although the distribution was skewed; the median was zero, and 4 participants reported that they owned businesses whose assets were worth $100,000 or more. Among small-business owners, average business assets was $10,000 (median $2,000), and 64 percent of small-business owners had business assets worth $5,000 or less. This suggests that most of the small businesses run by IDA participants in ADD were very small indeed.

Land or property. Two percent of participants reported owning land or property. The average value across all participants was $677, but, among owners of land or property, the average was $35,000 (median $25,000). (Three participants reported land or property worth more than $100,000.) Two-thirds of the participants who owned land or property also reported owning their homes. Overall, land and property accounted for 1 percent of the value of total assets.

Investments. About 14 percent of participants reported having investments, accounting for 4 percent of the value of total assets. Among owners of investments, the average value was about $4,800. About 40 percent of investors reported having less than $1,000. In general, these investments were probably mostly illiquid IRAs or 401(k) plans that were not likely to be directly shifted or reshuffled into IDAs. Like homes or cars, however, the presence of these investments may act as a proxy for the existence of unobserved characteristics that favor greater savings outcomes.

Total illiquid assets. On average, total illiquid assets for participants in ADD was $17,459 (table 4.6). For homeowners, the value of the home dominated. For a greater number of participants, however, the highest-value asset was a car. Overall, about three-fourths (72 percent) of participants owned at least one type of illiquid asset, and illiquid assets accounted for about 74 percent of the value of total assets.

Total assets. On average, participants in ADD had about $18,000 in total assets. A few very large figures skew the average upwards, however, and the median participant had about $3,000 in total assets, with only $125 of those in liquid bank accounts. While 4 percent of participants had total assets of $100,000 or more, 18 percent reported $100 or less, and 12 percent reported having exactly zero assets.

Participants who reported zero assets likely had unobserved characteristics that would be associated with low saving, with or without IDAs. Indeed, for this group, 23 percent were "savers" with net IDA savings of $100 or more (compared with 53 percent in ADD overall), and average net IDA savings per month for the group with zero assets were about $7 (versus $18 in ADD overall).

The main lesson from ADD is that the poor can save in IDAs; 53 percent of participants were "savers" with net deposits of $100 or more, and, across all participants, average net IDA savings per month was $16.60. Still, it appears that saving in IDAs was more difficult—though certainly not impossible—for participants who had saved less and accumulated fewer assets in the past.

Asset shifting and reshuffling. The typical (modal) participant enrolled in ADD owning a car, about $125 in bank-account balances, and little else in terms of financial or physical assets. Not only did this composite participant have few assets to shift into IDAs, but the low level of asset accumulation in the participant's lifetime before the advent of ADD also suggests that there was little scope to shift resources into IDAs by reducing non-IDA saving. Of course, some participants did have substantial assets (albeit often in illiquid forms), and for this minority of participants, asset shifts may account for at least part of their net IDA savings. Furthermore, any participant could have shifted assets into IDAs by increasing debt.

Did IDAs cause new saving? That is, did IDAs increase the difference between income and consumption, relative to what it would have been in the absence of IDAs? There are three possible approaches to answering this question. The first is to randomly assign access to IDAs to qualified participants or to eligible people. With randomization, new saving can be measured as the average differences in net worth between people with and without access (Manski, 1995; Royse, 1991). The experimental-design component of ADD adopted this experimental approach, but its results are not yet available. The second approach is to ask people what they did with IDAs that they would not have done without IDAs (Moore et al., 2001). This approach is not perfect, because even if people tell the truth, they might not be aware of any asset shifting or reshuffling that they might be doing. The third approach is to build a model based on assumptions about all unmeasured aspects (Schreiner et al., 2001). The next sections explore these last two approaches.

Model based on assumptions. Given the ADD data, very strong assumptions are required to estimate what share of IDA savings comes from new saving. Although the assumptions are so strong that the results should be taken with a grain of salt, the exercise is still interesting. The exercise makes three main assumptions.

First, the data must contain measures of both income and consumption. The ADD data include a measure of income but not of consumption. Because any difference between income and consumption will be reflected in changes in net worth, an alternative that is equivalent to measuring income and consumption is to measure all components of net worth. New saving is then the change in net worth caused by access or use of IDAs. But again, the measure of net worth from ADD—like the measure of net worth from all other data sources—omits social capital and human capital. For example, participants could shift resources out of human capital (health) by postponing doctor visits and depositing the money that they would have spent on health care in their IDAs. Likewise, participants could shift resources out of social capital by requesting small cash gifts from friends and family to be deposited in IDAs. Nevertheless, it is assumed here that net IDA savings was not affected by any component of net worth not recorded in the ADD data.

Second, the measurement of the "impact" of IDAs on net worth—that is, measures of new saving—require the measurement of participant net worth both with and without the use of IDAs. Of course, this is an impossible requirement; participants did use IDAs, so their net worth in the counterfactual case of non-use is unobservable. A *control group* is defined as non-participants whose net worth without IDAs serves as a proxy for the (unobserved and unobservable) net worth of participants, had they been without IDAs. But a good control group is hard to find. This is because participants are—in the absence of randomization or some other arbitrary assignment of eligibility—self-selected, and those people who choose to participate probably differ from non-participants in terms of characteristics that affect both net worth and the likelihood of participating (Schreiner, 2002c; Moffitt, 1991). For example, low-income people who are eligible for IDAs and who are "naturally thrifty" (that is, people who for some unobserved reason incur lesser mental costs or greater mental rewards when they increase income and/or decrease consumption so as to come up with more resources to save) are probably more likely to open an IDA and to have greater IDA saving than are other eligible people who are less naturally thrifty, precisely because a natural bent toward thrift makes it easier to save in IDAs. In the analysis here, participants at enrollment (before opening their IDAs) are taken as a control group for participants without IDAs. That is, it is assumed that, in the absence of IDAs, participants' net worth would not have changed from what it was at enrollment. Given the low net worth of most ADD participants (mean of about $4,000 and median of $360, table 4.6), this is not a terribly strong assumption. After all, if participants' net worth would have had a strong upward growth trend even without IDAs, then why was their net worth not already much higher than it was? No, IDA participants as a whole saved very little in their lifetimes prior to ADD, and it is a stretch to believe that—in the absence of IDAs—they suddenly would have started saving a lot more than ever before in the period covered by ADD.

Third, measures of changes in net worth through time are required. The MIS IDA data for ADD, however, record net worth only at enrollment. To come up with changes through time for this exercise, it is assumed that all net IDA deposits that could have come from shifts of liquid assets in passbook or checking accounts did come from such shifts, and furthermore that all other net IDA deposits came from new saving. That is, it is assumed that participants shifted as much as they could out of bank accounts but did not otherwise reshuffle anything.

Given these extremely strong assumptions, an estimate of new saving in IDAs in ADD is the non-negative difference between net IDA savings and liquid assets at enrollment. Excluding participants with less than $100 of net deposits (because asset shifts are irrelevant when net IDA savings are zero or close to zero), the per-participant mean of the maximum share of net deposits that could have been shifted to IDAs from liquid assets in bank accounts was 44 percent (median 33 percent). If the heroic assumptions made here are correct (and they most certainly are not), it would mean that—at the median—about two-thirds of net IDA savings in ADD came from new saving and that about one-third came from asset shifts.

Of course, not all IDA deposits that could have been shifted from liquid assets were shifted. Participants may have also shifted resources from other, less-liquid components of net worth. The true share of net deposits that were shifted or reshuffled could be much less (or much more) than one-third.

If IDAs are to promote both saving and asset accumulation, then they must not only provide matches for asset accumulation but also spark new saving (that is, cause an increase in the difference between income and consumption). Although the MIS IDA data do not permit reliable measurement of new saving, a survey of ADD participants and a series of case studies of ADD participants suggest that deposits into IDAs came both from new saving and from shifted assets. Still, the importance of each source in the mix is unknown.

Survey of participants. A straightforward way to estimate new saving caused by IDAs is to ask the participants themselves. Moore et al. (2001 and 2000) use a survey and case studies to analyze the saving strategies of participants in ADD. While useful in many ways, their research was not designed to measure new saving versus asset shifting. It asked about the presence of saving strategies, not how much was saved due to each strategy. Furthermore, the surveys and case studies did not encompass all the ways that participants might come up with new saving or shift assets. For example, the survey did not ask whether participants raided a bank account for funds to make IDA deposits. The analysis here simply looks for broad clues about how ADD participants say that they funded their IDAs. The results suggest that IDA deposits came from both new saving and shifted assets.

ADD participants created new saving when they used strategies that increased income and/or reduced consumption. For example, some participants in the survey said that they attempted to increase income by working more in the labor market. About 29 percent said that, because of IDAs, they worked longer hours, and 41 percent said that IDAs made them more likely to work more. About 59 percent said that IDAs made them more likely to work or to stay employed. Some participants in the case studies said that, because of IDAs, they did odd jobs to increase income or bartered services to reduce consumption expenses.

About 61 percent of surveyed participants said that IDAs made them more likely to increase income in ways other than working more hours. Furthermore, some case-study participants said that, because of IDAs, they put more effort into budgeting and money management.

In several ways, participants spent more time, effort, and human capital in household production so as to free up more cash for IDAs without concomitant cuts in consumption. For example, 70 percent of survey respondents said that, because of IDAs, they shopped more carefully for food. That is, they used greater time, effort, and skill in household production to maintain a given level of consumption while reducing their cash expenses. Some case-study participants said that, because of IDAs, they used coupons and searched for bargains. Of surveyed participants, 68 percent said that they ate out less, a straight substitution of household production for market purchases. (Sherraden, et al., 2004, also reports a couple of interviews with ADD participants in which they explained how they reshuffled to save in IDAs.)

The most common strategies (although not necessarily the most important or most effective) involved reducing the amount and/or the quality of consumption. For example, some case-study participants said that they conserved energy, cooked inexpensive meals, and cut back on treats. About 34 percent of those surveyed said that they spent less on alcohol and tobacco. (The share of participants who used alcohol or tobacco in the first place is unknown.) Kempson, McKay, and Collard (2003) also find that the poorest participants in matched-savings programs are more likely to use strategies that involving cutting back on consumption, treats, and vices.

Participants also said that they generated new savings through reduced quality of the consumption of leisure time. Among survey respondents, 64 percent said that they spent less on leisure, and 30 percent said that they had less money for leisure than they would have liked. Some case-study participants reported that, because of IDAs, they took fewer vacation trips.

In addition to generating new savings from increased income and/or decreased consumption, the survey and case studies reported in Moore et al. (2001 and 2000) suggest that ADD participants also funded their IDAs with shifted or reshuffled assets. For example, 35 percent of those surveyed said that, because of IDAs, they were less likely to save in other forms. Even if participants did not explicitly transfer balances from other bank accounts into IDAs, this response suggests that they still reduced additions to non-IDA bank accounts, and this is of course equivalent to an explicit asset shift.

Some IDA deposits were financed by debt. (The incidence of this strategy may be underreported because the surveys were conducted by program staff, and they generally had exhorted participants not to borrow to finance IDAs.) Of those surveyed, 7 percent said that they had financed IDA deposits by borrowing from family or friends, 3 percent by borrowing from another source, and 16 percent by postponing bill payment. Others—such as the 9 percent who reported that IDAs made it more difficult to pay bills—probably made implicit shifts from debt into IDA deposits. While they did not borrow cash with the explicit purpose of depositing that cash in IDAs, they did increase their debts beyond what they would have done in the absence of IDAs.

Resources in the form of household durables were also reshuffled into resources in the form of IDA deposits. Of those surveyed, 12 percent said that they had sold household or personal items to get cash for IDA deposits. Likewise, the 55 percent who said that—because of IDAs—they wore or bought used clothes (or postponed the purchase of new clothes) in effect shifted resources from clothes—a type of household durable—to IDAs.

Some participants postponed maintenance of other assets to finance IDAs. This is also a form of asset shifting. Of those surveyed, 17 percent said that, because of IDAs, they postponed visits to the doctor or dentist, and 8 percent said that they gave up food or other necessities. In the case studies, one participant cancelled membership in a health club. All of these are examples of asset shifts from human capital into IDAs.

In sum, the analysis here of data from Moore et al. (2001 and 2000) suggests that participants in ADD financed deposits with a mix of new saving and asset shifting. Unfortunately, the weight of each source in the mix is unknown. It is just as incorrect to assume that all resources put into IDAs were new saving as it is to assume that all resources put into IDAs came from shifted or reshuffled assets.

Debts. In many ways, debts are the opposite of assets. Assets are resources available in the future, while debts are resources already spoken for. Assets come from saving (when income exceeds consumption) but debt comes from dissaving (when consumption exceeds income). Assets pay interest, but debts cost interest. The saving that leads to assets requires current sacrifice in return for future rewards; the borrowing that leads to debt offers current rewards in exchange for future sacrifices. While assets spark hope, debts spawn worry.

Debt is expected to impede saving in IDAs for at least three reasons. First, debts reduce the resources available to be saved. Not only do debt repayments drain resources that might otherwise be put in an IDA, but interest on debt also increases expenses. (Although using unconsumed income to pay down debts is a form of "saving," it is not IDA saving.) This factor should be most relevant for debts that are large and long lasting, such as home mortgages.

Second, almost all debts (except informal ones from family or friends) entail fixed repayment obligations. A home mortgage, for example, implies a payment in all months, even months with unusually low income or unusually high expenses. This reduces flexibility, increases the risk of resource short-falls, and makes saving more difficult. Because debt repayments are "first in line," they can crowd out IDA deposits, which are neither fixed nor obligatory.

Third, just as the presence of assets signals past saving and thus serves as a proxy for unobserved characteristics (such as patience or foresightedness) that are probably causes of both greater past saving and greater current IDA saving, the presence of debt signals past dissaving and thus serves as a proxy for unobserved characteristics (such as impatience or shortsightedness) that are probably causes of both greater past borrowing and lesser current IDA saving. For example, the ADD data do not include a measure of participants' impul-siveness, defined as the tendency to make choices so quickly that small re-wards in the short term are misjudged relative to large costs in the long term. Greater impulsiveness is probably associated with greater debt; access to loans facilitates impulsive choices (Maital and Maital, 1994). Not only are impul-sive people more likely than deliberate people to borrow more, but they are also more likely—all else constant—to choose to save less because they mis-judge the trade-offs between the short-term costs of saving and the long-term rewards of asset accumulation. In sum, the presence of debt is associated with greater impulsiveness, and greater impulsiveness causes reduced IDA saving, so the presence of debt is associated with reduced IDA saving. As a proxy for these types of "negative" unobserved characteristics, the most-relevant types of debt are credit-card debt, overdue household bills, informal debts with family and friends, and overdue medical bills.

Debt can also be a way to reshuffle resources into IDAs (Schreiner et al., 2001). In the most obvious case, borrowed money is deposited in an IDA. Less directly (and perhaps unbeknownst even to the participants themselves), pay-ing the gas bill late (or paying for anything with credit instead of cash) can free up cash for IDA deposits. Likewise, a participant might stop adding an extra $50 to her monthly mortgage payment and instead deposit $50 in her IDA. Of course, the mere presence of debt is not necessarily a smoking gun that indi-cates that reshuffling took place, but it does at least show that participants had access to loans and that they therefore had the ability to reshuffle via debt.

"Of course, debt is not necessarily bad—as long as it is used to develop productive capacity" (Sherraden, 1991, p. 284). Indeed, most people use debt to finance at least part of their most important productive assets: homes, cars, and post-secondary education for human capital. Because assets beget assets and because loans can finance assets, loans can help people to break out of a low-asset trap. Like most things, debt can be used or abused.

Notwithstanding the discussion just above about debt, impulsiveness, and other unobserved characteristics that may cause both greater debt and reduced saving, the presence of debt may signal unobserved characteristics that cause greater saving. As the adage goes, "you cannot get a loan unless you do not need it." Would-be homeowners (or car buyers) cannot get a mortgage until they have saved up for a down payment. Furthermore, they must show that they will have enough steady income—that is, enough human capital—to make monthly repayments (perhaps for decades) and to pay for property taxes and up-keep. Likewise, student loans go only to those with enough human capital to attend post-secondary schools. In these ways, knowledge of the presence of debt may stand in for knowledge of unobserved characteristics that cause greater saving. As a proxy for these types of "positive" unobserved characteristics, the most-relevant types of debt are home mortgages, car loans, small-business debts, and loans for land or property.

Staff in IDA programs often advise deeply indebted participants to seek credit counseling before they attempt to save in IDAs. In particular, participants who plan to make a matched withdrawal for home purchase will probably also need to apply for a bank loan, and approval will require that they have their debt under control. In this sense, the out-of-control debtors may already have been screened out of ADD, increasing the likelihood that the presence of debt serves more as a proxy for unobserved characteristics that cause greater saving than as a proxy for unobserved characteristics that cause lesser saving.

Like the data on assets, the data on debts in ADD (or, for that matter, in any data set) are imperfect. Although participants proudly acknowledge their ownership of assets (even if they do not know the assets' value), they may be embarrassed by their debts. On the one hand, if they do acknowledge their debts, they may understate their value. On the other hand, the value of debt is usually well known and need not be "marked to market." In any case, the presence of debt is probably measured more precisely than the value of debt.

Home mortgages. On average, debt for home mortgages was $7,318 (table 4.9). About 16 percent of participants had home mortgages, accounting for 18 percent of the value of total debt. Among homeowners with mortgages, average mortgage debt was about $49,000 (median $40,000). About 1 percent of participants had mortgage debt of $100,000 or more, and 4 percent owned their homes free and clear.

Home equity (the participant-by-participant difference between the value of the home and the mortgage) averaged about $4,000 (median $0, as 84 percent of participants were not homeowners). Among the 16 percent of participants who were homeowners, average equity was about $16,700 (median $10,000). Average equity for the 4 percent of participants who owned their homes free and clear was $35,500 (median $30,000).

In sum, about one in six participants in ADD were homeowners. In general, the homes were modest, with a median asset value of $52,000, median debt of $40,000, and median equity of $10,000. (Median equity is not the difference between median asset value and median debt because it is calculated participant-by-participant.) About 4 percent of participants owned their homes free and clear, and these homes were even more modest, with a median value of $30,000.

Table 4.9
Participant Debts by Class

Debt Class	N	Mean ($)	Median ($)	Min. ($)	Max. ($)	Cases Missing	Participants with a Debt Class (%)	Distribution of Total Debt Value by Class (%)
Home Mortgages	2,347	7,318	0	0	185,000	3	16	18
Car Loans	2,330	1,857	0	0	30,000	20	26	20
Student Loans	2,343	1,946	0	0	140,000	7	18	15
Business Loans	2,345	247	0	0	130,000	5	2	1
Land or Property Mortgages	2,349	228	0	0	90,000	1	1	1
Family and Friends Debts	2,341	460	0	0	120,000	9	19	8
Household Bills	2,341	177	0	0	30,000	9	25	10
Medical Bills	2,344	506	0	0	150,000	6	23	10
Credit Cards	2,342	888	0	0	60,000	8	32	17
Total Debts	2,300	13,654	2,900	0	272,700	50	75	100
Total Assets	2,262	18,081	2,982	0	427,000	88	88	N/A
Net Worth	2,231	4,087	360	−230,550	349,000	119	N/A	N/A

Car loans. It was more common for participants to have debt for cars than for homes. About 26 percent had car debt, accounting for about 20 percent of the value of total debt (table 4.9). On average, car debt was $1,857 (median $0). About 7 percent of participants had car debt of $10,000 or more, and 41 percent owned their cars free and clear. Among owners with debt, the average was about $7,200 (median $6,000). MIS IDA did not record the number of cars owned.

For all participants, average car equity was $1,600 (median $500). For the 67 percent of participants who owned cars, average equity was $2,400 (median $1,500), and for the 41 percent who owned their cars free and clear, average equity was $2,900 (median $2,000).

In sum, two of three participants in ADD owned a car. Like their houses, their cars were modest; the median asset value was $3,000, median debt was $6,000, and median equity was $1,500. (Median debt exceeds median assets because indebted car owners had higher-value cars than debt-free car owners.)

Student loans. About one in five (18 percent) of ADD participants had student loans outstanding, accounting for 15 percent of the value of total debt (table 4.9). Among participants with student loans, the average debt was $10,800 (median $5,400).

Like home mortgages and car debt, student debt could signal high human capital (and therefore greater potential for saving) or—because of the need to make repayments—less free cash flow (and therefore lesser potential for saving). In the worst case, a participant took on student debt without graduating and therefore without obtaining the signal of high human capital that is a post-secondary degree.

Business loans. The average participant had business debts of about $250 (table 4.9). The vast majority of participants (98 percent) had no business debt, however, and business debt averaged 1 percent of the value of total debt. Among business owners with debt, average debt was $12,000 (median $4,000).

For all business owners, average business assets were about $2,000 (median $0) and average business equity was about $8,000 (median $1,700). Thus, most small businesses owned by ADD participants were very small and were financed not with loans but with the owners' savings; median assets were $2,000, median debt was $0, and median equity was $1,700.

These figures on business debt suggest two lessons. First, many small businesses were very small. This suggests that although some fear that assets accumulated in IDAs are too little to make a difference (Bernstein, 2003), they may well be enough to help many small businesses. Second, most small businesses are financed mostly with the owners' savings. This suggests that the microenterprise movement—both in the United States and worldwide—may be placing too much emphasis on improved access to loans and too little emphasis on improved access to saving services (Schreiner, 2004b; Schreiner and Woller, 2003; Schreiner and Morduch, 2002; Adams and Von Pischke, 1992).

Land or property mortgages. About half of all owners of land or property (1 percent of ADD participants) had mortgages on those assets, accounting for 1 percent of the value of total debt (table 4.9). Among property owners, average debt was $12,700 (median $0), average assets were $35,500 (median $25,000), and average property equity was $22,800 (median 10,000).

Family and friends debt. Almost one in five (19 percent) of ADD participants owed money to family or friends for informal loans. Average informal debt was $460, accounting for 8 percent of total debt. Most informal debts were $1,000 or less; for participants with informal debts, the mean was $2,360 (median $750).

Among small-business owners, about one-third (31 percent) had informal debts. In contrast, about one-sixth of small-business owners (16 percent) had formal business debts. Although there is no way to know for certain whether the informal loans were used for small business, it seems likely that many of them were, given informal debts were more common among business owners (31 percent) than among participants in general (19 percent). Most likely, informal loans were a more common source of small-business finance than formal loans. This is hardly surprising, as it is well-known that informal finance dominates for microenterprises in non-industrialized countries (Levenson and Maloney, 1996; Adams and Fitchett, 1992; Meyer and Nagarajan, 1992). Still, it again highlights the low importance of formal loans for microenterprises in the United States.

Household bills. About one-fourth (25 percent) of ADD participants owed money on overdue household bills (table 4.9). Such late bills averaged $177 per participant and accounted for 10 percent of the value of total debt. For participants with overdue bills, the average was $700 (median $300). More than 90 percent of these participants with overdue bills owed $1,000 or less.

Overdue bills may be a particularly strong signal of financial distress (and thus of low saving potential). For example, people probably pay their rent, gas, and electricity bills before they pay their medical bills, credit-card bills, or student loans. Still, overdue bills may not serve as a strong signal of "negative" unobserved characteristics because the distress may last only a short time.

Medical bills. Almost one-fourth (23 percent) of ADD participants owed money on overdue medical bills (table 4.9). The average debt for all participants was about $500, accounting for 10 percent of the value of total debt. Among participants with overdue medical bills, the average amount owed was $2,200 (median $570).

The presence of medical debt could serve as a proxy for unobserved characteristics that cause low saving in at least two ways. First, the debt may signal financial distress. Second, the debt may signal long-term medical problems.

Credit-card debts. About one-third (32 percent) of ADD participants had credit-card debts (table 4.9). The average value across all participants was almost $900, and credit-card debt accounted for 17 percent of the value of

Figure 4.4
Distribution of Participant Net Worth

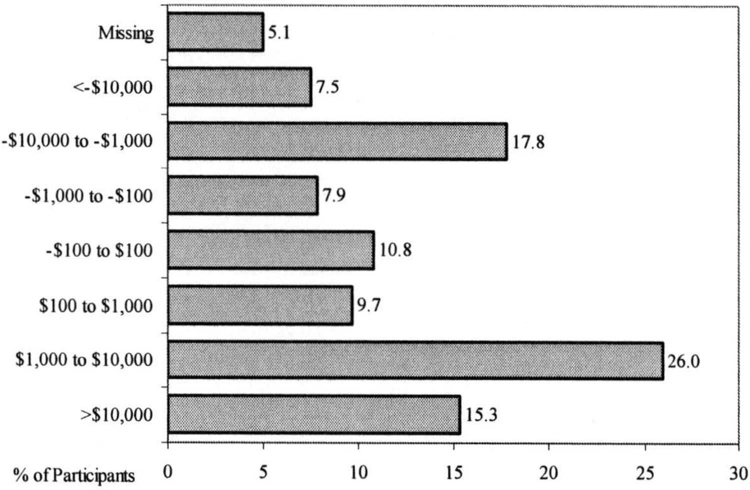

total debt. Among debtors, the average value was $2,800 (median $1,000). The ADD data do not record whether a participant had a credit card, only whether a participant had credit-card debt.

Bird, Hagstrom, and Wild (1997) report on credit-card usage by households under 200 percent of the federal poverty guideline in the 1995 Survey of Consumer Finances. About 26–45 percent of these households had credit-card debt, and their balances averaged $2,000 to $2,700. Furthermore, the average ratio of monthly income to credit-card debt was 26–36 percent. For comparison in ADD, 32 percent had credit-card debt, the average balance was $2,800, and the average ratio of credit-card debt to monthly income was 73 percent. Overall, participants in ADD were more heavily indebted than this comparison group from the 1995 SCF under 200-percent of the poverty line, but this may reflect differences between 1995 and 1999–2001, as the trend has been toward greater indebtedness, especially among the poor (Black and Morgan, 1998; Bird, Hagstrom, and Wild, 1997).

Net worth. The difference between assets and debt is net worth. Average net worth in ADD was about $4,000 (table 4.9). A few extreme values skewed the distribution, so median net worth was much smaller ($360). About 28 percent of participants had net worth that was essentially zero (between –$1,000 and $1,000, figure 4.4), including about 7 percent of participants who reported net worth of exactly zero. Net worth was negative for about 25 percent of participants, positive for 41 percent. (Net worth was missing for five percent of participants.) All in all, slightly more than half of participants in ADD had zero or negative net worth, and most of the rest had less than $10,000.

Insurance Coverage

ADD recorded whether participants carried health or life insurance. (These questions were added to MIS IDA after ADD started, so about 62 percent of participants have missing values.) In theory, insurance might be linked with saving in several ways, but the direction of the association is indeterminate.

Insurance coverage affects saving both through premiums (an expense) and through pay-outs (a source of income). On the one hand, premiums drain resources and so may decrease saving. This is especially relevant for health insurance because, compared with life insurance, it is more likely to be billed monthly. On the other hand, pay-outs for covered medical events decrease expenses and so may increase saving. (The death of an IDA participant and a subsequent life-insurance pay-out may increase the household's saving but of course cannot increase the dead participant's saving.) Before the fact for a given person, it is unknown whether insurance will be a net source of resources or a net drain, although, on average, insurance is a net drain because of the insurer's operating costs and profit.

Insurance coverage may also predict saving because it acts as a proxy for unobserved characteristics that are associated with either greater or lesser saving. For example, people who purchase life insurance show foresight and future orientation; they incur an expense now in exchange for a possible future benefit to others, should the insured die. In this sense, the presence of life insurance could signal unobserved characteristics that cause greater saving. Likewise, health insurance could signal unusual foresight and future orientation. The presence of health insurance could also, however, signal the presence of health problems, and this would put downward pressure on saving, both through increased expenses for uncovered medical bills, decreased income due to diminished human capital, and decreased future-orientation due to a shortened expected life span.

Finally, the presence of insurance dampens precautionary motives to save at the same time that it signals strong bequest motives. On the one hand, people with health insurance may save less because they know that, if they get sick, insurance will pay the bills. Likewise, people with life insurance may save less because they know that, when they die, their heirs will inherit at least the insurance pay-out. (Among the poor, life-insurance policies are often small and are seen as burial insurance.) On the other hand, the presence of life insurance reveals a strong bequest motive. The policy may substitute for the need to save for bequests and so decrease saving. Alternatively, the policy may signal such strong bequest motives that, even after accounting for the insurance pay-out, the person saves more than otherwise.

Table 4.10
Insurance Coverage and Relationships with the Host Organization

Participant characteristic	%
Health-Insurance Coverage	
Private or Medicaid	66
None	34
Life-Insurance Coverage	
Covered	42
None	.58
Referred by a Partner Organization	
Yes	30
No	70
Previous Relationship with the Host Organization	
Yes	59
No	41
Employee of the Host Organization	
Yes	2
No	98

Note: Cases with missing values are excluded.

Health-insurance coverage. About two in three (66 percent) of ADD participants with non-missing data had private health insurance or Medicaid (table 4.10). Among those with health insurance, one in four (25 percent) had overdue medical bills (average value $622), while 29 percent of those without health insurance had overdue medical bills (average value $585). In this simple analysis, a lack of health insurance did not seem to lead to more overdue medical bills.

Life-insurance coverage. About 42 percent of ADD participants with non-missing data had life insurance. Looking at health and life insurance together, 36 percent of participants had both types of coverage, 30 percent had only health insurance, 6 percent had only life insurance, and 28 percent had no insurance coverage at all.

Relationship with Host or Partner Organizations

As noted above, participants in ADD were both program-selected and self-selected. Program selection took place in two ways. First, the IDA program established its target group (see chapter 3). Second, the host organization (and its partner organizations) referred potential participants who fit the target-group requirements to the IDA program. Compared to participants without referrals, those with referrals should save more. The referring organization should refer only people whom they believe will succeed, and these beliefs are likely founded at least in part on participant characteristics that are observed by the referring organization but that are unobserved in the ADD data. Thus, the existence of a referral may act as a proxy for unobserved characteristics that cause greater saving. For example, a home-ownership program might refer to an IDA program only those clients who show an unusually strong desire to own a home (a characteristic not recorded in the ADD data) because the home-ownership program believes that these people will put forth greater effort to save and will thus have a greater chance to eventually make a matched withdrawal for home purchase. This is why participants who arrived with a referral—all else constant—should save more.

Of course, not all else is constant. In particular, participants may know themselves and their chances to successfully save better than the referring organization, so the effects of unobserved characteristics associated with self-selection could overwhelm the effects of unobserved characteristics associated with program selection. Furthermore, the non-referred/self-selected may feel more committed to making their choice succeed than those who enroll because someone else told them that it would be a good idea. Finally, being referred means that the participant was receiving some non-IDA social services and thus may have unobserved characteristics that depress saving. In the end, participants with a referral might save more than others, but the reverse could also turn out to be true.

Referred by partner organization or previous relationship with the host organization. Among ADD participants with non-missing data, 30 percent reported having been referred to the IDA program by a partner organization (table 4.10). In addition, about 59 percent had received other social services from the host organization before ADD. In all likelihood, many of these participants were referred to the IDA program. Overall, 69 percent of participants had a prior relationship either with the host organization or with a partner organization.

Employee of host organization. About 2 percent of participants were employees of the host organization; in a few cases, they even worked for the IDA program itself. Immersed as they were in the IDA institution, these employee-participants should have experienced the strongest social/institutional effects. Host organizations sometimes have high turn-over, however, and employees who left the host may also have felt compelled to drop out of the IDA program and thus to register low saving.

ADD Participants versus the General Low-Income Population

This section compares ADD participants with people in the U.S. population below 200 percent of the income-poverty threshold. As discussed before, differences between the two groups result largely from two factors. First, host organizations in ADD usually targeted people who were employed and who were below 200 percent of poverty. Within this target group, ADD participants probably reflected the clientele already served by the host organizations, as more than two-thirds had a previous relationship with the host organization or had been referred by a partner organization.

Second, ADD participants were self-selected; they themselves chose to participate. (Even if they were referred, they chose to follow-up on the referral.) People who expected greater benefits from IDAs were more likely to choose to participate. Because people know their own characteristics and because these characteristics affect saving, the people who chose to enroll in ADD probably differed systematically from the general low-income population and probably differed even from the overall clientele served by the host organizations in ADD. In particular, self-selected participants are more likely to possess characteristics that cause greater saving.

The analysis here comes from Sherraden et al. (2000) and uses the Survey of Income and Program Participation from the U.S. Census Bureau. The data come from the ninth wave of the 1993 panel and refer to September 1995. The sample includes individuals eighteen years old and older in households with income below 200 percent of the family-size adjusted poverty threshold (not guideline). Annual income was taken as twelve multiplied by household income in September. Employment status refers to the first week of September 1995. The "bank use" variable identifies individuals in households in which someone had a passbook or checking account in the first quarter of 1995. The data are weighted by person-level weights provided by the Census Bureau. The steep decline in poverty in the United States as a whole since 1995 suggests that, all else constant, participants in ADD were probably more disadvantaged than the general population under 200 percent of the poverty line in 1995.

In terms of gender, race/ethnicity, and marital status, ADD participants were more disadvantaged than the general low-income population (table 4.11). ADD participants were disproportionately female (80 percent versus 59 percent). Likewise, ADD had fewer Caucasians (37 percent versus 64 percent) and more African Americans (47 percent versus 16 percent). Finally, ADD had more people who had never been married (44 percent versus 28 percent) and fewer people who were married (15 percent versus 42 percent).

In terms of education, employment, and bank use, however, ADD participants were more advantaged. Compared to the education of the general low-income population, ADD participants were less likely not to have completed high school (15 percent versus 35 percent), less likely to have only a high-school diploma or a GED (24 percent versus 39 percent), more likely to have attended college without graduating (37 percent versus 18 percent), and more likely to have a college degree (24 percent versus 8 percent).

Table 4.11
Characteristics of ADD Participants Versus the General Low-Income Population

Characteristic	ADD (%)	General Low-Income (%)
Gender		
Female	80	59
Male	20	41
Race/Ethnicity		
African American	47	16
Caucasian	37	64
Hispanic	9	16
Asian American, Native American, or Other	8	4
Marital Status		
Never-married	44	28
Married	15	42
Widowed, divorced, or separated	32	30
Education		
Did not complete high school	15	35
High-school diploma or GED	22	39
Attended college but did not graduate	39	18
Graduated college (2-year or 4-year)	24	8
Employment		
Employed full-time	58	31
Employed part-time	20	11
Unemployed	7	6
Not working or student	15	52
Bank Use		
Passbook and/or checking account	79	67
No bank account	19	33

ADD also had a higher proportion of employed people (table 4.11). Whereas more than half (52 percent) of the general low-income population was not working or were students, the figure in ADD was 15 percent. About 78 percent of ADD participants were employed full-time or part-time, compared with 42 percent for the general low-income population.

Finally, ADD participants were more likely to have a passbook savings account and/or a checking account (in addition to their IDA). One in three (33 percent) in the general low-income population was "unbanked," compared with one in five (19 percent) in ADD.

Overall, perhaps the best way to describe the ADD population is that it was "working poor." This was by design—most programs in ADD targeted the "working poor," so a high proportion of participants worked. This is probably explains much of the higher level of education among ADD participants as well as the higher proportion who owned bank accounts.

The disproportionate representation of women, African Americans, and never-married people probably reflects the characteristics of the broad clientele served by the host organizations and their partner organizations who referred their clients to IDA programs in ADD. These markers of disadvantage (female, African American, and never-married) suggest that, among the "working-poor" target group, somewhat more disadvantaged people enrolled in ADD.

These figures lead to a question: Do IDAs work only for people who, while poor, are nonetheless relatively advantaged in terms of employment, education, and bank experience? Although almost 90 percent of participants in ADD were employed or were students, the ADD data cannot answer this question. Most programs in ADD targeted the "working poor" and made employment a prerequisite for participation. Given that the unemployed were usually ineligible, their low numbers in ADD says little about whether IDAs fit the employed better than the unemployed. For policy purposes, it would be useful to know who would open an IDA if all people had access and then how they would save, but ADD cannot answer this question.

Single Mothers in ADD versus in the General Low-Income Population

This section compares the characteristics of single mothers in ADD with those of single mothers in the general U.S. population at or below 200 percent of the income-poverty threshold. This is an important comparison for two reasons. First, more than half (52 percent) of ADD participants were single mothers. Second, single mothers with children are the focus of welfare reform and of many other programs meant to relieve poverty.

The analysis here comes from Zhan (2003). Single mothers are defined as unmarried females of at least eighteen years of age who live in a household with at least one child under eighteen years of age. Comparison statistics are for single mothers in households with income under 200 percent of the family-

Table 4.12
Characteristics of Single Mothers in ADD Versus
in the General Low-Income Population

Characteristic	ADD (%)	General Low-Income (%)
Sample size	1,215	850
Race/Ethnicity		
African American	56	54
Caucasian	31	38
Hispanic, Asian American, Native American, and Other	13	8
Receipt of AFDC/TANF		
Yes	45	68
No	55	32
Education		
Did not complete high school	14	20
High-school diploma or GED	27	50
Attended college	59	30
Bank Use		
Passbook and/or checking account	77	42
No bank account	23	58
Home Owner		
Yes	10	30
No	90	70

sized adjusted poverty threshold in interview year 2000 of the National Longitudinal Survey of Youth.

Like ADD participants overall, single mothers in ADD were more disadvantaged vis-à-vis single mothers in the general low-income population in terms of race/ethnicity (31 percent Caucasian versus 39 percent, table 4.12). Single mothers in ADD were also more disadvantaged in that they were less likely to own their home (10 percent versus 30 percent).

Also like ADD participants overall, single mothers in ADD were better educated than single mothers in the general low-income population (59 percent had attended at least some college, versus 30 percent). Furthermore, single mothers in ADD were more likely to have a passbook savings account or a checking account (77 percent versus 42 percent). Single mothers in ADD were also more advantaged in terms of receipt of AFDC/TANF (45 percent versus 68 percent).

Overall, the comparison of single mothers in ADD and single mothers in the general low-income population resembles the comparison between ADD participants overall and the overall general low-income population. Single mothers in ADD tend to be "working poor" and disadvantaged in terms of race/ethnicity and homeownership but advantaged in terms of education, bank use, and receipt of public assistance.

Summary

Participants in ADD were poor; the median participant was just above the poverty line in a household with income of about $18,000 per year. Four in five participants were female, and about half were African American. More than half were single mothers, and more than half had received some form of means-tested public assistance. One in six were married. Within measurement error, median net worth was zero.

Participants in ADD were not among the "poorest of the poor"; almost two-thirds had attended college, almost 90 percent were employed or were students, and about four in five owned a bank account. About one in five owned a home, and about two of three owned a car. Most homes and cars were modest. There was a high concentration of small-business owners and aspiring entrepreneurs, and they financed their businesses more with their own savings than with debt.

The characteristics of the 2,350 participants in ADD matter for two reasons. First, they suggest for whom IDAs might be a good fit. Although the ADD data here cannot give a conclusive answer because its participants are both program-selected and self-selected, ADD participants tended to be among the more disadvantaged of the "working poor." While they were highly educated and had high rates of employment and bank-account ownership, they were disproportionately female, African American, and never-married. They were not middle-class, nor were they among the "poorest of the poor."

Second, participant characteristics may affect how the institutional characteristics of IDAs affect saving. If decision-makers understand how participant characteristics interact with program characteristics, then they have more powerful levers with which to adjust policy.

Later chapters use regression analysis to test the various theories discussed here about how participant characteristics may be associated with savings outcomes. First, however, the next chapter discusses savings outcomes: net IDA savings and withdrawals, both matched and unmatched.

5

Savings Outcomes in ADD

This chapter analyzes deposits and withdrawals by IDA participants in ADD. It also presents new ideas about ways to measure saving. Finally, it discusses aspects of the normative question of what types of uses should be matched. The main result reported in this chapter—and the main result of ADD overall—is that poor people can indeed save and accumulate assets in IDAs.

The central measure of savings outcomes is *net IDA savings*, defined as the value of matched withdrawals (excluding matches) plus any IDA balances available for possible future matched withdrawals. Across all 2,350 participants in ADD, net IDA savings per month was $16.60, equivalent to annual net IDA savings of about $200. The average participant had net IDA savings of $558, and 52 percent of participants were "savers," defined as those with net IDA savings of $100 or more. The average IDA saving rate (net IDA savings as a share of income) was about 1.1 percent. Participants made a deposit in about one of every two months in which an IDA was open, and they saved about forty-two cents for every dollar that could have been matched. The average participant moved 1,090 dollar-years through time, equivalent to 363 dollar-years for each year eligible for matchable deposits.

As of the cut-off date for data collection, about 31 percent of participants had made at least one matched withdrawal. Among those without a matched withdrawal, about 31 percent could have made a matched withdrawal from matchable balances of at least $100 after the time cap. Given an average match rate of 1.88:1 and assuming that all matchable balances were eventually taken out as matched withdrawals, the average ADD participant accumulated $1,609 through IDAs. Given an average of 33.6 months between account opening and the time cap, participants accumulated assets at a rate of about $48 per month, equivalent to $576 per year.

Among participants with matched withdrawals, 27 percent bought a home, 23 percent microenterprise, 19 percent post-secondary education, 20 percent home repair, 8 percent retirement savings, and 2 percent job training. Among "savers" yet to make a matched withdrawal, 52 percent planned for home purchase, 16 percent post-secondary education, 21 percent microenterprise, 5 percent job training, and 4 percent home repair. Thus, the three most-common uses were home purchase, post-secondary education, and microenterprise. Excluding matches, the average value per matched withdrawal was highest ($702) for retirement savings, followed by home purchase ($559) and home repair ($491). The average matched withdrawal for post-secondary education and small business was about $245.

As of the data cut-off date, about two-thirds of participants (64 percent) had made at least one unmatched withdrawal. The average participant in this group made 4.1 unmatched withdrawals worth a total of $504. Given an average match rate for these participants of about 1.77:1, these unmatched withdrawals—if consumed—represented lost potential asset accumulation of about $1,400 per participant who made an unmatched withdrawal.

Moreover, 48 percent of all participants were "low savers" with net IDA savings of less than $100. The commonness of low saving and of unmatched withdrawals suggests three lessons for policy. First, even with matches and the supportive institutional structure of IDAs, it is still not easy for the poor to save. Second, there may be room to improve IDA design to be more supportive, in particular by making access to IDAs permanent. Third, poor savers apparently often need to take out at least part of their IDA savings. Thus, unmatched withdrawals should be unrestricted so that the poor cannot harm themselves by saving in IDAs.

What uses should be matched? Matches should be provided for assets that are difficult to convert into consumption, that improve productivity, and that have strongly positive personal and social impacts. If a matched use meets these criteria and is already subsidized for the non-poor, then subsidies for the poor through IDAs will likely be seen as fair and enjoy the support of the public.

By these standards, IDAs should provide matches for the three "cornerstone" uses of home purchase for first-time buyers, post-secondary education and job training, and microenterprise. Furthermore, IDAs should also match retirement savings, car purchase, computer purchase, and medical expenses for those without access to group health insurance. The non-poor already have access to subsidies for all of these assets, except for cars and computers. While all programs in ADD matched the three "cornerstone" uses, only some matched retirement savings, and none matched car purchase, computer purchase, or medical expenses. Some programs in ADD provided matches for home repair, but this use scores poorly against the standards suggested here.

This rest of this chapter has two parts. The first presents measures of savings outcomes in ADD, covering both deposits and withdrawals, both matched and unmatched. This first part starts with a broad framework for thinking about the process of saving in terms of three stages: "putting in" (depositing), "keeping in" (maintaining a balance through time), and "taking out" (withdrawing).

This framework highlights how the act of saving can be seen as moving resources through time. Based on this framework, several measures of saving—many of them new—are defined and then applied to IDAs in ADD. The second part of the chapter looks at matched withdrawals by use in ADD. It also discusses what types of asset purchases IDAs should match.

A Framework for Saving as Moving Resources through Time: Putting In, Keeping In, and Taking Out

Development—that is, long-term improvement in well-being—depends on saving. But what exactly is saving, and how is it measured? Following Schreiner (2004c), this section gives a precise definition of saving and describes several measures of financial savings. The proposed measures take into account the passage of time and the three stages of saving: "putting in" (depositing), "keeping in" (maintaining a balance), and "taking out" (withdrawing). Together, the measures provide a rich description of how people move financial resources through time. While the concepts are illustrated for the example of IDAs in ADD, they are general, and so they may be usefully applied to the measurement of almost any form of subsidized financial savings, including 401(k) plans and Individual Retirement Accounts.

Saving as Moving Resources through Time

As discussed in chapter 2, consumption uses up resources, resources come from income, income comes from production, and production requires natural resources, physical capital (tools), and human capital (time, effort, and skill). These factors of production come from *saving*, defined as moving resources through time rather than using them up now. Without saving, people would be hunters and gatherers living hand-to-mouth. With saving, humankind can build steadily on the past to improve the future. In short, saving drives development.

Although saving is required for long-term improvement in well-being, measures of financial saving—let alone measures of non-financial saving—tend to be rudimentary. The two typical measures of financial saving are "deposits in a time frame" and "balances at a point in time." As discussed below, these common measures—while useful—fail to capture some key aspects of the process of moving resources through time.

Stages of Financial Saving

Financial saving is moving dollars through time. This process can be seen in three stages.

The first stage is "putting in," the one-shot act of changing non-financial resources into dollars or—for the case where "putting in" means "depositing"—changing cash into bank-account balances. Although "depositing" is often equated with "saving," "depositing" is a far narrower concept than "saving." For example, paying down home-mortgage debt is saving, but it is saving in the form of a house, that is, cash converted into physical capital. Likewise, attending school is saving through the conversion of time and effort into the form of human capital. (Of course, before "putting in" can happen, a person must have income that exceeds consumption. This essential preliminary stage of financial saving is taken for granted here.)

The second stage of financial saving is maintaining balances, or "keeping in." Usually, "keeping in" is an act of omission rather than commission; most of the time, people do not think about whether they should close out their bank account and consume the proceeds. Still, they could close their account at any time, and sometimes they do think about closing it (and sometimes they close it). Thus, the absence of withdrawals—whether due to active decision or passive default—helps to move resources through time and thus is saving.

The third stage of financial saving is "taking out." Resources "taken out" may be consumed (dissaved) or converted and kept in another form (saved). For financial saving in bank accounts, "taking out" means making withdrawals.

Each of these three stages captures a distinct aspect of financial saving in a time frame. Saving might be high in one stage but low in another, and different stages are more or less prominent at different times. Thus, the best measures of saving encompass all three stages. The common measures of "deposits in a time frame" and "balances at a point in time" are simple and appropriate for personal financial management. From the perspective of describing and understanding how people move resources through time, however, these common measures miss some key aspects of saving.

For example, savers who make large deposits in a time frame may have high saving in terms of "putting in." If they quickly "take out" withdrawals, however, then they may have low saving in terms of "keeping in." In the same way, savers with low deposits in a time frame might nonetheless maintain their balances for a long time, registering low saving in terms of "putting in" but high saving in terms of "keeping in." Finally, withdrawals that are "taken out" and consumed lead to different saving—in terms of moving resources through time—than withdrawals that are "taken out" and converted into other forms of assets.

On the one hand, the common measure of saving as "deposits in the time frame" describes resources "put in" without saying how long the resources are then "kept in" before being "taken out." On the other hand, the common measure "balances at a point in time" focuses narrowly on resources "kept in" at a specific moment, ignoring how long ago the resources were "put in" and also ignoring how long they last until being "taken out."

As an example, suppose two people hold IDAs in no-interest, no-fee passbook savings accounts. The first saver puts in a deposit of $100 on January 1 and keeps a balance of $100 all year, taking out everything in a matched withdrawal on December 31. The second saver puts in a deposit of $200 on May 1 and keeps a balance of $200 for two months, taking it all out in an unmatched withdrawal on June 30. (These savings patterns are pictured in figure 5.1.) Who saved the most? In other words, who moved the most resources through time?

The common measures of "deposits in a time frame" (a flow) and "balances at a point in time" (a stock) do not provide a complete answer to this question because—as shown above—stocks and flows do not completely describe the three stages of putting in, keeping in, and taking out. What is needed is a "flowing stock" such as "dollar-years moved." (One dollar-year means one dollar was moved through twelve months of time, or two dollars were moved through six months, etc.) This new measure—as well as the average annual balance per year in a given time frame (another name for "dollar-years moved per year")—is sensitive to all three stages of putting in, keeping in, and taking out.

Consider the first example saver. The flow of deposits "put in" in the year was $100 on January 1, the balance of resources "kept in" was $100 throughout the year, and the flow of resources "taken out" as a matched withdrawal was $100 at the end of the year. The average balance for the year was $100 ($100 x 12 months), implying a measure of saving as a "flowing stock" of 100 dollar-years. In the context of the example's one-year time frame, saving was 100 dollar-years per year.

Figure 5.1
Two Example Saving Patterns

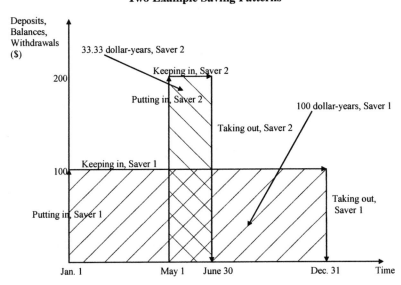

Now consider the second example saver. In the year, the flow of deposits "put in" was $200 on May 1, the balance of resources "kept in" was $200 for two months, and the flow of resources "taken out" as an unmatched withdrawal was $200 on June 30. Compared with the first saver, the second saver had higher deposits in the year and—at least in May and June—higher balances. The average balance for the second saver, however, was $33.33 ($200 x 2 months / 12 months), so the measure of saving as a "flowified stock" was 33.33 dollar-years. (In the context of the one-year time frame, this is equivalent to 33.33 dollar-years per year).

Compared with the first saver, the second saver had higher deposits and (at some points in time) higher balances. Still, after considering the three stages of saving as well as the time context, the first saver moved more resources through time and saved more. Furthermore, because the first saver made a matched withdrawal that is assumed to be converted into other forms of assets while the second saver made an unmatched withdrawal that is assumed to be consumed, the first saver will have greater saving (and greater asset accumulation) going forward in the next year.

Measures of Saving in Subsidized Accounts

This section describes a system of measures of financial saving in subsidized accounts. The measures account for time and—taken as a whole—they cover all three stages of saving. The measures require monthly data on deposits and withdrawals. While illustrated for IDAs in ADD, the measures could also be applied to 401(k) plans or Individual Retirement Accounts.

These measures of saving matter not only because they offer insight into how people save in IDAs but also because they may inform policy efforts to expand access to IDAs. For example, depository institutions that might hold the passbook savings accounts used for IDAs can take advantage of the figures to forecast the probable frequency and size of deposits and withdrawals. Likewise, new IDA programs can use the figures to plan, set benchmarks, and make budgets.

Participation

The most basic measure of saving in subsidized accounts is participation; non-participants cannot save in subsidized accounts. ADD had 2,350 *participants* (table 5.1), defined as enrollees who opened an IDA and who had at least one account statement recorded in MIS IDA.

Participation in 401(k) plans and in Individual Retirement Accounts has been widely studied (Munnell, Sundén, and Taylor, 2002; Madrian and Shea, 2001; Bassett, Fleming, and Rodrigues, 1998; Clark and Schieber, 1998; General Accounting Office, 1997). ADD, however, collected data only on participants, so—beyond the simple descriptive comparisons of the characteristics

Table 5.1
Participation in ADD

Line	Item	Formula	Value
Aa	Participants	Data	2,350
Ab	Months eligible to make matchable deposits	Data	78,962
Ac	Months IDA open and eligible to make matchable deposits	Data	60,982
Ad	Months eligible per participant	Ab/Aa	33.6
Ae	Months with an IDA open per participant	Ac/Aa	26.0

Table 5.2
Gross Deposits in ADD

Line	Item	Formula	Value
Ba	"Regular" cash deposits	Data	$2,682,620
Bb	Interest	Data	$43,669
Bc	Fees	Data	$4,846
Bd	Gross deposits	Ba+Bb–Bc	$2,721,443
Be	Gross deposits per participant	Bd/Aa	$1,158
Bf	Gross deposits per month eligible	Bd/Ab	$34.47
Bg	Gross deposits per month with an IDA open	Bd/Ac	$44.63
Bh	Months with a deposit	Data	30,719
Bi	Deposit frequency in months with IDA open (%)	100x(Bh/Ac)	50
Bj	Gross deposits per month with a deposit	Bd/Bh	$88.59

of ADD participants versus the overall low-income population in chapter 4—little can be said here about who among those eligible to participate in ADD did end up participating.

Each participant in ADD faced a *time cap*, defined as the number of calendar months eligible for making matchable deposits after opening an IDA. In ADD, the average participant had a time cap of 33.6 months (table 5.1). While it was possible to make matched and/or unmatched withdrawals after the time cap from deposits put in before the time cap, it is not possible to make matched withdrawals from deposits put in after the time cap.

About half of participants in ADD closed their IDAs before the time cap (51 percent, 28 percent of whom had made a matched withdrawal). The average participant had an IDA open for twenty-six months in which deposits were eligible for matching. The decision to close an IDA—regardless of whether a matched withdrawal had been made—was equivalent to the decision to deposit nothing in all future months up to the time-cap deadline nor to make any (additional) matched withdrawals.

Gross Deposits

Looking at the "putting in" aspect of saving, *gross deposits* are defined as cash flows into a subsidized savings account. This is the sum of "regular" deposits (cash put in) plus interest earnings, net of any account fees. In ADD, aggregate "regular" cash deposits for all participants in all months were $2,682,620, interest earnings were $43,669, and account fees were $4,846 (table 5.2). Thus, aggregate gross deposits in ADD were $2,721,443, corresponding to gross deposits per participant of about $1,158.

The measure of aggregate gross deposits depends on the number of participants; all else constant, if ADD had had more participants, then the aggregate measure would have been larger. But the number of participants in ADD depended mostly on the funds available for matches and program expenses. For policy purposes, a measure of saving that depends on the ability to fund-raise is not ideal, as it reflects policy choices as well as IDA design and participant saving. In this sense, the measure of gross deposits per participant is more useful than aggregate gross deposits, as it controls for the size of ADD and thus does not depend directly on fund-raising. For this same reason, "per-participant" measures are generally more meaningful than aggregate measures.

Going another step with the same logic, the measure of gross deposits per participant depends on the length of ADD; if ADD had been longer—that is, if participants had had longer time caps and thus more months available to make matchable deposits—then gross deposits per participant would have been larger. But again, the length of ADD and participants' time caps were at least partly a function not of optimal IDA design but of funding constraints. Thus, an even more policy-relevant measure of saving in terms of "putting in" is gross deposits per month eligible to make matchable deposits. In ADD, this was $34.47 (table 5.2).

For depository institutions contemplating the financial costs and benefits of their potential involvement with IDAs, it may also be useful to know that in months in which an IDA was open and eligible to receive matchable deposits, the average gross deposit was $44.63. In months in which ADD participants made a deposit, the average gross deposit was $88.59.

Gross deposits and the EITC. In tax season, many poor households receive tax refunds, a large share of which comes from the Earned Income Tax Credit (Berube et al., 2002). (According to Barrow and McGranahan, 2002, the vast majority of poor households receive their refunds in February or March.) These tax refunds are often the largest lump sum that poor households receive in a year, and theory suggests that a large share of such lump sums are likely to be saved (Browning and Collado, 2001; Souleles, 1999). Indeed, poor households carefully plan how to use their tax refunds (Romich and Weisner, 2000), and Barrow and McGranahan (2000) estimate that 80 percent of refunds are saved for at least one month and that receipt of the EITC increases household spending on durables in the months following the tax season. Poor households also often use tax refunds to make life changes such as moving, buying a car, or switching schools (Smeeding, Phillips, and O'Conner, 2000). Not surprisingly, policy makers, researchers, and financial intermediaries have asked how they might somehow tap this lump sum to help the "unbanked" to open accounts (Beverly, Romich, and Tescher, 2003; Beverly, Tescher, and Marzahl, 2000). For IDAs, the question is whether IDAs can help poor households to save a larger share of their tax refund and then put the savings to good use (Smeeding, 2000).

Some programs in ADD explicitly encouraged their participants to make deposits into IDAs from their tax refunds. Gross deposits in ADD did increase sharply in tax season (figures 5.2 and 5.3).

Were these unusually high gross deposits in tax season wiped out by unusually high unmatched withdrawals after tax season? An analysis of changes in net IDA savings by month (similar to that in figures 5.2 and 5.3 for gross deposits) suggests that IDA deposits from tax season were no more likely than IDA deposits in other months to be taken out in unmatched withdrawals. Thus, saving part of tax refunds appears to have been an effective strategy for increasing IDA savings.

Figure 5.2
Gross Deposits per Participant by Calendar Month and Year of Participation for ADD Participants with Annual Match Caps

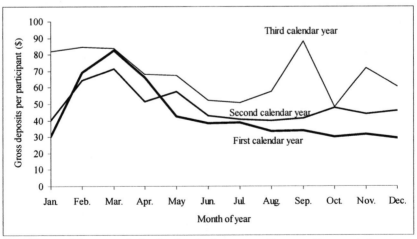

Note: Few participants reached a fourth calendar year, so those results are not shown.

Figure 5.3
Gross Deposits per Participant by Calendar Month and Year of Participation
for ADD Participants with Lifetime Match Caps

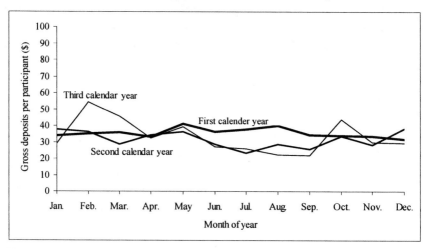

Note: Few participants reached a fourth calendar year, so those results are not shown.

The increase in gross deposits in tax season was clear and consistent in all years for participants with annual match caps, but it was present only in the third year for participants with lifetime match caps. Unfortunately, the data do not reveal why the match-cap structure was linked with saving from tax refunds. Perhaps annual match caps impressed on participants the need to deposit some of this year's refund before it was too late, but lifetime match caps allowed participants to put off saving from their tax refunds until their final deadline was approaching.

Gross deposits and deadlines. Figure 5.4 provides some support for the procrastination hypothesis. For participants with annual match caps, gross deposits spiked in months 12, 24, and 36, the last months before the annual match caps. In contrast, there were no such spikes for participants with lifetime match caps. Perhaps annual deadlines help poor people save in IDAs (just as they help non-poor people save in Individual Retirement Accounts) by forcing them to make a use-it-or-lose-it decision that cannot be put off.

Deposit Frequency

Deposit frequency is the share of months in which an IDA was open and in which a "regular" (cash) deposit was made. (Deposits of interest are not counted; if they were, then deposit frequency would always be 100 percent.) Deposit frequency matters because the common wisdom—repeated by nearly all fi-

Figure 5.4
**Gross Deposits per Participant in ADD by Months since Account Opening,
by Match-Cap Structure**

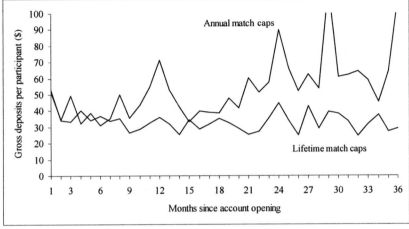

Note: Few participants had more than 36 months to make match-eligible deposits, so months 36–48 are not shown.

nancial planners—is that slow and steady wins the saving race. That is, consistent monthly deposits—even if small—builds both balances and habits that, in the long term, build assets. The idea is that it is better for savers to force themselves to save a small-but-consistent amount each month than to wait to save until there is a month-end surplus. Across all participant-months in ADD, deposit frequency was 50 percent in months in which an IDA was open (table 5.2).

Deposit frequency was strongly correlated with average (per participant) net IDA savings per month eligible for matchable deposits (figure 5.5). Participants with a deposit in 0–10 percent of months averaged net IDA savings per month of $1.62, whereas those with deposit frequencies of 81 percent or more averaged about $32. Correlation does not imply causation, however, so the data do not reveal whether frequent deposits led to high saving or whether high saving led to frequent deposits. Most likely, both forces were at work to some degree.

The strength of the measure of deposit frequency is its simplicity. Unfortunately, this simplicity is also its weakness; for example, deposit frequency is the same whether deposits are $10 in each month for four months or whether they are $1, $19, $15, and then $4. This weakness of the measure of deposit frequency may not matter much if, for learning to save, the key is not the size of deposits but rather their mere existence.

Figure 5.5
Average Net IDA Savings per Month by Deposit Frequency in ADD

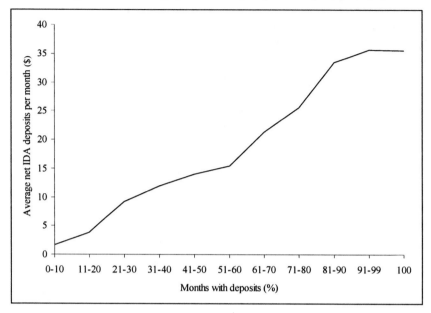

Excess Balances

Excess balances are gross deposits that are ineligible for matches because they exceed the match cap. As of the data cut-off date, IDA participants in ADD had aggregate gross deposits in excess of the match cap of $646,432 (table 5.3). Of these excess balances, $530,096 had been withdrawn (without matches), and $116,336 remained in the IDAs. (These figures omit gross deposits that exceeded an annual match cap when first put in but that later became matchable at the start of a new participation-year.) Excess balances are not counted as part of net IDA savings because they are not eligible for matches.

Is the definition of IDA savings in this book is too conservative because it excludes excess balances? After all, excess balances were put in the IDA and kept in for some time. But while excess balances in an IDA are certainly *savings*, they are not matchable and so are not *IDA savings*. If non-matchable balances counted as IDA savings, then the concept would logically have to include not only all balances in IDAs but also all balances in passbook or checking accounts. For comparison, non-poor savers in Individual Retirement Accounts and 401(k) plans do not get tax breaks for excess balances in those subsidized savings accounts, and excess balances there are not considered by researchers nor government as IRA or 401(k) savings.

Table 5.3
Gross Deposits in Excess of the Match Cap in ADD

Line	Item	Formula	Value
Ca	Excess balances still in IDAs	Data	$116,336
Cb	Withdrawals of excess balances	Data	$530,096
Cc	Gross deposits in excess of the match cap	Ca+Cb	$646,432
Cd	Participants with gross deposits in excess of the match cap	Data	832
Ce	Share of participants with excess balances (%)	100x(Cd/Aa)	35
Cf	Gross deposits in excess of the match cap per participant with gross deposits in excess of the match cap	Cc/Cd	$777

Gross deposits in excess of the match cap were not unusual; about one-third (35 percent) of participants had excess balances at some point. Participants in this group averaged gross deposits in excess of the match cap of $777. This is a large figure, considering that the average participant had gross deposits (whether above or below the match cap) of $1,158 (table 5.2) and that about 48 percent of participants were "low savers" with net IDA savings of less than $100.

There are several possible explanations for the presence and extent of excess balances in ADD. First, some participants apparently used their IDAs as transaction accounts, for example, by depositing their paychecks in IDAs and then making frequent unmatched withdrawals. (About 7 percent of participants with excess balances had twenty or more unmatched withdrawals.) Among these "transactors," gross deposits in excess of the match cap averaged $2,611, equivalent to about one-fourth of the aggregate value of excess balances. These "transactors" would be expected to be concentrated among the 21 percent of "unbanked" participants who did not have a bank account before ADD. It turns out, however, that average gross deposits in excess of the match cap were $253 for the "unbanked" and $281 for others. While the average number of unmatched withdrawals was 3.3 for the "unbanked" and 2.4 for others, there is not much evidence that most "transactors" were "unbanked" before ADD.

Second, some participants used their IDAs as a place to "park" large sums. For example, 8 percent of participants with excess balances put in gross deposits in excess of the match cap of $2,000 or more in a single month. These "parkers" accounted for about 61 percent of the aggregate value of excess balances. Many "parkers" probably used their IDA to consolidate a down payment on a house, as 47 percent of them made matched withdrawals for home purchase. Furthermore, tax refunds probably account for some large excess balances, as 27 percent of "parkers" had their largest gross deposit in excess of the match cap in February or March, the months in which most low-income people receive tax refunds (Barrow and McGranahan, 2000).

Third, many IDA participants with excess balances (about 43 percent) just barely exceeded the match cap. Most of these (64 percent) made matched withdrawals, so the excess may simply be what Moffitt (1990) calls "optimization error," that is, the choice to err on the side of putting in a little too much rather than risk getting caught a little short when going to take out a matched withdrawal for a specific purchase. Among this group of "over-flowers," the average excess was about $66, less than the average gross deposit ($89) in a month with a deposit (table 5.2). Among participants with net IDA savings equal to the match cap, 98 percent had some excess balances. For many of these, the excess likely resulted from interest deposited into the IDA in months after the participant had saved up to the match cap.

Fourth, among the 65 percent of participants without excess balances, about 64 percent were "low savers" with net IDA deposits of less than $100. Given that about 48 percent of all participants were "low savers," this suggests that those with excess balances may simply have been those who managed to be "savers."

In sum, participants with excess balances can be grouped (non-exclusively) as "transactors" who used the IDA as their day-to-day bank account, "parkers" who used the IDA for short-term storage of tax refunds or down payments for a house, "over-flowers" who saved a little bit more than the match cap, "savers" with $100 or more in net IDA savings, and/or "others."

Does the presence of excess balances mean that IDA participants would save more if match caps were loosened? The analysis of the ADD data in this chapter cannot answer this question. With a higher match cap, "over-flowers" almost certainly would have saved more in their IDAs, but "transactors" and "parkers" may or may not have saved more, and most "low savers" would probably still have had net IDA savings of less than $100. The regression analysis in the next chapter addresses this question directly by looking at how net IDA savings varied with variations in the match cap, controlling for many other program and participant characteristics.

The discussion so far has focused on gross deposits, but—for several reasons—the measurement of saving should not focus exclusively on the first step of "putting in." First, gross deposits in IDAs are matchable only up to the match cap. Gross deposits in excess of the cap are still savings, but they are not matchable IDA savings. Second, deposits put in IDAs may be withdrawn to finance consumption or to be converted into other forms of assets. Third, as shown above, some participants are "transactors" who treat their IDAs almost like checking accounts, making frequent deposits and frequent withdrawals without much long-term accumulation. This churning leads to high "putting in" but low "keeping in." Thus, it is better to consider both deposits and withdrawals, whether unmatched or matched.

Table 5.4
Unmatched Withdrawals in ADD

Line	Item	Formula	Value
Da	Value of unmatched withdrawals	Data	$763,903
Db	Number of unmatched withdrawals	Data	6,138
Dc	Value of average unmatched withdrawal	Da/Db	$124
Dd	Participants with an unmatched withdrawal	Data	1,515
De	Share of participants with an unmatched withdrawal (%)	100x(Dd/Aa)	64
Df	Number of unmatched withdrawals per participant	Db/Aa	2.6
Dg	Value of unmatched withdrawals per participant	Da/Aa	$325
Dh	Number of unmatched withdrawals per participant with unmatched withdrawals	Db/Dd	4.1
Di	Value of unmatched withdrawals per participant with unmatched withdrawals	Da/Dd	$504
Dj	Match rate per dollar taken out in unmatched withdrawal	Data	1.77:1
Dk	Lost matches per participant with unmatched withdrawals	Di x Dj	$892

Unmatched Withdrawals

Unmatched withdrawals are funds taken out of an IDA for a purpose for which matches are not provided. ADD placed no formal restrictions on unmatched withdrawals. (AFIA sites and a few other programs in ADD were joint owners of the IDA with the participant, so program staff had to sign off on any unmatched withdrawals. Apparently, program staff approved all requests without any fuss other than trying to take advantage of a "teachable moment." Other nominal formal restrictions on unmatched withdrawals in ADD were probably enforced only rarely.) Participants were always free to make unmatched withdrawals, reducing the chance that IDAs could somehow cause participants to harm themselves by saving too much when they needed the resources for subsistence. The average participant in ADD made 2.6 unmatched withdrawals worth a total of $325 (table 5.4).

The typical unmatched withdrawal was not large ($124). Indeed, one-fourth of the value of unmatched withdrawals by participants in months with an unmatched withdrawal was $28 or less, and one-half were $100 or less. Although ADD did not collect data on the use of unmatched withdrawals, most unmatched withdrawals were small, perhaps suggesting that they were often used for short-term subsistence needs (such as paying bills) and that participants tried to take out as little as possible.

While the typical unmatched withdrawal was not large, the average participant with an unmatched withdrawal made 4.1 unmatched withdrawals worth a total of $504 (table 5.4). Furthermore, any unmatched withdrawal exacted a steep opportunity cost in terms of lost matches. The average match rate for participants with an unmatched withdrawal was 1.77:1, so unmatched withdrawals cost each of these participants about $892 in lost matches. Seen across all participants, average unmatched withdrawals were about $325, and net IDA savings (deposits that were matched or could still be matched after the data cut-off date) were about $558. Thus, about one-third (37 percent) of all deposits in ADD that might have been matched were taken out in unmatched withdrawals. Finally, about 48 percent of ADD participants were "low savers," having net IDA savings of less than $100.

Did "low savers" make too few gross deposits or too many unmatched withdrawals? Among "low savers," average gross deposits were $687, and average unmatched withdrawals were $430. (The difference is mostly due to withdrawals of gross deposits in excess of the match cap which are not counted as unmatched withdrawals from matchable balances.) Among "savers" with net IDA savings of $100 or more, average gross deposits were $1,584, and average unmatched withdrawals were $230. Thus, "low savers" had both lower gross deposits and higher unmatched withdrawals, and the two factors probably reinforced each other. That is, participants with low deposits may have become discouraged, making unmatched withdrawals easier for them. Furthermore, whatever factors caused low deposits in the first place were probably also likely to cause emergencies and the need to make unmatched withdrawals.

Given the high opportunity costs of lost matches and the supportive institutional environment of IDAs, the extent of unmatched withdrawals (and of "low savers") in ADD was a surprise and a concern. When IDA participants make an unmatched withdrawal, they forego a high rate of return from the match (and lose future ownership of an asset) in exchange for cash that is likely used up in current consumption. As usual, the ADD data provide results and not reasons, so it is not possible to know exactly how or why unmatched withdrawals and "low saving" happened. But theory suggests a few speculative possibilities.

The first idea—and probably the most important—is simply that saving is difficult for the poor. Some participants may not only be very close to subsistence but also subject to sharp variations in their streams of income and expenses. If income dips (for example, due to job loss) or if expenses spike (for example, due to illness), then the short-term need for cash may outweigh the long-term costs of unmatched withdrawals. Furthermore, even if participants themselves do not suffer shocks to income or expenses, members of their social networks may suffer such shocks and then ask for cash gifts, leading to unmatched withdrawals (Chiteji and Hamilton, 2002). Of course, it is also possible that some participants are simply shortsighted or unwise; that is, to the detriment of their own long-term well-being and with full knowledge of the consequences, they make unmatched withdrawals in response to tempting short-term consumption opportunities. In the end, it is unknown—and probably does not matter—whether the poor's difficulty in saving stems more from the closeness of income to physical subsistence needs, from shortsighted choices, or from institutional factors such as downwardly skewed world views or habits ingrained by asset-limits on means-tested public assistance. All these factors probably matter to some extent. In any case, it should come as no surprise that while ADD shows that the poor can save in IDAs, ADD also shows that even saving in IDAs is difficult for many poor people and that IDAs are not a panacea.

Second, about 49 percent of the participants who made matched withdrawals also subsequently made unmatched withdrawals, averaging about $434 per participant in this group and accounting for about 20 percent of the aggregate value of unmatched withdrawals. Some unknown share of these unmatched withdrawals came from "extra" IDA savings left over after a matched purchase and thus represent not failed attempts to save in IDAs but rather savings in excess of what was required for a desired matched use.

Third, participants may have decided at some point after enrollment that, from their perspective, there was no worthwhile matched use for their IDA savings. For example, a participant might have enrolled hoping to save the full matchable amount to use for a down payment on a house. If—for whatever reason—the participant ended up saving less than had been hoped, such a down payment might have no longer been feasible. Of course, IDA participants were always free to change their minds and make a matched withdrawal for some purpose other than what they had planned at enrollment, but such switches may have been difficult if participants had enrolled thinking of only one or two of the possible matched uses. Thus, if plans had to change, some participants may have preferred to close the IDA with an unmatched withdrawal rather than switch to a different matched use.

The point is that, at a given point in time, only one or two possible matched uses may be relevant for a given IDA participant. For example, most of the 20 percent of participants in ADD who owned a home at enrollment probably did not want to make a matched withdrawal for home purchase (in any case, some programs in ADD limited such matched withdrawals to first-time buyers, and any permanent, universal IDA policy would probably have to do likewise). Furthermore, homeownership is not a one-shot event that ends with purchase; some participants who would have been able to save for a down payment on a house through IDAs may have nonetheless have decided that they preferred not to encumber themselves with the on-going responsibilities of maintenance and monthly mortgage payments. In the same way, matched withdrawals for home repair were probably irrelevant for most of the 80 percent of participants who did not own a home at enrollment. Likewise, most older participants—especially those without college-age children or grandchildren—may not have seen matched withdrawals for post-secondary education as an attractive option. Even those interested in matched withdrawals for post-secondary education likely realized that such a program of training does not end with a single purchase and that completing post-secondary education entails a large, long commitment. Microenterprise also may have lacked wide appeal. About 78 percent of ADD participants had wage jobs at enrollment, and self-employment is usually much more difficult than wage employment, especially for low-income people (Schreiner, 1999a and 1999b; Bates, 1997; Balkin, 1989). The only matched use with potential for universal appeal is the "roll-over" of the IDA plus match into a Roth IRA, as this is a one-shot use that is possible for almost any participant of any age, educational level, self-employment status, or homeownership status. Still, only four programs in ADD provided matches for retirement savings, and, in any case, many younger people—regardless of income—may see retirement as too far off to be relevant.

All this suggests that unmatched withdrawals from IDAs in ADD were probably least likely for participants who—even before enrollment—were already planning (and perhaps saving) to buy a house, obtain post-secondary education, start or expand a microenterprise, or repair their home. In these cases, access to IDAs could still have had an impact if it accelerated and/or augmented the asset accumulation that was already underway or being planned. Of course, IDAs could still have been useful for people who, before they heard of IDAs, had never dreamed of buying a house, getting post-secondary education, or being self-employed. The institutional structure of IDAs certainly does suggest to people that they can (and perhaps should) do things that they had not previously considered doing. But because no more than one or two matched uses were usually relevant for a given participant, unmatched withdrawals were probably more likely for people who opened their IDAs with a single goal in mind and then found—for whatever reason—that they had to make a change to their plans.

Unmatched withdrawals and matches for retirement savings. A simple way to help IDA participants to reduce unmatched withdrawals is to offer matches for "roll-overs" of IDAs into Roth IRAs. This would not only promote greater retirement savings for the poor but also encourage post-secondary education and homeownership, as Roth IRAs may be tapped for either of these two uses at any time without tax penalties. If IDAs can be "rolled-over" into Roth IRAs, then IDA participants who enroll hoping to make a down payment for a home or to pay for college can still accumulate towards those long-term goals even if the short-term deadlines of the IDA program arrive before the participant is ready for a matched withdrawal. Matches for "roll-overs" into 529 College Savings Plans (Clancy, 2003; Clancy and Sherraden, 2003) might also help to "extend" IDAs meant to fund post-secondary education. In fact, Oregon and Pennsylvania already allow such "roll-overs" of IDAs into 529 plans (Clancy, Orszag, and Sherraden, 2004).

Some state and federal policies already provide matches for savings by the poor in Roth IRAs for retirement and in 529 College Savings Plans for post-secondary education. The 2001 tax act created the Saver's Tax Credit that acts somewhat like a match; contributions (up to a limit) by low-income taxpayers to an IRA or 401(k) plan qualify for a non-refundable 50 percent tax credit (Orszag and Hall, 2003). In 529 College Savings Plans, five states (Louisiana, Maine, Michigan, Minnesota, and Rhode Island) offer matches for contributions by low-income savers (Clancy, Orszag, and Sherraden, 2004).

Unmatched withdrawals and IDA design. Should IDA programs use formal rules to discourage or even prevent unmatched withdrawals? On the one hand, if participants expect that they will fail to resist tempting short-term consumption opportunities, then IDA programs would do participants a favor by restricting unmatched withdrawals. These restrictions would allow enrollees to commit to protect themselves from their own shortsightedness. Angeletos et al. (2001), Shefrin and Thaler (1988), and Maital (1986) describe how people—poor or non-poor—are often shortsighted and fail to do what is in their own long-term best interest even though they know better. Some ADD participants reported that they had an appreciation for institutional restrictions on unmatched withdrawals because they believed that the restrictions helped to protect them against moments of weakness (Moore et al., 2001). Restrictions on unmatched withdrawals may also be useful if people are not aware of ways to meet their household's short-term financial demands without resorting to an unmatched withdrawal. If unmatched withdrawals are not simple and easy, participants under duress may put more effort into looking for alternative solutions.

On the other hand, if unmatched withdrawals are tightly restricted and if some participants expect that they may end up wanting to make unmatched withdrawals in an emergency, then those potential participants may choose not to enroll in an IDA program at all, or they may choose—less extremely—to delay making deposits until the last minute before the time-cap deadline. That way, if they do suffer a shock, they will avoid the transaction costs of an unmatched withdrawal. Results in Schreiner et al. (2005) and earlier in this chapter suggest that deposits in ADD did tend to increase just before annual time-cap deadlines, leading to the plausible speculation some participants in ADD did wait until the last moment to put in their deposits. If restrictions on withdrawals lead participants to save outside of IDAs until just before time-cap deadlines, however, then net deposits may decline because cash kept outside of an IDA is more likely to "burn a hole in a pocket" and be spent before the time-cap deadline rolls around, regardless of emergencies or restrictions on withdrawals (Beverly and Sherraden, 1999; Bernheim, 1997; Caskey, 1997; Thaler, 1990).

For the poor, crises are a fact of life. One of the few ways that IDAs might do harm would be to put the poor's savings of out of their reach. At the same time, some light, informal constraints on unmatched withdrawals may help some participants to "keep in" their deposits. The institutional structure for IDAs in ADD, with informal discouragement of unmatched withdrawals but no enforced formal restrictions, may be a good model of a compromise that manages to capture some of the benefits of restrictions on withdrawals without imposing any formal restrictions. That is, informal or merely nominal restrictions may increase the "mental costs" of unmatched withdrawals and thus help deter some unwise choices without increasing costs so much that savings are unreachable even when they are truly needed. One example of an informal restriction is an explicit expectation that participants first discuss any planned unmatched withdrawal with IDA staff. Not only would participants try to avoid unmatched withdrawals so that they can avoid the embarrassment of discussing the issue with staff, but the discussion might lead to ideas for alternative ways to deal with the crisis without resorting to an unmatched withdrawal. In addition, financial-education classes and IDA promotional literature can highlight that unmatched withdrawals should be made only with extreme caution and in extreme cases because of their high costs in terms of lost matches. Consistent with the "libertarian paternalism" of Thaler and Sunstein (2003), such informal or nominal restrictions on unmatched withdrawals allow participants to make their own choices while also facilitating the choice generally considered as "wise."

Another simple adjustment to program design that might help to reduce unmatched withdrawals takes advantage of "mental accounts" (Milligan, 2002; Prelec and Loewenstein, 1998; Thaler, 1992). The idea is to provide—alongside the IDA that is labeled for long-term asset accumulation—a second savings account explicitly labeled for emergencies. Even if participants do not save more in the two accounts together than they would save in an IDA alone, the mere existence of the second "emergency" account (and its label) may help to preserve IDA balances if it helps participants to see IDAs as long-term savings. Furthermore, the existence of the "emergency" account may have an awareness effect that prompts participants to save more for emergencies, again decreasing pressure on the IDA for unmatched withdrawals.

The regression results in the next chapter suggest that in ADD, the joint-ownership of the IDA by the participant and the program as mandated in the AFIA sites was associated with a higher likelihood of being a "saver," perhaps due to the minor inconvenience of having to request a signature from program staff for an unmatched withdrawal (even though this signature was always granted).

Still, from a practical standpoint, joint account ownership is problematic. For one thing, it is cumbersome to administer and takes time from program staff. For another thing, such seeming heavy-handedness is absent from subsidized savings programs aimed at the non-poor. For example, 401(k) plans and Individual Retirement Accounts qualify for tax breaks even though the government is not a co-owner on the account, and withdrawals (possibly with a tax penalty, akin to the loss of matches) do not require any co-signer. Furthermore, requiring the program's signature increases the danger that a participant will be unable to take out savings quickly in an emergency, for example on a weekend or when IDA staff are on vacation. Finally, joint ownership leaves open the danger that a staff member will be tempted to find a way to embezzle participants' IDA savings.

Deadlines, "kick-outs," and IDA policy. Unlike subsidized-savings programs such as 401(k) plans and Individual Retirement Accounts for the non-poor, programs in ADD (like most IDA programs so far) imposed deadlines both for making matchable deposits (the time cap) and for making matched withdrawals (usually six to twelve months after the time cap). Beyond these deadlines, deposits were not matchable and matched withdrawals were not possible.

If the goal is to improve the long-term well-being of the poor, however, then these deadlines are dysfunctional. Some IDA participants might be content to save for years without a specific purchase in mind, and it makes little sense to force them to make a matched withdrawal in a brief time frame. A better design would allow savings to accumulate for as long as participants wish.

Furthermore, some unknown number of unmatched withdrawals in ADD resulted from "kick-outs." Program staff forced some participants with low and/or infrequent deposits to close their IDAs with unmatched withdrawals. While "kick-outs" did have low net IDA savings, they did not choose to quit. Rather, IDA staff made that choice for them, based not on their desire for the well-being of that particular participant but rather the program's wish to make room for other participants who might save more (and perhaps benefit more). This can be seen as a tough-love choice, and—given constraints on funds in ADD—may have improved overall social well-being. Also, program staff were not unaware that replacing "kick-outs" may have helped to improve the numbers that the program could report to funders and thus may have improved the likelihood of securing further funding for their IDA program. While "kick-outs" may make sense to programs surviving on soft funds, however, they do not make sense from a developmental perspective. Like deadlines, "kick-outs" are dysfunctional. Furthermore, the MIS IDA data from ADD suggest that it was not uncommon for participants who were not kicked-out to have low saving at first or to have gaps of twelve to eighteen months between deposits but yet to end up being "savers" and/or making matched withdrawals.

Both deadlines and "kick-outs" are symptoms of the short-term nature of funding for IDA demonstrations. Private funders simply and quite sensibly will not commit to funding IDAs over participants' lifetimes—only the government can do that. Given their short-term funding, IDA programs must set deadlines for matchable deposits and matched withdrawals because, eventually, unused funds revert to the funders. Likewise, if budget constraints limit the number of participants, "kick-outs" can make room for others who might save and benefit more.

Unfortunately, funding constraints has led some people—and some IDA staff—to see IDAs merely as short-term savings instruments. Of course, this was never the intent; it is but an artifact of the nature of policy demonstrations. For a developmental perspective, the policy goal should be to allow people to save in IDAs until they are ready to make a matched withdrawal. In addition, the transformation of IDAs into short-term programs seems inconsistent with subsidized savings programs for the non-poor. For example, 401(k) plans and Individual Retirement Accounts do not kick out participants or restrict access to tax breaks if participants miss a deadline, suspend contributions for long periods, or even wait for decades to open an account. No, everyone has permanent access to these programs, regardless of their past saving.

How long should IDA programs last? Sherraden's (1991) original IDA proposal calls for universal, permanent accounts, opened at birth, with greater subsidies for the poor. In this sense, IDAs were never meant to be "programs" with ending dates any more than 401(k) plans or Individual Retirement Accounts were. In practice, IDAs have been time-limited because advances in the field—funded as demonstrations—have preceded creation of a permanent policy (Edwards and Mason, 2003). If, however, the goal of IDA policy is to improve the long-term well-being of the poor, then many practices that are necessary in demonstrations—such as setting deadlines for matched withdrawals or kicking out low savers—are counterproductive. A better design would allow IDA participants to save and keep balances for as long as they wish. Some participants would be content to save for years without making a matched withdrawal, sometimes depositing regularly, sometimes not depositing, and sometimes making unmatched withdrawals in emergencies. But everyone would have an account (even if the balance were zero), and everyone would receive annual statements that would act as gentle reminders of the possibility of saving, much as annual Social Security statements serve to remind people that Social Security is not meant to be their sole source of retirement income.

Matched Withdrawals

Matched withdrawals are funds taken out of an IDA for a purpose for which matches are provided. In ADD, every program provided matches for home

Table 5.5
Matched Withdrawals in ADD

Line	Item	Formula	Value
Ea	Value of matched withdrawals	Data	$672,577
Eb	Number of matched withdrawals	Data	1,874
Ec	Value of average matched withdrawal	Ea/Eb	$359
Ed	Participants with a matched withdrawal	Data	729
Ee	Share of participants with a matched withdrawal (%)	100 x (Ed/Aa)	31
Ef	Number of matched withdrawals per participant	Eb/Aa	0.8
Eg	Value of matched withdrawals per participant	Ea/Aa	$286
Eh	Number of matched withdrawals per participant with a matched withdrawal	Eb/Ed	2.6
Ei	Value of matched withdrawals per participant with a matched withdrawal	Ea/Ed	$923
Ej	Match rate per dollar taken out in a matched withdrawal	Data	1.81:1
Ek	Matches on matched withdrawals	Ea x Ej	$1,217,364
El	Matched withdrawals plus match	Ea+Ek	$1,889,941
Em	Average matched withdrawal plus match	El/Eb	$1,009
En	Average matched withdrawal plus match per participant with a matched withdrawal	El/Ed	$2,593

purchase, post-secondary education, and microenterprise. Eleven programs provided matches for job training and technical education (uses which might be included under the rubric of "post-secondary education"), eight programs matched home repair and remodeling, and four matched retirement savings. Outside ADD, some IDA programs provide matches for car purchase or computer purchase.

Matched withdrawals convert assets in the form of IDA balances into assets in other forms (for example, physical capital through home purchase, human capital through post-secondary education, or business capital through microenterprise). Only the purchases of specific types of assets are matched, and the matches themselves are usually disbursed directly to vendors.

As of the data cut-off date, 31 percent of participants in ADD had made a matched withdrawal. Participants in this group averaged 2.6 matched withdrawals worth a total (without matches) of $923 (table 5.5). (In ADD overall, the average matched withdrawal was $359, and the average participant had 0.8 matched withdrawals worth—without matches—$286.) Given an average match rate for these participants of 1.81:1, the average matched withdrawal (with matches) was worth $1,009, or $2,593 per participant who made a matched withdrawal.

As a measure of saving, matched withdrawals "taken out" of an IDA is useful but incomplete. First, at a point in time, some match-eligible balances are still in the IDA, waiting to be taken out as matched withdrawals. Second, because resources are fungible, the assumption that resources transferred in matched withdrawals are converted into the asset purchased is not always completely correct. In some cases, the participant would have made the same purchase even without assistance from an IDA, although the purchase may have been smaller or later in time. In these cases, the matched withdrawal is converted not into the asset purchased but rather into whatever the participant purchased (assets and/or consumption goods) which would not have been purchased without an IDA. (This holds even though the match is disbursed directly to the vendor and even if the matched withdrawal is carried directly from the depository institution to the vendor.) The MIS IDA data from ADD, however, do not reveal what would have happened in the absence of IDAs, so the analysis here cannot determine to what extent resource fungibility meant that matched withdrawals did not cause the purchase of the associated matched assets.

Match-eligible balances. Participants in ADD generally had six to twelve months after the time-cap deadline to make matched withdrawals from matchable deposits that had been made before the time cap. The data cut-off date, however, was at the time cap. Thus, the figures for matched withdrawals discussed so far do not tell the whole story, as many ADD participants held *match-eligible balances*—matchable deposits yet to be taken out in matched withdrawals—that do not show up in the data as matched withdrawals but that may have been taken out as matched withdrawals after the data cut-off date. In particular, match-eligible balances are likely to be common and large for participants planning for home purchase, as that matched use involves a single, large matched withdrawal that must be coordinated with a lengthy, complex process of home search. Not only does finding an appropriate house take time, but saving a larger amount—all else constant—also requires a longer time. Thus, many expectant homebuyers may have had most or all of their savings still in their IDA as of the time cap.

Indeed, aggregate match-eligible balances in ADD were $638,531 (table 5.6), almost as high as aggregate matched withdrawals of $672,577 (table 5.5). As of the data cut-off date, about 47 percent of participants had match-eligible balances (table 5.6), of whom 74 percent had match-eligible balances of $100 or more. Among participants with match-eligible balances, the average level was $578, and, given an average match rate for these participants of 1.96:1, these match-eligible balances would—if taken out in matched withdrawals—

Table 5.6
Match-Eligible Balances in ADD

Line	Item	Formula	Value
Fa	Match-eligible balances	Bd–Cc–Da–Ea	$638,531
Fb	Participants with match-eligible balances	Data	1,105
Fc	Share of participants with match-eligible balances (%)	100 x (Fb/Aa)	47
Fd	Match-eligible balances per participant	Fa/Aa	$272
Fe	Match-eligible balances per participant with match-eligible balances	Fa/Eb	$578
Ff	Match rate per dollar of match-eligible balances	Data	1.96:1
Fg	Possible matches on match-eligible balances	Fa x Ff	$1,251,522
Fh	Match-eligible balances plus possible matches	Fa+Fg	$1,890,053
Fi	Match-eligible balances plus possible matches per participant	Fi/Aa	$804
Fj	Match-eligible balances plus possible matches per participant with match-eligible balances	Fi/Fb	$1,710

lead to asset accumulation of $1,710 per participant in this group. Aggregate potential asset accumulation from match-eligible balances plus potential matches was $1,890,053 (table 5.6), almost exactly equal to aggregate matched withdrawals plus matches of $1,889,941 (table 5.5). (Of course, these figures overstate asset accumulation to some unknown degree, as some share of match-eligible balances taken out after the time cap were not matched but rather unmatched.)

Among the 35 percent of participants who were "savers" with match-eligible balances of $100 or more, 72 percent had yet to make a matched withdrawal. Of those who had yet to make a matched withdrawal, 52 percent planned for home purchase. Those participants who planned to buy homes had average match-eligible balances of $897, whereas other participants who were planning for other uses averaged $797. Thus, most participants with match-eligible balances were planning to buy a house, and they likely were waiting as long as they could so as to maximize their down payment.

Net IDA Savings

Net IDA savings are deposits in IDAs that were matched or that might have been matched after the time-cap deadline. That is, net IDA savings are the sum

Table 5.7
Net IDA Savings in ADD

Line	Item	Formula	Value
Ga	Net IDA savings	Ea+Fa	$1,311,108
Gb	Match rate per dollar of net IDA savings	Data	1.88:1
Gc	Possible matches on net IDA savings	Ek+FG	$2,468,886
Gd	Net IDA savings plus possible matches	Ga+Gc	$3,779,994
Ge	Net IDA savings per participant	Ga/Aa	$558
Gf	Net IDA savings plus possible matches per participant	Gd/Aa	$1,609
Gg	Net IDA savings per month eligible for matchable deposits	Ga/Ab	$16.60
Gh	Net IDA savings per month with IDA open and eligible for matchable deposits	Ga/Ac	$21.50

of matched withdrawals plus match-eligible balances. Net IDA savings is the central measure of savings outcomes in ADD because it reveals the amount saved and matched (or available to be matched). The measure omits matches themselves because the match rate and the match cap were set not by participants but by the program. Because net IDA savings depends on the length of time available to save—people with shorter time caps save less, all else constant—the measure is most useful in the context of the number of months eligible for matchable deposits. In ADD, net IDA savings per month eligible for matchable deposits was $16.60 (table 5.7).

This is how it is known that low-income people can save in IDAs; on average in ADD, they saved $16.60 per month in which deposits were eligible for matches. With an average of 33.6 months eligible for matchable deposits per participant, net IDA savings averaged $558. Given an average match rate of 1.88:1, net IDA savings plus (possible) matches per participant (that is, asset accumulation through IDAs) was $1,609. (The next two chapters look at links between net IDA savings and the characteristics of programs and participants.)

That poor people can save is a major result. After all, many public policies—in spite of the fundamental importance of saving and asset accumulation for long-term improvement in well-being as discussed in chapter 2—seem to assume that the poor cannot (or should not) save. ADD shows not only that the poor can save to improve their long-term lot in life but also that they can do at least some of that saving through the institutional vehicle of IDAs. From a policy perspective, seeing the poor as savers is a breakthrough, and proving that the poor can save in IDAs provides an institutional means to encourage saving and asset accumulation by the poor.

Of course, while the poor's saving is big news, it is not the end of the story. In particular, to say that the poor saved in IDAs is not to say that the poor could not save without IDAs. Indeed, at least in non-industrialized countries, one of the main lessons of the microfinance movement has been that the poor are desperate to save and that their saving is restrained mostly by a lack of access to adequate institutions (Robinson, 2001; Rutherford, 2000; Adams, 1978).

Nor is saying that the poor saved in IDAs the same as saying that the poor saved more in IDAs than they would have saved otherwise. Unfortunately, the MIS IDA data from ADD cannot reveal the impact of IDAs because they do not show whether the poor saved more with IDAs than they would have saved otherwise. Whether or not IDAs had an impact on overall saving by the poor, they may have had an impact on asset accumulation and/or on the types of assets accumulated. The MIS IDA data cannot address any of these possible impacts because they cover only what happened to ADD participants with IDAs, not what would have happened to ADD participants (or what did happen to equivalent non-participants) without IDAs.

In general, the evaluation of any social-policy intervention looks at three tiers of impacts. The first tier—and the most important from a policy perspective—is the impact on eligible people. How would access to IDAs change outcomes for poor people, if all poor people had access? Even if impact on participants were known—and in the case of ADD this impact is not known—impact on eligibles cannot be extrapolated directly from impact on participants because participants probably differ systematically from eligibles. In particular, participants are probably drawn disproportionately from among those for whom IDA impacts are likely to be largest. The MIS IDA data from ADD cannot indicate impact on eligibles not only because it cannot measure impact on participants but also because it did not collect data on eligible non-participants.

The second tier is impact on participants. How do IDAs change outcomes for eligibles who participate? This second tier matters because impact on participants usually drives the greatest part of impact on eligibles, which is after all a weighted average of impact on participants and impact on eligible non-participants. As discussed above, the MIS IDA data from ADD cover outcomes for participants, not changes in outcomes for participants with-versus-without IDAs.

The third tier—and the least informative from a policy perspective—is impact on "successful" participants. In the case of IDAs, this tier asks how IDAs change outcomes for people who consummate their IDA participation with a matched withdrawal. This third tier matters because impact on "successful" participants usually drives the greatest part of the second tier of impact on all participants, which in turn usually drives most of the first tier of impact on eligibles. The MIS IDA data from ADD do not reveal impact on "successful" participants, as it is unknown how participants with a matched withdrawal would have fared without IDAs.

Table 5.8
"Savers" in ADD

Line	Item	Formula	Value
Ha	"Savers" with net IDA savings of $100 or more	Data	1,233
Hb	Share of participants who were "savers" (%)	Ha/Aa ·	52
Hc	Net IDA savings for "savers"	Data	$1,238,295
Hd	Months eligible to make matchable deposits for "savers"	Data	38,169
He	Net IDA savings per month eligible to make matchable deposits for "savers"	Hc/Hd	$32.44

"Savers"

What is "success" in an IDA? One perspective looks at having saved, that is, having moved resources through time. The discussion below of "dollar-years moved" looks at IDAs through this lens. Another perspective—one that captures IDAs' goals for both saving and asset accumulation—looks at having made a matched withdrawal (or, in the case of match-eligible balances, being able to make a future matched withdrawal).

"Savers" are defined as participants with net IDA savings (matched withdrawals plus match-eligible balances) of $100 or more. "Savers" either made a matched withdrawal of $100 or more before the cut-off date of the ADD data or were able to make such a matched withdrawal after the cut-off.

"Low savers" are defined as those with net IDA savings of less than $100. Almost all "low savers" did save something—that is, they did move some resources through time in IDAs—but they either did not make a matched withdrawal before the time cap or they could not possibly make a matched withdrawal worth $100 or more after the time cap.

About 52 percent of participants in ADD were "savers" (table 5.8). Naturally, net IDA savings per month was much higher for "savers" ($32.44) than for the average participant ($16.60) and for "low savers" ($3.19).

These outcomes for "savers" must be placed in context. Advocates may be tempted to focus on *outcomes for successful participants*, perhaps implicitly (or explicitly) equating them with *changes in outcomes for eligibles*. While "savers" are an important group, they are not the only group, and focusing only on them is a mistake. Changes in outcomes for eligibles are almost always much smaller than changes in outcomes for successful participants, and in any case the MIS IDA data from ADD reveal nothing about changes in outcomes for any group.

To glean lessons about the types of IDA designs that were linked with savings outcomes in ADD, the next chapter uses regression analysis to look at how program characteristics were associated with the likelihood of being a "saver" and then—for "savers"—with the level of net IDA savings. The chapter after that then analyzes linkages between participant characteristics, the likelihood of being a "saver," and the level of net IDA savings for "savers."

Dollar-Years Moved

Two final measures—dollar-years moved, and dollar-years moved per year—look directly at saving, that is, resources moved through time. These new measures recognize that even "low savers" moved some resources through time. In one sense, the new measures are not so new at all—after all, they are based on average balances through time—but this is their first presentation as a theoretically consistent way to measure saving viewed as moving resources through time. None of the other measures discussed so far does this. Furthermore, the new measures account for both the size and timing of both deposits and withdrawals; none of the other measures does this as completely.

To see the usefulness of the new measures, return to the two hypothetical IDA participants whose patterns of putting in deposits, keeping in balances, and taking out withdrawals are illustrated in figure 5.1. As discussed earlier, the first saver put in deposits $100 on January 1 and kept a balance of $100 all year, taking it out in a matched withdrawal at the time cap on December 31. The second saver put in deposits of $200 on May 1 and kept a balance of $200 for two months, taking it out in an unmatched withdrawal on June 30. Who saved more?

Intuition suggests that although both saved something, the first person saved more. But the typical measures do not consistently reflect this. For example, net IDA savings are higher for the first saver ($100 versus zero), but gross deposits are higher for the second saver ($200 versus $100).

Both measures miss part of the full picture because they look at only the "putting in" and "taking out" stages of saving and ignore the "keeping in" stage. Accounting for the "keeping in" stage requires a "flowing stock." Such a measure is *dollar-years moved*, defined as the sum of annual average net IDA savings. In this example, the first saver had annual average net IDA savings of $100 in the first and only year, and the second saver had annual average net IDA savings of $33.33 (net IDA savings were $200 for 2 months before going to zero after the unmatched withdrawal). Thus, the first saver moved $100 through one year of time, and the second saver moved $200 through two months, equivalent to moving $33.33 through twelve months. (For the purposes of measuring dollar-years moved in IDAs, resources taken out from IDAs in matched withdrawals are assumed not to be consumed but rather to be transformed into other forms of assets, so they still represent resources moved through time, at least until the time cap. Resources taken out of IDAs in un-matched withdrawals are assumed to be consumed and not to lead to asset accumulation.) As this example shows, a strength of this measure of dollar-years moved is that it recognizes that all IDA participants—even "low savers," almost all of whom had some gross deposits at some point in ADD—moved at some resources through time.

For ADD, dollar-years moved per participant was 1,090. The average "saver" moved 1,810 dollar-years, and the average "low saver"—despite ending up with net IDA savings of less than $100—moved 296 dollar-years. Apparently, many "low savers" who ended up with less than $100 in net IDA savings nevertheless had made deposits and held non-negligible balances for some time before taking them out in unmatched withdrawals. Perhaps some share of "low savers" made deposits and kept them in IDAs for a while before unex-pected rough times forced them to liquidate their IDAs to meet current needs. In addition, some share of participants may have had non-negligible savings in their IDAs before they despaired of being able to make and sustain a "large" asset purchase—such as home purchase, post-secondary education, or microenterprise—that requires on-going maintenance and continued investment.

Measures of dollar-years moved by different participants are most straight-forwardly compared when the measures pertain to time periods of equal length. All else constant, participants with longer time caps will move more dollars through more time. In ADD, of course, different participants had different time caps. The measure *dollar-years moved per year* adjusts for the time available to save. It is defined as the ratio of dollar-years moved to the number of years in which resources could be saved in an IDA. In ADD, the average participant moved 363 dollar-years per year. The average "saver" moved 597 dollar-years per year, and the average "low saver" moved 104.

Summary of Saving and Asset Accumulation through IDAs in ADD

Table 5.9 summarizes the components of aggregate and per-participant saving and asset accumulation through IDAs in ADD. The average participant in ADD put in gross deposits of $1,158. Of these, $275 were in excess of the match cap and so did not count as "IDA savings." In addition, the average participant took out unmatched withdrawals of matchable depos-its worth $325.

Net IDA savings can be seen as gross deposits net of excess balances and net of unmatched withdrawals. Alternatively, net IDA savings can be seen as the sum of matched withdrawals ($286 per participant) and match-eligible bal-ances ($272 per participant). Either way, net IDA savings per participant in ADD was $558, or $16.60 per month eligible for matchable deposits. About 52 percent of participants were "savers" with net IDA savings of $100 or more.

Table 5.9
Summary of Saving and Asset Accumulation in ADD

Line	Item	Formula	Aggregate	Per Participant
Ia	Gross deposits	Bd	$2,721,433	$1,158
Ib	Gross deposits in excess of the match cap	Cc	$646,432	$275
Ic	Unmatched withdrawals	Da	$763,903	$325
Id	Net IDA savings	Ia–Ib–Ic	$1,311,108	$558
Ie	Matched withdrawals	Ea	$672,577	$286
If	Match-eligible balances	Fa	$638,531	$272
Ig	Net IDA savings	Ie+Fa	$1,311,108	$558
Ih	Matches and possible matches	Gc	$2,468,886	$1,051
Ii	Asset accumulation in IDAs	Id+Ih	$3,779,994	$1,609

Note: Slight differences from previous tables are due to rounding.

Asset accumulation in IDAs was $1,609 per participant, the sum of net IDA savings of $558 plus matches (including possible matches after the time cap) of $1,051.

Figure 5.6 shows the evolution of the various components of IDA savings and asset accumulation over the course of ADD from December 1997 through December 2001. Of course, the absolute magnitude of the aggregate numbers depends on the size of ADD—the number of participants and the length of the time caps—but figure 5.6 still helps to illustrate how the components of savings and asset accumulation changed through time, how they relate to each other, and their relative importance as the cut-off date of December 31, 2001.

Was asset accumulation in IDAs enough to make a difference? For the non-poor, a few hundred dollars—or even a few thousand dollars—may not seem like much. For example, Bernstein (2003) worries that IDAs, while a good idea, do not go far enough. In this sense, Ackerman and Alstott (1999) propose that all youth receive an $80,000 "stake" on their twenty-first birthday. Are IDAs too small too matter?

More than half of ADD participants, did (or could) use their IDAs to save and to purchase the types of key assets that often mark turning points in the life course and that are generally expected to have high personal and social returns. Perhaps more importantly, qualitative research from ADD reports that participants say that they believe that saving in IDAs improved their outlook on life (Sherraden et al., 2004; McBride, Lombe, and Beverly, 2003). That is, IDAs seem to have helped to uplift downwardly skewed worldviews. With something to look forward to, IDA participants reported that they had more

Figure 5.6
Evolution of Components of Saving and Asset Accumulation
in the Course of ADD

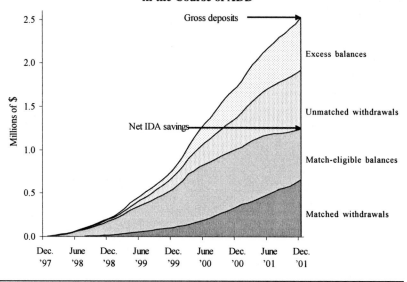

Note: These figures differ slightly from those in table 5.9 because they omit data from one program in ADD (CAPTC Large-scale) which had a time cap for some participants after December 31, 2001.

hope. Perhaps what matters is not only the amount saved but also the process of saving and the simple existence of savings.

It is also worth mentioning that IDA savers tend to make modest investments in modest assets. They go to community colleges, not the Ivy League. They move into older, smaller houses in non-fashionable parts of town, not McMansions in the suburbs. They run very small, often part-time businesses in low-prestige, blue-collar service sectors such as child-care, janitorial services, food service, and landscaping. IDAs do not pretend to catapult poor people instantly to the middle class; rather, they offer a hand up to the first—and often the highest—rung of a ladder.

The average participant in ADD had net IDA savings of $558. For perspective, liquid assets in bank accounts at enrollment averaged $555 (median $125). Median illiquid assets (mostly houses and cars) were $2,500, median debt was $2,982, and median net worth was $360. (Median net worth is participant-by-participant, not median assets minus median liabilities.) If all net IDA savings were used in matched withdrawals, then the average participant in ADD would have accumulated $1,609 in IDAs. Thus, as a share of participants' assets at enrollment, IDA accumulations are large, even in the unlikely case

Figure 5.7
Saving Rate from Income by Income Decile in ADD

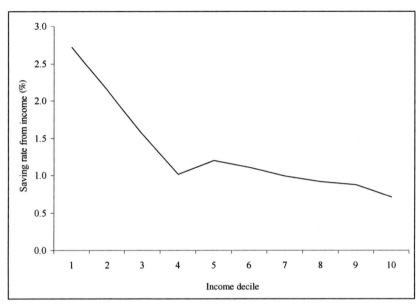

that IDAs did not cause any "new" savings through increases in income and/or decreases in consumption.

Net IDA Savings Compared with Other Benchmarks

This section attempts to put savings outcomes in ADD in context through two final measures that compare net IDA savings with two benchmarks, the participant's monthly household income at enrollment and the program-imposed match cap.

IDA saving rate. The *IDA saving rate* is defined as the rate at which inflows of resources (income) were converted into net IDA savings. In ADD, this is the ratio of net IDA savings per month divided by monthly household income at enrollment. Average monthly income was $1,494, and net IDA deposits per month were $16.60. Thus, the IDA saving rate was 1.1 percent. (For "savers," the IDA saving rate was 2.0 percent.) While not particularly high in absolute terms, this is not so different from the overall U.S. household saving rate. Surprisingly, poorer participants had higher IDA saving rates (figure 5.7). While chapter 7 discusses the relationship between income and net IDA savings in detail, the central finding there is that less income—all else constant—did not mean a lower absolute level of IDA saving and that the very poor saved a greater relative share of their income in IDAs than did the less-poor.

What might explain this? First, a host of measurement issues may have depressed measured income more for the very poor than for the less-poor (Schreiner et al., 2001). These measurement problems might have induced a spurious negative correlation between income and the IDA saving rate. Second, censoring of desired savings at the match cap could also have induced a spurious negative correlation. In other words, because the match cap drove a wedge between observed savings and desired savings for about one-fifth of participants, desired savings may have increased with income even if observed savings did not. Third, the institutional features of IDAs—matches, targets, deadlines, automatic transfer, financial education, restrictions on withdrawals, and staff support—may have not only overshadowed the economic effect of income but also have been strongest for the very poor (Sherraden, Schreiner, and Beverly, 2003). For example, the pull of the savings target may have been greater for those furthest away from the target. Likewise, the match is a larger share of total resources for the very poor than for the less-poor. Furthermore, the very poor may have had more to learn about how or why to save, so, in response to given a level of financial education, they may have changed their behavior more. Likewise, the very poor may have benefited more from social support. All three factors—measurement noise, censoring at the match cap, and institutional effects—probably were at work in ADD, but it is not possible to disentangle them from the MIS IDA data. Still, the broad lesson is that—at least for IDAs in ADD—less income did not imply less savings.

Net IDA savings as a share of the match cap. For every dollar of match-eligibility in ADD, 42 cents were saved. That is, net IDA savings were 42 percent of the match cap. Given an average match rate of 1.85:1 and an average match cap of $1,329, the average participant was $771 under the match cap, leaving $1,426 in matches "on the table". Most unused match eligibility was associated with "low savers." Among "savers," net IDA savings were 69 percent of the match cap.

For some participants, the match cap was not a limit but a target; had there been no match cap, they would have had lower net IDA savings. This happened in a couple of ways. First, program staff explicitly asked participants to save up to the match cap; they created the social expectation that the match cap represented what a "good" participant would save. Second, apart from staff expectations, some participants probably took the match cap as a normative guideline for how much they should save. Much as the non-poor likely assume that they will have saved enough for retirement if they "max out" their contribution eligibility in 401(k) plans and Individual Retirement Accounts, many IDA participants likely assumed that they would have saved enough for their planned matched purpose if they saved up to the match cap. In this sense, increasing the match cap would increase IDA saving by implicitly holding participants to a higher standard of expectation.

For other participants, the match cap was a limit that constrained net IDA savings; if the match cap had been higher, then they would have saved more in IDAs. For participants constrained by the match cap, desired net IDA savings exceeded the level of observed net IDA savings that the program would match. For policy purposes, however, the outcome of interest is desired savings, as observed savings depends not only on the participant but also on the match cap and other aspects of program design. Unfortunately, desired savings is unobserved (censored) for participants who saved up to the match cap. It is known that desired savings exceeded the match cap, but not by how much. This hampers attempts at policy analysis because it obscures the true links between desired net IDA savings and the characteristics of programs and participants.

As an extreme example, imagine that two IDA programs differ only in the match cap: one matches up to $100, the second matches up to $1,000. If all participants have desired savings of $500, observed savings equals desired savings in the program with a $1,000 match cap but is constrained to equal the $100 match cap in the other program.

Now imagine that both programs increase their match rates from 1:1 to 2:1 and that this increases desired net IDA savings for all participants from $500 to $700. At the program with a $1,000 match cap, observed savings equals desired savings, so the $200 change in desired savings due to the increase in the match rate is observed. In the program with a $100 match cap, however, observed savings remains constrained by the match cap at $100, even though the higher match rate increased desired savings. If censoring at the match cap were ignored, it would appear that increasing the match rate had no effect at this program; the match cap completely masks the increase in desired savings sparked by the increase in the match rate.

In ADD, there was censoring at the match cap, so observed net IDA savings were smaller than desired net IDA savings by some unknown amount. About one-fifth (19 percent) of participants saved up to the match cap. (Among "savers," one-third—34 percent—were at the match cap.) The analysis here does not control for censoring, but it does attempt to point out when censoring might matter and the likely direction of bias. Compared with unobserved desired net IDA savings, censoring biases observed net IDA savings downward.

Summary of Measures of Savings Outcomes

Saving means moving resources through time. Financial saving and asset accumulation depend on three stages: putting in, keeping in, and taking out. Various measures of saving through these three stages have been illustrated for IDAs in ADD.

Resources "put in" are measured as gross deposits. Net IDA savings are gross deposits net of unmatched withdrawals and net of gross deposits in excess of the match cap. Alternatively, net IDA savings can be seen as matched (or matchable) savings, that is, the sum of matched withdrawals and match-eligible balances. In turn, asset accumulation is the sum of net IDA savings and matches. Finally, dollar-years moved—a new measure—reflects saving seen as moving resources through time; it shows that even "low savers" still did some saving.

Why bother with so many measures? First, the concrete effects of subsidized saving policies depend directly on asset accumulation. For example, some minimum level is required to make a down payment on a house (or to pay tuition, or buy a business). Until savings exceed a threshold, a desired asset may be out of reach. Capturing the process of asset accumulation requires measuring not only "putting in" but also "keeping in" and "taking out."

Second, the social/psychological/behavioral effects of asset ownership—what Sherraden (1991) calls "asset effects"—depend not on the consumption of resources but on the contemplation of resources (Schreiner et al., 2001). The idea is that when people think about their assets and how they might use them—when they savor their savings—they feel more in control of their lives, make better choices, and thus have greater well-being. The new measure of dollar-years moved per year indicates how much assets were owned and for how long, suggesting the likely strength of "asset effects."

Third, measures of savings outcomes matter not only because they suggest how people saved through IDAs in ADD but also because they inform efforts to expand access to IDAs. For example, financial intermediaries that might hold IDAs want to know the likely number, frequency, and size of deposits and withdrawals. Likewise, new IDA programs can use the figures to plan and to set benchmarks.

Uses of Matched Withdrawals

How do savings outcomes differ across matched uses? And what uses should be matched? To address these questions, this section analyzes the use of matched withdrawals in ADD. Beyond the three "cornerstone" uses of home purchase, post-secondary education, and microenterprise, some IDA programs in ADD provided matches for job training, retirement savings, and home repair. Furthermore, it has sometimes been suggested that IDAs should provide matches for cars, household durables, medical expenses, for paying-down debt, or even for any unrestricted use.

Complicating Factors

The analysis of matched withdrawals by use must deal with several complicating factors. First, 15 percent of participants with matched withdrawals had more than one type of matched use. For example, 6 percent of participants who made a matched withdrawal had matched withdrawals for both home purchase and home repair. Second, even among participants who made matched withdrawals for only a single use, 44 percent made more than one matched withdrawal for that use. For example, one participant in ADD made twenty matched withdrawals for microenterprise, and another made twenty-one matched withdrawals for home repair. Third, as of the data cut-off date, 40 percent of "savers" had not yet made a matched withdrawal. Fourth, one-fifth (21 percent) of participants who made a matched withdrawal did so for a different use than what they had declared as their intent at enrollment. There is nothing "wrong" with this, but it does impede extrapolating from the planned use at enrollment to the probable matched use for "savers" who had not yet made a matched withdrawal. Fifth, beyond the three "cornerstone" uses of home purchase, post-secondary education, and microenterprise, not all programs in ADD provided matches for job training, retirement savings, or home repair. Thus, not all participants in ADD had access to all types of matched uses. Sixth, some programs in ADD—because of the mission of their host organizations—had disproportionate concentrations of participants interested in one or two specific matched uses. WSEP in Chicago, for example, is a microenterprise program and thus its IDA participants were disproportionately interested in matched withdrawals for self-employment. Likewise, Foundation Communities in Texas is an affordable-housing organization, so its participants were more likely to plan for homeownership. Taken as a whole, these complicating factors mean that the patterns of matched uses in ADD may be particular to this specific set of programs and participants rather than representative of what might happen in a permanent, universal IDA policy.

Besides these measurement issues, the analysis of the uses of matched withdrawals is complicated by the fact that—as discussed briefly earlier in this chapter—most participants at a point in time consider as relevant only one or two of the available types of matched uses. The relevance of a given use for a given participant hinges on seven aspects of the matched asset.

The first is *divisibility*, that is, whether the asset can be acquired in parts and/or over time. For example, a home is indivisible; a participant must buy the whole thing or none at all. Buying just the bathroom and the kitchen is not an option. Furthermore, home purchase is indivisible in time; buyers must not only purchase all of a home, but they must purchase it all at once. In contrast, post-secondary education (and job training) are relatively divisible. For example, a student can make a matched withdrawal to buy a single textbook. Likewise, microenterprise assets may be acquired piecemeal. For example, a child-care business might buy a set of playground equipment this year, a van to transport children next year, and cookware for snacks the following year. Most microentrepreneurs do not buy existing businesses whole but rather build up their own small firms from scratch. Asset accumulation for post-secondary education and microenterprise are also divisible in time. Students build human capital over time, the same way in which businesses accumulate plant and equipment. Likewise, home repair is a divisible use; a participant can make a matched withdrawal to replace a roof today and then to buy a can of paint next month. Finally, retirement savings is almost completely divisible; participants can make deposits of whatever size as frequently as they want. All else constant, divisible matched uses are easier to make because they are possible sooner and with less saving.

The second factor that affects the relevance of a potential matched use is the extent of the required *post-purchase commitment* to on-going maintenance. A home, for example, is a high-commitment asset. After purchase, a home requires additional resources to meet monthly mortgage payments, perform physical maintenance, and pay insurance and property taxes. Post-secondary education also requires some ongoing commitment. A student, for example, must invest time and effort to attend class after paying tuition and/or to read textbooks after buying them. Still, post-secondary education probably demands less commitment than home purchase. For example, an associate's degree from a community college can be completed in two to three years, and courses for job training or for licenses such as truck driving or cosmetology are even shorter. Students can also go to school on and off, full time or part time, accumulating academic credit as their situation allows. Microenterprise also requires some mid-level commitment. Most self-employed participants are not starting new small businesses but rather expanding their existing activities. Therefore, while they must use the asset in the business to get value from it, they already have at least some complementary assets. Of course, microenterprise start-up requires a greater additional commitment than microenterprise expansion. For its part, retirement savings requires almost no post-purchase commitment; after being opened, the Roth IRA exists on its own, and withdrawals for any use are always possible even before retirement (subject to a 10 percent penalty). Home repair also requires little commitment beyond what is already entailed in homeownership. All else constant, matched purchases with little post-purchase commitment are easier because they require only saving for the asset purchase rather than also making additional investment in the future.

The third factor is the *complexity of the asset purchase* itself. Home purchase, for example, is a more complex event than is tuition payment for post-secondary education or job training. Buying a home takes time and involves a home search, loan application, inspection, title search, buyer's agents, seller's agents, loan officers, movers, and others. In contrast, most students navigate the enrollment process in a day or so without professional help, and of course they buy books on their own. For small-business owners, IDA programs sometimes require a written business plan as evidence that the proposed venture is legitimate and well thought out, but business owners usually make the actual asset purchase alone. Retirement savings is even less complex. Participants with an existing Roth IRA simply make a deposit into it. Participants without an existing account can open one at almost any bank, on the Internet, or at local brokerage storefronts. While there is a bewildering variety of investment options, only three make sense—a money-market fund, a bond-index fund, or a stock-index fund—and getting the money into a Roth IRA is simple. Home repair is also simple. Again, the IDA program may require two to three written estimates from independent contractors for the proposed repair work—to ensure both that the homeowner shops around and that matched withdrawals for do-it-yourself work are in line with the size of the job—but the homeowner gets the work done in a relatively short time. The less complex the process of buying a matched asset, the easier are matched withdrawals.

The fourth factor is the asset's *convertibility*. Given time, effort, and transaction costs, a resource in any form can be converted into a resource in any other form. Illiquid resources—such as a home or an improved home, thanks to home repair—require heavy transaction costs to convert to other forms. Human capital from post-secondary education or from job training is also illiquid, convertible to other resources only with work through time. Microenterprise likewise is an illiquid, difficult-to-convert resource. After all, the market for "used" small businesses is very thin, and income from self-employment—like income from the employment of human capital in a wage job—comes only after time and work. Retirement savings, in contrast, are relatively liquid. Balances in a Roth IRA can be taken out at any time (subject to a 10 percent penalty), with the resulting cash easily converted into an asset or a consumption good. All else constant, IDA participants would rather make a matched withdrawal for a convertible asset than for a non-convertible asset.

The fifth factor is the participant's *life-cycle stage*. For example, home purchase is probably a more salient option for people aged twenty to fifty than for youth or the elderly. On the other hand, post-secondary education and job training are probably more relevant for youth and young people. Small-business owners—at least successful ones—tend to be older (Åstebro and Bernhardt, 2003). Retirement savings, of course, is more salient as participants age.

The sixth factor is *existing asset accumulation*. For example, current homeowners may not be interested (or eligible) in matched withdrawals for home purchase, and home repair is mostly irrelevant for renters. Likewise, post-secondary education and job training are probably less salient for people who already have a college degree. Microenterprise is difficult and risky, and most people with wage employment do not think much about the possibility of self-employment. Retirement savings, in contrast, is generally relevant for all IDA participants. Anyone with earned income can contribute to a Roth IRA, and few low-income people already have adequate retirement savings (Hubbard, Skinner, and Zeldes, 1995 and 1994). In short, people who already own a matched asset are not likely to make a matched withdrawal to buy that same asset, although almost everyone can use matched withdrawals for retirement savings.

The seventh factor is psychological: the asset's immediate *tangibility*. A home is probably the most tangible matched asset, changing a new homeowner's life in many ways. Furthermore, homeownership is ingrained in the American psyche; a young couple who rent is liable to feel somehow that they have not yet "made it." Self-employment is likewise part of the American Dream, and people who leave a wage job for self-employment (or who slowly move their employment mix away from wage work and toward microenterprise) experience an immediate change in their day-to-day lives. In contrast, retirement savings is quite intangible, except perhaps for people on the threshold of retirement. For young people, however, retirement is decades away. The adequacy or inadequacy of retirement savings has no short-term visceral consequences, except, of course, for the sacrifice involved in saving via reducing current consumption and/or increasing income. Post-secondary education (job training excepted) also produces an intangible asset whose rewards must wait for the future. Few students have deliberately chosen to invest their time and effort in forming human capital now so as to reap the rewards later. Rather, they study because they enjoy it or because they have the habit and/or feel a duty. All else constant, IDA participants will make more matched withdrawals for immediately tangible assets than for assets whose benefits arrive in the future.

In sum, the use of matched withdrawals varies with the characteristics of the matched asset, that is, with the divisibility (in purchase and in time), the post-purchase commitment to further investment, the complexity of the purchase itself, and the asset's convertibility and immediate tangibility. The characteristics of the participant also matter, in particular life-cycle stage and existing asset ownership. For most people, home purchase is probably the most difficult use; it is salient mostly for renters, and it is indivisible, complex, and illiquid, with heavy post-purchase commitments. On the plus side, home purchase leads to a large and immediately tangible life change. At the other end of the continuum, retirement savings are simple, divisible, and liquid. Furthermore, retirement savings require little post-purchase commitment, and this matched use is possible regardless of age or existing assets. On the minus side, retirement savings (like post-secondary education) provide few tangible benefits in the here-and-now to offset their immediate costs. Somewhere between the high cost and immediate rewards of home purchase and the low cost but delayed rewards of retirement savings appear home repair, post-secondary education, and job training.

Most IDA participants do not sit down with the program's brochure before enrollment and carefully weigh the pros and cons of each possible type of matched withdrawal. Rather, given their existing age, education, employment situation, and wealth, they probably narrow the menu down quickly to one or two possible uses. This has a few implications.

First, the analysis of matched withdrawals cannot presume that observed uses result from choices in which every possible matched use started out on a level playing field with all others. Some matched uses were easier, some were more rewarding, and their costs and benefits depended not only on the characteristics of the matched use itself but also on the characteristics of the participant. In a given case or in the aggregate, disentangling the various forces may not be possible.

Second, a given participant's characteristics change through time. A renter becomes a homeowner, a high school graduate goes back to school, a wage worker strikes out on her own, and a youth becomes a young adult, then middle aged, and finally elderly. In turn, the preferred matched use likely changes through time. Thus, even if only one or two matched uses are relevant now, different matched uses may be relevant later. If access to IDAs were permanent, participants may find themselves saving and making matched withdrawals for different uses over the life span.

Third, if the participant's first choice for a matched use does not pan out and if access to IDAs is temporary, then the participant may very well decide to take out an unmatched withdrawal rather than make a matched withdrawal for some other use that lacks much current relevance. If access were permanent, the balance could remain in the IDA—perhaps for years or decades—until some type of matched use became relevant.

Distribution of Matched Withdrawals by Use

As discussed above, 31 percent of participants in ADD had a matched withdrawal for some type of asset purchase as of the data cut-off date. Participants who made matched withdrawals averaged 2.6 matched withdrawals each, worth a total (without matches) of $923 (table 5.5). With an average match rate of 1.81:1, the average participant in this group had asset accumulation through IDAs of $2,593.

Numbers of matched withdrawals. The most common type of matched withdrawal was for microenterprise (26 percent, table 5.10), followed by home repair (22 percent), home purchase and post-secondary education (both 21 percent), retirement savings (7 percent) and job training (2 percent). Thus, two-thirds (68 percent) of all matched withdrawals were made for the three "cornerstone" uses, and nine in ten (90 percent) were for the three "cornerstone" uses plus home repair. Matched withdrawals for job training were rare.

On average, the largest matched withdrawals were for retirement savings ($702), home purchase ($559), and home repair ($491). The average matched withdrawal for post-secondary education and microenterprise was about $245, or half the average matched withdrawal for home repair. The smallest average matched withdrawals ($133) were for job training.

In terms of average match rates, retirement savings was about 1:1, home repair was 1.5:1, and the other four uses were about 2:1. These match rates probably reflect the beliefs of the IDA programs and their funders about which

Table 5.10
Aspects of Matched Withdrawals by Use in ADD

Use	Share of matched withdrawals (%)	Value per withdrawal ($)	Match rate
Home purchase	21	559	2.11:1
Post-secondary education	21	249	1.96:1
Microenterprise	26	243	1.96:1
Retirement savings	7	702	1.07:1
Job training	2	133	2.03:1
Home repair	22	491	1.51:1
Total	100	373	1.78:1

matched uses "deserve" greater encouragement. In particular, the convertibility of retirement savings and home repair may have meant that they were more likely to be seen as closer to personal consumption (and thus less socially valuable) than home purchase, microenterprise, and post-secondary education and job training.

Access to matches for specific uses. The numbers in table 5.10 do not tell the whole story, however, because while all ADD participants could make matched withdrawals for the three "cornerstone" uses, some did not have access to matched withdrawals for some of the other matched uses. For example, 35 percent of all participants had access to matches for retirement savings, 70 percent had access to matches for job training, and 56 percent had access to matches for home repair (table 5.11). A further complication is that some "savers" had yet to make a matched withdrawal as of the data cut-off date.

The ranking of the frequency of the types of matched withdrawals changes after controlling for access and counting "savers" as if they had made matched withdrawals as they planned as of enrollment. Home purchase is now the most common use; one in five (21 percent) of all participants who could have made a matched withdrawal for home purchase either did so or were "savers" who planned to do so after the data cut-off date. Among those ADD participants with access to matches for home repair, 15 percent either made such a matched withdrawal or were "savers" who planned to do so. About 12 percent of participants made matched withdrawals for retirement savings, and another 12 percent made matched withdrawals for microenterprise. (Before controlling for access and the planned use of "savers" yet to make a matched withdrawal, microenterprise was the most common matched use.) Post-secondary education was 11 percent, and job training was 2 percent.

These rankings may reflect that withdrawals for home repair, retirement savings, microenterprise, and post-secondary education are relatively easy, given their divisibility, simplicity, convertibility, and low post-purchase com-

Table 5.11

Share of ADD Participants with a Matched Withdrawal for a Given Use among Participants with Access to Matches for that Use as of the Data Cut-Off Date, for All Participants and for "Savers" yet to Make a Matched Withdrawal

Use	Share of participants with access (%)	Share of participants with access who also made a matched withdrawal (%)	Share of "savers" with access who plan a matched withdrawal (%)	Share of all participants with access who either made a matched withdrawal or who are "savers" who plan to do so (%)
Home purchase	100	10	19	21
Post-secondary education	100	8	14	11
Microenterprise	100	8	14	12
Retirement savings	35	9	17	12
Job training	70	1	2	2
Home repair	56	13	23	15

Note: Some participants with a matched withdrawal have made matched withdrawals for more than one use. For "savers" who have yet to make a matched withdrawal, MIS IDA records only a single planned use.

mitment. In the cases of home repair and retirement savings, these advantages apparently compensate for their lower match rates. In contrast, home purchase is the most common use in spite of its relative difficulty. Apparently, the higher match rate and participants' desire to own a home overwhelmed its other disadvantages.

Among "savers" yet to make a matched withdrawal, more than half (52 percent) were planning for home purchase (table 5.12). About 21 percent planned for microenterprise, and 16 percent planned for post-secondary education. Perhaps prospective homebuyers—especially those with higher match rates—wanted to make sure that they took advantage of all months eligible for matchable deposits to build a down payment. Among "savers" yet to make matched withdrawals, the largest potential was for retirement savings ($1,099) and home repair ($916), followed by home purchase ($903) and post-secondary education ($899). Potential matched withdrawals were smaller for microenterprise ($650) and job training ($712).

These patterns reinforce the idea that home purchase is both difficult and highly desired. In contrast, retirement savings and home repair seem easier, as participants made these matched withdrawals more quickly. Furthermore, regression results in chapter 7 suggest that retirement savings and home repair may also be easier in that older people (who are more likely to save for retirement) and homeowners (who are more likely to save for home repair) also tend to save more, regardless of the type of matched use. Post-secondary education and microenterprise were between the two extremes, having smaller but more-frequent matched withdrawals.

Existing wealth and matched uses. The figures just reported control for access and for the planned use of "savers" yet to make a matched withdrawal, but they still ignore that the relevance of some matched uses depends partly on participants' existing wealth. For example, home purchase was more salient for renters than for homeowners. In ADD, 84 percent of participants were renters at enrollment, and 26 percent of these made a matched withdrawal for home purchase or were "savers" planning their first matched withdrawal for home purchase. In contrast, among the 16 percent of participants who were homeowners at enrollment, 9 percent made a matched withdrawal for home purchase or were "savers" planning for it. (Some programs in ADD did not restrict matches to first-time homebuyers.) Thus, among all renters (including "low savers") who were potential first-time homebuyers, about one-fourth made a matched withdrawal for home purchase or were "savers" planning to do so. More than half (52 percent) of renters were "low savers," so among renters who were "savers," more than half made a matched withdrawal for home purchase or were planning to do so.

Just as home purchase was more relevant for renters, post-secondary education was more relevant for young people. (Surprisingly, matched withdrawals for post-secondary education in ADD varied little with education at enroll-

Table 5.12

Aspects of Potential Matched Withdrawals by Planned Use Recorded at Enrollment for "Savers" without a Matched Withdrawal in ADD as of the Cut-Off Date in the Data

Planned Use	Share of "savers" without a matched withdrawal (%)	Net IDA savings per "saver" without a matched withdrawal ($)	Match rate
Home purchase	52	903	2.20:1
Post-secondary education	16	899	2.17:1
Microenterprise	21	650	1.91:1
Retirement savings	5	1,099	1.26:1
Job training	2	712	1.96:1
Home repair	4	916	1.13:1
Total	100	855	2.04:1

Figure 5.8

**Share of ADD Participants of a Given Age or Younger Who Made a
Matched Withdrawal for Post-Secondary Education or Who Were "Savers"
Planning for Such a Matched Withdrawal**

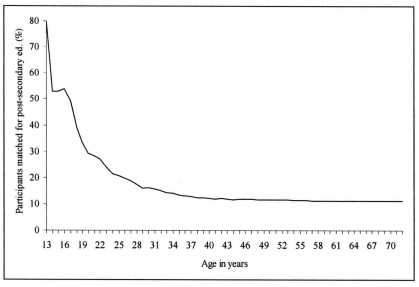

ment.) The likelihood of making a matched withdrawal for post-secondary education (or of being a "saver" planning for such a matched withdrawal) was highest for youth and then decreased with age (figure 5.8). For example, 29 percent of participants aged 20 or younger made a matched withdrawal for post-secondary education or were "savers" planning for it. This figure fell to 21 percent for those aged twenty-five or younger, and it was 16 percent for those aged thirty or younger. About 3 percent of those aged fifty-four or older used IDAs for post-secondary education for themselves, their children, or their grandchildren. Given that 59 percent of participants aged twenty-five or younger were "low savers," more than half of ADD participants in this group who were "savers" made matched withdrawals for post-secondary education or were planning to do so.

Expanding an existing small business is easier than starting a new small business from scratch, so matched withdrawals for microenterprise were more relevant for those who were already involved in self-employment at enrollment. Among the 7 percent of participants who reported small-business assets at enrollment, almost half (47 percent) made a matched withdrawal for microenterprise or were "savers" planning to do so (table 5.13). Likewise, among the 2 percent of participants who reported small-business debts, 44 percent made a matched withdrawal for microenterprise. About 11 percent of participants said that they "owned a business" (even if they did not report any

Table 5.13
Use of Matched Withdrawals for Microenterprise among Participants
with Some Involvement in Microenterprise at Enrollment

Involvement	Share of all participants (%)	Share of participants with a given involvement in microenterprise who made a matched withdrawal for microenterprise or who were "savers" planning for it (%)
Owned small-business assets	7	47
Had small-business debts	2	44
Said he/she owned a small business	11	40
Reported self-employment income	17	30
Any of the above	19	30

business assets, debts, or income), and about 40 percent of these made a matched withdrawal for microenterprise. Among the 17 percent who reported small-business income, 30 percent made a matched withdrawal for microenterprise. Finally, among the 19 percent of participants who said that they owned a business or who reported some business assets, debts, or income, 30 percent made a matched withdrawal for microenterprise. In this broad class, 61 percent were "savers," so almost half (49 percent) of "savers" involved in self-employment at enrollment made a matched withdrawal (or planned to do so) for microenterprise.

Retirement savings was more relevant for older participants than for younger ones, probably because older participants were closer to retirement and because they were less likely to go back to school and more likely to own a home already. Looking only at participants with access to matches for retirement, the likelihood of a matched withdrawal for retirement increased with age (table 5.14). While one in twenty participants who were twenty-five years old or younger at enrollment made a matched withdrawal for retirement (or were "savers" planning to do so), almost half of participants aged fifty-six years or older did so. Furthermore, the average value of matched withdrawals for participants who made a matched withdrawal for retirement was highest for the oldest segment.

Finally, just as home purchase was more relevant for renters, home repair was more relevant for homeowners. Looking at participants with access to matches for home repair, 3 percent of renters made matched withdrawals for home repair, compared with 45 percent of homeowners. (Here, "homeowners" includes renters who made a matched withdrawal for home purchase and who

Table 5.14
Use of Matched Withdrawals for Retirement Savings in ADD by Age

Age	Share of all participants with access (%)	Share of participants with access who made a matched withdrawal for retirement or who were "savers" planning to do so	Average value of matched withdrawals for participants with matched withdrawals for retirement or "savers" planning for retirement ($)
13 to 25	14	5	1,611
26 to 35	35	7	1,251
36 to 45	35	16	1,528
46 to 55	12	21	1,462
56 or older	4	46	1,820
Total	100	13	1,514

then made a second matched withdrawal for home repair.) About 77 percent of participants who were homeowners at enrollment were "savers," so 58 percent of homeowners who were "savers" made (or planned to make) a matched withdrawal for home repair.

To sum up, participants' age and existing assets were correlated with their use of matched withdrawals. For example, about one-half of renters who were also "savers" ended up making (or planning) a matched withdrawal for home purchase. The likelihood of a matched withdrawal for post-secondary education decreased with age, while the likelihood of a matched withdrawal for retirement savings increased with age. About half of "savers" who were already involved in self-employment at enrollment made matched withdrawals for microenterprise, and more than half of "savers" who were homeowners made matched withdrawals for home repair.

Matched withdrawals per participant with a matched withdrawal. The two previous sections described matched withdrawals and then matched withdrawals by use, regardless of whether the matched withdrawals were made by participants with one matched withdrawal, with multiple matched withdrawals for a single use, or with multiple matched withdrawals for multiple uses. About 52 percent of participants with matched withdrawals had a single matched withdrawal. Among the 48 percent with multiple matched withdrawals, about 27 percent also had multiple uses. Table 5.15 looks at matched withdrawals per participant according to the type of the first matched withdrawal made by a participant.

Table 5.15
Aspects of Matched Withdrawals per Participant with a Matched Withdrawal in ADD, by First Use

First use	Share of participants with first matched withdrawal (%)	Average total value of matched withdrawals per participant ($)	Number of matched withdrawals per participant	Value per matched withdrawal ($)	Match rate
Home purchase	30	1,075	2.2	484	2.05
Post-secondary education	21	675	2.4	278	1.95
Microenterprise	22	745	2.9	256	1.91
Retirement savings	8	1,259	2.0	608	1.09
Job training	2	438	3.0	146	2.05
Home repair	16	1,110	3.1	359	1.57
Total	100	921	2.6	358	1.81

The most common use for a first matched withdrawal was home purchase (30 percent), followed by microenterprise (22 percent), post-secondary education (21 percent), home repair (16 percent, without adjustment for access), retirement savings (8 percent), and job training (2 percent). Although the average total value of matched withdrawals (as well as the average value per matched withdrawal) includes multiple types of matched withdrawals in about 15 percent of the cases, the patterns generally follow what has already been seen, with retirement savings being the largest type of matched withdrawal followed by home repair and home purchase. As before, job training was the smallest, and microenterprise and post-secondary education were in the middle range. The average number of matched withdrawals per participant was highest for home repair, job training, and microenterprise, probably reflecting the divisibility of those asset types.

In ADD, the "cornerstone" uses of home purchase, post-secondary education, and microenterprise comprised about three-fourths (73 percent) of all first matched withdrawals. Often, home repair was a second use. This makes sense, as a homeowner who made a matched withdrawal for some other use (including homeownership) and who had some "extra" IDA savings could easily have found some small repair job to absorb remaining matchable balances.

Multiple matched withdrawals for multiple uses. About 15 percent of participants with matched withdrawals as of the data cut-off date had made multiple matched withdrawals for multiple uses. Table 5.16 shows the patterns of changes from the first matched use by a given participant to the second. The most common second matched uses were home repair, post-secondary education, retirement savings, and microenterprise. These were all more common second uses than home purchase, probably reflecting their advantages in terms of divisibility, complexity, and post-purchase commitment.

The most common pattern (27 percent of cases) was to make a first matched withdrawal for home purchase and then to make a second matched withdrawal for home repair. This is more or less equivalent to buying a higher-quality home with a single, larger matched withdrawal.

Changes from planned use to actual use. For 23 percent of participants, the use of the first matched withdrawal differed from the planned use that they had declared at enrollment. Table 5.17 shows the patterns of changes from planned use to actual use. The most-common pattern (11 percent of cases) was to switch from home purchase to post-secondary education. The data show forty participants switching from home repair to home purchase, but thirty-three of these were renters at enrollment, so these probably reflect data-entry mistakes.

The most commonly abandoned planned use was home purchase, probably reflecting its difficulty in terms of divisibility, complexity, and post-purchase commitment. For example, a participant who enrolled planning for home purchase may have ended up saving too little. Or the participant's credit record may have made it difficult to get a home loan.

Table 5.16
Distribution of Patterns of First and Second Matched Uses for ADD Participants with Multiple Uses of Matched Withdrawals

	Second Use						
First Use	Home purchase	Post-second. ed.	Microenterprise	Retirement	Job training	Home repair	Total
Home purchase		6	5	3	1	30	45
Post-second. ed.	2		3	4		5	14
Microenterprise	4	2		2		8	16
Retirement		1				4	5
Job training	2		4			1	7
Home repair	5	11	2	6			24
Total	13	20	14	15	1	48	111

Note: Figures indicate the number of participants with a given use for their first type of matched withdrawal and a given other use for their second type of matched withdrawal. As of the cut-off date of the data, 111 ADD participants had made matched withdrawals for more than one use. Twelve participants had three or more uses of matched withdrawals, but only the first two uses are shown here.

Table 5.17
Distribution of Changes in Planned Matched Use at Enrollment to Actual Use of Matched Withdrawals in ADD

Planned Use	Actual Use						
	Home purchase	Post-second. ed.	Microenterprise	Retirement	Job training	Home repair	Total
Home purchase		19	11	10	1	6	47
Post-second. ed.	7		2	3	2	7	21
Microenterprise	9	6		2	4	6	27
Retirement	7	5	3			5	20
Job training	1			1			2
Home repair	40	5	4	3	1		53
Total	64	35	20	19	8	24	170

Note: Figures indicate the number of participants with a given planned use for matched withdrawals at enrollment and a different use for their first actual matched withdrawal.

Microenterprise was the second most-common abandoned use, probably reflecting the difficulty of small-business start-up. Indeed, many microenterprise programs see their first task as giving aspiring—and perhaps dreamily optimistic—entrepreneurs a "cold shower" in the risks and hard knocks of self-employment (Kosanovich and Fleck, 2001; Balkin, 1989).

On the other side, the use into which participants switched was most frequently post-secondary education, followed by home repair and home purchase. Post-secondary education and home repair are both easy uses. Home purchase is a difficult use, but perhaps some participants found themselves saving more than they had expected.

What Uses Should Be Matched?

The above discussion has been an empirical examination of the uses of matched withdrawals by IDA participants in ADD. What follows is more normative, addressing what types of uses should be matched.

Beyond the three "cornerstone" uses of home purchase, post-secondary education, and microenterprise suggested by Sherraden (1991) and adopted in AFIA, there is little agreement (or explicit rhyme or reason) about what uses should be matched. While there are many "good" things that people would like to have matched, a line must be drawn somewhere, lest IDAs stray from their original vision as a relatively leak-proof way to help poor people acquire life-changing assets. In general, these three "cornerstone" types of asset-building subsidies are already available to the non-poor and thus enjoy broad political support.

Missing are criteria for what uses should be eligible for matches. Such criteria should come from a well-specified theory of the role of assets in development, and they should also take into consideration practical policy issues that can derail otherwise ideal proposals. In the absence of an explicit theory and criteria, proponents and opponents tend to talk past each other, each judging a possible matched use by implicit (and perhaps vague or ill-formed) sets of standards. Ultimately, agreement about what uses should be matched first requires agreement on a set of standards and then agreement of how possible uses meet those standards.

The discussion below presents various proposed matched uses and an explicit set of standards for evaluating them. It then applies the standards to various proposed uses.

Proposed Matched Uses

The assets proposed at one time or another for matching in IDAs can be classified in four groups: physical capital, human capital, business capital, and financial capital.

Types of physical capital that might be matched include housing, cars, computers, and household durables such as computers. Matches for home purchase might be limited to free-standing homes or might also be allowed for manufactured (trailer) homes; limited to inexpensive homes or also allowed for expensive homes; limited to first-time home buyers (individuals in households that do not currently own a home) or allowed for all home buyers; limited to home purchase or also allowed for home repair; and/or limited to down payment and closing costs or also allowed for paying down mortgage debt. For cars, matches might be limited to first-time buyers (individuals in households that do not currently own a car) or allowed for all car buyers. Matches might be limited to car purchase or also allowed for car repair. Likewise, matches for computers (or other household durables such as refrigerators, washers and dryers, or air conditioners) could be limited to first-time purchase or also allowed for repair.

Types of human capital that might be matched include job training as well as primary, secondary, and post-secondary education. Of course, life itself is the most basic form of human capital, so savings earmarked for health care might also be matched.

Types of matchable business capital might be limited to purchases of plant and equipment or also allowed for any business expense. Although not often recognized, any decrease in business expenses serves to increase business profits and so increases the assets of the business owner. Thus, matched withdrawals used to cover business expenses (such as payroll, inventory, or rent) would increase business saving. Of course, this same logic applies to matches for personal and household expenses; matched withdrawals for groceries, cable TV, or even vacations increase—at least for a time—household assets, unless the household would not have paid the bill or incurred the expense in the absence of IDAs.

Finally, types of financial capital that might be matched could be limited to retirement savings or also allowed for paying down debts and perhaps even for general-purpose, un-earmarked savings.

Standards for Evaluating Potential Matched Uses

How should these possible matched uses be judged? The first step is to establish a core set of standards that a matched use should meet. After all, any matched use benefits its recipient; the real question is which matched uses— given political and other constraints—offer the most social development bang for the buck.

One oft-mentioned criterion is economic *appreciation*; IDAs should provide matches only for assets that appreciate in value. Usually, this standard is used to argue against matches for cars, computers, or manufactured homes. Unfortunately, all types of assets can and often do depreciate, including free-standing homes, human capital, businesses, and retirement savings. (In the short term, human capital—the physical body—requires maintenance just like any other asset. For example, as a person gets hungry, tired, and thirsty, the quality of the use of human capital diminishes until it gets food, drink, and rest. In the long term, the body dies.) In the end, everything depreciates, so appreciation is not a very useful yardstick for distinguishing among possible matched uses.

Fairness is a fundamental standard; a matched use is seen as "fair" not so much if it levels outcomes across people but if it levels access to opportunities (Haveman, 1988). Indeed, IDAs explicitly aim to level the playing field (Sherraden, 2005; Sherraden, 1991). If the non-poor have access to subsidies to save and build assets, then why not the poor? Of course, almost no one openly opposes a level playing field, but some argue that the poor—who pay low or no income taxes—already have the field tilted in their favor against the non-poor for whom asset-building tax breaks are seen merely as incomplete offsets to higher income taxes. This view sees differences in outcomes as due more to choice than to constraint. The judgment here, however, is that differences in access to opportunities result more from luck and constraint than from choice. Thus, the poor are poor less because they choose that path and more because they were born poor (probably because their parents were born poor) or because they saw no better choice. Thus, if the non-poor have access to asset-building subsidies, then so should the poor. As it stands, the poor lack access; they cannot choose to take advantage of asset-building tax breaks. Of course, fairness also rules out "double-dipping" on subsidies for a single asset.

The second standard is *non-convertibility*; it should be difficult to sell matched assets and then consume the proceeds. After all, IDAs are meant for saving and asset building. While consumption support is sometimes needed, it is not the domain of IDAs. (IDAs and means-tested transfers for consumption are complements, not substitutes.) Thus, matched assets should be illiquid. Illiquid assets are also less susceptible to fraud and to perversions of their intended purposes.

Non-convertibility also requires that "saving in an IDA" means something more than merely going through the motions of keeping a few dollars in an IDA just long enough to qualify for matches. After all, IDAs aim to create savers as well as savings (Sherraden, 2000). This purpose is subverted if matches are provided for uses for which "saving up" is easy or unnecessary, for example, because an asset purchase does not require accumulating a large lump sum, because the saving has already been done, or because the asset purchase would have been made anyway. The best matched uses are those that are possible with an IDA but that would be very difficult and take a very long time for poor people saving on their own.

The third standard is *productivity*; whether in the household or in the labor market, a matched asset should help a person do more in less time and with less effort. Households produce and consume both necessities and non-necessities, but non-necessities are not believed to merit public support and are seen as having smaller personal and social impacts. Of course, "necessity" is partly socially and culturally defined. Also, most household assets facilitate the production of both necessities and non-necessities.

Personal impact is the fourth standard; the matched use should cause a non-marginal, quantum change in a person's life. To achieve personal impact, IDAs must prompt people to save and build assets when they otherwise would not (or to save more and/or faster). That is, personal impact requires "new" saving via increases in income and/or decreases in consumption. While most IDA participants "shift" or "reshuffle" some existing assets into IDAs, the larger the asset purchase (and the poorer the participant), the more likely the saving and asset accumulation is "new." Furthermore, larger assets are more likely to make large impacts. In this sense, matches should be limited to uses that must be "saved up for" rather than for uses that can be made without a person's changing much what would have been done anyway.

Social impact is the fifth standard; a matched use should improve the well-being not only of the participant but also of non-participants. Most subsidies improve the well-being of their recipients, but the real challenge is to structure subsidies to maximize spillover effects that improve the well-being of non-recipients. In general, production has greater positive spillovers than consumption, partly justifying the standards of non-convertibility and productivity.

The sixth standard—one that in some sense encompasses all the others—is *political feasibility*. Permanent IDAs will require government funding, so viable matched uses must—at least in the long term—attract broad public support. Matched uses that pass the tests of fairness, non-convertibility, productivity, personal impact, and social impact may also be more politically feasible.

Evaluating Possible Matched Uses

The second step in evaluating possible matched uses is to test them against the standards. Physical assets—homes, cars, computers, and other household durables—are discussed first, followed by human capital, business capital, and financial capital.

Home purchase. Fairness argues for providing matches for home purchase. While all homeowners with mortgage debt can deduct the interest from their taxes, the poor get smaller subsidies than the non-poor because not only are they in lower tax brackets but also because they buy less-expensive homes and so get smaller loans.

A home is also illiquid, so it is difficult to convert into consumption. Of course, a participant might buy a home with a matched withdrawal and then turn around and sell it. Given the transaction costs of purchase and sale, however, such arbitrage would not yield much profit. Also, most people buy a home to live in it, so most users of matched withdrawals for home purchase would not quickly sell their home even if they could profit from it.

The common wisdom is that homeownership has great personal and social impacts (Katz Reid, 2004; Boshara, Scanlon, and Page-Adams, 1998; Green and White, 1997; Scanlon, 1996; Kingston, 1994). While some share of the observed correlation between homeownership and positive outcomes is surely due to pre-existing characteristics of the owner that cause both the positive outcomes and the homeownership, homeownership itself undoubtedly exerts some independent influence as well.

While homes do not produce goods or services for the market, they do produce shelter—a necessity—for the household. Everyone has to live somewhere, perhaps explaining the political support for current subsidies for homeownership. In short, home purchase fulfills all six criteria for matched uses.

The same argument holds for trailer homes. They are homes, they are illiquid, they have positive personal and social impacts, they provide shelter, and they face no particular political opposition. In general, manufactured homes make homeownership more affordable, and in rural areas and small towns with thin rental markets, trailer homes can allow homeowners to move with their work. If matches for free-standing homes make sense, then so do matches for trailer homes.

Matches for home purchase for current homeowners probably have little impact. While there is some evidence that the switch from renting to owning has positive social impacts, the same cannot be said for moves from one home to another (although a move to a "better" neighborhood may have high personal impacts). In any case, almost all subsidies for home purchase for the non-poor (other than the mortgage-interest tax deduction) are limited to first-time buyers. It is not clear that the public would support IDA matches for current owners wanting to move up.

Likewise, IDA matches for expensive homes would likely be seen as unfair and thus would lack political support. Indeed, most current low-income homeownership programs are limited to less-expensive homes. Sherraden (1991) proposed limiting matches to homes priced under the local median. As he says (p. 250), "If people want to live in above-average style, they are free to do so, but tax dollars should not be used to support personal luxury." (This same principle, of course, should also apply to the mortgage interest tax deduction, but it does not.)

Matched withdrawals for home repair were common in ADD, and Sherraden (1991, p. 250) supports matching "capital improvements" to homes. The idea is that this helps poor people to stay homeowners during maintenance emergencies such as a leaky roof or broken furnace. Still, this use stacks up poorly against the standards suggested here. Home repair is not subsidized for the non-poor, so subsidizing it for the poor cannot be justified on fairness grounds. Furthermore, the life change implied by, say, replacing a carpet or fixing a leaky sink is much smaller than that implied by the shift from renter to owner. Even if home repair has some personal impacts, its social impacts are probably weak. In addition, home repair jobs are often small. Thus, compared with larger asset purchases, home repair is less likely to be "caused" by access to IDAs. That is, home repair is rather convertible. For example, suppose a homeowner was going to save to repair the roof. With an IDA, the homeowner can save less than what would have been saved without an IDA and yet—because of the match—make exactly the same roof repair. The IDA does not "cause" the repaired roof, as it would have been repaired even in the absence of the IDA. Rather, the IDA "causes" whatever additional saving or consumption was done with the IDA that not have been done without it. Of course, such implicit diversion can and does happen with any matched use, but the likelihood is higher for smaller uses and for uses that are common even in the absence of IDAs. Home repair does improve the production of shelter, but by the rest of the standards set forth here, it scores poorly.

In ADD, the rationale for matching home repair was not stated. Probably, the intent was to support viable homeownership by the poor. Certainly, home repair was an easy matched use. For participants, it was divisible and relevant for most homeowners. For programs, it leveraged existing relationships with homeowners, many of whom likely bought their home with the help of the host organization before the advent of IDAs and who had already proven themselves to be the type of model participants that the IDA program wanted to work with. But a matched use cannot be justified simply by its convenience for participants and programs; after all, if convenience were the criteria, then straight grants would always be preferred.

Finally, IDAs might provide matches for savings used to pay down mortgage debt. Of course, this does not produce more or better shelter, the non-poor get no similar subsidy, except perhaps in exceptional cases through the mortgage-interest deduction. Of course, the home whose debt is being paid down has already been bought, so there is no impact from switching renters to owners. Furthermore, debt pay-down is highly convertible, so while matching it may have personal impact by keeping cash in the pockets of homeowners that would otherwise have gone to debt service, social impact is probably low. Even if such matched withdrawals were disbursed directly to the lender, the end result would be to transfer cash to participants. Any funds put in an IDA by a participant could have been used to pay down debt, so matches simply transfer resources to qualifying homeowners who run saving that they would have done anyway through an IDA. IDAs aim to prompt greater saving and asset accumulation, not to serve as a cover for cash transfers to those who can jump through the hoop of parking some savings briefly in an IDA.

In sum, providing matches makes sense for first-time home purchase, whether for free-standing or manufactured homes, provided that they are not too expensive. Matches do not make sense for home repair nor for paying-down mortgage debt.

Car purchase. The United States is a relatively young country, most of it built-up since the advent of the automobile. In most cities—and especially in rural areas and small towns—a car is a virtual necessity (Kim, 2002; Beverly, 1999; Ong, 1996). Cars are needed not only to get to work but also for a host of necessary household-production tasks such as grocery shopping, taking children to school, and going to the doctor. In the United States, a car is a productive asset.

So should car purchase be matched? As large purchases usually made with a loan whose down payment must be "saved up for," cars are fairly non-convertible. Cars can also have large personal impacts, for example, by helping to find and keep a better job distant from home (Kasarda, 1995). Through these labor-market effects, cars can have large economic and social impacts.

While cars are productive, non-convertible, and have positive personal and social impacts, they are not subsidized for the non-poor. (Indeed, cars are the largest of the very few large assets owned by households that are not subsidized.) In this sense, matches for car purchase may struggle to find political support. Furthermore, many Americans do not see cars as necessities, and they may fear that subsidized cars would be used for non-productive purposes other than driving to work, school, or the doctor. (Of course, homeowners also use their subsidized homes both for household production and for less socially valuable uses such as entertainment and status.) Public opinion, however, seems to be slowly shifting in favor of cars being necessary assets, just as houses are seen as "necessary" assets. Almost half of states no longer count the value of a first car in asset tests for means-tested cash assistance, and almost all states have relaxed asset tests on cars (Hurst and Ziliak, 2004). In addition, the personal-property exclusion in bankruptcy laws usually protects a car from creditors (Agarwal, Liu, and Mielnicki, 2003). Also, IDAs funded by the Office of Refugee Resettlement already provide matches for car purchase (Johnson, 2000). In all likelihood, most cars bought with the aid of IDAs will be older, inexpensive used cars.

Matches for car repair—like matches for home repair—do not score well on the criteria here.

Computers and other household durables. Some IDA programs—including those funded by the Office of Refugee Resettlement—provide matches for personal computers, and Johnson (2000, p. 1252) argues that IDAs should provide matches for other household durables as well because "televisions, appliances, furniture, and computers are necessities of modern life."

As noted earlier, the definition of "necessity" is partly social and cultural, and most Americans would view life without a bed or a refrigerator as Spartan at best. And as Johnson (2000) argues, if public assistance is to go beyond minimal support for bare subsistence, then—in agreement with the developmental perspective that spawned IDAs—it might make sense to help the poorest to purchase household durables.

Matches for savings used to buy household durables, however, are unlikely to attract much political support. Such purchases are not subsidized for the non-poor, so matches for the poor might seem unfair. Many households—poor or not—live contentedly and productively without personal computers, and some get by without a television. Most appliances (beyond refrigerators and stoves) and most furniture (beyond beds, tables, and chairs) aim to reduce labor (dish washers or clothes washers) or to entertain or provide comfort (televisions and air conditioners). Food and sleep are necessities, but avoiding all drudgery is not. While household durables undoubtedly have great personal impact—the change in sleep quality when moving from the floor to a mattress cannot be discounted—the vast majority of poor people (though not the poorest) already own (or rent with their shelter) the basic items, so matches for household durables might be seen as facilitating ease rather than as alleviating suffering or promoting development.

Furthermore, household durables—while more expensive than most consumption items—still require relatively less "saving up." Considered in conjunction with the positive personal impact of household durables, this means that even poor people usually already own the most important items or are already saving for them. Thus, household durables are relatively convertible. This is not to say that poor people would use matches to buy beds or refrigerators just to sell them off but rather that IDAs are unlikely to cause much first-time purchase.

In any case, the proper form of assistance for those who lack beds or refrigerators is almost certainly not IDA matches but rather straight grants in-kind or in-cash.

Computers may be one exception. The public worries that a "digital divide" will leave poor people without computers behind as information and communication grow in importance. While a computer is little more than a glorified video game for some households, for others it is a central learning tool. And in the future, the internet will probably replace libraries and perhaps even deliver some educational services that currently provided through schools. Children without computers at home will not have access to the same opportunities to build human capital. As mentioned above, the Office of Refugee Resettlement already funds IDAs that provide matches for personal computers, so political support is possible.

Education. Besides age and experience, human capital is developed through job training and through primary, secondary, and post-secondary education. Human capital—life itself—is also maintained through health care. Human capital is productive, cannot be instantly liquidated (it can be "cashed-out" only slowly through work), and has well-recognized private and social impacts. Thus, the question of whether investments in human capital should be matched hinges on fairness and political considerations.

Post-secondary education. People see matches for post-secondary education as fair. The government already subsidizes much of the cost of public and private colleges and universities (Dynarski, 2002). Still, much of the benefit goes to the non-poor, most fundamentally because the poor, after a lifetime of lower-quality grade schools and high schools, are less likely to attend college. If the poor do go to college, they are more likely than the non-poor to qualify for financial aid (Kafer, 2004), but that aid increasingly takes the form of subsidized loans. Furthermore, because aid is based on "financial need" (the difference between costs and an estimate of ability to pay), saving for post-secondary education may reduce aid (Long, 2003; Hurley, 2002; Feldstein, 1995). Non-poor students at expensive private schools can qualify for aid just like poor students at inexpensive public schools. Although saving for post-secondary education is already subsidized through Roth IRAs, Coverdell Education Savings Accounts, and 529 College Savings Accounts, these policies provide their subsidies through tax breaks that are mostly irrelevant to the poor.

Matches for post-secondary education are fair because the poor cannot take advantage of existing college-savings subsidies to the same extent as the non-poor; they are politically feasible because no seems to oppose subsidies—for the poor or non-poor—for post-secondary education. Indeed, Boshara and Sherraden (2004) report that matched-savings initiatives for post-secondary education are underway or planned in Canada, Australia, the United Kingdom, and Western Europe.

Primary and secondary education. In contrast to matches for post-secondary education, matches for primary and secondary education are seen as unfair. Grade school and high school are already highly subsidized—indeed, free—to all students. Thus, matches would be seen largely as a way to help the non-poor opt out of the public school system. The rich and religious can do this if they wish, but not with public funds. Matches are not like vouchers because vouchers go to everyone but matches go only to those who save and then make a matched purchase. Thus, while vouchers are relevant to everyone, matches are more relevant to households paying tuition to private or parochial schools. While even public-school students must bear some out-of-pocket costs for transport, clothes, supplies, and books, these small items do not require much "saving up."

Health care. Human capital requires maintenance both in the short term and the long term. Without it, both health and vigor decline. Public policy already recognizes the immense personal and social impacts of health care—as well as the productivity and non-convertibility of the asset that is a healthy body—through the tax-deductibility of health-insurance premiums and health-care expenses beyond a certain level. But, for a couple of reasons, the poor are less likely to have access to these subsidies. First, the subsidies work through tax breaks that are worth less to the poor. Second, subsidized health-care plans are run through employers, and many employers—especially the ones most likely to employ the poor—do not sponsor health-care plans or they set rules that tend to exclude low-wage employees.

Currently, people without access to subsidized group health plans through their employers can open Medical Savings Accounts. Contributions are tax deductible, and withdrawals are permitted for the types of reparative health-care costs that are counted as "medical expenses" by the Internal Revenue Service. (As usual, preventative health care is excluded.) Upon retirement, unused balances in a Medical Savings Account may be withdrawn for any purpose. Still, the subsidies are provided through tax breaks, so poor people get low (or no) subsidies.

In general, the public supports subsidies for health care, and they also view tying these subsidies to employers as unfair. Thus, the payment of direct expenses for reparative health care and the payment of non-group insurance premiums are consistent with the standards here for matched uses. Matches for health-care expenses should be limited to poor people who, because they are unemployed or self-employed or because their employer does not offer them a group health plan, have no access to existing health-care subsidies. Ineligibles would include the non-poor (for whom Medical Savings Accounts are relevant), those who can get health insurance through their employer, and those who qualify for Medicaid or Medicare.

Business capital. On the whole, Americans like to think of themselves as a do-it-yourself bunch who are liable to go off and start their own businesses at the slightest provocation. They abhor stories of "corporate welfare" and sympathize with family and friends who farm or run local stores or repair shops. Many Americans are immigrants or had immigrant ancestors for whom farming or microenterprise was the only option. Furthermore, Americans pay attention to research that says that small businesses create most new jobs (Birch, 1979) while ignoring research that finds that small-business failures destroy most lost jobs (Finlayson and Peacock, 2003). Americans want to believe in the positive personal and social impacts of the small-business dream.

While admiring those who seem to have pulled themselves up by their own bootstraps, the general public also supports subsidies for small business. (Successful entrepreneurs encourage this by founding think-tanks and policy institutes that trumpet the benefits of small business and that lobby for subsidies.) For example, small businesses benefit from government set-asides and are exempt from many labor and safety laws as well as some equal-opportunity requirements. These subsidies are seen as fair because small businesses—due to their small size—have greater difficulty diluting the more or less fixed costs of full regulatory compliance. Furthermore, small businesses face greater relative costs to find and exploit tax loop-holes. If small businesses have less access to subsidies than do large businesses, then microenterprises have the least access of all. This is why matches for microenterprise are seen as fair.

Whether or not they produce jobs on net, microenterprises are directly productive in the market. If not, they soon go out of business. In addition, microenterprise assets are relatively non-convertible, especially if they are large and business-specific. On the one hand, a matched withdrawal used to buy, say, a silk-screen machine is unlikely to have the effect of merely freeing up cash for other uses that would otherwise have been invested in plant and equipment. On the other hand, matched withdrawals for a box of shirts, some cans of paint, or a new mop are straightforward to convert and less likely to have a large impact. Thus, most IDA programs limit matched withdrawals for microenterprise to "start-up or expansion," reasoning that, compared with small changes, large changes are more likely to be "caused" by IDAs. Of course, microenterprises themselves are notoriously illiquid; most could not find an arm's-length buyer for any price higher than salvage value. By the set of criteria here, providing matches for microenterprise assets—that is, plant and equipment—makes sense.

Should IDAs also provide matches to microenterprises for buying inventory or for paying expenses such as payroll, rent, or utilities? Although some IDA programs do match business expenses (as well as the pay-down of business debt), this use fails the test of non-convertibility. Matching the business's light bill, for example, is not much different from matching the owner's purchase of corn flakes or movie tickets. The match increases free cash flow—less of the owner's "own money" must go to expenses—and so increases profit. Furthermore, matches for expenses do not change current purchases but rather pay for past purchases.

Financial capital. The final type of asset that might be matched through IDAs is financial capital. The most common form of subsidized financial capital is retirement savings, but subsidies could also go for paying down debts and or for general-purpose, un-earmarked savings.

RETIREMENT SAVINGS. Asset-building transfers to the non-poor through the tax system are a pillar of what Sherraden (1991) calls the "grand welfare state." These transfers—although highly regressive (Seidman, 2001; Howard, 1997; Sherraden, 1991)—are hugely popular and are seen as fair for several reasons. First, the non-poor do not see them as "something-for-nothing welfare" but rather as "keeping more of what they earned" (Sherraden, 1991, p. 75). Second, because many people fail to plan (Bernheim, 1997; Hubbard and Skinner, 1996) and/or push unpleasant thoughts (such as their future old age) out of their minds (Slemrod, 2003), they tend to save too little for retirement. If they arrive at old age short of savings, then they will turn to the state for help, and the state at that point will not be able to say "no" (Hubbard, Skinner, and Zeldes, 1995). Thus, subsidies for retirement savings help reduce reliance on public assistance in old age. Third, many people believe that they will get less Social Security retirement benefits than they have paid in, so subsidies for retirement savings help even things out (Bernheim, 1995). Fourth and finally, because subsidies for retirement savings work through tax breaks without any cash explicitly changing hands, their regressivity is easily overlooked. Means-tested public assistance for the poor, in contrast, is progressive but involves the explicit transfer of cash.

As noted above, tax breaks are weak incentives for the poor (Joulfaian and Richardson, 2001; Engelhardt, 1996). Thus, matches for retirement savings for the poor are seen as a fair way to level the playing field, and the idea already has political support. For example, the new Saver's Tax Credit provides a non-refundable tax credit for low-income retirement savers. Other design flaws, however, have rendered this well-meant policy mostly irrelevant in its current form (Orszag and Hall, 2003).

Retirement savings are also illiquid, at least before retirement, because early withdrawal triggers a substantial tax penalty. Furthermore, retirement savings are productive inasmuch as they increase the economy's capital stock. In retirement, of course, they are typically converted into consumption, maintaining life but often not producing much else.

In general, it is not clear whether subsidies for retirement savings have high personal and social impacts. In the case of IRAs and 401(k) plans for the non-poor, a long-standing debate asks whether subsidies cause people to save more than they otherwise would have. One camp uses data and tests that may be biased against finding "new" savings. Unsurprisingly, they fail to reject the hypothesis that all subsidized savings are reshuffled from existing assets (Engen, Gale, and Scholz, 1996; Gale and Scholz, 1994). A second camp uses data and tests that may be biased toward finding "new" savings. Again unsurprisingly, they fail to reject the hypothesis that all subsidized savings come from increases in income and/or reductions in consumption (Poterba, Venti, and Wise, 1996).

While some people undoubtedly save just as much (or less) with subsidies than they would have saved without subsidies, some others surely save more, and there must be some people who are prompted to save something by subsidies but who would not have saved anything without subsidies. Thus, common sense and simple economic theory suggests that, on average, subsidized savings—whether in IRAs, 401(k) plans, or IDAs—are some mix of both "new" savings and "reshuffled" assets, even for people who started with no assets at all (Orszag and Greenstein, 2004; Schreiner et al., 2001). Skinner (1997) surmises that, on net, the weight of evidence suggests that "new" savings account for between 20 to 40 percent of all subsidized retirement savings by the non-poor.

Whatever the impacts of subsidies on "new" savings, they are likely stronger for the poor. Benjamin (2003), Engelhardt (2001), Engen and Gale (2000),

Bernheim (1997), Joines and Manegold (1991), and Venti and Wise (1986) all find that subsidies for retirement savings are more likely to spark "new" saving among the poor than the non-poor. Sherraden and Barr (2004) and Sherraden (1991) point out that the poor are less likely to reshuffle simply because they have less existing assets available for reshuffling in the first place.

On the whole, then, matching for retirement in IDAs fulfills the criteria here. It has political support because of its fairness, and it probably has high personal and social impacts, at least for the poor. Also, retirement savings (before retirement) are illiquid and productive.

PAYING DOWN GENERAL DEBTS. As discussed previously, matches for debt service do not meet the standards here. To be fair, there is not wide agreement on this issue in the IDA field. Three points are made in favor of matching debt service. First, paying down debt is a form of saving because it increases net worth and requires an increase in income and/or a decrease in consumption. Thus, matches for debt service are matches on saving. Second, the non-poor get tax deductions for interest on student loans and home mortgages. Because the poor get little benefit from tax breaks, matching debt service is a way to level the playing field. Third, clearing up old debts is often a prerequisite for other types of asset-building, especially homeownership.

These are all valid points, but matching debt service still does not meet all six standards. Fundamentally, such matches are less likely to have strong personal or social impacts. For one thing, the debt being cleared up may have served not to purchase large, life-changing assets but rather to buy clothes, vacations, or beer. Furthermore, matching post-purchase rather than pre-purchase increases the likelihood that the match just transfers cash rather than increasing investment. This convertibility of debt service—coupled with its weak impact—implies that matching for debt pay-down is less likely to boost household or market productivity. Thus, even if matches for debt service for student loans and home mortgages are fair, they are nevertheless unlikely to attract wide political support. After all, households could run up credit-card debt on flings and splurges today, counting on matches from IDAs to help them pay off the debt tomorrow.

GENERAL-PURPOSE SAVINGS. The United Kingdom allows non-deductible contributions of up to £5,000 per person per year into "Individual Savings Accounts" with tax-free earnings and unrestricted withdrawals (Milligan, 2002). Similarly, President Bush proposed "Lifetime Savings Accounts" in the 2004 budget. If implemented, these would be like Roth IRAs, only with higher contribution limits and unrestricted withdrawals.

Still, the subsidy works through tax breaks, so it will not benefit the poor. Should IDAs then provide matches for general-purpose savings? After all, if the non-poor have access to such unrestricted savings subsidies, voters might approve of unrestricted matches in IDAs. Overall, however, unrestricted matches do not score well against the standards here.

Un-earmarked savings are highly convertible. There is no pretense—for the poor or non-poor—that they would be used for large, productive asset purchases with positive social impacts. All withdrawals would be matched, whether for college tuition or for Spring Break. If people know what is best for themselves and make sensible plans that they successfully carry out, then such unrestricted savings subsidies would increase personal income and thus have high personal impacts. But if people are myopic, lack self-control, change their minds, forget things, and in general make mistakes (Thaler, 2000), then matching only large asset purchases can help people do what they wish they would do, if only the flesh were as strong as the spirit.

Compared with tax breaks on accumulated earnings, unrestricted matches are less likely to be seen as fair. After all, such tax breaks are small (or zero, or negative) in the short term. Furthermore, the longer savings are held, the greater the increase in the capital stock (increasing social impact) and the more likely the savers are to develop—and stick to—a sensible plan for using the savings (increasing personal impact) (Americks, Caplin, and Leahy, 2002; Sherraden, 1991). Matches, in contrast, are instant. If all withdrawals were matched, then the poor and the non-poor might see IDAs as free-money machines; make a deposit today, make a matched withdrawal for any use tomorrow. Instead of being an institution that helps the poor to save and accumulate assets for their long-term development, IDAs could turn into little more than a thinly disguised cover for unrestricted cash transfers, a hoop to jump through in exchange for an increase in income equal to the annual match eligibility.

Overall assessment of matched uses. IDAs differ from means-tested cash transfers (such as Food Stamps or Temporary Assistance for Needy Families) by focusing on saving and asset accumulation rather than immediate consumption. (For this reason, IDAs complement means-tested cash transfers.) One way that IDAs do this is by restricting matched withdrawals to purchases of illiquid, productive assets with high personal and social impacts. If a matched use meets these standards and gives the poor access to a savings subsidy previously reserved for the non-poor, then it has a good chance of being perceived as fair and of receiving public support.

By these standards, IDAs should provide matches for the three "cornerstone" uses of home purchase for first-time buyers, post-secondary education and job training, and microenterprise. Furthermore, IDAs should also match retirement savings, car purchase, computer purchase, and medical expenses for those without access to group health insurance. The non-poor already have access to subsidies for all of these assets (except for car and computer purchase). While all fourteen programs in ADD provided matches for the three "cornerstone" uses, only some programs matched retirement savings, and no programs matched car purchase, computer purchase, or medical expenses. Some programs in ADD provided matches for home repair, but this use appears to score poorly against the standards set forth here.

Chapter Summary and Looking Ahead

Poor people saved and accumulated assets in IDAs in ADD. While the data do not reveal whether participants saved more overall than they would have in the absence of IDAs, the mere fact that they saved something dispels many myths about the inability and/or unwillingness of the poor to sacrifice short-term consumption to build assets that improve long-term well-being.

On average, net IDA savings per month in ADD was $16.60, equivalent to about $200 per year. Given an average of 33.6 months of eligibility, the average participant had net IDA savings of $558. With an average match rate of 1.88:1 and assuming that all matchable balances were eventually taken out as matched withdrawals, the average participant in ADD accumulated assets in IDAs at a rate of about $48 per month, equivalent to $576 per year.

Looking at saving through the lens of a new measure proposed in this chapter, the average IDA participant in ADD moved 1,090 dollar-years through time, equivalent to 363 dollar-years per year eligible. This new measure is useful because it is consistent with the view of saving as moving resources through time, and it also recognizes that even participants who did not make a matched withdrawal still saved and kept balances in an IDA for some time.

As of the data cut-off date, about 31 percent of participants had made a matched withdrawal. Among the other 69 percent, about one-third were "savers" with match-eligible balances of at least $100. Assuming that all matchable balances were eventually taken out as matched withdrawals, the average ADD participant accumulated $1,609 in IDAs.

Among participants with access to a given type of matched withdrawal, the share who made that type of matched withdrawal (or who planned to do so and had at least $100 of match-eligible balances) were 21 percent for home purchase, 11 percent for post-secondary education, and 12 percent for microenterprise. These three "cornerstone" uses enjoy broad political support and are seen as fair because these assets are heavily subsidized for the non-poor and because these assets are illiquid, productive, and have high personal and social impacts. Retirement savings also satisfies these standards, and 12 percent of participants in ADD made matched withdrawals for this use (or planned to do so). Although home repair does not satisfy the standards for matchable uses set forth in this chapter, it was the second-most popular use in ADD (15 percent). No program in ADD provided matches for car purchase or medical expenses, but these two uses satisfy the criteria here. In dollar terms, the largest matched withdrawals (excluding matches) were for retirement savings, followed by home purchase and home repair.

Although poor people saved within the supportive institutional structure of IDAs in ADD, it was not easy. As of the cut-off date for the data, about two-thirds of participants had made at least one unmatched withdrawal, representing lost potential asset accumulation per participant in this group of about

$1,400. The presence of these withdrawals, in spite of their high opportunity costs in terms of lost matches, may in part reflect the difficulty of moving resources through time for people who, due to their poverty, face frequent emergencies.

Other angles also suggest that saving was difficult for some participants. For example, the average IDA saving rate from income was about 1.1 percent, participants made a deposit in about half of the months in which an IDA was open, and they saved about forty-two cents for every matchable dollar. Moreover, 48 percent of all participants were "low savers" with net IDA savings of less than $100. Whether the proverbial glass is better viewed as half empty or half full is less relevant than the question of how to use knowledge from ADD to improve the design and structure of IDAs so as to more effectively encourage saving and asset accumulation by the poor.

The rest of this book tackles this subject. The next chapter examines links between saving in IDAs in ADD and variation in account design and program structure. This offers lessons for policy choices about the match rate, match cap, match-cap structure, time cap, facilitation of automatic transfer, restrictions on unmatched withdrawals, and provision of financial education. To date, such design choices have been largely shots in the dark. Program design is the main lever available to policy, so knowing what worked in ADD may make this lever more useful.

The chapter after the next then looks at links between saving in IDAs and participant characteristics, including gender, race/ethnicity, age, marital status, education, employment status, receipt of public assistance, income, and debts and assets at enrollment. The analysis also looks at how savings outcomes varied with participants' planned use of matched withdrawals. While policy cannot change participants' characteristics, knowing how these characteristics are linked with saving can provide hints about who has more difficulty saving in IDAs and perhaps why, again leading to lessons for policy, account design, and program services.

6

IDA Design, Program Structure,
and Savings Outcomes

The analysis of ADD data in the previous chapter shows that the poor can save in IDAs. With access to subsidies and facilitating institutions like those enjoyed by the non-poor, perhaps the poor will turn out to be not so different after all.

From a policy perspective, knowing that the poor can save matters because it may shift the focus from reforming the poor to reforming savings institutions. Such a shift is eminently practical, as policy has a direct influence on institutions but only an indirect (via institutions) influence on people. In a sense, policy is all about institutional design.

Rossi (1984) emphasizes that social interventions are usually limited to transfers of resources or changes in constraints and are thus unlikely to change people. Failure to focus on what policy can do leads to what Rossi calls the "Iron Law of Program Evaluation," that is, that "the expected value of any net impact assessment of any large-scale social program is zero" (p. 4). According to Rossi (1985, p. 11), "the major problem with much basic social science is that social scientists have tended to ignore policy-related variables in building theories because policy-related variables account for so little of the variance of the behavior in question." To avoid these mistakes for the case of IDAs, this chapter not only focuses on policy-related variables but also links them with basic social-science theory and shows that they are correlated with a large share of the variance in savings in ADD.

How are the institutional aspects of IDAs—account design and program structure—associated with savings outcomes? This chapter addresses this question with regression analysis and the ADD data. As expressed by Choi, Laibson, and Madrian (2004, p. 3) in the context of 401(k) plans, "Making good plan-design decisions requires an understanding of the relationship between plan rules and participant savings outcomes."

In ADD, different programs (and sometimes different participants within a program) had different IDA designs. The associations between differences in the institutional aspects of IDAs and the differences in savings outcomes can provide lessons for improving the effectiveness of institutions meant to facilitate saving and asset accumulation by the poor. On the one hand, if savings outcomes are associated mostly with economic incentives, then policy should focus on match rates and match caps. On the other hand, if savings outcomes depend mostly on institutions, then policy should focus on other aspects of IDA design such as match-cap structures, financial education, and explicit and implicit expectations communicated to participants about how much they "should" save.

The analysis here associates institutional aspects of IDAs in ADD with two participant-level savings outcomes: being a "saver" (having net IDA savings of $100 or more), and net IDA savings per month eligible for matchable deposits. The institutional aspects in the regression are the match rate, match cap, match-cap structure, use of automatic transfer, months eligible for matchable deposits, hours of general financial education, and finally the set of rules relevant for participants funded by the Assets for Independence Act (AFIA). In addition to these program characteristics, the regressions also control for a wide array of participant characteristics (discussed in the next chapter).

Many aspects of IDA design in ADD had strong associations with savings outcomes. Thus, policy may have much to say about how well the poor save and build assets in IDAs. For example, higher match rates were associated with a greater likelihood of being a "saver," although, among "savers," they were associated with lower monthly net IDA savings. Higher match caps were associated with higher savings; as they tried to "max out" their IDAs, ADD participants turned limits into targets. The use of automatic transfer was associated with a greater likelihood of being a "saver." Longer time caps were associated with a greater likelihood of being a "saver" but with lower monthly net IDA savings. Finally, each hour of financial education (up to 10) was associated greater monthly net IDA savings for "savers."

After describing the analytical strategy and the statistical model, this chapter discusses the associations between savings outcomes and the institutional aspects of IDAs, relating them both to the theoretical predictions of chapter 2 as well as to possible lessons for policy.

Analytical Strategy and Statistical Model

Regression analysis provides estimates of the sign, size, and statistical significance of associations between a savings outcome ("saver" status or monthly net IDA savings for "savers") and a given institutional aspect of IDAs. At the same time, regression controls for associations between savings outcomes and all other program and participant characteristics included in the regression. Because regression controls for all correlations among the savings outcomes and all included characteristics, it is less subject to the "cross-tab fallacy." That is, associations derived from regressions are more likely than associations derived from cross-tabs to be close to the "true" associations. Regressions are preferred to cross-tabs because their estimates are more likely to have a larger causal element.

As a primer for the rest of this chapter and the next, this section briefly discusses how regression analysis works and how to interpret the regression results. It also presents a formal two-step "Heckit" regression model and the reasons for its use here. Finally, it describes several caveats on interpreting regression results in the context of ADD. These matter because policy seeks causes—what aspects of IDA design change outcomes—rather mere correlations.

Cross-Tabs

Cross-tabs are a simple way to associate a characteristic with a savings outcome. For example, the cross-tab in table 6.1 associates the match rate in ADD with monthly net IDA savings for "savers." It shows that—all else in the cross-tab constant—higher match rates were associated with lower net IDA savings. On average, "savers" with a 1:1 match rate had net IDA savings of $37.54 per month, but "savers" with a 2:1 match rate saved about $10 less ($26.92), and "savers" with match rates above 2:1 saved about $15 less ($21.85).

Why would higher match rates be associated with lower savings? If many participants saved for a fixed goal, then higher match rates could cause lower saving. But other explanations are also plausible. For example, perhaps ADD participants with higher match rates also had lower match caps. If so, then censoring at the match cap could have made observed savings lower for "savers" with higher match rates even if desired savings increased with the match rate. Or perhaps match rates were correlated with a third factor that caused low saving but is not held constant in the cross-tab. For example, suppose that being a woman was a causal factor of low savings, and suppose further that women in ADD were more likely to be assigned higher match rates, perhaps because programs expected women to save less and tried to compensate by assigning higher match rates to women. Then, even if match rates caused higher savings, cross-tab analysis could still show a negative correlation. In general, even if match rates do not cause low savings, they may be correlated with low savings through their correlation with other factors that do cause low savings.

Thus, while cross-tabs are simple and useful, their assumption that all else is constant is usually untenable. For example, the cross-tab in table 6.1 does not control for the possibility that gender was correlated with both match rates and net IDA savings. The cross-tab in table 6.2, however, does control for both match rates and gender. It shows that women in ADD were more likely than men to be assigned higher match rates, and furthermore that—for a given match rate—women saved less than men. This suggests that some (but not all)

Table 6.1
Cross-Tab Analysis of the Association between Match Rates
and Net IDA Savings per Month for "Savers" in ADD

Match rate	N	Ave. monthly net IDA savings ($)
1:1	368	37.54
2:1	566	26.92
>2:1	299	21.85

Table 6.2
Cross-Tab Analysis of the Association between Match Rates, Gender,
and Net IDA Savings per Month in ADD

		N		Ave. monthly net IDA savings ($)	
	Gender	Men	Women	Men	Women
Match rate					
1:1		105	263	37.99	37.36
2:1		103	463	32.75	25.67
>2:1		51	248	23.42	21.50

of the apparent correlation between match rates and net IDA savings was due not to match rates' causing savings but rather to the correlation between match rates and gender and then the correlation between gender and net IDA savings.

Is gender then a causal factor of savings? The two-way cross-tab in table 6.2 holds more constant than does the one-way cross-tab in table 6.1, but a third factor (say, receipt of means-tested public assistance) may still have been correlated with gender and have been a cause of low savings, even if gender was not a causal factor at all. Indeed, the regression analysis in the next chapter suggests that after controlling for a wide range of other factors, gender was not associated with net IDA savings in ADD, even though table 6.2 suggests that women saved much less than men.

While three-way (or four-way, or n-way) cross-tabs are possible, the approach soon reaches its limits. First, the tables get too large and complex to be analyzed. The regression later in this chapter, for example, includes eight institutional characteristics and thirty-five participant characteristics. In contrast, the human brain (and printed tables) cannot handle more than three or four dimensions, let alone forty-three. Second, the number of cases in a given cell (say, men who received public assistance and who had match rates of greater than 2:1) shrinks with each additional dimension. Eventually, almost all the cells have too few cases to provide a reliable estimate of average monthly net IDA savings for cases in the cell (and most cells are completely empty). Third, non-categorical (continuous) variables such as age or income can be cross-tabbed only if they are first cut up into bins. Not only does this discard information, but it is difficult to select cut-points wisely (Hand and Adams, 2000). Fourth, a user of cross-tabs who seeks knowledge of an independent correlation (say, between the match rate and net IDA savings) must somehow mentally adjust for the correlations between match rates and all other characteristics in all other dimensions of the cross-tab. While this is possible for two-way or three-way cross-tabs, it is very difficult in higher dimensions.

These problems of n-way cross-tabs are mitigated by regression. For each characteristic, regression provides one estimate of the independent correlation between the characteristic and the savings outcome, accounting for all the correlations among all the characteristics in the regression with each other and with the savings outcome.

Omitted Characteristics

Of course, regression cannot control for characteristics omitted from the regression. All too commonly, researchers act as if all else is successfully held constant once they control for a handful of boilerplate demographic characteristics. Social-science outcomes, however, are usually related with a whole host of characteristics; age, gender, race/ethnicity, and income do not completely describe a person. Just like cross-tabs, regressions can mislead if they omit some characteristics and thus fail to hold all else constant (Kennedy, 1998; Greene, 1993). The advantage of regression over cross-tabs is mostly that regression omits fewer characteristics.

Still, all regressions inevitably omit some relevant characteristics, if only because some relevant characteristics are absent from the data. (The literature calls these *unobserved characteristics*. In fact, many are observed and appear in the data, although not the regression.) The existence of omitted characteristics has several consequences for drawing policy lessons from regression analysis.

First, regression estimates—like cross-tabs—do not necessarily indicate causality. It is always possible—and usually plausible—that an included characteristic is correlated with some omitted characteristic that is also a cause of the outcome. While most characteristics generally are causes of most outcomes, the share of an estimated association from a regression that represents causality is usually different (perhaps weaker, perhaps stronger) than a naïve interpretation of the estimate would suggest.

Second, there are ways to minimize bias due to omitted characteristics. The simplest and most straightforward technique (although rarely used) is to include more characteristics (Schreiner, 2004d; Benjamin, 2003; Breiman, 2001). In practice, few regression studies include all the characteristics that are in the data and that theory suggests as relevant. Another way to minimize omitted-characteristic bias is randomization. If access to IDAs were randomly assigned, then the distribution of characteristics—whether or not observed or included in the regression—would be the same (on average in repeated samples) for the treatment group and the control group. Then, any post-IDA differences could be causally attributed to differences in access to IDAs rather than differences in pre-IDA characteristics. While randomization is the gold standard for simply and incontrovertibly establishing causality (Orr, 1999; Burtless, 1995; Manski, 1995), running a randomized study requires more resources than analyzing existing data. Although access to IDAs was randomized across qualified applicants at one program in ADD, the MIS IDA data cover only the treatment group, so the analysis here cannot take advantage of the randomization. Finally, the most common technique (and the most complicated, and probably the least effective) for minimizing omitted-characteristic bias uses statistical models and assumptions to represent omitted characteristics via proxies derived from included characteristics.

Third, policy development requires knowledge of causes. To fine-tune the institutional aspects of IDA design to maximize saving and asset accumulation by the poor, policy makers need to know more than that higher match rates are correlated with lower savings; they need to know whether higher match rates cause lower savings. If match rates are merely associated with lower savings (perhaps because women are assigned higher match rates, and being a woman causes lower savings), then policy makers would want to adjust not match rates themselves but rather the gender-related assignment of match rates.

In the absence of randomization, omitted characteristics are inevitable, so the ADD data cannot establish beyond a shadow of a doubt exactly how (or whether) institutional aspects caused savings outcomes. Does this make the regression analysis irrelevant for policy? Even though it is not the final word, the analysis is still useful. For one thing, there is little other research associating IDA design and program rules with savings outcomes in IDAs. Incomplete knowledge is better than no knowledge, guesses, or propaganda from proponents or opponents. Policy development marches on, and the analysis here may help inform policy choices, even if it cannot do all the hard work for policymakers. Furthermore, all the estimates represent some mix of causes and non-causal correlations. While they are all reported as correlations, some are probably more on the causal side, and sometimes there are clues to encourage (or discourage) such a view. As usual, the best that can be done is to be explicit about the analytical assumptions and caveats (Schreiner, 2002c). This encourages reasoned, productive discussion about the areas still subject to debate and makes it easier for future work to find improvements and to offer more certainty.

It is unfortunate that the ADD data cannot reveal the optimal IDA design once and for all. To pretend that ADD had all the answers might advance a particular agenda and might perhaps even improve social well-being within an imperfect political process. But it would be lying (and possibly incorrect).

The job of policy research is not to spin or dumb-down research results until policymakers will support specific interventions. Rather, policy research should be clear and accurate (Easterly, 2003; Bardach, 2002; Aaron, 2000; Bonnen and Schweikhardt, 1999). This can only improve the likelihood that policy will accomplish its goals.

The analysis here attempts to limit omitted-characteristic bias in two ways. First, the regression includes an unusually wide array of characteristics (eight for programs, thirty-five for participants). This regression omits fewer characteristics than most. Also, the included characteristics are likely correlated to some degree with omitted characteristics and thus serve as proxies for them (Benjamin, 2003). Second, the regression has two steps, allowing the construction of a proxy for omitted characteristics that might influence both the likelihood of being a "saver" and—for "savers"—the level of monthly net IDA savings. As an additional control for omitted program characteristics, the regressions include a set of indicator variables for each specific program in ADD.

A characteristic was included in the regression if theory suggested an association with net IDA savings, if the characteristic appeared in MIS IDA, and if the characteristic had sufficient variation across participants. Counting both steps in the two-step regression, all classes of categorical variables, splines for continuous variables, and controls for missing data, the regression estimated 215 parameters. This is an unusually large regression, but with 2,350 participants, there was no shortage of degrees of freedom. Although the results are presented in a series of figures in this chapter and the next, they all come from a single two-step regression.

Two-Way Causation

In addition to bias due to omitted characteristics, any regression analysis must guard against bias due to two-way causation. Of course institutional characteristics can affect savings outcomes, but how can savings outcomes affect institutional characteristics? Suppose that an IDA program believes—correctly or incorrectly—that higher match rates cause higher savings. If this program notices that savings are low, then it might try to compensate by raising match rates in midstream. This makes low savings a cause of higher match rates. All else in the analysis constant, the two-way causation biases the regression-derived estimate of the association between match rates and savings.

Even if programs do not change their rules in midstream, two-way causation is still possible. For example, suppose that an IDA program sets its match rate based on how it expects the target group to save. If the program expects that its target group will have difficulty saving and if the program expects that higher match rates will boost saving, then it might set a higher match rate from the outset than would an otherwise equivalent program that does not expect its target group to have as much difficulty saving. If a program's expectations for savings are correlated with eventual savings outcomes, then there is two-way causation; not only does the match rate cause savings, but expected savings also cause the match rate.

There are three ways to control for two-way causation. The first is to include pre-enrollment characteristics in the regression rather than post-enrollment characteristics. While this simple technique works for program and participant characteristics that may change after enrollment as a function of savings outcomes, it does not control for program characteristics affected by pre-enrollment expectations for post-enrollment outcomes.

The second way to control for two-way causation is randomization. Just as programs could have randomly assigned access to IDAs to participants, ADD could have randomly assigned institutional characteristics (such as match rates and match caps) to programs or to participants. Such randomization breaks any causal relationship between pre-enrollment expectations for savings outcomes and institutional features. For administrative reasons, however, ADD did not randomize institutional characteristics across participants. Programs would have found it difficult to apply different rules to different participants, and participants would likely have viewed such an arrangement as unfair. In the name of giving programs latitude to experiment and find "best practices," ADD also did not randomize institutional features across programs.

The third way to control for two-way causation is statistical modeling. This requires an "instrument," that is, a third characteristic that is correlated with one side of a two-way causal relationship but not the other. Good instruments are hard to find; the most common one is randomization itself, as it is perfectly correlated with access and perfectly uncorrelated with everything else. The ADD data contain no obvious candidates for instruments. For example, any characteristic that affected IDA design through a program's pre-enrollment expectations for participants' post-enrollment savings would probably also have affected post-enrollment savings.

Two-way causation was possible in ADD. Each IDA program developed its own rules and account structures. (AFIA legislated rules for the participants that it funded, but AFIA started only after all the ADD programs had already set their rules for participants with non-AFIA funding.) While there is no direct evidence, programs may have set some of their rules partly in response to their expectations for participants' saving (Sherraden et al., 2000). The analysis here cannot control for this, but it does note when bias from two-way causation may matter. Furthermore, some programs in ADD changed rules in mid-stream in response to savings outcomes. Indeed, ADD encouraged programs to revise designs as they "learned what worked." While this may have facilitated the qualitative evaluation of the effects of program design by introducing variation through time, it impeded quantitative evaluation such as in the regression analysis here.

To avoid two-way causation from midstream rule changes in response to savings outcomes, this analysis uses pre-enrollment program characteristics. If most participants believed that the original rules were in force most of the time, then the original rules are the most relevant.

Some ADD programs offered different match rates for different uses, so there was also two-way causation between savings outcomes and the match rate. For example, one program offered a 2:1 match rate for home purchase and a 1:1 match rate for all other uses. Thus, the type of matched use (and thus the match rate) could be caused by savings outcomes. For example, someone who saved $200 could usefully make a matched withdrawal for microenterprise but probably not for home purchase. To control for this, the analysis here uses the match rate for the planned use recorded by the participant at enrollment, regardless of whether this planned use was ever realized. This assumes that the participant expected to receive the match rate that corresponded to the planned matched use that was declared at enrollment.

Finally, the regressions use pre-enrollment participant characteristics, eliminating the possibility that savings outcomes caused participant characteristics. The downside is that the pre-enrollment data for participants in MIS IDA were less clean. MIS IDA provided no way to distinguish between corrections of pre-enrollment characteristics versus post-enrollment updates of characteristics which changed with time (possibly due to savings outcomes). Because two-way causation may have contaminated post-enrollment updates, the regressions use pre-enrollment participant data.

A Two-Step Heckit

The analysis here uses a two-step regression for two reasons. First, this permits the construction of a proxy for omitted characteristics associated both with the likelihood of being a "saver" and with the level of monthly net IDA savings for "savers." As mentioned above, this helps minimize omitted-factor bias. Second, the associations between characteristics and the likelihood of being a "saver" may differ from the associations between those same characteristics and the level of monthly net IDA savings for "savers." For example, higher match rates might be associated with a higher probability of being a "saver" (perhaps because they increase the reward to saving) while simultaneously being associated with lower monthly net IDA savings for "savers" (perhaps because they permit target-savers to save less and still reach their goals). In a one-step analysis that simply regresses match rates on monthly net IDA savings for all participants, the net estimated association would be some unknown mix of the association with the likelihood of being a "saver" with the association with the level of net IDA savings for "savers." This net estimate could be positive, negative, or zero, and it would be extremely difficult to derive policy lessons. (Examples of single-step analysis with the ADD data include Grinstein-Weiss and Sherraden, 2004; Grinstein-Weiss, Zhan, and Sherraden, 2004; Ssewemala and Sherraden, 2004; Zhan and Schreiner, 2004; Zhan, 2003; Curly and Grinstein-Weiss, 2002; Grinstein-Weiss and Curley, 2002; and Sherraden et al., 2000). In the regression here, it is not uncommon for associations to differ in sign between the two steps.

This two-step technique was introduced by Heckman (1979 and 1976). Analogously to "Probit" and "Logit," it is called the "Heckit." The first step encompasses all 2,350 participants in ADD. Because being a "saver" is a yes/no dichotomous outcome, the first step uses a Probit regression. The second step includes only the 1,232 "savers." Monthly net IDA savings is a continuous outcome that for a given participant can take any value between zero and the match cap, so the second step uses ordinary least-squares regression. The set of included characteristics in the second step is augmented by a proxy constructed from the first step that represents omitted characteristics correlated with being a "saver" that may also be correlated with monthly net IDA savings.

The first step. Knowledge of the characteristics associated with being a "saver" (net IDA savings of $100 or more) matters because participation is costly. Not only do programs lose their administrative investment in participants who are not "savers," but the participants lose potential matches and may even become discouraged with saving in general. Knowledge of how program and participant characteristics are associated with being a "saver" might help policy makers and program staff to improve IDA design so that more participants are "savers." For example, program staff can use the first-step regression results to predict at enrollment who is likely to be a "saver" (Schreiner and Sherraden, 2005; Eberts, 2001). Programs could then target extra help to at-risk participants. Research on 401(k) plans (Chang, 1996; Poterba, Venti, and Wise, 1995) has revealed little about why any participants—let alone poor participants—leave subsidized savings programs.

Following Greene (1993), participant i is a "saver" in the first-step Probit if the participant's net benefits of being a "saver" z_i^* are positive. The level of net benefits z_i^* is unobserved, but its sign is observed. A participant is a "saver" if net benefits are positive ($z_i = 1$ if $z_i^* > 0$). Otherwise, net benefits are negative and the participant is not a "saver" ($z_i = 0$ if $z_i^* \leq 0$):

$$z_i = 1 \text{ if } z_i^* = \alpha' W_i + u_i > 0,$$
$$z_i = 0 \text{ otherwise.} \tag{1}$$

Here, W_i is a vector of eight program characteristics and thirty-five participant characteristics, α' is a vector of coefficients to be estimated and that is common across all participants, and u_i is an error term with a Normal distribution.

To construct a proxy for omitted characteristics associated with being a "saver," let α^* represent the estimated coefficients common to all participants, let $\varphi(\cdot)$ represent the Normal probability distribution function, and let $\Phi(\cdot)$ represent the Normal cumulative distribution function. For participant i, the predicted probability of being a "saver" is $\Phi(\alpha^{*'}W_i)$. Then the ratio $\lambda_i = \varphi(\alpha^{*'}W_i) / \Phi(\alpha^{*'}W_i)$ decreases as the predicted probability of being a "saver" increases. (The literature often refers to λ_i as the "Inverse Mill's Ratio.")

"Savers" with high λ_i are "surprises"; based on the characteristics included in the regression, they were not predicted to be "savers." Given that they were in fact "savers" even though their included characteristics made being a "saver" unlikely, it must be that their omitted characteristics favored being a "saver." In contrast, "savers" with low λ_i were not "surprises"; based on their included characteristics, they were predicted to be "savers." Thus, λ_i tends to be higher for "savers" whose omitted characteristics most strongly favored being a "saver."

The first-step Probit fit the ADD data well. The "–2 log-likelihood" measure was 2,463.04, and the coefficients as a whole were statistically significant with 99 percent confidence ($p = 0.01$). For 81.3 percent of pairs in which one case was a "saver" and the other was not, the predicted likelihood of being a "saver" was higher for the "saver."

The second step. The level of monthly net IDA savings for "savers" is a direct measure of saving and asset accumulation in IDAs. Again, knowledge of how characteristics are associated with the level of savings matters because it may help policy makers and program staff to craft IDA designs that are more supportive of saving and asset accumulation by the poor.

The match cap drives a wedge between observed and desired net IDA savings for "savers" who "max out" their IDAs. The ordinary least-squares regression here, however, ignores this censoring and instead simply assumes that the monthly net IDA savings y_i of "saver" i is associated with a vector X_i of nine program characteristics and thirty-five participant characteristics. Monthly net IDA savings y_i is also assumed to be associated with λ_i, the proxy for omitted characteristics associated with the likelihood of being a "saver" from the first-step Probit. If β and θ are vectors of coefficients to be estimated (common to all "savers"), and if ε_i is an error term with a Normal distribution, then the second-step regression is:

$$y_i = \beta'X_i + \theta\lambda_i + \varepsilon_i \qquad (2)$$

The estimates of the standard errors of the estimated coefficients β and θ are adjusted to reflect that λ_i is an estimated characteristic.

The coefficient θ is expected to be positive. That is, the omitted characteristics that favor being a "saver" are expected also to favor higher levels of monthly net IDA savings. It turns out (table 6.3) that θ, while positive, was statistically insignificant ($p = 0.94$). Perhaps the regression included so many characteristics that the "flat max" kicked in (Lovie and Lovie, 1986; Dawes, 1979; Wainer, 1976).That is, the included characteristics in X_i may be correlated with the same omitted characteristics as is λ_i, so including λ_i did not add any explanatory power.

Indeed, adjusted R^2 for the second-step regression was 47.5 percent, a very high level of explanatory power for cross-section data on savings. That is, included characteristics were associated with about half of the variation in the level of monthly net IDA savings for "savers."

Censoring. The two-step "Heckit" specified here ignores censoring at the match cap. The regression in Schreiner (2004d) does control for censoring, and the estimates there are remarkably similar to those here. Thus, the estimates here—which technically pertain to observed savings—differ very little from those for desired savings.

Missing values. Like most data, the MIS IDA data for ADD contain many missing values. For example, 62 percent of participants did not report whether they were covered by either life or health insurance, and 35 percent had missing values for the receipt of Food Stamps at enrollment (table 6.3).

The standard approach is to omit all cases in which any included characteristic has missing values, assuming that missing values were sprinkled across participants at random. (This is sometimes called "list-wise deletion.") With so many characteristics included in the regression, however, this approach would discard about 72 percent of participants, precluding most analyses. This seems like a waste; the values of most characteristics are present for all participants, so why not use them?

To avoid wasting information, the analysis here uses "modified zero-order regression." As described in Orme and Reis (1991), each characteristic which sometimes had missing values was associated with a corresponding zero/one indicator variable. When the value of the "original" characteristic was non-missing, then the corresponding indicator was set to zero. When the value of the "original" characteristic was missing, however, then the corresponding indicator was set to one and the "original" characteristic was set to zero. Both the "original" characteristic and the corresponding indicator variable were then included in the regression. Modified zero-order regression cleanses the estimates of the effects of missing values and also avoids decimating the data. This is equivalent to what is sometimes called "pair-wise deletion." It is also equivalent to replacing missing values with the mean of non-missing cases (Greene, 1993). Like most common treatments of missing data, this assumes that missing values occur at random. The coefficients on the indicator variables (table 6.3) have no useful interpretation, although they can aid in prediction (Lewis, 1990).

Splines. Regressions usually assume that continuous characteristics such as age are linearly associated with outcomes. But little in life is linear. As people traverse the life cycle, for example, their desire and ability to save in

Table 6.3

Associations between Savings Outcomes and IDA Design and Program Structure: Match Rates, Match Caps, Match-Cap Structure, and Use of Automatic Transfer to the IDA

Independent variable	Prob.("Saver")			Net IDA savings/month		
	Mean	Δ% pts.	p-value	Mean	Δ$	p-value
Intercept	1.0	–30.7	0.10	1.0	+9.86	0.18
Omitted characteristics favoring being a "saver" (Lambda)				0	+0.28	0.94
Modified zero-order regression indicators						
Use of automatic transfer	0.06	–28.6	0.01	0.03	–3.03	0.37
Marital status	0.01	+18.3	0.26	0.01	+2.51	0.57
Number of children	0.00	+33.0	0.16	0.00	+5.68	0.30
Existing relationship with host organization	0.06	+0.4	0.97	0.03	–8.21	0.08
Referred by partner organization	0.21	–43.2	0.01	0.21	+2.09	0.68
AFDC or TANF before enrollment	0.01	–13.4	0.39	0.01	+1.19	0.83
Received SSI at enrollment	0.34	+22.3	0.02	0.37	+4.47	0.15
Received food stamps at enrollment	0.35	+5.8	0.55	0.38	–2.10	0.47
Recurrent income	0.02	–57.4	0.03	0.03	+4.60	0.51
Passbook balances	0.03	+12.6	0.13	0.03	+1.09	0.68
Checking balances	0.04	–15.0	0.03	0.04	–0.37	0.87
Financial investments	0.00	+25.7	0.33	0.00	+1.60	0.82
Car	0.00	–7.7	0.82	0.00	–1.42	0.89
Presence of some type of debt	0.01	+21.5	0.29	0.01	+4.97	0.33
Insurance coverage	0.62	–12.6	0.01	0.61	+0.16	0.91
Variables with rare missings	0.01	–4.4	0.76	0.01	+1.13	0.82
Intermittent income				0.00	+1.26	0.83
General financial education				0.06	+11.99	0.06

Note on regression fit: For the first-step Probit, –2 multiplied by the log-likelihood was 2463.04, and the percentage of pairs correctly predicted was 81.3. For the second-step ordinary least-squares, R^2 was 52.2 percent, and adjusted R^2 was 47.5 percent.

subsidized forms changes, with youth saving mostly in human capital, young people saving mostly in housing, middle-aged people saving mostly for retirement, and the elderly mostly dissaving. The change in a given form of savings associated with an additional year of age varies with age, so the relationship is non-linear.

Some regressions represent non-linear relationships with polynomials, for example including not only age but also age-squared and perhaps also age-cubed. Polynomials allow the data to determine the turning points of the curve, but they are fragile with respect to outliers and may also introduce multicollinearity (Miranda and Fackler, 2002).

Rather than polynomials, the regressions here use series of spliced lines. Such *splines* (Friedman, 1991; Smith, 1979; Suits, Mason, and Chan, 1978) are simple to interpret (the coefficient on each segment is the slope of the "curve" for that segment), do not cause multicollinearity, allow multiple changes of direction, and are robust to outliers.

Statistical Significance

This chapter and the next discuss the precision of the estimated associations between savings outcomes and the characteristics of programs and participants partly in terms of their statistical significance. Therefore, before presenting the estimates and policy implications, this sub-section reviews the use and meaning of statistical significance.

Estimates are *statistically significant* if they are unlikely to be due to sampling variation. Compared with statistically insignificant estimates, statistically significant estimates matter more for policy because they are more likely to represent "real" associations that will happen again rather than non-repeatable aberrations due to chance.

All samples are imperfect representations of their larger underlying populations, and estimated associations deviate from the "true" population associations in different ways from sample to sample. Statistical significance indicates the likelihood that an estimated association does not represent the population but rather merely a particular, non-representative sample.

Larger samples are more likely to be representative of the population. Thus, all else constant, a larger sample increases the likelihood that an estimate is statistically significant. For example, a fair coin lands on "heads" in 50 percent of the population of tosses. If a coin of unknown fairness lands on "heads" in six of ten tosses, there is not extremely strong evidence of unfairness. According to the binomial distribution, even a fair coin comes up "heads" six or more times in 17 percent of ten-toss samples. Here, 0.17 (17 percent) is the "p-value," the probability that a fair coin would land on "heads" at least as often as it did in the sample. The lower the "p-value," the greater the statistical significance and the lower the risk that the estimate comes from a non-representative sample. If a hundred tosses produces sixty "heads," then the p-value would be 0.017 (1.7 percent), as a fair coin would rarely produce that many "heads" in that many tosses.

The likelihood that an estimate is statistically significant also increases with the strength of the "true" association. For example, a coin that is "heads" in 70 percent of its population is more likely to be detected as unfair than is a coin that is "heads" in 60 percent of its population. The 70 percent coin will have sixty or more "heads" in 98 percent of a hundred toss samples, but the 60 percent coin will have sixty or more "heads" in 46 percent of a hundred toss samples. The stronger the "true" association, the more likely is high statistical significance.

Statistical significance is expressed as the degree of confidence that the estimate is not due to a non-representative sample. For example, if a coin lands on "heads" in sixty of a hundred tosses, there is 98.3 percent confidence that it is an unfair coin rather than a fair coin that happened to draw a non-representative sample.

The *p-value* is the complement of the confidence level, expressed as a probability rather than a percentage. For example, 98.3 percent confidence implies a p-value of 0.017. In general, if the confidence level is x percent, then the p-value is $(100-x)/100$. The higher the confidence, the lower the p-value. To avoid the appearance of false precision, p-values expressed here are rounded up to units of hundredths (for example, 0.017 becomes 0.02), and p-values below 0.01 are expressed as 0.01.

In standard practice, estimates are deemed "statistically significant" only if the confidence level exceeds 90 or 95 percent (equivalently, if the p-value is less than 0.10 or 0.05). Most researchers act as if estimated associations that do not achieve this level of confidence are the same as zero. Unfortunately, this is mechanical use of statistical significance (McCloskey, 1985; Cowger, 1984). The degree of confidence required of an estimate should depend not on the number of fingers or toes that humans happen to possess but rather on the expected changes in social well-being due to changes in decisions due to correctly or incorrectly taking the estimate as representative of the population. Confidence levels that are lower (or higher) than 90 percent are sometimes sufficient, and each case requires reasoned discussion. For example, if a regression indicated that an increase in the match rate from 1:1 to 2:1 was associated with an increase in monthly net IDA savings of $10 with 85 percent confidence (p-value 0.15), the standard response would be to forge ahead as if the match rate had no association with savings at all. But such an estimated association is "large" from a policy perspective, that is, compared with what an average IDA participant saves in a month, compared with what share of IDA savings are probably "new" rather than "reshuffled," and compared with the possible strength of other non-match-rate aspects of IDA policy. And 85 percent confidence is a lot, at least compared with the confidence available about most other aspects of public policy. Furthermore, it makes little sense to assume that the association is zero when there is an 85 percent chance that the estimated non-zero association is not simply the artifact of a non-representative sample. In "government work" and elsewhere, regression estimates can be useful even if they fail to achieve statistical significance at conventional levels.

The choice of the expected "default" association also matters. Are policymakers so convinced that match rates are not associated with IDA savings that they require more than 85 percent confidence to budge from this version of the status quo? Or are they so convinced that match rates are indeed associated with IDA savings that the 15 percent chance that there is no association is not enough to change their minds?

This brief review of the use of statistical significance in policy work wraps up with three caveats. First, statistical significance depends on both the sample size and the strength of the "true" association. In small samples, high levels of statistical significance are less likely, regardless of the strength of the "true" association. In large samples, high levels of statistical significance are more likely. In any sample, high levels of statistical significance are more likely if the "true" association is strong. Policy work must consider not only statistical significance but also sample size and the strength of the expected and estimated "true" associations.

Second, statistical significance implies nothing about causality. Furthermore, statistical significance does not imply policy significance. A statistically significant estimate might not provide any useful information for policy, and statistical insignificance might not imply policy insignificance. For example, a statistically insignificant association between the match rate and savings might provide a useful policy lesson (such as "look elsewhere for policy levers").

Third and finally, statistical significance measures imprecision due to non-representative samples while ignoring all other sources of bias such as omitted characteristics, two-way causation, censoring, and linear representations of non-linear associations. Statistical significance is a measure of sampling variation, and nothing more; the analyst must still do the hard work of discussing what the estimate might mean for policy.

These caveats do not imply that "statistical significance" should be reserved only for very high levels of confidence, as if demanding extreme precision in terms of sampling variation could somehow compensate for a lack of knowledge of other sources of imprecision. After all, imprecision from sampling variation has no specific relationship with imprecision from other sources (King, 1986). Rather than lean on statistical significance, a better approach is to describe all known sources of imprecision and then to discuss their potential implications.

An example witnessed at a recent conference shows how the (mis-)use of statistical significance can have policy consequences. The presenting researchers asked whether their university discriminated by paying African-American professors less than otherwise equivalent Caucasian professors. The sample was small, covering all professors at the university in a recent year, few of whom were African American. Despite the long and continuing history of pervasive discrimination against African Americans in the United States (Arrow, 1998; Darity and Mason, 1998; Ladd, 1998; Loury, 1998; Yinger, 1998), the researchers nonetheless took "no discrimination" as the "default" or "status quo" standard against which estimates would be judged. The regression estimates suggested that African-American professors were paid about $8,000 less than Caucasian professors, a large share of the average salary. The p-value, however, was 0.20, so there was 80 percent confidence that the "true" association was greater than zero and that the estimate was not an aberration from a non-representative sample. Still, because they lacked 90 percent confidence, the researchers concluded that there was "no evidence" of discrimination and that the university could continue business as usual. Yet, given the small sample, the regression estimates might fail to achieve 90 percent confidence even if the true association were large. Furthermore, both the expected and estimated associations between race and salary were large. Finally, it seems like a stretch to equate 80 percent confidence of an $8,000 difference with "no evidence." Statistical significance is not a substitute for thought.

Match Rates

As discussed in chapter 3 and in accord with most participant-level evidence from 401(k) plans (Clark et al., 2000; Clark and Schieber, 1998; General Accounting Office, 1997; Bayer, Bernheim, and Scholz, 1996), higher match rates are expected to increase the reward to saving and so should increase the likelihood of being a "saver" in ADD with net IDA savings of $100 or more. For "savers," however, theory does not unambiguously predict how higher match rates affect monthly net IDA savings (matched withdrawals plus matchable balances divided by the number of months eligible to make matchable deposits). On the one hand, the "substitution effect" suggests that higher match rates increase saving by rewarding participants who shift resources out of consumption and into saving. On the other hand, the "fixed-goal effect" suggests that higher match rates decrease saving by allowing participants to achieve a given asset-accumulation goal with less saving. Bernheim and Scholz (1993) suggest that the poor are more likely to save for fixed goals and so savings subsidies may decrease their saving. (They also argue that the general response of saving to the rate of return—equivalent to the match rate—grows stronger with income.) Still, few policy makers or programs believe that higher match rates (or matching in general) could depress IDA saving. Indeed, a basic premise of IDAs is that matching per se (regardless of the level of match rates) increases saving, and research on matching in 401(k) plans strongly supports this view (Even and Macpherson, 2003; Cunningham and Engelhardt, 2002;

Munnell, Sundén, and Taylor, 2002; Bassett, Fleming, and Rodrigues, 1998; Even and Macpherson, 1997; General Accounting Office, 1997; Ippolito, 1997; Bayer, Bernheim, and Scholz, 1996; Papke, 1995; Papke and Poterba, 1995; Even and Macpherson, 1994; Andrews, 1992). Because all ADD participants were eligible for matching, the analysis here cannot test the associations of matching per se. Because match rates vary across and within programs in ADD, however, the regression here can test whether higher match rates were associated with a higher likelihood of being a "saver" as well as whether the "substitution effect" was stronger than the "fixed-goal effect" for the level of monthly net IDA savings for "savers."

Why Match Rates Matter

Matching is one of few ways to include the poor in asset-building policies. The poor are in low tax brackets, so tax breaks—the typical subsidy mechanism for asset building—provide weak incentives. Without an alternative subsidy mechanism, the worldwide policy shift toward asset building may exclude the poor (Sherraden, 1997 and 2003).

Matches may help to include poor people in saving and asset building in three ways. First, matches increase the reward to saving. For poor people with low consumption, increasing saving by further decreasing consumption is more difficult than for non-poor people with higher consumption. By boosting the return to saving, matches can help to compensate for the short-term sacrifice.

Second, matches increase asset accumulation. Given a level of savings, higher match rates translate into a higher level of asset accumulation, perhaps producing a large-enough lump sum to enable the purchase of a life-changing asset such as a house or a college education.

Third, matches act as a mental focal point for participants. Often, the match is what first attracts participants to IDAs (Johnson et al., 2003; Moore et al., 2000). Participants often identify IDAs with the match; in their minds, other institutional aspects take a distant backseat. Participation may be based less on a conscious plan that sees IDAs as a means to a specific end than on a rule of thumb that says, "It only makes sense to take advantage of the match." Matching makes saving in IDAs a "no-brainer."

For these reasons, matching is central to IDAs. Indeed, IDAs are defined as *matched* savings structures for the poor. Thus, it matters how match rates are associated with savings outcomes. Still, little is known about how people—poor or not—respond to match rates.

Cross-Tab Analysis

In ADD, about one-fourth of participants had match rates of 1:1, about half had match rates of 2:1, and about one-fourth had match rates greater than 2:1

(table 6.4). In simple cross-tabs, higher match rates were not associated with a greater likelihood of being a "saver." The share of participants with 1:1 match rates who were "savers" (56 percent) was greater (p = 0.01) than for participants with 2:1 match rates (50 percent). About 53 percent of participants with match rates greater than 2:1 were "savers." The 1:1 versus >2:1 comparison had a p-value of 0.33, and the 2:1 versus >2:1 comparison had a p-value of 0.15. If anything, this simple cross-tab analysis suggests that higher match rates in ADD were associated with a lower likelihood of being a "saver."

For "savers," the cross-tabs associated higher match rates with lower net IDA savings. Monthly net IDA savings was $37.54 for "savers" with a 1:1 match rate, $26.92 for "savers" with a 2:1 match rate, and $21.85 for "savers" with match rates greater than 2:1.

Does this mean that higher match rates depressed savings outcomes in ADD? Not necessarily, for four reasons. First, correlation does not imply causality. Second, the cross-tabs omit many characteristics. Regression estimates that control for more characteristics may or may not reproduce these patterns. Third, two-way causation could explain these patterns. For example, higher match rates could increase the likelihood of being a "saver" and also increase monthly net IDA savings for "savers" and yet be negatively correlated with savings outcomes. This could happen if IDA programs in ADD assigned higher match rates to participants whom they expected to have greater difficulty saving, if these participants did in fact end up having greater difficulty saving, and if the increase in the match rate was not enough to fully compensate for the greater difficulty experienced by these groups. Fourth, the cross-tabs do not control for censoring at the match cap nor for associations between match rates and match caps.

Absent randomization, there is no way to distinguish correlation from causality, although the weight of causality grows with the number of characteristics held constant. Likewise, there is no way to cleanse estimates of bias due to two-way causation other than to control for the participant characteristics that first led programs to expect participants to have greater difficulty saving. Still, the possible bias from two-way causality—bias whose direction cannot be signed without knowledge of the "true" relationship between savings and match rates—makes the results here are less conclusive than otherwise. Schreiner (2004d) argues that bias from two-way causality in ADD is not likely to be strong.

Censoring may also be an issue in ADD. About 42 percent of "savers" saved up to the match cap (table 6.4), so their unobserved desired net IDA savings may have exceeded their observed net IDA savings. To further complicate matters, programs in ADD coupled higher match rates—as in 401(k) plans (VanDerhei and Copeland, 2001; Even and Macpherson, 2003 and 1997)—with lower match caps. The match cap per month eligible for matchable deposits (the "savings target") averaged $56.12 for "savers" with a 1:1 match rate,

Table 6.4

Savings Outcomes, Match Caps, and Censoring by Match Rate in ADD

Measure	All	Match rate		
		1:1	2:1	>2:1
Participants (%)	100	28	48	24
Share of participants who were "savers"	52	56	50	53
"Savers" only				
Net IDA savings per month eligible for matchable deposits ($)	29.08	37.54	26.92	21.85
Match cap per month eligible for matchable deposits ($)	42.23	56.12	35.94	27.20
Share censored at ≥95% of the match cap (%)	42	28	44	57

$35.94 for "savers" with a 2:1 match rate, and $27.20 for "savers" with a match rate greater than 2:1. (All the pair-wise comparisons had p-values of 0.01 in t-tests for differences in means.) As the match rate increased, the match cap decreased, and the share of "savers" who were censored increased (28 percent with 1:1, 44 percent with 2:1, and 57 percent with greater than 2:1). With this pattern of censoring, higher match rates could have increased desired savings while simultaneously being associated with decreased observed savings. For example, suppose that match rates have no association with net IDA savings and that all "savers" have desired net IDA savings of $60 per month. They would all be censored at the match cap. "Savers" with higher match rates also have lower match caps, so they would have lower observed savings. This produces a spurious negative correlation between match rates and savings.

Failure to adjust for censoring at the match cap biases estimates of match-rate effects downward. Most studies of match rates in 401(k) plans do not adjust for censoring, and they often find (perhaps spuriously) that higher match rates are associated with lower levels of savings as a share of income (Munnell, Sundén, and Taylor, 2002; VanDerhei and Copeland, 2001; Clark et al., 2000; Papke, 1995; Andrews, 1992). This result could reflect two-way causation in which employers—correctly—expect their employees to have difficulty saving and thus try—but do not completely succeed—to compensate by setting a higher match rate (Even and Macpherson, 2003). In contrast, specifications that do adjust for censoring (Engelhardt and Kumar, 2003; Cunningham and Engelhardt, 2002) find that higher match rates are associated with higher savings. According to Choi, Laibson, and Madrian (2004, p. 15), "The widely divergent empirical results in the literature on matching appear to result from empirical analysis that does not carefully account for the effect of both the match rate and the match threshold."

The regression here does account for both the match rate and the match cap. While it does not control for censoring, its results are very similar to those of a regression in Schreiner (2004d) that does control for censoring. Thus, censoring does not appear to be an important source of bias here. Furthermore, the regression here controls for an unusually wide array of program and participant characteristics, decreasing the severity of omitted-characteristic bias.

Regression Results

The associations between match rates and savings outcomes in ADD appear in table 6.5. The three columns on the left side of the figure under the heading "Prob.("Saver")" pertain to the first-step Probit that associates program (and participant) characteristics with the probability of being a "saver" with net IDA savings of $100 or more. The column headed "Mean" lists the average value for a given characteristic. The means of indicator variables are between 0 and 1. With all other characteristics included in the regression held constant, the column headed "Δ% pts." reports the percentage-point change in the likelihood of being a "saver" associated with a unit change in the value of a given program characteristic. (A percentage point is equivalent to 1/100, or 0.01. The percentage-point changes are derived from the estimated Probit coefficients α^*, but the estimated coefficients themselves are not reported because they do not have a straightforward interpretation.) Computed at the means of the characteristics, these percentage-point "marginal effects" are consistent estimators of the partial derivatives of the predicted likelihood of being a "saver" with respect to a given characteristic. Positive estimates mean that higher values of a given characteristic were associated with a greater likelihood of being a "saver," and negative estimates mean the converse. The column headed "p-value" displays the probability that the estimate could have come from a non-representative sample in which the "true" population association was zero. As always, lower p-values denote greater degrees of confidence. The standard errors of the percentage-point changes were derived with the "delta method" (Greene, 1993).

The three columns on the right side of table 6.5 under the heading "Net IDA savings/month" pertain to the ordinary least-squares regression in the second step of the "Heckit" that associates program (and participant) characteristics with the level of monthly net IDA savings for "savers" in ADD. With all other characteristics included in the regression constant, the column "Δ$" reports the estimate of the change in monthly net IDA savings associated with a unit change in the value of a given characteristic.

The first-step Probit suggests—in contrast with the patterns in simple crosstabs but consistent with theory—that higher match rates were associated with a greater likelihood of being a "saver." Compared with the 28 percent of participants with a 1:1 match rate, the 48 percent of participants with a 2:1 match rate were 8.9 percentage points more likely to be "savers." Considering that about half (52 percent) of all participants in ADD were "savers," this association was very large, and its statistical significance was high (p = 0.07).

The pattern continued as match rates increased. Participants with match rates greater than 2:1 were 15.8 percentage points more likely to be "savers" than those with match rates of 1:1 (p = 0.03). Furthermore, participants with match rates greater than 2:1 were 6.9 percentage points (15.8 − 8.9) more likely to be "savers" than those with match rates of 2:1. (The p-value of 0.06 for this second comparison does not appear in table 6.5).

While a regression with these data cannot establish causality with certainty, the estimates probably do mean that higher match rates increased the likelihood of being a "saver" in ADD. First, they accord with theory; it makes sense that higher match rates would prompt more participants to be "savers." Also, empirical research on 401(k) plans unanimously finds the same association. Second, the regression controls for a wide array of other characteristics, so—at least compared with most analyses—there are few potential omitted

Table 6.5
Associations between Savings Outcomes and IDA Design and Program Structure: Match Rates, Match Caps, Match-Cap Structure, and Use of Automatic Transfer to the IDA

Independent variable	Prob. ("Saver")			Net IDA savings/month		
	Mean	Δ% pts.	p-value	Mean	Δ$	p-value
Match rate						
1:1	0.28			0.30		
2:1	0.48	+8.9	0.07	0.46	-4.71	0.01
>2:1	0.24	+15.8	0.03	0.24	-0.80	0.77
Match cap						
Limit on matchable deposits ($/month)	41	+0.1	0.26	42	+0.57	0.01
Match-cap structure						
Lifetime	0.48			0.50		
Annual	0.52	+21.4	0.03	0.50	-5.93	0.07
Use of automatic transfer to IDA						
No	0.94			0.93		
Yes	0.06	+16.7	0.01	0.07	+0.32	0.84

Note: All regression estimates were derived from a single two-step "Heckit" regression. The first step was a Probit (n=2,350, k=104) for the likelihood of being a "saver." The second step was ordinary least-squares (n=1,232, k=111) for net IDA savings per month for "savers." Means were taken over non-missing observations.

characteristics that might both cause participants to be "savers" and be correlated with match rates. Finally, censoring and two-way causation cannot explain the estimates. In the first-step Probit, censoring at the match cap is irrelevant. Two-way causation between match rates and the expected likelihood of being a "saver" could account for a negative estimated association, but it could not account for a positive one. The policy lesson is simple and clear: higher match rates increase inclusion in IDAs by increasing the share of participants who are "savers."

For "savers," the theoretical effect of higher match rates on the level of monthly net IDA savings is ambiguous; either the "substitution effect" or the "fixed-goal effect" could win out. Holding constant other included characteristics in the second-step ordinary least-squares regression (table 6.5), participants with match rates of 2:1 had monthly net IDA savings of about $4.71 (p = 0.01) less than participants with match rates of 1:1. This is a large association, equivalent to about 16 percent of $29.08, the average monthly net IDA savings for "savers" in ADD.

"Savers" with match rates greater than 2:1 had—all else in the regression constant—$3.90 more monthly net IDA savings than "savers" with match rates of 2:1. (The p-value of 0.09 is not shown in table 6.5.) Compared with "savers" with 1:1 match rates, "savers" with match rates greater than 2:1 had monthly net IDA savings of $0.80 less. This estimate could have resulted from sampling variation (p = 0.77), so match rates of 1:1 and greater than 2:1 in ADD were associated with about the same level of monthly net IDA savings.

In contrast to the estimates from the first-step Probit for all participants in ADD, these estimates from the second-step ordinary least-squares for "savers" might reflect censoring or two-way causation. Indeed, both these sources of bias tend to induce a negative correlation between match rates and observed savings. Still, a regression that controlled for censoring (Schreiner, 2004d) produced very similar results, and two-way causation in ADD probably was weak. For example, program staff did not report purposely setting higher match rates for groups expected to have difficulty saving. Instead, they said that they set match rates according to constraints on enrollment and funding. In addition, the regression includes indicator variables for each program. These "fixed effects" should soak up much of any program-specific variation due to two-way causation.

At least for match rates of 1:1 versus 2:1 in ADD, the "fixed-goal effect" seems to have dominated the "substitution effect." For poor people saving for a "lumpy" purchase—precisely the case for IDAs in ADD—this is not implausible. The opportunity cost of lost matches due to not saving an additional $100 is the same at $1,900 as at $2,100, but, if a home requires a down payment of $2,000, participants may stop saving once they can buy the house, either because they need the cash for closing costs or because the marginal utility of current consumption exceeds the opportunity cost of lost matches.

The increase in monthly net IDA savings associated with a match rate of 2:1 versus a match rate greater than 2:1 may indicate a non-linear association; as match rates increase past 2:1, the strength of the "substitution effect" may grow and eventually swamp the "fixed-goal effect." At the same time, match rates greater than 2:1 had little within-program variation in ADD (Schreiner, 2004d), so policymakers should hesitate to lean heavily on this estimate.

Policy Implications

In ADD, higher match rates were strongly associated with a greater likelihood of being a "saver." For "savers," the "fixed-goal effect" seems to have dominated the "substitution effect" (at least in the most policy-relevant range of match rates of 1:1 to 2:1). Thus, higher match rates were associated with lower levels of monthly net IDA savings. From a policy perspective, these estimates may foreshadow possible conflicts between the three goals of inclusion, saving, and asset accumulation.

Higher match rates encourage inclusion because they make participants more likely to be "savers" able to make a meaningful matched withdrawal. Furthermore, given a level of IDA savings, a higher match rate obviously increases asset accumulation. At the same time, higher match rates were associated in ADD with lower IDA savings. Thus, higher match rates could be associated with either higher or lower monthly asset accumulation per participant (not per "saver"). On the one hand, an increase in the likelihood of being a "saver" would be associated with an increase in monthly asset accumulation per participant. On the other hand, a decrease in monthly net IDA savings by "savers" would be associated with a decrease in monthly asset accumulation per participant.

To check the net association, a simulation was done assuming that the match-rate estimates from ADD represented pure causal effects. In the simulation, all characteristics from ADD were left at their actual values, but the match rate for all participants was set to 1:1. The first-step Probit estimates α^* were then applied to the characteristics and the 1:1 match rate to predict the likelihood of being a "saver." This same process was also used to predict monthly net IDA savings for "savers" based on the second-step ordinary least-squares estimates β^* and θ^* (Positive predicted values were capped at each participant's match cap, and negative predicted values were capped at zero.) This process was then repeated, this time with all participants assigned a match rate of 2:1.

The simulation indicates that if all participants in ADD had had a match rate of 1:1, 46.6 percent would have been "savers" (table 6.6). With a match rate of 2:1, 53.1 percent would have been "savers," an increase of 6.5 percentage points. (The 6.5 percentage-point figure differs from the 8.9 percentage-point estimate in table 6.5 due to the non-linearity of the Probit model and due to the non-uniform distribution of participant and program characteristics

Table 6.6
Simulated Changes in the Likelihood of Being a "Saver,"
Monthly Net IDA Savings per "Saver," Monthly Net IDA Savings
per Participant, and Monthly Asset Accumulation per Participant in ADD
with a Match Rate of 1:1 versus a Match Rate of 2:1

Measure	Match rate		
	1:1	2:1	Change
Share of participants who were "savers" (%)	46.6	53.1	+6.5
Monthly net IDA savings per "saver" ($)	30.04	26.01	−4.03
Monthly net IDA savings per participant ($)	14.00	13.81	−0.19
Monthly asset accumulation per participant ($)	28.00	41.43	+13.43

Note: Simulated figures are based on estimates from two-step "Heckit" regressions for participants in ADD in which all characteristics are kept at their values from ADD but in which the match rate is set first for all participants to 1:1 and then to 2:1. Simulated monthly net IDA savings are constrained to be positive and no greater than the match cap for a given participant.

across match rates.) For "savers," the simulated shift in match rates from 1:1 to 2:1 produced a decrease in monthly net IDA savings of $4.03, from $30.04 to $26.01. (The $4.03 figure in the simulation differs from the $4.71 in table 6.5 due to censoring the predicted value at zero and at the match cap as well as the uneven distribution of characteristics across match rates.)

On net, the increase in the likelihood of being a "saver" and the decrease in monthly net IDA savings per "saver" combined to produce a decrease in monthly net IDA savings per participant. But the decrease is small ($0.19). Of course, given an increase in match rates from 1:1 to 2:1 and essentially no change in monthly net IDA savings per participant, monthly asset accumulation (net IDA savings plus match) increases a lot (by $13.43, from $28.00 to $41.43).

What does this mean for IDAs as a possible universal, lifelong, progressive asset-building policy? If participants in ADD do not resemble participants in an inclusive policy or if the regression estimates represent mostly correlations rather than causes, then this simulation may mean little. If ADD is somewhat representative, however, and if the regression estimates represent mostly causes, then the simulation highlights some trade-offs among the basic policy goals of IDAs. Higher match rates would increase inclusion and increase asset accumulation per participant, but they would decrease net IDA savings per "saver." Net IDA savings per participant would be essentially unchanged.

Which policy goals matter more? Most likely, inclusion and asset accumulation take precedence over saving. IDAs are first and foremost about inclusion

(Sherraden, 2005). Without participation, IDAs cannot help the poor to save and build assets. Also, asset accumulation—ownership through time—produces the "asset effects" described in chapter 2. Saving is clearly important, but, especially for the poor, saving is but a means to the end of asset accumulation and the purchase of large, lumpy, life-changing assets such as a home, post-secondary education, or microenterprise. From the perspective of America's anemic national saving, IDAs are probably not the solution. Even though ADD participants were poor, at least some of their IDA savings were "reshuffled" rather than "new" (Schreiner et al., 2001). Even if all IDA savings were "new," $16.60 per participant per month (about 1 percent of income for these low-income households) probably would not boost the U.S. household saving rate by much.

In qualitative work, ADD participants say that participation in IDAs sparked hope and helped them focus on future goals (Sherraden et al., 2003a). These reported effects were stronger for "savers" than for others (Moore et al., 2000). Also, preliminary estimates from the one program in ADD that randomized access to IDAs across qualified applicants suggest that IDAs accelerated asset accumulation—relative to a control group—for the three "cornerstone" matched uses of home ownership, post-secondary education, and microenterprise. All this argues for higher match rates. In ADD, higher match rates were associated with improved inclusion and asset accumulation with little harm to saving.

In a study of more than 800,000 employees eligible for 401(k) plans at 647 employers, Huberman, Iyengar, and Jiang (2003) found results remarkably similar to those here: the presence of a match (and higher match rates) were associated with increased participation and increased contributions. Furthermore, the increases were much higher for low-income employees than for others; indeed, higher match rates were associated with a decrease in contributions for high-income employees. Huberman, Iyengar, and Jiang (2003, p. 22) conclude that something resembling a universal, permanent IDA with higher match rates for the poor will boost saving and asset accumulation: "Voluntary participation and contributions in individual retirement accounts are likely to increase if the government were to match contributions. Moreover, the match will have the strongest impact on low-income members of society. And, if policy makers find it desirable to limit the subsidy to high-income people, match rates could be set to decline with income." If inclusion and saving in asset-building policy are primary policy goals, then the estimates from ADD suggest that similar lessons would apply to IDAs and the poor.

Match Cap (Savings Target)

The match cap determines the level of IDA savings eligible for matches. In ADD, the average match cap was $1,329, or about $39.56 per month. (The mean in table 6.5 of $41 is the participant-by-participant match cap per month.)

Economic theory typically predicts no match-cap effect on net IDA savings. In contrast, behavioral theory predicts a positive effect. Which view is supported in the ADD data, and what are the implications for policy?

In most economic models, participants have complete knowledge and effortlessly make rational decisions. Under this assumption, match caps are mere limits and so are not associated with desired net IDA savings (before or after accounting for censoring) nor with observed net IDA savings (after accounting for censoring). For participants whose desired net IDA savings exceed a given match cap, an increase in the match cap relaxes censoring and so causes an increase in observed net IDA savings. Under mainstream assumptions, however, desired net IDA savings remain unchanged. For example, if a participant has desired net IDA savings of $550 but observed net IDA savings are capped at $500, an increase in the cap to $600 increases observed net IDA savings to $550 but leaves desired net IDA savings unchanged. For participants whose desired net IDA savings do not exceed a given cap, a higher cap is not even associated with observed net IDA savings, let alone desired net IDA savings. For example, a participant who saves $300 with a $500 cap still saves $300 with a $600 cap. If match caps are mere limits, then match caps and desired net IDA savings should have no association in a regression that controls for censoring and that includes all characteristics that cause saving and that are correlated with match caps. Under mainstream economic assumptions, higher match caps increase observed net IDA savings and asset accumulation for participants who otherwise would have "maxed out" the IDA by saving up to the cap. For all other participants, however, increasing match caps does not affect observed net IDA savings nor asset accumulation. For all participants, higher match caps are unrelated to desired net IDA savings. If these assumptions hold, then the choice for policy makers is between lower match caps (and lower outlays for matches) versus higher match caps (and higher observed net IDA savings and asset accumulation for participants who would be constrained by a lower cap).

Behavioral theory assumes that participants can change the match cap—technically a limit—into a goal or target. Thus, the match cap is not only mechanically related with observed net IDA savings but also causally (and positively) related with desired net IDA savings. In short, the match cap becomes a savings target. This happens because *homo sapiens*—unlike *homo economicus*—has incomplete knowledge and must expend effort to figure out how much to save (Thaler, 2000). Financial decisions are especially difficult because they involve the future, uncertainty, and math. Rather than engage in costly and uncomfortable decision-making, people often prefer to fall into choices that they believe that wiser minds have selected (Huberman, Iyengar, and Jiang, 2003; Thaler and Sunstein, 2003; Bernheim, 2002). In effect, participants "interpret defaults as implicit advice" (Choi et al., 2003). For example, research on Individual Retirement Accounts and 401(k) plans finds that many non-poor people prefer to let someone else make their savings decisions for them or to save according to rules of thumb worn smooth by social convention or handed down from family or friends (Choi, Laibson, and Madrian, 2004; Benartzi and Thaler, 2002; Lusardi, 2000; Bernheim, 1998 and 1997). Apparently, a common rule of thumb is simply "save up to the match cap" (Milligan, 2003; Bernheim, 2002). According to Bernheim (1997, p. 30), "Individuals may attach significance to contribution limits . . . on the grounds that these limits reflect the judgment of experts." Many non-poor participants in 401(k) plans are bunched at the match cap, which they appear to use as a focal point (Choi, Laibson, and Madrian, 2004; Bernheim, 1999). (Of course, some bunching is due to the kink in the budget constraint at the match cap, see Moffitt, 1990, and Pudney, 1989.) When participants in 401(k) plans must opt out of a default contribution rate chosen by the plan sponsor rather than choose their own, they tend to stick with the default. In one case, 70 percent stayed with the default (Choi, Laibson, and Madrian, 2004). According to Gokhale, Kotlikoff, and Warshawsky (2001, p. 8), "Those employers who offer a defined-contribution plan with an employer match on employee contributions up to, say, 5 percent of pay are, perhaps unwittingly, suggesting that their workers contribute no more than 5 percent of their salary." Applied to the non-poor and put another way, the "power of suggestion" (Madrian and Shea, 2001) of IDA design means that, because participants tend to turn match caps into savings targets and then try to "max out" their match eligibility, match-cap policy may induce participants to save more than they otherwise would have done on their own. Indeed, most programs in ADD presented the match cap as a target and explicitly asked participants to try to save enough each month to "max out" their match eligibility. In turn, participants reported that they tried to respond to this expectation (Sherraden et al., 2004; Johnson et al., 2003).

Milligan (2003, p. 278) tests whether participants in Canada's Registered Retirement Savings Program turned limits into goals. Controlling for the censoring of desired savings at the match cap, a $1 increase in the match cap was associated with a fifty-cent increase in savings. This huge association is consistent with participants' turning limits into targets.

Did participants in ADD also do this? Stated another way, were match caps associated with desired net IDA savings? The absence of an association would support the hypothesis that limits are just limits. In contrast, the presence of an association would support the behavioral hypothesis that participants turn limits into goals. In this case, policy could increase not only observed IDA savings but also desired IDA savings by increasing match caps.

The average match cap in ADD was about $41 per month (table 6.5). A $10 increase in the monthly match cap was associated with a 1 percentage-point increase in the likelihood of being a "saver." While positive, this was not a strong association, and the estimate was not very precise ($p = 0.26$). This is consistent with the economic assumption that match caps were just limits. From a behavioral perspective, perhaps higher match caps exerted a "pull" on some participants that encouraged them to make a greater effort to be "savers" while discouraging others who found themselves saving less than what they believed was the "proper" amount as signaled by the match cap.

For "savers," a $1 increase in the monthly match cap was associated with an increase in monthly net IDA savings of $0.57 (p = 0.01). Given that monthly net IDA savings for "savers" in ADD averaged $29.08, this is a large association, and it strongly supports the idea that participants in ADD turned match caps into savings targets and thus that policy could increase desired savings by increasing the match cap.

Censoring or two-way causation might also have contributed to this estimated association, but they probably are not the most important factors. Schreiner (2004d) controls for censoring and finds that a $1 increase in the monthly match cap is associated with a $0.50 increase in monthly net IDA savings. As argued above, two-way causation was also weak, as match caps (and match rates) were determined mostly by funding conditions rather than the programs' expectations about how participants would save. Thus, the estimate here probably mostly represents participants' turning the match cap into a savings target.

Of course, the match cap is just one aspect of IDA design. In particular, program designers typically couple higher match rates with lower match caps (table 6.4). In the example of ADD, the average match cap for "savers" was $56.12 with a 1:1 match rate, $35.94 with a 2:1 match rate, and $27.20 with a match rate greater than 2:1.

How might the interaction of match caps and match rates be associated with IDAs' three goals of inclusion, saving, and asset accumulation? Simulations are a simple way to sort through the consequences of match rates' negative association with match caps, match rates' positive association with being a "saver," match rates' negative association with monthly net IDA savings, and match caps' positive association with monthly net IDA savings.

Two scenarios were simulated. In the first, participant and program characteristics were kept at their actual values from ADD, but the match rate was set to 1:1 and the monthly match cap was set to $56.12 (the average cap for "savers" with 1:1 match rates in ADD). The estimated coefficients α^*, β^*, and θ^* from the two-step "Heckit" were then used to compute the likelihood of being a "saver" and the value of monthly net IDA savings for "savers." (As usual, positive predicted values were capped at each participant's match cap, and negative predicted values were capped at zero.) The second scenario repeated this process with a match rate of 2:1 and a monthly match cap of $35.94.

Table 6.7 shows that the simulated move from a low-match-rate/high-match-cap regime to a high-match-rate/low-match-cap regime was associated with a

Table 6.7
Simulated Changes in the Likelihood of Being a "Saver,"
Monthly Net IDA Savings per "Saver," Monthly Net IDA Savings
per Participant, and Monthly Asset Accumulation per Participant
in ADD with a Match Rate of 1:1 and a Match Cap of $56.12 versus
a Match Rate of 2:1 and a Match Cap of $35.94

Measure	Combination of match rate and match cap		
	1:1 and $56.12	2:1 and $35.94	Change
Share of participants who were "savers" (%)	47.9	52.6	+4.7
Monthly net IDA savings per "saver" ($)	39.13	22.85	−16.28
Monthly net IDA savings per participant ($)	18.74	12.02	−6.72
Monthly asset accumulation per participant ($)	37.48	36.06	−1.42

Note: Simulated figures are based on estimates from two-step "Heckit" regressions for participants in ADD in which all characteristics are kept at their values from ADD but in which the match rate and match cap is set first for all participants to 1:1 and $56.12 and then to 2:1 and $35.94. Simulated monthly net IDA savings are constrained to be positive and no greater than the match cap for a given participant.

4.7 percentage point increase in the likelihood of being a "saver." This is no surprise, as match rates were strongly associated with being a "saver" while match caps were weakly associated with that outcome. If the goal is inclusion and if match rates and match caps must have an inverse relationship, then high match rates and low match caps are better than low match rates and high match caps.

In the regression, both the movement from a 1:1 match rate to a 2:1 match rate and the movement from a $56.12 match cap to a $35.94 match cap were associated with a decrease in monthly net IDA savings per "saver." The combined decrease was $16.28 (table 6.7), equivalent to more than half the average monthly net IDA savings of $29.08 for "savers."

How were the two simulated regime changes associated with IDA's second goal of saving? For these specific match-rate/match-cap regimes, the decrease in monthly net IDA savings per "saver" dominates the increase in the likelihood of being a "saver." Compared with a regime of 1:1/$56.12, a regime of 2:1/$35.94 was associated with a decrease in monthly net IDA savings per participant of $6.72. Relative to $16.60, the average monthly net IDA savings per participant in ADD, this is a large change.

How were simulated changes in the match-rate/match-cap regime associated with IDA's third goal of asset accumulation? It turns out that the increase in the likelihood of being a "saver" and the increase in the match rate more or less balanced out against the decrease in the level of asset accumulation per participant. In the 1:1/$56.12 regime, monthly asset accumulation was $37.48, whereas in the 2:1/$35.94 regime, it was $36.06, a difference of $1.42.

These simulations highlight possible trade-offs between the three goals of IDAs and the match-rate/match-cap regime. Higher match rates (usually coupled with lower match caps) were associated with greater inclusion via a higher likelihood that participants were "savers." But higher match rates (and lower match caps) were also associated with lower saving. On net, the changes in the likelihood of being a "saver" and the changes in the level of saving more or less balanced out and so were not strongly associated with changes in asset accumulation.

Of course, these two specific match-rate/match-cap combinations are particular to ADD and do not necessarily represent the only policy-relevant regimes. If budgets permit, high match rates could be combined with high match caps. In general, however, there are budget constraints. The two specific cases here had about the same monthly asset accumulation per participant, but the 1:1/$56.12 regime implied lower outlays for matches ($18.74 versus $24.02) than the 2:1/$35.94 regime. If saving, asset accumulation, and cost matter more than being a "saver," then these simulations suggest that a higher match cap and a lower match rate are better than the converse.

Match-Cap Structure

About 52 percent of ADD participants had annual match caps. For these participants, unused eligibility was lost with each passing year, although excess balances were carried forward and became matchable in the new year. Thus, annual match caps created a "use-it-or-lose-it" incentive. For example, suppose a participant has a $500 annual match cap, a two-year time cap, and deposits of $300 in year 1 and $700 in year 2. At the start of month 13, $200 of unused match eligibility is lost, so total matchable deposits after two years are $800 ($300 in year 1 and $500 in year 2, with $200 of excess balances after year 2). If deposits are $700 in year 1 and $300 in year 2, the $200 of excess balances at the end of year 1 are carried forward and become matchable in year 2, so total matchable deposits after two years are $1,000 with no excess balances after year 2. In the United States, Individual Retirement Accounts and 401(k) plans have what amount to annual match caps.

The other 48 percent of participants in ADD had match caps defined over the lifetime of the demonstration. For example, suppose that a participant has a $1,000 lifetime match cap, a two-year time cap, and deposits of $300 in year 1 and $700 in year 2. Total matchable deposits in the two years are $1,000 (with no excess balances after year 2), just as they would be if the entire $1,000 were deposited on the day of enrollment or on the last day before the time cap.

Match-Cap Theory

Was match-cap structure associated with savings outcomes in ADD? In most economic theory, the match-cap structure is irrelevant. Rational, self-disciplined participants with annual caps use loans and the ability to carry excess balances forward to work around the annual cap and so end up saving as much as they would have saved with a lifetime cap. (The only real effect of annual caps is to delay some matched withdrawals because match eligibility is released only over a stretch of several years rather than all at once upon enrollment.)

Behavioral theory posits four factors that contribute (in different directions) to the relevance of match-cap structure. First, some participants with annual caps can save as much as they want only if they take full advantage of their match eligibility in some (perhaps all) years. Yet, because income and expenses fluctuate from year to year, their saving may come up short in some years. To meet their goals in spite of the annual match-cap structure, they must get loans and deposit the proceeds in their IDAs before they lose that year's match eligibility. But they may not be able to get a loan, or they may not want to borrow, or they may not even consider borrowing as an option. Thus, borrowing constraints coupled with annual caps may depress savings outcomes.

Second, participants may sometimes lack perfect self-discipline. Behavioral theory recognizes that people procrastinate, especially when it comes to saving. From the perspective of their own long-term well-being, people often place inconsistently and disproportionately high value on immediate costs and benefits relative to future costs and benefits (Frederick, Loewenstein and O'Donoghue, 2002; Angeletos et al., 2001; Maital, 1986; Ainslie, 1984). In the case of saving, the sacrifices are immediate and the rewards are delayed, exacerbating the urge to put off for tomorrow what could be saved today. Lifetime match caps permit (and may encourage) procrastination; participants can let themselves avoid extra effort today in the belief or hope that saving will be easier tomorrow. In contrast, the "use-it-or-lose-it" nature of annual caps may help deter procrastination and thus improve savings outcomes.

Third, "use-it-or-lose-it" incentives may help participants to mentally "lock away" savings in IDAs. Taking cues from external institutions set up by policy and from internal rules set up by themselves and by social norms, people tend to assign resources to "spendable" or "untouchable" accounts (Prelec and Loewenstein, 1998; Beverly, 1997; Shefrin and Thaler, 1988; Thaler and Shefrin, 1981). For example, cash is usually considered "spendable." To keep cash from "burning a hole in their pockets," some people purposely avoid holding cash, for example through "envelop budgeting" or direct deposit of paychecks (Beverly, McBride, and Schreiner, 2003). Resources are less likely to be consumed when being out-of-sight puts them out-of-mind. Participants usually consider IDAs balances as "untouchable," mentally earmarking them for specific future asset purchases. Exhortations from program staff (and sometimes explicit program rules) encourage this view. The "use-it-or-lose-it" nature of annual caps helps participants to put resources in the "IDA lockbox" sooner than do lifetime caps. A participant with a lifetime cap might wait to put resources into the IDA because such delays do not forfeit match eligibility but do help to avoid the hassle of making an emergency unmatched withdrawal. Funds kept outside an IDA, however, are more likely to be spent on consumption, emergency or otherwise. Annual caps may boost savings outcomes by encouraging participants to mentally "lock away" their resources sooner.

Fourth, the "use-it-or-lose-it" nature of annual caps may breed "saving habits." The received wisdom from financial planners and consumer-economics extension agents is that steady saving leads to greater asset accumulation. To encourage regular deposits, a few IDA programs outside of ADD have even gone so far as to impose *monthly* match caps. The idea is that having saved once decreases the mental effort of saving again, perhaps even to the point of making saving mindlessly automatic. As with mental lockboxes, saving habits decrease the temptation to consume. Compared with lifetime caps, annual caps do more to encourage participants to save something sooner and thus are more likely to promote a habit that decreases the cost of constantly having to choose whether to save or consume.

In sum, lifetime match caps afford greater flexibility. For *homo economicus*, greater flexibility means greater well-being. In contrast, annual match caps impose a "use-it-or-lose-it" constraint. For *homo sapiens*, such constraints may improve savings outcomes and well-being by helping participants to overcome their imperfect self-discipline and—through mental lockboxes and habit formation—by decreasing participants' need for self-discipline.

Match Caps in ADD

The ADD regressions associate savings outcomes with match-cap structures based on within-program variation in match-cap structure. Unfortunately, only two programs (Near Eastside and Shorebank) exhibit such variation (table 6.8). At Near Eastside, the variation was perfectly correlated with participants' AFIA status. This means that the regression estimates might plausibly reflect not the causal effects of the match-cap structure but rather omitted characteristics correlated with savings outcomes at these two programs (perhaps different omitted characteristics at each program) that happen to affect savings outcomes in the same direction. Thus, policy design should not place too much emphasis on the estimates here.

In the first-step Probit, having an annual cap rather than a lifetime cap was associated with a 21.4 percentage-point ($p = 0.03$) increase in the chances of being a "saver" (table 6.5). About 52 percent of ADD participants were "savers," so this is a huge association. It is also somewhat surprising. While annual match caps may improve savings outcomes by discouraging procrastination, locking savings away, and fomenting habits, their "use-it-or-lose-it" feature could also discourage participants who save little at first and who thus have low match eligibility in later years. In contrast, participants with lifetime match

Table 6.8

Distribution of ADD Participants by Match-Cap Structure and AFIA Status and by Program

Program	Number of Participants	Match-cap structure			AFIA status	
		Annual	Lifetime	non-AFIA	AFIA
ADVOCAP	82	82	0	64	18
CAAB	142	0	142	86	56
CVCAC	154	0	154	98	56
Near Eastside	190	68	122	68	122
Heart of America	91	0	91	91	0
Mercy Corps	118	118	0	118	0
MACED	65	0	65	65	0
CAPTC Small-scale	163	163	0	163	0
Shorebank	203	129	74	203	0
WSEP	231	0	231	134	97
Alternatives FCU	91	0	91	91	0
Foundation Communities	125	125	0	122	3
Bay Area	239	0	239	184	55
CAPTC Large-scale	456	456	0	456	0
Total:	2,350	1,141	1,209	1,943	407

Note: Only two programs (Near Eastside and Shorebank) have within-program variation in the match-cap structure among their participants. In contrast, 6 programs have significant variation in AFIA status.

caps might press on even if they saved nothing at first, knowing that they can still take full advantage of their match eligibility at any time before the deadline. In any case, the estimate may very well be a spurious correlation due to sparse within-program variation in match-cap structure in the ADD data.

In the second step for "savers," annual caps were associated with almost $6 less net IDA savings per month (p = 0.07). The greater flexibility of lifetime caps may explain this large association. It is most likely spurious, however, due lack of variation in the data. It seems unlikely that annual caps could be positively and strongly associated with being a "saver" and at the same time negatively and strongly associated with monthly net IDA savings for "savers." These estimates may merely reflect omitted factors at Near Eastside and Shorebank and should not be taken as a definitive guide to policy.

If IDAs are to be a permanent policy, however, then the question of match-cap structure is probably moot. Annual caps—or perhaps hybrid caps—are more feasible. For three reasons, "lifetime" caps of the kind found in ADD are likely possible only in short-lived programs, not in permanent policies.

First, lifetime caps might allow blatant asset shifts or other subversions of IDAs. In principle, people could save nothing and then borrow (or otherwise use a confederate's money), put in a deposit equal to lifetime match eligibility, buy an asset with a matched withdrawal, sell the asset, and then split the profit with the confederate. (No such cases have been identified in ADD, but they are possible, and the incentives grow with the level of match eligibility. Banks and other lenders would have strong incentives to make loans to fund IDAs if they had large lifetime match caps.) On the front end, if people fear that the IDA policy will not last, then they may try to use up all their lifetime match eligibility before the policy is revoked. If many households rush to buy subsidized assets while they still can, saving and asset accumulation may increase, but it may also strain the fisc and bid up the prices of match-eligible assets, much as asset subsidies for the non-poor have done for housing (Englehardt, 1993), stocks, and agricultural land.

Second, lifetime match caps for the poor might be perceived as unfair, given that most current asset subsidies for the non-poor have annual caps. (Whether this perception of unfairness is itself unfair—given the massive asset subsidies for the non-poor—is another question.)

Third—and probably most importantly—annual caps are simpler to administer and to budget for (Gokhale, Kotlikoff, and Warshawsky, 2001). Annual caps can be managed through current-year tax returns. Lifetime caps, in contrast, would require linking savings for a given person across all previous years since birth.

A hybrid annual/lifetime cap might feasibly capture the advantages of both types of match-cap structures. The key is to accrue match eligibility through time (so that younger people cannot subvert the policy on the front end) and to limit total accrued match eligibility (so that older people cannot subvert the policy on the back end). For example, people might accrue $1,000 of match eligibility at birth and then an additional $1,000 of eligibility with each birthday until death. Unused eligibility could be carried forward, up to some limit (for example, $20,000). Canada and the United Kingdom already have asset-building accounts with this hybrid structure (Milligan, 2003).

Use of Automatic Transfer

Participants in ADD could request that their depository institution move funds from their passbook or checking accounts into their IDAs at some set interval (usually monthly). Participants could also request that their employers use direct deposit to put their paychecks into their IDAs.

As discussed in chapter 3, the use of automatic transfer should improve savings outcomes by reducing the transaction costs of physically putting money in an IDA, removing the need to remember to make a deposit, removing the need to make recurrent choices to save, and helping people to "pay themselves first."

Even if automatic transfer per se does not cause greater savings outcomes, its use may be correlated with omitted characteristics (such as financial sophistication, experience with depository institutions, or employment at a large firm) that do cause greater savings outcomes. That is, people who tend to save more—for whatever reason—are probably also more likely to use automatic transfer. This induces a spurious positive correlation between savings outcomes and the use of automatic transfer.

It is also possible that participants who use automatic transfer might end up saving less. This might happen if they choose to transfer very small amounts because they fear overdrawing the source account, desire to keep funds (mentally) liquid and to reserve some ongoing control, prefer to "feel" they are actively saving by hand-carrying cash to the depository institution, and fail to add to their automatic transfers with ad hoc deposits when they can because of inertia.

Regardless of these possible "negative" factors, financial planners and consumer-economics extension agents unanimously believe that automatic transfer improves savings outcomes. In 401(k) plans (the largest subsidized savings-account policy for the non-poor), all deposits—by law—are made by the employer via direct deposit.

In ADD, the use of automatic transfer was associated with a 16.7 percentage-point increase in the likelihood of being a "saver" (p = 0.01, table 6.5). Given that 52 percent of all participants were "savers," this is a large association. While automatic transfer may partly serve as a proxy for omitted characteristics that improve savings outcomes, the use of automatic transfer per se probably improves outcomes as well.

How can program design take advantage of this? At the least, the financial-education classes required of IDA participants can discuss the advantages of automatic transfer and perhaps walk participants through the initial paperwork. It is possible that many ADD participants did not use automatic transfer simply because they never considered using it. Classes can also ask employed participants to check with their employers on the availability of direct deposit as well as show participants where they can find the account numbers and bank-identification numbers needed to set up direct deposit. Some IDA programs might even want to require the use of automatic transfer, helping unbanked enrollees set up a passbook or checking account into which they make deposits (perhaps direct deposits of paychecks) and from which the IDA receives automatic transfers. This "liquid" account would complement the "illiquid" IDA, perhaps providing the "silken handcuffs" that help participants mentally commit to long-term saving while also allowing unfettered access to funds in an emergency. Finally, classes could also cover basic account management to mitigate the risk of overdrawing the source account.

For "savers" in ADD, the use of automatic transfer was not associated with monthly net IDA savings (p = 0.84, table 6.5). This is surprising, not only because theory and received wisdom predict a positive association but also because the use of automatic transfer was strongly and positively associated with being a "saver," and whatever forces are at work there should work in the same way for the level of savings. There are some theoretical reasons why automatic transfer might not increase savings, but these seem unlikely to dominate. About 6 percent of all IDA participants—and 7 percent of "savers," or ninety-two people—used automatic transfer, so the small sample may have contributed to the statistically insignificant estimate.

Why did so few ADD participants use automatic transfer? The data provide a few clues. At least some participants did not have a choice. For example, the 23 percent of participants who were unbanked at enrollment could not have used automatic transfer without first opening a non-IDA account. Likewise, employed participants could not have used direct deposit unless their employers offered it. About 83 percent of ADD participants were employed, but the share of these with access to direct deposit is unknown. Among participants who used automatic transfer, 93 percent owned another account, and 89 percent were employed. All but one user of automatic transfer reported owning a passbook or checking account or being employed.

Participants who used direct deposit probably had to put all their take-home pay in the IDA. They were likely reluctant to do this, both because IDAs were labeled for long-term savings and because programs imposed (mild) restrictions on unmatched withdrawals. If participants put all their pay into IDAs, they would have had to hassle with constant unmatched withdrawals to cover regular expenses. Thus, direct deposit into IDAs—even when available—was probably rarely a relevant option. (Of course, participants could have had direct deposit to a passbook or checking account and then made automatic transfers from there to IDAs.)

The bulk of automatic transfers in ADD probably came from passbook or checking accounts. But even though 77 percent of participants held such accounts at enrollment, many had such low balances that using automatic transfer would have meant risking overdrafts. Among account holders, the median in the highest-balance account at enrollment was $200, and 90 percent had less than $1,400. Furthermore, some participants may have held their savings at a different depository institution than the IDA, complicating the set-up of automatic transfer. For most ADD participants, automatic transfer from a passbook or checking account was probably not a very relevant option.

In sum, three known factors contributed to infrequent use of automatic transfer in ADD. First, some participants lacked access because they did not own non-IDA accounts or their employers did not offer direct deposit. Second, direct deposit of all take-home pay would have required constant unmatched withdrawals. Third, most participants with passbook or checking accounts had low balances and thus little to transfer.

Given the regression estimates from ADD, these factors suggest two policy options for boosting savings outcomes, both in IDAs and in general. First, employers could be required to offer direct deposit. Second, employers could be required to permit employees to split their pay among a check and any number of direct deposits, for example to 401(k) plans, IDAs, and other passbook and checking accounts. Currently, employers who sponsor 401(k) plans and/or who offer direct deposit routinely make these sorts of splits. Allowing employees to split pay across more accounts does not pose any special technological hurdles. (The largest payroll-processing firm already offers this capability, although it seems likely that few employers are aware of this and that even fewer facilitate the use of the option for their employees.) Such splits would allow direct deposit to an IDA without forcing the participant to put in (and then take out) all his or her take-home pay.

By the same logic, IDA saving would increase if tax refunds could be split across multiple accounts. (Refunds in tax year 2003 could be direct-deposited only to a single account.) People are more apt to save (and to save more) from their annual tax returns than from their periodic wages (see chapter 5). Depositing tax refunds directly—without the cash passing first through a taxpayer's hands—should increase long-term saving and asset accumulation. Allowing the refund to be split across checks and direct deposits to multiple accounts would increase the use of direct deposit, and increased use of direct deposit would boost saving.

Months Eligible to Make Matchable Deposits

Unlike a permanent IDA policy, ADD set limits on the number of months in which a participant was eligible to make matchable deposits. The time cap varied both across programs and across participants in a given program. The average participant had a time cap of 33.6 months.

A longer time cap should increase the likelihood of being a "saver." The more time with an IDA, the more likely an "up" spell will make saving easier, if only temporarily. Also, participants with distant deadlines get less discouraged if they have saved little so far because they know that they still have time.

For "savers," a longer time cap should be associated with lower net IDA savings per month. First, putting resources in IDAs in the initial months or years might mean reshuffling existing assets from other forms into IDAs. As months pass, however, the stock available for reshuffling may dwindle (Feenberg and Skinner, 1989). Second, "new" saving requires extra effort and/ or additional time to reduce consumption and/or to increase the amount and/ or quality of production in the household and/or market. With time, participants get tired. Third, participants may be more motivated at first as they learn about IDAs and attend the required financial-education classes. As the newness wears off and the classes wind down, the spark may ebb. Furthermore, IDA staff may spend more time with new participants. Fourth, participants are more likely to enroll at a high point in their financial lives (for example, just after starting a new job or receiving a tax refund). With time, their finances may regress to a more typical state, leading to less saving.

Finally, a longer time cap could either increase or decrease long-term asset accumulation. Even though savings per month (per "saver" and possibly per participant) may fall with time, the increase in the months available to save may (or may not) compensate.

In the ADD regression, the time cap was represented by four indicator variables (twenty-four months or less, twenty-five to thirty-five months, thirty-six months, and thirty-seven months or more). In accord with expectations, longer time caps were associated with a greater likelihood of being a "saver." Compared with participants with time caps of twenty-four months or less, participants with time caps of thirty-seven months or more were 19.5 percentage points more likely to be "savers" ($p = 0.01$, table 6.9). The differences were also large—but less precise—for twenty-five to thirty-five months (10.6 percentage points, $p = 0.14$) and for thirty-six months (8.7 percentage points, $p = 0.36$). The estimate for time caps of thirty-seven months or more was statistically different from those for twenty-five to thirty-five months and for thirty-six months with p-values of 0.08 or less (tests not shown). In sum, the move from time caps of two years or less to time caps of up to three years was associated with an increase in the likelihood of being a "saver" of about ten percentage points. Moving to time caps of more than three years added about ten more percentage points. These large effects are consistent with the idea that a longer (perhaps permanent) program includes more participants as "savers."

In accord with expectations, longer time caps were associated with lower monthly savings. Compared with "savers" with time caps of twenty-four months

Table 6.9

Associations between Savings Outcomes and IDA Design and Program Structure:
Months to Make Matchable Deposits and Hours of General Financial Education

Independent variable	Prob.("Saver")			Net IDA savings/month		
	Mean	Δ% pts.	p-value	Mean	Δ$	p-value
Months to make matchable deposits						
24 or less	0.25			0.22		
25 to 35	0.19	+10.6	0.14	0.20	-4.64	0.04
36	0.28	+8.7	0.36	0.25	-5.32	0.07
37 or more	0.28	+19.5	0.01	0.33	-6.45	0.01
Hours of general financial education						
Zero				0.09		
More than zero				0.91	-1.14	0.78
1 to 10 (spline)				9.0	+1.16	0.01
10 to 20 (spline)				2.3	+0.06	0.76
20 to 30 (spline)				0.4	+0.18	0.51

Note: All regression estimates were derived from a single two-step "Heckit" regression. The first step was a Probit (n=2,350, k=104) for the likelihood of being a "saver." The second step was ordinary least-squares (n=1,232, k=111) for net IDA savings per month for "savers." Means were taken over non-missing observations.

Table 6.10
Simulated Changes in the Likelihood of Being a "Saver,"
Monthly Net IDA Savings per "Saver," Monthly Net IDA Savings
per Participant, and Net IDA Savings per Participant in the Lifetime of ADD
with a Time Cap of 24 Months versus a Time Cap of 37 Months

| | Time cap | | |
Measure	24 months	37 months	Change
Share of participants who were "savers" (%)	45.2	59.9	+14.7
Monthly net IDA savings per "saver" ($)	31.81	26.33	−5.48
Monthly net IDA savings per participant ($)	14.38	15.77	+1.39
Net IDA savings per participant in lifetime of ADD ($)	345	583	+238

Note: Simulated figures are based on estimates from two-step "Heckit" regressions for participants in ADD in which all characteristics are kept at their values from ADD but in which the time cap is set first for all participants to 24 months and then to 37 months. Simulated monthly net IDA savings are constrained to be positive and no greater than the match cap for a given participant.

or less, other "savers" had about $4.50–$6.50 less net IDA savings per month. (The three estimates for caps longer than two years are not statistically different from each other.) Given more months to save, participants in ADD saved less per month.

How were longer time caps associated with asset accumulation? A simulation is used to sort out the consequences of the positive association with being a "saver" and the negative association with monthly net IDA savings for "savers." In the two scenarios, ADD participants were assigned first a time cap of twenty-four months and then a time cap of thirty-seven months.

The simulated move from a twenty-four-month cap to a thirty-seven-month cap was associated with an increase in the share of participants who were "savers" of 14.7 percentage points and with a decrease in monthly net IDA savings per "saver" of $5.48 (table 6.10). This translates to an increase in monthly net IDA savings per participant of $1.39. Given this increase and that longer time caps give participants more months to save, simulated net IDA savings per participant over the lifetime of ADD with a thirty-seven-month time cap was $238 more than with a twenty-four-month time cap ($583 versus $345).

In sum, longer time caps were associated with greater achievement of all three IDA goals. More participants were "savers," and this inclusion more than compensated for lower monthly net IDA savings per "saver," leading to higher monthly net IDA savings per participant. With more months to save and with more saving per month, longer time caps were associated—for a given match rate—with more asset accumulation over the lifetime of ADD.

From the perspective of long-term development, this analysis supports longer time caps. The longest possible time cap would be permanent, from birth to death. For example, Individual Retirement Accounts and 401(k) plans for the non-poor are permanent, available to anyone with earned income and—for 401(k) plans—a sponsoring employer.

In general, "use-it-or-lose-it" incentives mean that responses to transitory policies are stronger (per unit of time and/or per person) than responses to permanent policies (Garfinkle, Manski, and Michalopoulos, 1992). At least in the range of time caps in ADD, however, the increased likelihood of being a "saver" compensated for weakened monthly savings. This may or may not hold in a permanent policy (no more than 100 percent of participants can be "savers," and monthly savings could fall so far that even complete inclusion would not compensate). Longer time caps, however, can only increase lifetime asset accumulation per participant.

As importantly, a permanent policy might make saving and asset accumulation for the poor a social norm. People would grow up knowing that saving in IDAs was a "good thing." They could plan matched withdrawals for years or decades, buying different assets at different stages in the life cycle (Sherraden, 1991). Families at reunions and co-workers at the water-cooler would discuss the pros and cons of different saving strategies (Bernheim, 2002). Asset building for the poor might become part of the "American way of life," something that people do and accept without thinking. While such long-term social impacts of asset-building policy are nearly impossible to predict or quantify, belief in them has been reinforced over and over (but not for the poor).

Financial Education

Subsidized saving for the poor through IDAs differs in two main ways from subsidized saving for the non-poor through Individual Retirement Accounts and 401(k) plans. First, IDAs provide subsidies via matches rather than tax breaks. Second, IDAs come bundled with mandatory financial education. ADD required all participants to attend financial-education classes. Was this financial education associated with improved savings outcomes?

Beyond the "does it work?" question, a policy of required financial education faces two other challenges. First, it is paternalistic. If the poor are not so different from the non-poor, then why do they need financial education? While both the poor and the non-poor benefit from financial education, the benefits are larger for the poor, probably because they have more to learn. Second, the skilled labor required to provide financial education is costly. IDA-program costs are a concern (Schreiner, 2004a; Sherraden, 2000), especially for a permanent, universal policy. Financial education—if not highly effective—might be one place to cut costs.

This section presents a rationale for financial education, reviews the goals of financial education, summarizes research on the effectiveness of financial education in 401(k) plans, and discusses financial education in ADD. Each additional hour (up to ten) of attendance at general financial-education classes was associated with an increase in monthly net IDA savings for "savers" of $1.16. Beyond ten hours, more financial education was not associated with higher IDA savings. For policy, this suggests not only that financial education may be important but also that its costs may be contained—without trading-off effectiveness—by limiting the number of hours required.

Why Require Financial Education?

According to Beverly and Sherraden (1999, p. 464), "The extent to which an individual understands the process and benefits of asset accumulation is likely to affect her willingness to save." To this end, financial education in IDAs aims to increase awareness of saving as a wise choice and to strengthen future orientation. It conveys the rules of IDAs and practical techniques for how to save. Classes also provide, as a by-product, an opportunity for participants to receive (and give) peer support.

Financial education in IDAs is mandatory rather than optional because people—poor or non-poor—tend to underestimate its benefits. As stated by Bernheim (1994, p. 59), "Unsophisticated individuals may not recognize or acknowledge the need for advice in the first place." Simply put, people do not know what they do not know. (Of course, this is the same rationale for compulsory schooling and required subjects; few students are good judges of what they will need to know as adults.) In qualitative interviews, ADD participants often reported that financial education did indeed turn out to be in their best interests even though they said that they would not have attended classes on their own (Johnson et al., 2003).

The poor in particular are vulnerable to "inadvertent ignorance." People usually learn about finances, saving, and asset accumulation via rules of thumb that they pick up by observing and listening to friends and family or by making their own mistakes in the "school of hard knocks" (Lusardi, 2000; Bernheim, 1995). The friends and family of the poor, however, are less likely to serve as knowledgeable sources of financial information or as positive examples of saving and asset accumulation. As argued in chapter 2, saving and asset accumulation may drift to the fringes of the worldview of the poor because they grow up in a context were saving and asset accumulation are rare. For example, Sherraden et al. (2004) report that, thanks to financial education, ADD participants interviewed at the one program with an experimental design were more likely to track their workplace 401(k) balances. Some members of the control group, in contrast, did not even know that their 401(k) balances were savings.

Financial education is indeed paternalistic in that it assumes that people save less than they should. If people can judge what is best for them, then it is wasteful to require financial education or to spend public funds on it. Still, after the fact, most people say that they wish that they had saved more (Lusardi, 2000; Bernheim, 1995). Americans rarely oppose the constant stream of self-interested advertising urging them to consume more, so it seems inconsistent to worry that public-service campaigns urging them to consume less would somehow infringe on personal freedom. Except perhaps in deep economic depressions, saving also has positive macroeconomic spillovers, and few Americans have qualms about government efforts to promote saving in times of crisis (for example, the "buy bonds" campaign in World War II). Even simple financial-education messages may be able to turn the tide of national saving. For example, Bernheim (1994) attributes much of the high personal saving rate in Japan to a postwar government campaign that told citizens that they should save one-fifth of their income.

Requiring attendance at financial-education classes may also serve a latent targeting role. By increasing the cost of participation in terms of time, requiring classes may screen out non-poor people who, compared with the poor, have less time relative to non-time resources (Besley and Kanbur, 1991). Classes may also have a latent political role; some people may want the poor to "pay" for their IDA subsidies by attending required classes.

Goals of Financial Education

A central goal of financial education is *financial literacy*, the ability to understand financial terms and concepts and to translate knowledge into behavior, including such skills as balancing a checkbook and managing cash flows in other accounts, preparing a budget and tracking spending, managing debt, and saving and investing (Beverly, 2004; Beverly and Burkhalter, 2003; Jacob, Hudson, and Bush, 2000). As they transfer these skills, mandatory financial-education classes for IDA participants aim to instill awareness of the importance of finances and of financial choices, to strengthen future orientation, and to transfer psychological and behavioral saving strategies.

Awareness. Financial education aims to make people more aware of the choices that they might make, the various possible consequences of those choices, and the likelihood of realizing those consequences. For example, classroom lessons might highlight that a household can make a budget and track spending and that this may spark a newfound awareness of financial issues that may, in turn, decrease consumption and increase saving (Ameriks, Caplin, and Leahy, 2002; Caskey, 2001). Or classes might point out that frequent deposits tend to increase asset accumulation, or that saving is less psychologically taxing for participants who take the monthly choice of whether to save "out of their hands" by using automatic transfer or by making an internal rule to treat monthly deposits as if they were bills.

When it comes to saving, people in general—and the poor in particular—often lack accurate models of how choices are connected with outcomes (Bernheim, 1994). The temporal space between the short-term costs of saving and the long-term benefits only drive a bigger wedge between perceptions and reality. Furthermore, the links between current sacrifice and future gain tend to be uncertain, subtle, and difficult to discern or imagine. Even the non-poor—most of whose wealth comes from gifts of assets from Nature or from prior generations (see chapter 2)—often misperceive these links. Of course, the poor have fewer chances to see how saving might affect long-term well-being. Financial education might help move subjective worldviews closer to objective reality. For example, it could discuss the long-term costs of renting versus owning or the effects of post-secondary education on lifetime income. Classes could also play a role in informing participants of the rules for means-tested public assistance. For decades, low asset limits sent a message that the poor could not (or should not) save. Recent changes have relaxed asset limits on public assistance—and explicitly exempted IDA balances in some states—but many poor people do not realize this (Hogarth and Lee, 2000).

Future orientation. Weak imagination—for all people, poor or non-poor—works against saving (Frederick, Loewenstein, and O'Donoghue, 2002; Becker and Mulligan, 1997; Ramsey, 1929). The poor may stay poor in part because they miss opportunities to exchange small current costs for large future benefits because they fail to appreciate (via imagination) the future benefits. Financial education in IDAs aims not only to make participants aware of saving as a wise choice but also to focus their attention on the future and to prod them to imagine what might be if they save now. Classes "would be designed to structure people's thoughts of their own economic life in the long term" (Sherraden 1991, p. 204). As people think more about the future, they tend to place greater value on their future well-being (Becker and Mulligan, 1997). In turn, this decreases the cost of future consumption in terms of current consumption and thus increases saving. (Becker and Mulligan's model also predicts that greater wealth—from greater saving—will increase future orientation.) Sherraden et al. (2004) report that ADD participants say that financial education helps to structure their mind-set in just this way.

Although asset ownership may spark greater future orientation because the resources in IDAs give people more to look forward to (Sherraden, 1991), some degree of future orientation—as well as beliefs that current choices can affect future outcomes—are required if people are to save and maintain assets in the first place (Becker and Mulligan, 1997; Clancy, 1995). One way financial education might encourage this is through exercises in strategic personal financial planning. Making a plan for matched withdrawals or drawing up a budget helps participants to direct their thoughts toward the future. Such plans make explicit links between current choices and future opportunities. Classes might also spark participants to think about the future simply by asking them to list goals and to describe what they would have to do to reach them. In essence, asking people to think about the future may boost future orientation.

How to save. Even if people know that saving is a wise choice and even if they can imagine its future benefits, they may still not know how to do it. Financial education in IDAs teaches saving techniques. Beverly, McBride, and Schreiner (2003) describe two broad types of strategies—psychological and behavioral—commonly taught in financial-education classes.

Psychological strategies change minds. They build a conceptual understanding of resource flows, saving goals, and self-imposed mental constraints. Classes may ask participants to use psychological strategies through setting a saving goal, proposing a budget, or earmarking income from some source (for example, a second job or tax refunds) for saving rather than as "spending money." Using such slogans as "Pay yourself first," classes might suggest that participants use the psychological strategy of treating monthly deposits as bills that must be paid rather than as something to be done only if money is "left over." Labeling accounts might also help participants to set IDAs psychologically apart from funds seen as available for consumption (for example, by calling an account a "home buyer's IDA" rather than simply an "IDA").

Once minds are changed, *behavioral strategies* change actions. They aim to help people to follow through on their plans to control consumption, make deposits, and refrain from withdrawals. Behavioral strategies might include limiting consumption quality ("buy only generic brands") or quantity ("buy no more than one cup of coffee a day"). They include internal rules about spending more time and effort in household production (for example, "eat out no more than once a week" or "clip coupons"). Behavioral strategies also include commitments that put resources out of reach, for example, by signing up for automatic transfer, choosing to receive the Earned Income Tax Credit in a lump-sum or withholding too much income tax, cutting up ATM cards or credit cards, waiting to cash checks, or locking funds up in an account that threatens a substantial penalty for early withdrawal. Another behavioral strategy is to work more in the labor market.

Financial Education for Non-IDA Saving

Research on 401(k) plans and other types of saving consistently finds that financial education improves savings outcomes. Furthermore, the improvements are greatest for poorer participants. For example, case studies of 401(k) plans indicate that increased financial education is associated with increased participation rates and contribution rates (Richardson, 1995; Borleis and Wedell, 1994).

In academic work, Bayer, Bernheim, and Scholz (1996) find that more frequent corporate-sponsored retirement seminars were associated with both higher participation rates and with higher levels of contributions to 401(k) plans. The associations were strongest among non-highly compensated employees.

Bernheim and Garrett (2003) also report positive associations between educational offerings and participation in 401(k) plans. Participation rates were twelve percentage points higher in firms that offered financial education. In these firms that offered financial education, participation rates were twenty percentage points higher for employees who attended classes. Bernheim and Garrett (2003) estimate that financial education at work was associated with a 1.7 percentage-point increase in the overall—not just 401(k)—rate of saving from income. Low-income and/or low-wealth savers were the drivers behind this finding: "Education encourages saving among those who save too little but not among those who already save enough" (Bernheim and Garrett, 2003, p. 1508). People who attended financial education on the job also tended to listen to friends and family less for financial advice, so financial education may help to expand worldviews.

Bernheim, Garrett, and Maki (2001) analyze the long-term asset accumulation of people who grew up in states that had mandated consumer-education curricula—many of which included financial education—in public grade schools and high schools. Compared with others, people who grew up in states with these mandates had greater wealth in adulthood. Because the mandates were probably uncorrelated with the omitted characteristics of the survey respondents, this is strong evidence that financial education causes higher asset accumulation and that the effects last a long time (although they may also take a long time to build up). The effects were large: "Net worth is higher by roughly one year's worth of earnings for the typical individual who was exposed to a mandate" (Bernheim, Garrett, and Maki, 2001, p. 460). Furthermore, financial-education classes may substitute for "financial education" at home (as indicated by having "frugal" parents). This encourages the hope that financial education can help the poor to "catch up" in spite of their asset-sparse environment.

Financial Education in ADD

IDA programs in ADD provided two types of financial education, general and asset-specific.

General Financial Education

All programs in ADD required that participants take some general financial education. Some programs required some classes before opening an IDA, and all programs required that a participant fulfill the general financial-education requirement before making a matched withdrawal. Chapter 3 details the specific requirements at each of ADD's fourteen programs.

General financial education in ADD covered broad financial-literacy topics such as the benefits of saving, budgeting, saving strategies, compound interest, credit management, and how IDA balances count against asset limits on means-tested public assistance. Programs also used general financial-education classes to communicate the rules of IDAs.

Each program in ADD selected or developed its own general financial-education curriculum. The programs also chose the form of class sessions (seminars, workshops, peer-discussion groups, and/or one-on-one counseling). The data record the hours required by each program and hours attended by each participant, omitting the form of the class, student/teacher ratio, content of sessions, types of materials used, and quality of teaching. All hours of financial education in ADD were not the same, but the analysis here can only assume that they were.

Asset-Specific Financial Education

In ADD, asset-specific financial education aimed to prepare participants for matched withdrawals. In many ways, non-financial assets require more skills to purchase, manage, and maintain than financial assets. For example, the process of home ownership only starts with purchase; buyers usually commit to monthly mortgage payments (and maintenance, and property taxes) for the next thirty years.

Asset-specific education for home purchase in ADD usually involved one-on-one counseling and reviews of credit reports to ensure that participants who planned to buy a house had a good chance of being approved for a loan. In a study of homebuyers in a Freddie Mac affordable-lending program, Hirad and Zorn (2001) find that pre-purchase home-ownership counseling was associated with lower post-purchase delinquency rates. They also found that one-on-one counseling was more effective than self-study or classroom training.

Asset-specific education for microenterprise in ADD aimed to equip participants to wear the multiple hats of the self-employed. The classes also had a preventative component to help participants avoid unusually risky types of business ventures. In the same way, asset-specific classes for post-secondary education aimed to steer participants clear of diploma mills. Classes for retirement savings discussed compound interest, types of investments, and portfolio diversification.

Program staff in ADD did not always record attendance of asset-specific education. Therefore, the analysis here focuses on general financial education.

Costs

In general, financial education is costly for both programs and participants (Clancy, 1996). For example, time after work is scarce for participants, and they may also lack good, inexpensive child care. To adjust, programs may hold classes at night or on weekends, perhaps also providing snacks and babysitters. Programs might also need to convince some participants that classes can help, especially if they did not find school useful in the past. Also, some IDA participants may lack strong skills in math, reading, and/or English. Programs may offer classes in languages other than English, and they may base exercises on guided discussions of life experiences rather than on abstract ideas from textbooks or lectures. Lessons must put the obscure, abstract, and complex language of finance in clear, concrete, and simple terms while still conveying the correct message. Programs must also ensure that the message does not get lost in cultural gaps. Unlike traditional education, financial education for low-income people requires that the teacher adjust the style and format of the class to meet students where they are (Hogarth and Swanson, 1995).

This accommodation and personal attention requires skilled labor, so financial education is costly. Excluding matches, costs at the largest program in ADD were in the ballpark of $3 per $1 of net IDA savings (Schreiner, 2004a). With these costs, a permanent, universal IDA policy would not be sustainable (Sherraden, 2000). While the cost of financial education in ADD is unknown, it surely was not the main source of costs. Still, the cost of financial education is not trivial, and—especially if IDAs are run from for-profit financial-service firms—classes may be at the top of the cost-cutting list.

Was financial education in ADD worth the cost? In a survey and in case studies, ADD participants said that the classes taught them psychological and behavioral saving techniques (Moore et al., 2000). In addition, 85 percent agreed or strongly agreed with the statement "The IDA classes helped you to save" (Moore et al., 2001). Based on qualitative interviews, Johnson et al. (2003) report similar results. When asked, ADD participants usually said that financial education was helpful.

Still, the mere presence of benefits does not make financial education worthwhile; benefits must exceed costs, and the costs for financial education in ADD are unknown. Furthermore, participants may have said that classes helped them even if classes had no effect, either because they confused enjoyment with learning or because they wanted to give an answer that they thought would please the interviewers. Without data on costs, even rough estimates of benefits are not enough to evaluate whether financial education in ADD was worthwhile.

Regression Estimates

To avoid bias from possible two-way causation, hours of attendance at general financial-education classes in ADD were excluded from the first-step Probit on the likelihood of being a "saver" and included only in the second-step ordinary least-squares regression on monthly net IDA savings for "savers."

Two-way causation. There may have been two-way causation between savings and hours of attendance of general financial education in ADD. Participants who were not "savers" could not make matched withdrawals worth $100 or more. Programs required that participants complete classes before making a matched withdrawal, but this was a weak incentive for participants who were not "savers" and for whom matched withdrawals were unlikely. Indeed, many of these participants who were not "savers" closed their IDAs without fulfilling financial-education requirements. Also, programs kicked out some unknown number of participants for not attending classes, and hours were more likely to be under-reported for participants who were not "savers." Thus, participants who were not "savers" were more likely to have fewer hours of financial education. For them, not only may low attendance have caused low savings, but also low savings may have caused low attendance.

To eliminate bias from this possible two-way causation, the first-step Probit regression for the likelihood of being a "saver" does not include hours of financial education. The second-step ordinary least-squares regression for the level of monthly net IDA savings for "savers" does include hours of financial education. Did causation run only from hours of education to savings for "savers"? Perhaps only the "savers" with the greatest savings (or those who made matched withdrawals) bothered to fulfill financial-education requirements. Such two-way causation would induce a spurious positive correlation between savings and hours of attendance.

It turns out that in all ADD programs but three, 80 to 90 percent of "savers" met the financial-education requirements (table 6.11). The exceptions were CAAB (where hours were set to missing because CAAB said they were unreliable), Heart of America (where the 45-hour requirement was not enforced), and CAPTC Large-scale (where 76 percent of "savers" met requirements). The share is higher for "savers" with matched withdrawals. Furthermore, average hours of attendance by "savers" was close to program requirements everywhere except CAAB and Heart of America; this suggests that "savers" who failed to meet requirements were almost always short by one or two hours. Overall, this means that all but one program usually enforced their requirements and that "savers" usually fulfilled them. Thus, causality in ADD ran from education to savings.

Two-way causation may still have crept in if programs who expected their participants to have greater difficulty saving tried to compensate by requiring more financial education. If such expectations were correct and if the additional financial education did not fully compensate for the target group's greater difficulty in saving, then it would induce a spurious negative correlation between savings and hours of attendance at financial education.

Bayer, Bernheim, and Scholz (1996) and Bernheim and Garrett (1996) discuss this issue, noting that workplace financial education for 401(k) participants is almost always "remedial" in that it is implemented or stepped up when

Table 6.11
Fulfillment of General Financial-Education Requirements by all "Savers" and by "Savers" with Matched Withdrawals by Program in ADD

Program	Share completing requirements for general financial education (%)		Average hours of general financial education for "savers"	
	"Savers"	"Savers" with matched withdrawals	Required	Attended
ADVOCAP	93	91	10	9.8
CAAB	NA	NA	NA	NA
CVCAC	91	92	12	11.7
Near Eastside	85	92	9	8.4
Heart of America	0	0	45	9.2
Mercy Corps	89	89	8	7.7
MACED	83	97	12	11.7
CAPTC Small-scale	82	90	6	5.5
Shorebank	92	97	8	6.7
WSEP	92	89	16	15.0
Alternatives FCU	81	82	10	9.1
Foundation Communities	94	87	10	9.9
Bay Area	98	100	10	9.8
CAPTC Large-scale	76	83	12	11.0

Note: Data on financial education for CAAB were known to be unreliable and so were set to missing. Heart of America reported that they did not enforce their requirement of 45 hours of general financial education, although they stated that hours attended were reported accurately in MIS IDA. For all programs, the actual hours of financial education attended were capped at the program requirement before computing the program average.

savings are thought to be too low. In a sample of ADD participants, Moore et al. (2001) find that those who said that they were helped by financial-education classes had saved less (at the time of survey) than those who said that the classes did not help them. This is consistent with the hypothesis that those who benefited most from financial education were those who had the most to learn. Even if they learned a lot, however, they were unlikely to catch up all the way. Thus, requiring more financial education of those who needed it the most could have generated a negative correlation between class attendance and saving, even if—in the absence of two-way causation—attendance increased saving.

This possible two-way causation affects the analysis only if the estimated association between education and savings is negative. If the estimated association is positive, then financial education must have increased savings (supposing causality) so much that it overwhelmed any effects of two-way causation working in the opposite direction.

Estimated associations. In ADD, each additional hour (up to ten) of attendance of general financial education was associated with an increase in monthly net IDA savings for "savers" of $1.16 ($p = 0.01$, table 6.9). This is a large association. For example, the change in monthly net IDA savings associated with a move from six to ten hours of financial education was $4.64 (4 x $1.16).

After ten hours, additional classes were not associated with monthly net IDA savings. From ten to twenty, each hour was associated with an increase of $0.06, but the p-value was 0.76. From twenty to thirty, each hour was associated with an increase of $0.18, again with low confidence.

Figure 6.1 is derived from the regression estimates in table 6.9. It uses splines to depict the estimated relationship between monthly net IDA savings and hours of attendance. (The use of splines to represent non-linear relationships in regression is discussed in Friedman, 1991; Smith, 1979; and Suits, Mason, and Chan, 1978.) Figure 6.1 shows that more hours were associated with higher savings until attendance reached ten hours.

In regressions not reported here, the estimated associations were not qualitatively different when hours of attendance at Heart of America—where requirements were not enforced—were set to missing. Likewise, the estimates were qualitatively the same when each individual's hours were capped at the program requirement. This suggests that hours of general financial education in excess of program requirements—hours likely to be positively correlated with omitted factors that increase savings—did not drive the estimates here.

Policy. IDAs targeted to the poor differ from other subsidized-savings policies targeted to the non-poor in that IDAs work through matches and require financial education. Theory suggests that financial education should increase saving, and ADD participants said that they found classes helpful. Regression estimates support this; additional hours—up to ten—were associated with

Figure 6.1
Association between Monthly Net IDA Savings
and Hours of Attendance of General Financial Education

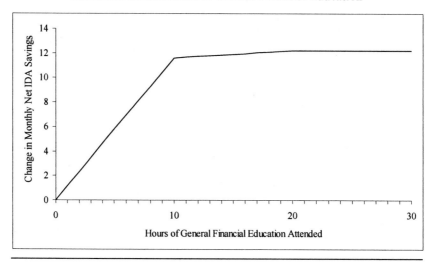

Note: Derived from regression estimates in table 6.9.

large increases in monthly net IDA savings. After ten hours, the association disappeared.

Financial education, however, is costly to provide. Did benefits exceed costs? Without cost estimates, there is no way to know for certain, but a simulation may provide a rough benchmark. Compared with no financial education, a ten-hour requirement was associated with an increase in monthly net IDA savings for "savers" in ADD of $11.60 (10 hours x $1.16 per hour). Over three years of participation, the increase would be $417 (36 months x $11.60 per month). Research on 401(k) plans suggests that it would not be far-fetched to believe that at least half of this (say, $200) is "new" saving. Assuming that a dollar of "new" saving is a dollar of benefit and noting that about half of participants in ADD were "savers," then costs and benefits would more or less balance out if classes cost about $10 per participant per hour ($200 of benefit per "saver" / 10 hours / 2 participants per "saver"). If classes cost less—including both program outlays and opportunity costs for participants—then, given the assumptions of this simulation, benefits would exceed costs and financial education in IDAs would be worthwhile.

Restrictions on Withdrawals (AFIA Rules)

Research on 401(k) plans suggests that participants save more when they have the option of taking their savings out via a loan, even though—once they put deposits in—few take advantage of the loan option (General Accounting Office, 1997; Holden and VanDerhei, 2001; Choi et al., 2004). At the same time, an ADD participant quoted in Sherraden et al. (2004, p. 22) reports that restrictions on unmatched withdrawals "are necessary because otherwise people would be raiding (the IDA) every other week." These two observations suggest that a well-designed saving policy should provide participants with structures that balance liquidity in case of emergency with illiquidity in case of loss of self-control (Ashraf et al., 2003).

ADD participants governed by the Assets for Independence Act (AFIA) were 17.4 percentage points more likely to be "savers" than non-AFIA participants (table 6.12). (AFIA "savers" had about the same monthly net IDA savings as non-AFIA "savers.") As discussed in chapter 3, AFIA sites required joint ownership of accounts, so program staff had to sign off on all withdrawals (matched or unmatched). Furthermore, unmatched withdrawals were supposed to be limited to "emergencies." While staff at AFIA sites in ADD signed off on all withdrawal requests, they also used the opportunity to discuss the reason for the desired unmatched withdrawal with the participant. Furthermore, the trouble and embarrassment of having to talk with staff about the unmatched withdrawal may have deterred some participants from making unmatched withdrawals. While AFIA sites had some other known differences vis-à-vis non-AFIA sites (allowed uses of matched withdrawals, income limits, and waiting periods), these differences were either controlled for in the regression or were probably not related with being a "saver." Thus, while there is no way to know exactly what aspect—or combination of aspects—of AFIA rules was associated with being a "saver," the best candidate was the restrictions on unmatched withdrawals implied by joint ownership of the IDA.

Because AFIA sites started later than non-AFIA sites, their participants had less time to make unmatched withdrawals. In regressions (not reported here) that include only the first twenty-four months of all participants' eligibility, the estimated association between AFIA sites and being a "saver" was even stronger than in table 6.12. This rules out "lack of time to make unmatched withdrawals" as an explanation why AFIA participants were more likely to be "savers."

Program staff at two AFIA sites attributed the increased likelihood of being a "saver" to greater program experience. Because AFIA sites started after non-AFIA sites and because most ADD programs started with no IDA experience, staff may have learned with time how to screen out potential participants who were very unlikely to become "savers." As they grew in experience, staff may have also provided more effective post-enrollment support, possibly because they became more efficient in program administration, freeing up their time to work with participants. Because ADD funds were once-off while AFIA funds were potentially renewable, AFIA sites who wanted to attract future AFIA funding may also have had greater incentives to ensure that high shares of participants were "savers."

Table 6.12
Associations between Savings Outcomes and IDA Design and Program Structure: Specific IDA Program

Independent variable	Prob.("Saver")			Net IDA savings/month		
	Mean	Δ% pts.	p-value	Mean	Δ$	p-value
Funded by Assets for Independence Act (AFIA)						
No	0.83			0.83		
Yes	0.17	+17.4	0.01	0.17	+1.83	0.34
Program						
ADVOCAP	0.03	+34.8	0.05	0.04	-4.71	0.41
CAAB	0.06	+63.8	0.01	0.06	-8.14	0.34
CVCAC	0.07	+33.2	0.01	0.09	-8.01	0.03
Near Eastside	0.08	+8.4	0.53	0.07	-5.65	0.22
Heart of America	0.04	+45.5	0.01	0.06	-6.64	0.19
Mercy Corps	0.05	+3.4	0.75	0.04	-3.40	0.32
MACED	0.03	+16.8	0.33	0.03	-14.72	0.01
CAPTC Small-scale	0.07	+9.0	0.32	0.08	-8.17	0.01
Shorebank	0.09	+28.2	0.01	0.08	-3.04	0.43
WSEP	0.07	+9.3	0.61	0.04	-10.43	0.07
WSEP AFIA	0.03	-0.7	0.97	0.02	-16.73	0.01
Alternatives FCU	0.04	+48.0	0.01	0.06	-3.64	0.52
Foundation Communities	0.05	-11.5	0.26	0.04	+1.73	0.62
Bay Area	0.10	+75.9	0.01	0.12	-5.39	0.45
CAPTC Large-scale	0.19			0.17		

Note: All regression estimates were derived from a single two-step "Heckit" regression. The first step was a Probit (n=2,350, k=104) for the likelihood of being a "saver." The second step was ordinary least-squares (n=1,232, k=111) for net IDA savings per month for "savers." Means were taken over non-missing observations.

But this is all speculation. Based on what is known from the data and AFIA rules, our best guess is that AFIA's restrictions on unmatched withdrawals increased the likelihood of being a "saver," although the optimal strength and formality of such restrictions are unknown. On the one hand, participants welcome "silken handcuffs" as a way to deter unwise withdrawals. On the other hand, participants sometimes do need to make unmatched withdrawals, and the prospect of having to go through hoops to do so may lead them to keep back funds from IDAs. Our opinion—not based on the ADD data—is that mild, informal restrictions may achieve the best of both worlds. If IDAs are jointly owned, then programs should always immediately sign off on requests for unmatched withdrawals.

Omitted Characteristics Correlated with Specific Programs

Although the regression includes a wide range of program (and participant) characteristics, it cannot control for everything. As a second-best, it controls—with indicator variables—for associations between savings outcomes and omitted factors correlated with each program. Examples of such omitted factors include program characteristics (such as the strictness of rule enforcement or the quality of financial education), average participant characteristics (such as future orientation), and other characteristics (such as the state of the local economy) that may affect savings outcomes while also being correlated with the specific program.

The estimates in table 6.12 reflect the combined effects of all omitted characteristics that are correlated with a specific program. The reference point is CAPTC Large-scale, whose estimate is set to zero. For example, compared with omitted factors at CAPTC Large-scale, omitted factors at Mercy Corps were associated with an increase of 3.4 percentage points in the likelihood of being a "saver" ($p = 0.75$) and a decrease of $3.40 in monthly net IDA savings for "savers" ($p = 0.32$). Many of the comparisons with CAPTC Large-scale are large and statistically significant. Of course, other programs could have been used as the reference point. This would not change the magnitudes, signs, or statistical significance of the pair-wise estimates of differences between programs.

These estimates do not necessarily rank IDA programs by quality. While they do depend in part on omitted program factors (such as quality of staff support), they also depend on omitted participant factors (such as future orientation) and omitted local factors (such as the economy). Which factors are omitted and how much each one matters is unknown.

Chapter Summary

Given that the poor can save, the next question for policy is *how* do they save? This chapter describes estimated associations between savings outcomes and institutional characteristics. Several aspects of IDA design—match rates, match caps, use of automatic transfer, months to make matchable deposits, financial education, and restrictions on unmatched withdrawals—were strongly associated with savings outcomes in ADD. Although correlation does not imply causation, the "Heckit" regression here controls for an unusually wide range of factors, lending weight to causal interpretations except where otherwise noted.

Higher match rates were associated with a greater likelihood of being a "saver" and—for "savers"—a lower level of monthly net IDA savings. This suggests possible trade-offs between IDAs' three goals of inclusion, saving, and asset accumulation. While higher match rates were associated with an increase in inclusion for participants, they were associated with a decrease in savings by "savers." On net, however, higher match rates had little association with the level of savings by participants (not just "savers"). Ignoring costs, higher match rates are preferred because they improve inclusion and asset accumulation with little harm to saving.

A $1 increase in the match cap was associated with a $0.57 increase in net IDA savings. Apparently, ADD participants tried to "max out" their match eligibility, turning match caps into saving targets. One way to increase saving and asset accumulation is to increase the match cap.

Like 401(k) plans, IDAs in ADD coupled higher match rates with lower match caps. Are high match rates and low match caps better than the converse? High match rates improve inclusion, but high match caps improve savings (both per "saver" and per participant) as well as asset accumulation per participant. At the same time, high match rates cost more than high match caps. If funds allow, of course, high match rates could be coupled with high match caps.

The match-cap structure—whether annual or lifetime—varied little within programs in ADD, so the data offer little guidance for policy. In theory, lifetime caps are more flexible, while annual caps can help curb procrastination and build saving habits. A hybrid annual/lifetime structure might give the best of both worlds, allowing people to accrue match eligibility through time (providing flexibility to save when ready) while limiting total accrued match eligibility (providing mild "use-it-or-lose-it" incentives). Canada and the United Kingdom have subsidized asset-building accounts with such a hybrid match-cap structure.

Other factors in the regression constant, ADD participants who used automatic transfer were more likely to be "savers." This fits the advice of financial planners to "pay yourself first" and "tie your own hands." Public policy could facilitate automatic transfer in three ways. First, it could educate people about the benefits of automatic transfer and how to set it up. Second, it could require employers to offer direct deposit of paychecks. Third, it could require employers and the Internal Revenue Service to allow employees and taxpayers to split paychecks and tax refunds across a check, a deposit to a 401(k) plan, and deposits to multiple savings accounts (including IDAs). The technical capability is already in place; employers and the Internal Revenue Service need but offer the service.

In ADD, months eligible to make matchable deposits was positively associated with being a "saver" and negatively associated with monthly net IDA savings per "saver." On net, the increase in inclusion as "savers" led to higher monthly net IDA savings per participant and higher net IDA savings per participant over the lifetime of ADD. Overall, longer time caps were associated with better outcomes for all three IDA goals. From the perspective of long-term development, this supports longer (perhaps permanent) time caps. The United States has precedents for permanent time caps in Individual Retirement Accounts and 401(k) plans for the non-poor.

Among subsidized savings policies, IDAs are unique in requiring financial education. In ADD, each hour of class attendance (up to ten) was associated with an additional $1.16 of monthly net IDA savings. Beyond ten hours, more education was not associated with savings outcomes. For policy, this suggests not only that some financial education is valuable but also that costs may be contained—without losing effectiveness—by limiting the hours required. A very rough simulation exercise suggests that financial education may be worthwhile if costs per participant per hour are less than about $10.

In similar research that summarizes empirical associations between savings outcomes and the institutional aspects of 401(k) plans, Choi, Laibson, and Madrian (2004, p. 22) conclude that "the central finding that plan design matters . . . places a tremendous responsibility on both employers and government regulators." The same holds for IDAs. Institutional design matters, and this gives policy makers a number of levers with which to affect saving and asset accumulation by the poor.

7

Participant Characteristics and IDA Savings Outcomes

While characteristics of IDA design provide direct policy levers, characteristics of participants provide indirect policy levers. For example, policy cannot change a participant's age, but policy can adjust IDA design according to age. For example, if young people save less because they have not yet learned how to save, then more financial education might be targeted to them.

This chapter looks at the links between IDA savings outcomes and participant characteristics. While outcomes in ADD varied with some participant characteristics, poor people with all types of characteristics—including welfare recipients and the very poor—saved and built assets in IDAs. Furthermore, the results often suggest the presence of omitted factors that were correlated with both IDA savings outcomes and participant characteristics. Because IDA design may affect such omitted factors, knowing how IDA savings outcomes are linked with participant characteristics can suggest additional policy levers.

For example, participants who planned for home purchase were less likely to be "savers," perhaps because home purchase was an unusually difficult goal. If so, one possible implication is that participants who plan for home purchase might benefit from early one-on-one financial counseling. This would seek both to ensure that the participant can qualify for a loan before getting too far along in the home-buying process and also to guide the participant— if home purchase would be too difficult at this time—toward a more feasible goal. In this way, "planned use" is a participant characteristic whose link with IDA savings outcomes suggests a way that IDA programs might improve saving and asset building.

As another example, ADD participants with four-year college degrees had better IDA savings outcomes than others. This may partly reflect greater knowledge about the value of saving and about how to save. A possible implication is that IDA programs might focus financial education more directly on participants who do not have this background.

Of course, adjusting IDA design for different segments of participants comes at a cost, especially when it extends or intensifies services. Given knowledge of the links between characteristics and outcomes, however, IDA programs can target special services where they are most relevant. For example, college graduates might be excused from financial education, freeing up resources for more classes structured toward participants with less educational experience.

This chapter uses the same regression as in the previous chapter to associate participant characteristics in ADD with two IDA savings outcomes: being a "saver" (net IDA savings of $100 or more) and the level of net IDA savings per month for "savers." In addition to the aspects of IDA design discussed in the previous chapter, the regression includes a wide range of participant characteristics, including planned use of matched withdrawals, gender, marital status, location of residence, age, race/ethnicity, education, employment, receipt of public assistance, income, assets, liabilities, and insurance coverage. The analysis considers independent associations (how IDA savings outcomes varied at the margin across participants with different values of a given characteristic, keeping constant other characteristics in the regression) as well as dependent associations (how IDA savings outcomes varied on average across segments of participants defined by the values of a given characteristic, without keeping constant other characteristics in the regression).

There are two central lessons. In terms of independent associations, IDA programs can use knowledge of how IDA savings outcomes are associated with participant characteristics to target special services to those for whom they are most relevant. In terms of dependent associations, all segments of participants saved and built assets in IDAs, so it does not make sense to exclude some segments from access to IDAs based on the assumption that they would not be able to save.

Regression Analysis

As in the previous chapter, the column in table 7.1 headed "Δ% pts." is the percentage-point change in the probability of being a "saver" associated with a unit change in the value of a given participant characteristic (all other factors in the regression constant). As before, positive estimates indicate that higher values of the given characteristic were associated with a greater likelihood of being a "saver." In the column headed "p-value," lower values denote greater confidence that the estimate was not due to ADD participants' being a nonrepresentative sample from some population in which the true association was zero.

The three columns on the right side of table 7.1 under the heading "Net IDA savings/month" pertain to the second-step least-squares regression that associates participant characteristics with the level of monthly net IDA savings for "savers." Keeping other factors in the regression constant, the column "Δ$" is the estimated change in monthly net IDA savings associated with a unit change

Table 7.1

**Associations between Savings Outcomes and Planned Use
of Matched Withdrawals as Declared at Enrollment by Participants in ADD**

Planned use of matched withdrawals	Prob.("Saver")			Net IDA savings/month		
	Mean	Δ% pts.	p-value	Mean	Δ$	p-value
Home purchase	0.48			0.37		
Home repair	0.09	+36.7	0.01	0.13	+2.64	0.26
Post-secondary education	0.16	+17.7	0.01	0.18	−2.45	0.09
Job training	0.02	+4.7	0.59	0.02	−2.09	0.49
Retirement	0.06	+19.1	0.01	0.07	+0.11	0.96
Small-business ownership	0.19	+16.0	0.01	0.22	−2.44	0.07

Note: All regression estimates were derived from a single "Heckit"-type selection specification with two steps. The first step was a Probit (n=2,350, k=104) for the likelihood of being a "saver." The second step was ordinary least-squares (n=1,232, k=111) for net IDA savings per month for "savers." Means were taken over non-missing observations.

in the value of a given characteristic. The "p-value" is the likelihood that the estimate is non-zero only because the sample is not representative.

In sum, table 7.1 displays the sign (positive or negative), size, and statistical significance of estimated associations between IDA savings outcomes and a participant characteristic. While the estimates are displayed in a series of tables, they all (and all those in the previous chapter) come from a single "Heckit" regression.

Planned Use of Matched Withdrawals

At enrollment, 48 percent of participants planned to make matched withdrawals for home purchase, 19 percent for small-business ownership, 18 percent for post-secondary education or job training, 9 percent for home repair, and 6 percent for retirement savings.

These averages appear in the column "Mean" under the heading "Prob.("Saver")" on the left side of table 7.1. The averages cover all participants, as all participants enter the first-step Probit that associates participant characteristics with the probability of being a "saver" with net IDA savings of $100 or more.

Planned use might be linked with IDA savings outcomes in two ways. First, a given matched use might appeal to specific participant segments (chapter 5). If the regression omits characteristics associated with these segments, then the effects of the omitted characteristics show up in the estimated association between savings outcomes and planned use. For example, most ADD participants who planned for home repair already owned a home. These homeowners differed from renters in part because they possess characteristics (such as a tendency to plan, or an appreciation of the value of asset ownership) that not only caused them to save for home purchase in the first place but that also generally cause greater saving. Homeowners planning for home repair might also tend to be "tidy" people who care about their home's quality and appearance. This "tidiness" may reflect underlying traits that cause greater saving. While the regression controls for homeownership (and thus for omitted characteristics that differ between homeowners and renters), it does not control for differences in "tidiness" among homeowners. If tidy homeowners were more likely to plan for home repair, then the estimated association between planning for home repair and IDA savings outcomes partly reflected the effect of "tidiness" on saving. As another example, participants who planned for small-business ownership likely possess omitted traits that increase saving, because business owners, in general, save more (Caner, 2003). Thus, participants who did not yet own businesses but who planned to do so probably saved more than otherwise-similar participants who did not plan to open a business. Because the regression controls for current business ownership but not planned business ownership, the estimated association between savings outcomes and planning for business ownership at least partly reflects omitted characteristics that caused both business ownership and greater saving.

A second link between IDA savings outcomes and the planned uses of matched withdrawals is that some matched uses are "easier" than others. "Easier" uses are feasible with smaller lump sums, simpler purchase processes, shorter time frames, and/or less commitment to on-going maintenance and investment. For example, home purchase usually requires a large lump sum. In contrast, smaller sums are enough for post-secondary education or job training (matched withdrawals can pay for textbooks), home repair (most homes could use some small repairs), small-business ownership (an owner can always buy some small tools or a bit more inventory), or retirement savings (Roth IRAs accept even tiny contributions). Likewise, the process of home purchase is much longer and more complex than buying textbooks, finding a home-repair contractor, buying business equipment, or contributing to a Roth IRA. Furthermore, the smaller the required lump sum and the simpler the purchase process, the sooner a matched withdrawal is possible. This decreases the risk that participants will lose patience or suffer a negative shock leading to unmatched withdrawals that deplete the IDA. Short waits between deposits and matched withdrawals are especially relevant for participants who already are saving for home purchase, who already are post-secondary students, or who already are business owners. These participants already have a use for their funds, and they may not want to tie up resources in IDAs long enough to qualify for matches (Edgcomb and Klein, 2004). Finally, home purchase, post-secondary education, and small-business ownership entail on-going commitments to maintenance and investment. For example, homebuyers must pay off a mortgage, students must graduate, and entrepreneurs must keep up a going concern.

Home repair and retirement savings, in contrast, are once-off investments. Even if matched withdrawals can cover a down payment on a home or tuition for a freshman year, IDA participants might opt for an "easier" matched use if they worry about keeping up with on-going maintenance and investment.

On net, the expected relationship between planned-use "difficulty" and IDA savings outcomes is ambiguous. On the one hand, participants who plan "difficult" uses may get discouraged and end up saving less. On the other hand, participants who—due to factors omitted from the regression—expect to save less might self-select out of "difficult" uses, leaving in the "difficult" uses mostly participants who expect to save more (and who end up saving more).

The results for "savers" in ADD on the left side of table 7.1 favor the "discouragement" hypothesis over the "self-selection" hypothesis. On the high end of the spectrum were participants who planned for home repair; on the low end were participants who planned for home purchase. In the middle were those who planned for post-secondary education, small-business ownership, or retirement savings. Given that 52 percent of participants were "savers," the differences between different matched uses were huge. Compared with homebuyers, home repairers were 36.7 percentage points more likely to be "savers" (p-value = 0.01). Those who planned for post-secondary education, small business, or retirement were 16 to 19 percentage points more likely to be "savers" (these three estimates were not statistically different from each other).

The participants most likely to be "savers" were those with the "easiest" planned use (home repair), while those least likely to be "savers" were those with the most "difficult" planned use (home purchase). This fits the "discouragement" explanation; homebuyers set a large, all-or-nothing goal for themselves. Because reaching a "difficult" goal requires more effort when a given roadblock appears, this increased the risk of giving up. In contrast, if participants who were planning for home repair or other "easy" uses ran into a roadblock, they could still make small matched withdrawals. Some homebuyers may also have quit when they realized, after meeting with IDA staff to review their credit standing, that they might not qualify for a mortgage loan. Yet another factor came into play for the one-fourth of all ADD participants served by the two IDA programs at CAPTC in Tulsa, as CAPTC offered a 2:1 match rate for home purchase and a 1:1 match rate for other uses. The higher match rate may have swayed some participants who enrolled without a well-formed idea for the matched use to aim for home purchase. Given the difficulty of home purchase, these participants may have been more susceptible to discouragement, especially because they did not start out with a particularly strong commitment to home purchase. Finally, some ADD participants who planned for home purchase may have been almost ready to buy when they enrolled. Getting a match, however, required them to first complete financial education as well as to keep an IDA open for at least 6 months. Furthermore, participants with annual match caps had to wait for years to take full advantage of their match eligibility. Thus, some participants who entered ADD ready to buy a house may have opted not to wait to fulfill IDA rules. All these reasons point to a greater risk of discouragement among those planning for home purchase.

Among "savers" and with all else in the regression constant, monthly net IDA savings was highest for homebuyers and home-repairers (right side of table 7.1). Monthly net IDA savings was statistically the same among the other matched uses. Unlike the results for "savers," this result for the monthly net IDA savings fits the "self-selection" explanation: "savers" who expected to save less (and who ended up saving less) planned for "easier" uses.

This discussion of the regression estimates in table 7.1 looks at "independent associations" and shows how IDA savings outcomes were associated with planned use, holding other factors in the regression constant. Another approach looks at "dependent associations," that is, how IDA savings outcomes varied across segments of participants as defined by planned use, without holding other factors constant. This approach shows that even though participants who planned for home purchase were less likely to be "savers," 41 percent of them were "savers." Also, among homebuyers, net IDA savings per month was $12.82.

What does this suggest for policy? First, home purchase is the most popular matched use; about half of ADD participants planned for it. Thus, effective ways to support saving for home purchase are important. Mills et al. (2004) find that access to IDAs at the one ADD program with an experimental design had large impacts on first-time home purchase.

Second, saving in IDAs for home purchase is difficult (but not impossible). Participants with short time caps may get discouraged and then quit. Awareness of this risk might help programs combat discouragement, perhaps by reminding those who plan for home purchase that, should this specific goal turn out to be too difficult, they can always switch to a different matched use. The same one-on-one financial counseling that checks whether potential homebuyers are likely to qualify for a mortgage might also provide guidance on other feasible matched uses.

Third, longer time caps might reduce discouragement. Many participants who cannot accumulate a down payment in three years might nevertheless do so in four or ten. The short time caps in ADD were not part of the IDA design (Sherraden, 1991) but rather a side effect of time-limited funding. Sustainable improvement in the well-being of the poor is promoted most effectively by long (even permanent) programs.

Gender, Marital Status, and Household Composition

Gender

Four out of five participants in ADD were women (table 7.2), reflecting both programs' targeting and women's concentration among the poor. How might gender be associated with IDA savings outcomes? On the one hand, women face job-market discrimination and general social oppression and so—compared with men—have fewer resources available to save. On the other hand, oppression may strengthen precautionary motives to save, as women can expect more "rainy days."

Research on saving by the poor in low-income countries suggests that women tend to be better savers than men. While men may spend on food, drink, and games for themselves outside the home, women are more likely to cache food, cash, or valuables in the home (or in social networks, see Gugerty, 2003) in case food runs short, children need medicine, or they are abandoned or must leave an abusive husband (Dowla and Alamgir, 2003; Vonderlack and Schreiner, 2002).

All else in the regression constant, women in ADD were much more likely than men (6.8 percentage points, p-value of 0.04) to be "savers." This suggests that factors omitted from the regression (such as the need to save to prepare for shocks) that were associated with being a woman also caused greater IDA saving.

The 6.8-percentage-point estimate here is similar to the 6.5-percentage-point advantage of women over men for participation in 401(k) plans (Huberman, Iyengar, and Jiang, 2003). That study attributes women's higher participation to their husbands' having, on average, the higher income in the couple. In such cases, women's household income exceeds women's personal income. Because Huberman, Iyengar, and Jiang's regression controls only for personal income, any effects of household income show up in the estimates for gender. This explanation, however, does not work for ADD's gender effect, as 85 percent of female participants were not married.

With other factors in the regression constant, net IDA savings per month for "savers" was not linked with gender. When other factors are not constant, women participants had less monthly net IDA savings ($15.84) than men ($19.47). This means that factors in the regression that were associated with greater savings were also more strongly associated with men. Overall, this may suggest that women were less able (but more willing) to save. If factors in the regression were distributed equally across genders, then women would have saved more than men, because factors not in the regression that cause greater saving were more strongly linked with women.

What does this suggest for policy? Women—especially poor women—want to save. By increasing their ability to save (via matches and supportive institutional structures), IDAs might help even out gender-based wealth inequalities.

Still, women's greater willingness to save does not fully compensate for their lesser ability to save. Thus, equal access to IDAs might widen wealth gaps. (The analysis here cannot reveal how much IDA saving in any participant segment is "new," so it can only speculate on how IDAs might affect

Table 7.2

Associations between Savings Outcomes and the Gender, Household Composition, Number of Participants in a Household, and Marital Status for Participants in ADD

Independent variable	Prob.("Saver")			Net IDA savings/month		
	Mean	Δ% pts.	p-value	Mean	Δ$	p-value
Gender						
Male	0.20			0.21		
Female	0.80	+6.8	0.04	0.79	+0.12	0.91
Household composition						
Adults (18 or older)	1.5	+2.4	0.25	1.5	−0.40	0.53
Children (17 or younger)	1.7	−0.8	0.38	1.7	−0.18	0.56
Multiple IDA participants in household						
No	0.94			0.93		
Yes	0.06	−4.3	0.42	0.07	+0.97	0.55
Marital status						
Never-married	0.49			0.39		
Married	0.23	+7.9	0.05	0.27	+0.23	0.86
Divorced or separated	0.28	+0.7	0.83	0.30	−0.51	0.61
Widowed	0.03	+3.4	0.70	0.04	−5.26	0.04

Note: All regression estimates were derived from a single "Heckit"-type selection specification with two steps. The first step was a Probit (n=2,350, k=104) for the likelihood of being a "saver." The second step was ordinary least-squares (n=1,232, k=111) for net IDA savings per month for "savers." Means were taken over non-missing observations.

gender wealth gaps.) One way programs might mitigate this risk is by giving women higher match rates, higher match caps, and/or longer time caps. But targeting based explicitly on gender—like targeting based explicitly on race/ethnicity—complicates program administration and may spark political opposition. One simple way to target the most supportive IDA designs to women is simply to target them to the poor in general, as women are disproportionately poor. (Using this reasoning, Conley, 1999, recommends a similar approach for targeting greater asset-building support to racial/ethnic minorities.)

Does the positive association between being a woman and the likelihood of being a "saver" mean that IDA programs somehow discriminate against men in favor of women? Yes, if the classical reasoning in regression studies of discrimination is to be accepted (Blinder, 1973; Oaxaca, 1973). After controlling for some other factors, these studies interpret estimates linking worse outcomes with women as evidence of discrimination against women. Logically, estimates linking worse outcomes with men would be evidence of discrimination against men. This assumes, however, that the regression controls for all factors linked with both gender and outcomes. This assumption rarely holds (Dietrich, 2003; Heckman, 1998), and R^2 in these regressions is far from 100 percent. Instead, these estimates pick up the effects of omitted factors associated with both gender and savings outcomes.

The real issue is whether these omitted factors are due to discrimination. In the case of women and IDAs, the omitted factors do seem to be due to discrimination, but discrimination by society as a whole, not by IDA programs in ADD. Ironically, this discrimination may have increased saving by increasing its importance for women.

In general, a better indicator of discrimination is the difference in the distributions of characteristics—whether or not included in a regression—between men and women. While physical/genetic factors might explain a tiny share of these differences, the rest are due to social forces. Attributing effects associated with omitted factors to discrimination while assuming that discrimination does not explain the distribution of included factors not only ignores the sedimentation of inequality over time (Oliver and Shapiro, 1995) but also irrationally focuses on the least important forces of discrimination while ignoring the most important ones (Loury, 1998). After all, a regression that included all factors would produce an almost-zero estimated association between gender and savings outcomes. But this would hardly mean that society offers equal opportunities to women. Detecting discrimination with statistics makes sense only when combined with theory (that is, reasoned argument and evidence) that looks not only at the nature of the omitted characteristics associated both with gender and the outcome of interest but also the factors that caused the divergences in the distribution of included characteristics.

Household Composition

On average, households with ADD participants had 1.5 adults and 1.7 children (table 7.2). About 15 percent of households had one adult and no children, and 9 percent had two or more adults and no children. Also, 46 percent had one adult with children (in these single-parent households, 95 percent were headed by women), and 30 percent had two or more adults with children.

Household composition might affect IDA savings outcomes in several ways. For example, other adults may (or may not) contribute income and thus increase resources available to save. Because children consume without contributing much in economic terms, they probably decrease available resources, but children's presence might inspire parents to sacrifice now to build assets for the future. In general, any household member might support or obstruct IDA saving. Because there are economies of scale in household production (Deaton, 1997), more adults should improve savings outcomes. On the other hand, more children (and their attendant consumption) should dampen savings outcomes.

In the regression, the number of adults and number of children were not associated with IDA savings outcomes. Using indicator variables for each of the four types of households (one adult versus two or more, with or without children) did not change these results.

Multiple IDA Participants in a Household

IDAs are *Individual* Development Accounts, so a single household might have multiple participants. In ADD, about 6 percent of participants were in multiple-IDA households.

As discussed in chapter 4, having multiple participants in a household might reduce per-participant IDA saving by spreading total household IDA saving across two accounts. Still, it is unlikely to reduce total household IDA saving. A multiple-IDA household is different than a one-IDA household, even though all household members in one-IDA households can help the IDA participant. First, multiple accounts increase the "household" match cap. Because higher match caps—all else in the regression constant—spark greater saving effort (chapter 6), this increases desired IDA saving.

Second, the presence of multiple participants may mark households with extraordinarily strong desires to save (or other omitted characteristics that improve savings outcomes). For example, households with large existing stocks of assets may open multiple IDAs to increase the amount that they can "reshuffle." For these cases, the presence of multiple participants does not itself cause greater saving but rather signals the presence of other factors that are direct causes.

Third, participants in multiple-IDA households can give each other support. Simply put, the topic of saving and financial planning is more likely to come up at the dinner table. When one household member goes to the bank, he or she can make deposits in both IDAs. If one household member wants to spend unnecessarily, the other may act as the voice of conscience. Saving—like spending—tends to be a family affair.

Other factors in the regression constant, ADD participants in multiple-IDA households were 4.3 percentage points less likely to be "savers" (table 7.2). Given that 52 percent of all participants were "savers," the per-household likelihood of having at least one "saver" was higher in multiple-IDA households than in single-participant households, as "saver" status was far from perfectly correlated among participants in multiple-IDA households.

The second step of the regression shows that having multiple IDA participants in a household did not dilute per-participant monthly net IDA savings, let alone per-household IDA savings. A household with two "savers"—all else in the regression constant—saved about twice as much as a household with one "saver." The higher effective match cap (chapter 6) accounts for much of this, and the rest is due to omitted factors correlated with the presence of multiple accounts and to mutual support among participants in a multi-IDA household.

Will poor households with multiple IDA participants save more in IDAs than households with a single IDA participant? Very likely, although the increase would be smaller than in ADD, because ADD households self-selected into multiple participation based partly on omitted factors (such as an extraordinarily strong desire to save) that is probably weaker in average households.

Marital Status

About 23 percent of IDA participants in ADD were married, 31 percent were divorced, separated, or widowed, and 49 percent were never married (table 7.2). About 15 percent of female participants were married, and among not married women, 79 percent had children. In ADD overall, 52 percent of participants were single mothers.

As summarized by Grinstein-Weiss, Zhan, and Sherraden (2004, p. 3), there are several economic pathways through which marriage might facilitate saving and asset accumulation:

First, the total product of a married couple is larger than the sum of the outputs of each produced separately. Second, the institution of marriage involves long-term commitment in which a division of labor enables each spouse to specialize in specific skills and duties. This specialization increases the productivity and efficiency of the household. Third, economies of scale in consumption suggest that a married couple may achieve the same utility with less combined expenditure than the sum of their individual [utilities] if living apart. Fourth, the requirements and expectations of married (versus single) life may encourage people to buy a house, save for children's education, and acquire cars and other assets. Fifth, there is persistent evidence that married men earn more than unmarried men. Sixth, the institution of marriage expands social networks and social support, which may result in additional opportunities and benefits that lead to saving. Finally, married individuals may have access to benefits such as health and life insurance provided by a spouse's employment.

In addition, marital status might be linked with IDA savings outcomes because people select their spouses rather than marrying at random (Varian, 2004). Thus, being married might signal the presence of factors that, while omitted from the regression, make a person an attractive spouse and also improve savings outcomes. For example, if people choose spouses partly based on qualities such as future-orientation and follow-through on commitments, then married people will be more likely to have these qualities that also happen to cause greater saving.

Finally (and in contrast to the broad forces in the previous two paragraphs that suggest that married people will save more), unmarried people may have a greater precautionary motive to save, as they cannot count on a spouse to help in times of illness or unemployment.

Compared with never-married participants in ADD, married participants were—all else in the regression constant—about 8 percentage points more likely to be "savers." The estimates for the three other marital statuses (never-married, divorced or separated, or widowed) were not statistically different from each other. This association of marriage with greater IDA savings outcomes could be due to greater support in a married household or to greater stick-to-it-tiveness among people who were self-selected and spouse-selected into marriage.

Of course, non-married people still saved in IDAs in ADD. About 46 percent of never-marrieds were "savers," and non-married participants had monthly net IDA savings of $20.73. Among the divorced or separated, 55.2 percent were "savers," and these "savers" had monthly IDA net savings of $19.20. Indeed, the divorced or separated had above-average IDA savings outcomes, perhaps because they were motivated to save by their children or because they expected to have to depend on their own savings in the event of a downturn.

Controlling for factors in the regression, there were no large differences in monthly net IDA savings among "savers" in the three most common marital statuses. (Widowed "savers" saved about $5 less than others.)

To check how IDA savings outcomes in ADD were associated with the combination of gender, children, and marital status, an indicator for single mothers was added to the regression. Married participants (male or female, with or without children) were the most likely to be "savers," followed by single mothers. Never-married or divorced participants (male or female) without children were the least likely to be "savers." All else in the regression constant, women were more likely than men to be "savers."

What does this mean for IDAs? First, households headed by single mothers—the segment of the poor of greatest policy concern—had above-average

IDA savings outcomes. If all ADD participants were single mothers and none of their other characteristics changed, then the share of "savers" would increase from 52 percent to 55 percent. Poor single mothers can save in IDAs, and IDA programs targeted to welfare recipients might be a step toward Friedman's (1988) vision of "the safety net as ladder." Counting IDA balances in means-tests for public assistance would likely dampen IDA saving by some single mothers.

Second, married participants had better IDA savings outcomes; if all ADD participants were married, the share of "savers" would increase from 52 percent to 57 percent. While IDA programs cannot influence marital status, they might try to offer unmarried participants some of the social support that married participants get from their spouses. In ADD, for example, program staff frequently telephoned participants to discuss their IDA savings. Making these calls was costly, but they might be targeted only to unmarried participants.

Third, the results of the regression that includes an indicator for single mothers suggests that the greater likelihood of a woman's being a "saver" comes mostly from women who are mothers. Because children's consumption uses up resources that would otherwise be available to save, the presence of children seems to motivate greater savings effort. For example, matches for post-secondary education are more relevant for women with children, and the presence of children may also enhance the desire for homeownership. As in ADD, IDA programs might use this knowledge by providing matches for post-secondary education not only for the participant but also for the participant's children or grandchildren.

Location of Residence

The 13 percent of ADD participants living in areas with populations of less than 2,500 were considered "rural" (table 7.3). The programs that accounted for most rural participants were the Central Vermont Community Action Council, the Mountain Association for Community Economic Development in Kentucky, the Women's Self-Employment Project in Illinois, and Alternatives Federal Credit Union in Ithaca, New York.

Location might be associated with IDA savings outcomes for reasons related to the sparse populations and long distances that define rural places. For example, small business may be a more relevant matched use in rural areas (Edgcomb and Thetford, 2004; Bailey and Preston, 2003), in part because of the seasonality of farm work and in part because, with fewer businesses nearby, rural dwellers tend to be jacks-of-many-trades. Long distances—and the lack of public transport—mean higher transaction costs, providing a measure of protection for small rural businesses from urban competitors. But long distances also increase the cost of making IDA deposits or attending financial-education classes (Bailey et al., 2004). Distances may also preclude living at home while attending a post-secondary school, reducing the attraction of that

Table 7.3

Associations between Savings Outcomes and Location of Residence, Age, and Race/Ethnicity for Participants in ADD

Independent variable	Prob.("Saver")			Net IDA savings/month		
	Mean	Δ% pts.	p-value	Mean	Δ$	p-value
Location of residence						
Urban (pop. 2,500 or more)	0.87			0.84		
Rural (pop. less than 2,500)	0.13	+2.4	0.68	0.16	−1.33	0.43
Age						
14 to 20 (spline)	5.9	−7.3	0.01	5.9	−1.60	0.03
20 to 70 (spline)	16	+0.5	0.01	17	+0.08	0.10
Race/Ethnicity						
Caucasian	0.37			0.43		
African American	0.47	−2.3	0.49	0.39	−5.43	0.01
Asian American	0.02	+20.3	0.04	0.03	+3.87	0.13
Hispanic	0.09	+8.3	0.11	0.10	−0.83	0.60
Native American	0.03	−5.0	0.50	0.02	−5.39	0.03
Other race/ethnicity	0.03	+14.3	0.06	0.03	+1.26	0.57

Note: All regression estimates were derived from a single "Heckit"-type selection specification with two steps. The first step was a Probit (n=2,350, k=104) for the likelihood of being a "saver." The second step was ordinary least-squares (n=1,232, k=111) for net IDA savings per month for "savers." Means were taken over non-missing observations.

matched use. Home purchase may be an "easier" matched use, because if a rural IDA participant wants to buy a mobile home, the down payment may be smaller than for buying a non-mobile home in a city. The abundance of land and therefore the presence of agriculture may also expose rural people to the vagaries of weather and crop harvests and thus impress on them the need to save for rainy (or dry) days. The randomness of weather patterns also contributes to greater rural religiosity, a trait associated with greater future-orientation and thus better savings outcomes. Finally, social capital may be greater in rural areas; with fewer people around, the same people tend to run into each other again and again. This breeds affinity, and it also allows rural people to reinforce behavior—such as IDA participation—that strengthen community. With fewer people to share the costs and benefits of communal action, individuals are also more likely to find it worthwhile to contribute to public goods.

Overall, these many factors associated with rural locations might improve IDA savings outcomes, worsen them, or more or less cancel out. It turns out that, other factors in the regression constant, location of residence in ADD did not have a statistically significant association with IDA savings outcomes. As a segment (that is, without controlling for factors other than location of residence), 61 percent of rural participants were "savers" (compared with 52 percent of all participants), and these rural participants had monthly net IDA savings of $17.26 (compared with $16.60 for all participants).

Age

The average ADD participant was thirty-six-years-old. About 3 percent of participants were eighteen or younger, and 2 percent were sixty or older.

To allow for non-linearities, age was represented with a two-piece spline. Other factors in the regression constant, the likelihood of being a "saver" decreased from age fourteen to twenty by 7.3 percentage points per year, a large effect (table 7.3). After age twenty, the likelihood of being a "saver" increased by about 0.5 percentage points per year, another large, statistically significant effect. These results are depicted in figure 7.1. For example, compared with a twenty-year-old, the likelihood of being a "saver" for a fourteen-year-old was 44 percentage points higher. The likelihood was 7.5 percentage points higher for a thirty-five-year-old than for a twenty-year-old.

Age and monthly net IDA savings for "savers" followed a similar pattern. Net IDA savings fell from ages fourteen to twenty by $1.60 per year. Once past twenty, however, each additional year was associated with an increase in savings of eight cents ($p = 0.10$). This is depicted in figure 7.2. For example, the difference in monthly net IDA savings for a sixty-year-old versus a thirty-year-old—all else in the regression constant—was $2.40. In a study of savings in 401(k) plans, Huberman, Iyengar, and Jiang (2003, p. 13) also find a "V" pattern, with contributions decreasing until age forty and then increasing after that.

Figure 7.1
Association between Age and the Likelihood of Being a "Saver"
for IDA Participants in ADD

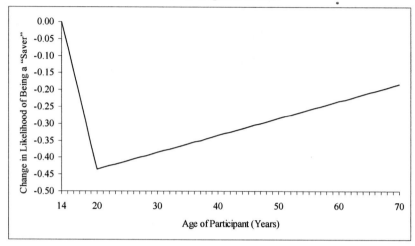

What drives this pattern? The best IDA savings outcomes for any age group in ADD—other regression factors constant—were for high schoolers. About 76 percent of participants aged eighteen or younger planned to make matched withdrawals for college, so IDA savings may have been especially salient to them. High schoolers may also have received help from parents or other family members. In addition, youth with part-time jobs may have had their entire paychecks at their disposal, with all "necessary" expenses covered by parents, perhaps making unusually high levels of resources available for IDA saving. High schoolers may also have been more comfortable with required financial education, having more free time and being more used to taking classes. Finally, some sub-programs in ADD may have given extra attention to youth.

While teenagers had the highest savings outcomes of any age group in ADD, college-age participants had the lowest, perhaps because only two matched uses were relevant to them. Among the 8 percent of all ADD participants who were aged 19 to 23, 2 percent were planning for retirement savings, and few were planning to open a business (13 percent) or repair a home (4 percent). A third were planning for post-secondary education, while almost half (46 percent) were saving for home purchase. Thus, home purchase was the most popular planned use among college-age participants, even among the 17 percent of college-age participants who were students. Most participants who planned for post-secondary education were older than "college age," even though they were concentrated among the young (average age of thirty versus thirty-six for all participants), reflecting perhaps the need for poor youth to take jobs straight out of high school rather than enroll directly in college.

Figure 7.2
Association between Age and Monthly Net IDA Savings for "Savers" in ADD

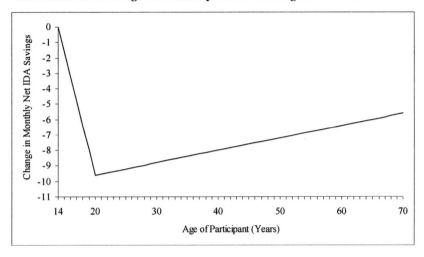

Given that most college-age participants (83 percent) were not students, they may have lacked some omitted characteristics (such as wealthy parents) associated both with college attendance and greater saving. If so, this would at least partly explain the college-age dip in IDA savings outcomes. (As a segment, college-age participants still saved in ADD; 38 percent were "savers," and monthly net IDA savings for college-age participants was $9.56).

As participants age, many matched uses become more relevant. The salience of post-secondary education for the poor, for example, apparently increases with age. Even after the participant is too old to go back to school, IDAs for post-secondary education may still be relevant for children or grandchildren. Likewise, home purchase becomes more salient once people have had more time to accumulate savings and perhaps buy a car. With age, relevance increases for home repair (because there are more homeowners), small-business ownership (because self-employment increases with age), and retirement savings (because retirement is closer).

Furthermore, older households tend to have more resources available to save, especially after children finish school and after they have accumulated basic consumer durables. Older participants also tend to have more liquid assets available to reshuffle into IDAs. Finally, older participants may know more about how to save and why to save. The improvement in IDA savings outcomes with age suggests that older people are more able and/or more willing to save.

What does this suggest for policy? First, the determination of what types of assets qualify for matches should consider how the relevancy of different uses changes over the life span. For the youngest or oldest participants, only one or two of the matched uses in ADD were relevant. More people would want to save in IDAs at more points in time if the range of matched uses were carefully expanded (chapter 5).

Second, IDA saving was lowest for people in their twenties. This group has less income than they will have later in life, and they are still acquiring basic consumer durables such as cars and furniture. At the same time, social expectations for consumption—and homeownership—are sharp, and they may be raising children. IDAs might be more relevant for this group if there were matches for car purchase or if time caps were longer so that younger participants could save for home purchase at a slower rate. In general, longer time caps would make IDAs more relevant at all ages, as participants could save even if they were not interested in any specific matched uses at the moment, knowing that they could wait to make a matched withdrawal when they are ready.

Third, youth in ADD had the best IDA savings outcomes of any age group, and three-fourths of them were planning for post-secondary education. This shows that at least some sub-set of youth is willing and able to save for college, perhaps with family help. One way to take advantage of this might be to link IDAs with 529 College Savings Plans (Clancy, Orszag, and Sherraden, 2004; Clancy, 2003).

Race/Ethnicity

In terms of race/ethnicity, most participants in ADD were African-American (47 percent) or Caucasian (37 percent). About 9 percent were Hispanic, 3 percent were Native American, 2 percent were Asian American, and 3 percent were "other." Compared with the general low-income population, ADD had a smaller share of Caucasians and a greater share of other groups.

Racial Wealth Gaps

African Americans are less wealthy than Caucasians (Altonji and Doraszelski, 2001; Blau and Graham, 1990). (Most research focuses on these two groups, in part because of small samples for other groups.) Compared with the median Caucasian, the median African American has six-tenths the income and one-tenth the net worth (Wolff, 2004). These gaps grew in the 1980s and 1990s (Wolff, 1998). For African Americans in 2001, median financial wealth was zero, and the homeownership rate was less than two-thirds that of Caucasians (Wolff, 2004). While 14 percent of Caucasians were "unbanked" in 1993, the figure for African Americans was 45 percent (Carney and Gale, 2001).

Research seems to conclude that African Americans have lower wealth even though they save a higher share of their income (Bernheim and Garrett, 2003, p. 1507; Blau and Graham, 1990). For example, Galenson (1972) attributes this to poor Caucasians' greater willingness to dissave (borrow) because, compared with poor African Americans, their low-income state is more likely temporary. In a historical study, Olney (1998) gives a similar reason, saying that African Americans in the 1920s saved more than Caucasians because they could not count on access to merchant credit for purchases of consumption goods.

A higher saving rate is not necessarily incompatible with the racial wealth gap, if the measure of saving does not net off dissaving and/or if African Americans' lower incomes mean that even their saving at a higher rate produces a lower absolute level of savings. The greater risks faced by African Americans—such as being the last hired and first fired—suggest that precautionary motives could explain high saving rates coupled with low asset accumulation. Precaution in the face of risk is consistent with the tendency of African Americans to hold low-risk (and low-return) investments (Badu, Daniels, and Salandro, 1999; Blau and Graham, 1990).

In ADD, Caucasians and African Americans had almost the same income (table 7.4). In contrast to the literature, the IDA savings rate from income was lower (0.8 percent) for African Americans than for Caucasians (1.6 percent, table 7.5). Furthermore, there was a pronounced racial wealth gap. Total assets for Caucasians averaged $18,700, versus $5,500 for African Americans (table 7.4), a ratio of 3.4:1. Mean net worth was $5,500 for Caucasians, versus $1,000 of African Americans, and median net worth for African Americans was zero. Caucasians were three times more likely to own a home, 1.5 times more likely

Table 7.4
Income and Asset Ownership for African-American and Caucasian Participants in ADD

Indicator	Caucasian	African American
Income		
Monthly household income ($)	$1,340	$1,400
Poverty/income ratio (%)	105	107
Asset ownership		
Total assets (average $)	18,700	5,500
Net worth (average $)	5,500	1,000
Net worth (median $)	1,000	0
Home-ownership rate (%)	27	8
Car-ownership rate (%)	81	53
Business-ownership rate (%)	15	8
Likelihood "unbanked" (%)	15	30

Table 7.5
IDA Savings Outcomes by Race/Ethnicity for Participants in ADD

IDA Savings Outcome	Caucasian	African American	Asian American	Hispanic	Native American	"Other"
Number of participants	877	1,094	44	208	62	65
Likelihood "saver" (%)	60	44	77	60	47	65
Net IDA savings per month for "savers" ($)	33.03	23.82	37.20	28.74	30.01	29.50
Net IDA savings per month per participant ($)	21.64	11.76	30.61	17.62	14.60	19.78
IDA savings rate from income (%)	1.6	0.8	2.2	1.2	1.0	1.5
Deposit frequency in months with IDA open (%)	52	43	50	45	49	48

to own a car, twice as likely to own a business, and half as likely to be "unbanked."

What explains the racial wealth gap? There are no intrinsic racial/ethnic differences in willingness or ability to save and build assets, so the ultimate cause must be discrimination, starting with slavery down to this day. The ancestors of most African Americans arrived as slaves with no assets, not even their own human capital. Even after Emancipation, African Americans—because of who they were, not because of what they did—were barred from many asset-building policies available to native-born Caucasians and European immigrants who, although poor on arrival, could take advantage of asset-building policies such as the Homestead Act (Williams, 2003). The Reconstruction promise to former slaves of "forty acres and a mule" was never kept. Furthermore, the descendents of European immigrants were eventually accepted as "mainstream" Americans, a status not yet accorded to the descendents of African slaves.

When African Americans did build assets, they often lost them to theft or destruction (Miller, 2003; Massey and Deaton, 1994). The lesson that savers would be punished was not lost on African Americans. For example, the Freedman's Bank, set up for newly freed slaves, collapsed due to mismanagement by its Caucasian board. Sherraden (1991, p. 134) quotes DuBois (1970, p. 39): "Not even ten additional years of slavery could have done so much to throttle the thrift of the freedmen as the mismanagement and bankruptcy of the series of savings banks chartered by the Nation for their especial aid."

In general, access to institutions for saving and asset building has varied by race (Shapiro, 2004; Oliver and Shapiro, 1995; Sherraden, 1991). For example, discrimination in credit and housing markets (Ladd, 1998; Munnell et al., 1996) has decreased access for African Americans to the home-mortgage interest subsidy, to mortgages as a saving-commitment device, and to homeownership as a source of capital gains. (Compared with Caucasian homeowners, African-American homeowners are less likely to benefit from appreciation, see Katz Reid, 2004). Labor-market discrimination—both in wage jobs (Darity and Mason, 1998) and in self-employment (Blanchflower, Levine, and Zimmerman, 1998; Cavalluzzo and Cavalluzzo, 1998)—has decreased access not only to remunerative work but also to asset-building subsidies in 401(k) plans. Self-employment—a quintessentially American path to wealth—has been for African Americans an economic detour (Bates, 1997). Segregation in housing and schooling—combined with local-school finance— means that African Americans receive smaller human-capital subsidies and then lower returns—thanks to labor-market discrimination—for their human capital. Finally, theft and murder by governments, businesses, mobs, and individuals have punctuated the history of African Americans, disrupting saving and asset building (Feagan, 2000). Even if these shames did not persist into the present, part of the "sedimentation of racial inequality" (Oliver and Shapiro,

1995) is that low assets beget low assets, so past inequality produces current inequality.

Not only does past discrimination percolate into current wealth gaps, but discrimination is still alive and well. The clearest evidence comes from "audit" studies in which a pair of matched testers, one Caucasian and one African American, interact one after the other with a given agent (Yinger, 1998). Audit studies show, for example, that car dealers give smaller discounts off sticker prices to African Americans, increasing the cost of this asset (Ayres and Siegelman, 1995). Likewise, real estate agents and appraisers discriminate in several ways, decreasing African-American homeownership (Galster, 1990; Yinger, 1986). Landlords contacted by phone are more likely to tell a caller with a black accent that an apartment is already rented (Massey and Lundy, 1998). Employers also discriminate, for example by responding half as frequently to written requests for interviews from people with stereotypically African-American first names (Bertrand and Mullainathan, 2003).

As argued in chapter 2 and in Bowles and Gintis (2002), a large share of wealth is inherited through inter vivos transfers of education (human capital), social networks, and other intangible assets. Parents with enough wealth (human capital and otherwise) to earn high incomes can reside in high-quality school districts and so bequeath to their children high levels of human capital. These children then get higher-paying jobs and thus enjoy greater lifetime resources. African Americans are systematically shut out of this process, not only because their parents and grandparents started with fewer resources but also because current discrimination and segregation keeps them in low-quality schools and low-paying jobs. Attaining a given economic status is more difficult for African Americans than for otherwise-similar Caucasians.

In other words, African Americans and Caucasians do not have access to the same asset-building institutions. The difference stems from actions (and continuing consequences) made by a Caucasian-controlled society. Education, homeownership, business ownership, hard work, thrift, and other factors related to asset-building do not produce outcomes in the same way for African Americans as for Caucasians.

In some cases (as argued in chapter 2), the dysfunction of the asset-building institutions available to African Americans has allowed knowledge of the possibility (and/or value) of asset-building to atrophy, much like many Cubans under the trade embargo have lost skill at driving cars simply because there are fewer cars.

Closing Racial Wealth Gaps

There are three broad approaches to closing racial wealth gaps: redistribution, reform, and education. Redistribution forms the basis of current calls for reparations, reasoning that if Caucasians stole resources from African Americans, then they should pay them back. This debt exists even if all theft involved now-dead people, because stolen advantages were passed from generation to generation. Redistribution does not address the need to improve the asset-building institutions available to African Americans.

Reform involves changing policies and programs so as to improve the asset-building institutions available to African Americans. Examples include abolishing local-school finance, pressuring banks to maintain branches in African-American neighborhoods and to avoid redlining, and eradicating discrimination from labor markets. Reform makes saving easier from now on, putting African Americans on a level playing field, but it does not wipe out the head start that Caucasians have inherited from the past.

Education—the third approach—focuses on knowledge of how to save and of the value of saving. This is not because African Americans blew their chance to learn but because, in a confiscatory society with inefficient asset-building institutions, they were taught a different lesson, one that rationally led them to let saving fade from their worldview. The consensus in the literature is that most people, regardless of race, need help learning how and why to save (Bernheim and Garrett, 2003; Bernheim, 2002; Bernheim, Garrett, and Maki, 2001; Thaler, 1992). Education without reform or redistribution, however, is a bit like providing Cubans with free driver's-education classes but no cars.

IDAs combine all three approaches for closing racial wealth gaps. IDAs are redistributive; matches take from taxpayers or private philanthropists and give to poor participants. IDAs also reform savings institutions, for example by asking banks to remove maintenance fees and minimum-balance requirements, by promoting looser asset limits on public assistance, and by increasing the financial return to saving. IDA's most important reform, however, is simply their existence, which suggests—to both the poor and non-poor—that the poor can and should save. Finally, IDAs educate not only through required classes but also through the provision of real-life experience in saving and building assets.

"Savers" and Race/Ethnicity

In the first-step Probit regression, African-American and Caucasian participants in ADD were equally likely to be "savers" with at least $100 in net IDA savings (table 7.3). If characteristics in the regression were uniformly distributed by race, then the same share of Caucasians and African Americans would have been "savers."

Still, discrimination and its legacy mattered, as characteristics in the regression were not uniformly distributed by race. For example, having a four-year college degree was strongly associated with being a "saver," and 11 percent of Caucasians had a four-year degrees, versus 5 percent of African Americans. Without controlling for factors in the regression, 60 percent of Caucasians were "savers," versus 44 percent of African Americans (table 7.5). The non-existent "independent association" from the regression contrasts with the large "dependent association" from cross-tabs. Race was not associated with omitted characteristics linked with "savers," but race was associated with included characteristics linked with "savers."

Compared with Caucasians and African Americans, Asian Americans in the regression were more likely to be "savers" (20 percentage points, table 7.3), as were Hispanics (8 percentage points) and "others" (14 percentage points). Native Americans were least likely to be "savers." This same pattern was reflected in the average share of "savers" by segment (table 7.5): 77 percent for Asian Americans, 65 percent for "others," 60 percent for Hispanics, and 47 percent for Native Americans. As for African Americans, IDA savings outcomes for Native Americans reflect a history of discrimination and asset stripping.

Of course, Asian Americans, Hispanics, and "others" have also suffered discrimination. Their better outcomes—all else in the regression constant—may reflect a concentration of first-generation Americans (or their children) who self-selected into immigration based on traits such as risk-taking and future orientation that also improve savings outcomes. Native-born Caucasians, African Americans, and Native Americans are not so highly self-selected.

Monthly Net IDA Savings and Race/Ethnicity

All else in the second-step least-squares regression constant, Asian-American "savers" in ADD had the highest levels of monthly net IDA savings, and Native-American "savers" had the lowest (table 7.3). Hispanic and Caucasian "savers" had higher levels than African-American "savers." All groups of "savers" had monthly net IDA savings of at least $23.82 (table 7.5), but differences in characteristics (omitted or included in the regression) led to large differences among groups.

For example, Caucasian "savers" had—without controlling for other characteristics—$33.03 of net IDA savings per month, while African-American "savers" had $23.82. About 40 percent of the $9.21 difference was due to differences in characteristics included in the regression, and 60 percent ($5.43) was due to differences in omitted characteristics.

On a per-participant basis, African Americans had the lowest monthly net IDA savings, ($11.76, table 7.5), followed by Native Americans ($14.60), Hispanics ($17.62), "others" ($19.78), Caucasians ($21.64), and Asian Americans ($30.61). The average for ADD overall was $16.60.

Discrimination

What does this suggest about discrimination, whether by ADD programs or by society? Most non-audit regression studies of discrimination follow Blinder

(1972) and Oaxaca (1972) in attributing to discrimination any association between outcomes and omitted characteristics correlated with race while not attributing to discrimination any racial differences in the distribution of the values of included characteristics (for example, Lindley, Selby, and Jackson, 1984; Black, Schweitzer, and Mandell, 1978). This assumes that associations between outcomes and included characteristics constitute acceptable non-discrimination (even if discrimination caused different races to have different distributions of included characteristics in the first place) but that associations between outcomes and omitted characteristics constitute unacceptable discrimination. This is mistaken on two counts. First, a regression might find an association between an outcome and race that is due to past discrimination, not current discrimination. For example, suppose that homeownership depends partly on knowing about the benefits of homeownership, which in turn depends partly on having grown up around homeowners. The legacy of discrimination means that African Americans are less likely to have grown up around homeowners, are less likely to know about the benefits of homeownership, and thus are less likely to become homeowners now. Even if there were no current discrimination, a regression that failed to control for "having grown up around homeowners" would find a negative association between being African American and homeownership. The standard approach would attribute this to current discrimination and then recommend ways to eliminate it, even if there is no current discrimination to eliminate. Second, if the regression controlled for "having grown up around homeowners," then there would be no link between race and homeownership indicating (correctly) that there is no current discrimination. In this case, however, housing-market outcomes still depend on a characteristic that was shaped by past discrimination, and the absence of current discrimination does not mean that past discrimination no longer produces unequal opportunities.

All this means two things. First, regressions can detect whether omitted characteristics were correlated with both race and outcomes, but this is not the same thing as detecting discrimination. For example, the statistically significant association for African Americans and Native Americans in the second-step regression does not necessarily mean that IDA programs (or society) discriminated against these groups while they participated in ADD. Likewise, the statistically insignificant association for African Americans in the first-step regression does not necessarily mean that IDA programs (or society) did not discriminate. In both cases, the results are about links between race and characteristics omitted from the regression and correlated with outcomes. The regressions do not say whether the omitted characteristics were due to discrimination, nor, if they were, who did the discrimination.

Second, the effects of past discrimination may linger—even in the absence of current discrimination—until differences in characteristics caused by past discrimination are eliminated. Thus, the regression results here do not mean that African Americans or Native Americans, for some reason related to their choices or abilities, save less than other groups. Rather, it indicates the effects of past (and current) discrimination.

African-American, Native American, and other non-Caucasian participants in ADD suffered and suffer from discrimination. This much is known. If statistics must be mustered, then the clearest evidence is not that regressions found statistically significant associations between race/ethnicity and IDA savings outcomes but rather that IDA savings outcomes (and the distribution of values of characteristics) differed by race/ethnicity. The IDA programs in ADD may or may not have discriminated (or reverse discriminated); there is no way for the regression to tell. Given that there is nothing intrinsically different among people of different racial/ethnic backgrounds beyond their groups' social histories, the most policy-relevant measure of discrimination is not the regression coefficient on race (something that depends, after all, on which characteristics are omitted from a regression) but rather group differences in outcomes and the distribution of characteristics.

IDAs and Racial Wealth Gaps

At enrollment, mean net worth in ADD was $5,500 for Caucasians and $1,000 for African Americans (table 7.4), a ratio of 5.5:1. How IDAs affected this gap depended on how much IDA savings was "new" (caused by access to IDAs) versus "reshuffled" (shifted into IDAs from other forms). The MIS IDA data cannot distinguish between "new" and "reshuffled" savings, so two polar cases are analyzed.

In the scenario least likely to close racial wealth gaps, all net IDA savings by African Americans are assumed to be "reshuffled" while all net IDA savings by Caucasians are assumed to be "new." The average match rate was 1.75:1 for Caucasians and 1.93:1 for African Americans, and net IDA savings per participant was $739 for Caucasians and $280 for African Americans. Given these assumptions, IDAs would have increased net worth by $2,032 for Caucasians and $540 for African Americans, decreasing the ratio gap to 4.9:1 while increasing the absolute gap by about $1,500. The simulated increase for African Americans represents 50 percent growth.

In the scenario most likely to close racial wealth gaps, all net IDA savings by African Americans are assumed to be "new" while all net IDA savings by Caucasians are assumed to be "reshuffled." (Results in Mills et al., 2004, suggest that IDA saving by African Americans may be more likely to be "new" than IDA saving by Caucasians.) Under these assumptions, net worth increases by about $1,300 for Caucasians and $820 for African Americans. The ratio of mean net worth falls to 3.7:1 while the absolute gap increases by almost $500. The simulated increase for African Americans represents 80 percent growth over their starting point.

What actually happened in ADD must be somewhere between the two polar cases, so IDAs reduced the ratio gap but expanded the absolute gap. The failure to shrink absolute wealth gaps even though mean net worth for African Americans increased by at least 50 percent highlights how the different distribution of characteristics by race impedes catching up.

Education

More education (and thus more human capital) might be linked with IDA savings outcomes because education increases financial sophistication and future orientation and/or because education signals the presence of such factors. In ADD, 16 percent of participants did not complete high school, 23 percent finished high school but did not attend college, 39 percent attended college but did not graduate, and 22 percent had a college degree of some sort (table 7.6).

Keeping other factors in the regression constant, IDA savings outcomes were best for four-year college graduates. (The regression estimates suggest that most college graduates for whom two-year/four-year status was unknown had four-year degrees.) Four-year graduates were twenty-one percentage points more likely to be "savers" than those who did not complete high school, and they were about sixteen percentage points more likely to be "savers" than high-school graduates who did not attend or finish college. Compared with other groups, four-year graduates who were "savers" also had about $3 more of net IDA savings per month.

From a policy perspective, this may highlight the potential benefit of financial education, especially for less-educated participants. For example, IDA programs might excuse college graduates from financial-education requirements, freeing up resources to improve classes for other IDA participants.

Without keeping other factors in the regression constant, less-educated participants in ADD saved less, although they still saved. For example, 42 percent of participants who did not complete high school were "savers," and participants who did not complete high school had monthly net IDA savings of $12.19.

Employment

Employment might be linked with IDA savings outcomes in several ways. First, employed participants may have more resources available to save, not only because they have earned income (a factor included in the regression) but also because employer-provided benefits may decrease their expenses (a factor omitted from the regression). Second, employment might serve as a marker for omitted characteristics (such as dedication or future orientation) associated both with employment and with greater saving.

Several IDA programs in ADD required that participants be employed, and about 91 percent of participants had jobs or were students (table 7.6). Keeping

Table 7.6

Associations between Savings Outcomes and Education and Employment Status for Participants in ADD

Independent variable	Prob.("Saver") Mean	Δ% pts.	p-value	Net IDA savings/month Mean	Δ$	p-value
Education						
Did not complete high school	0.16			0.13		
Completed high school or GED	0.23	+4.6	0.26	0.21	+0.11	0.94
Attended college but did not graduate	0.39	+6.3	0.12	0.38	+0.57	0.69
Graduated 2-year college	0.04	+4.4	0.55	0.03	−3.26	0.20
Graduated college, 2-year/4-year unknown	0.11	+18.3	0.01	0.14	+3.81	0.04
Graduated 4-year college	0.07	+21.1	0.01	0.10	+2.84	0.15
Employment						
Unemployed	0.05			0.05		
Homemaker, retired, or disabled	0.04	+2.2	0.79	0.05	−3.28	0.18
Student, not working	0.06	−6.3	0.41	0.04	+1.13	0.68
Student, also working	0.03	+14.4	0.11	0.03	+3.27	0.26
Employed part-time	0.23	+6.5	0.27	0.23	+0.82	0.68
Employed full-time	0.59	+7.0	0.23	0.60	−2.16	0.27
Employee of host organization						
No	0.98			0.97		
Yes	0.02	+5.4	0.52	0.03	+3.26	0.17

Note: All regression estimates were derived from a single "Heckit"-type selection specification with two steps. The first step was a Probit (n=2,350, k=104) for the likelihood of being a "saver." The second step was ordinary least-squares (n=1,232, k=111) for net IDA savings per month for "savers." Means were taken over non-missing observations.

other factors in the regression constant, "working" participants (full-time employees, part-time employees, and students with jobs) were more likely to be "savers" than "not working" participants (unemployed, homemakers, retired, disabled, and students without jobs). Among "savers," there were no statistical differences in monthly net IDA savings by employment status.

Without keeping other factors in the regression constant, employment was associated with saving, but the absence of employment did not preclude saving. "Not working" participants had monthly net IDA savings of $12.68, and 48 percent were "savers." This suggests that policy should not target IDA programs only to the "working poor," because the "not working poor" can also save in IDAs. Furthermore, targeting only the "working poor" may send the message that the "not working" poor cannot or should not save.

About 2 percent of IDA participants were employed by host organizations in ADD (table 7.6). In the regression, this was not linked with IDA savings outcomes.

Public Assistance

Can welfare recipients save? About 45 percent of ADD participants received some form of means-tested public assistance at some time, whether Aid for Families with Dependent Children or Temporary Assistance for Needy Families before enrollment (10 percent, table 7.7), AFDC or TANF at enrollment (38 percent), Supplemental Security Income or Supplemental Security Disability Income at enrollment (11 percent), and/or Food Stamps at enrollment (17 percent).

Receipt of public assistance might be linked with IDA savings outcomes for three reasons. First, eligibility for welfare depends on an asset test. Thus, welfare recipients have fewer assets available to reshuffle into IDAs. Furthermore, poor people—even if they do not currently receive public assistance—are aware of these limits. Thus, they may save less so that, in a downturn, they need not spend-down assets before qualifying for welfare (Ziliak, 2003; Powers, 1998; Moffitt, 1986). In contrast to IDAs, asset limits tell the poor that they should not or cannot save. Second, the prospect of using public assistance decreases saving, not only because of asset tests but also because the safety net weakens precautionary motives. Third, people on welfare might possess characteristics that are omitted from the regression and correlated with both savings outcomes and welfare receipt. For example, welfare receipt might produce a "culture of poverty" that decreases saving. Also, characteristics that cause a need for public assistance (say, alcoholism) may reduce saving.

For IDA participants in ADD, welfare receipt was not linked with being a "saver" (table 7.7). Except for Food Stamps, welfare was also not linked with monthly net IDA savings for "savers." Combining the four indicators for welfare receipt into a single indicator and rerunning the regressions produces estimates with p-values of 0.99. Also, removing controls for income (due to

Table 7.7

Associations between Savings Outcomes and Income and Receipt of Public Assistance for Participants in ADD

Independent variable	Prob.("Saver")			Net IDA savings/month		
	Mean	Δ% pts.	p-value	Mean	ΔS	p-value
AFDC or TANF before enrollment						
No	0.62			0.64		
Yes	0.38	+1.6	0.59	0.36	−0.09	0.92
AFDC or TANF at enrollment						
No	0.90			0.93		
Yes	0.10	−4.2	0.41	0.07	+1.77	0.32
SSI/SSDI at enrollment						
No	0.89			0.89		
Yes	0.11	+2.1	0.68	0.11	+2.29	0.15
Food Stamps at enrollment						
No	0.83			0.84		
Yes	0.17	+4.6	0.28	0.16	−2.75	0.06
Recurrent income (monthly $)						
0 to $1,500 (spline)	1,000	−0.003	0.41	990	+0.0015	0.19
$1,500 to $3,000 (spline)	155	+0.003	0.52	165	−0.0001	0.97
Intermittent income (monthly $)						
0 to $2,000 (spline)	210	+0.007	0.06	250 •	+0.0018	0.13
$2,000 to $3,000 (spline)	6	+0.014	0.51	8	−0.0052	0.33

Note: All regression estimates were derived from a single "Heckit"-type selection specification with two steps. The first step was a Probit (n=2,350, k=104) for the likelihood of being a "saver." The second step was ordinary least-squares (n=1,232, k=111) for net IDA savings per month for "savers." Means were taken over non-missing observations.

possible collinearity with welfare receipt) does not change the results. All in all, welfare receipt did not serve as a marker of omitted characteristics that affected IDA saving.

Of course, the values of included characteristics differed between welfare recipients and other participants, so, without regression controls, welfare recipients did have worse IDA savings outcomes. But they still saved; about 38 percent of participants who received TANF at enrollment were "savers," and these participants who received TANF at enrollment had monthly net IDA savings of $10.85. This suggests that it does not make sense for policy to exclude welfare recipients from IDAs on the assumption that they would not save anyway; even some people on welfare can save in IDAs.

Income

For IDA participants in ADD, household income was low, averaging 107 percent of the federal poverty guideline. The median participant was at the poverty line, and about 20 percent of participants were below 50 percent of the poverty line.

In classical economic theory, saving depends on "permanent income," a measure of expected lifetime resources. Changes to permanent income (perhaps due to access to matches in IDAs) might increase or decrease saving. When permanent income increases, the "substitution effect" increases saving because it decreases the price of future consumption in terms of current consumption. In contrast, the "fixed target effect" (also called the "income effect" or "wealth effect") decreases saving, as less saving is required to reach a target level of future consumption. In principle, either effect could dominate, and the net effect might depend on the level of income. For example, if income is so low that it must all be spent merely to subsist, then only the "substitution effect" is relevant and increased permanent income cannot decrease saving.

In 401(k) plans, higher income is associated with higher participation (roughly corresponding to a higher likelihood of being a "saver"). Higher income is also associated with higher 401(k) savings rates as a share of income (Huberman, Iyengar, and Jiang, 2003; VanDerhei and Copeland, 2001). But the relationship between income and 401(k) saving—even for low-income employees—need not indicate anything about the relationship between income and IDA saving. For one thing, IDA participants are poorer than 401(k) participants. Also, the financial pay-off to IDA saving comes sooner and is more concrete than the pay-off for 401(k) saving. Finally, 401(k) participants probably expect to have access to 401(k) plans for most of the rest of their lives, but participants in ADD did not expect permanent access to IDAs. The time limits on IDAs should—all else constant—increase participants' saving.

Economic theory also predicts that saving is more likely from temporary changes in income than from permanent changes. The MIS IDA data from ADD do not distinguish between the permanent and temporary parts of income.

Instead, sources of income were grouped as "recurrent" (wages, public assistance, pensions, and income from investments, accounting for 85 percent of income) and "intermittent" (self-employment, child support, gifts, and "other"). The assumption is that "recurrent" income corresponds to permanent income (with small effects on saving) and "intermittent" income corresponds to transitory income (with large effects on saving). This grouping also isolates sources of income that, due to their recurrence, are probably measured more accurately than intermittent sources of income.

To allow associations between income and IDA savings outcomes in ADD to vary with the level of income, both recurrent and intermittent income in the first and second steps of the regression were represented as two-piece splines. For the lowest levels of income, additional income was generally associated with (small) improvements in IDA savings outcomes. For participants close to subsistence, this is exactly what theory predicts, as only the "substitution effect" is operative.

For example, the level of recurrent income was not related with the likelihood of being a "saver" (table 7.7). In the range of 0 to $2,000, intermittent income was associated ($p = 0.06$) with greater chances of being a "saver." Still, the link was small (0.7 percentage points per $100). Additional intermittent income above $2,000 was not linked with being a "saver."

This same pattern held for income and monthly net IDA savings for "savers," albeit with less statistical significance and weaker associations. For recurrent income below $1,500, each $100 was associated with 15 cents more net IDA savings per month, with no link after $1,500. For intermittent income, the association was 18 cents per $100, leveling off after $2,000.

These estimates control for other factors in the regression and suggest that income did not have a strong independent association with IDA savings outcomes. Looking at dependent associations without controlling for other factors, 48 percent of participants below 50 percent of the poverty line were "savers." These participants averaged monthly net IDA savings of $14.91, and their IDA savings rate from income was 1.9 percent. For comparison, 56 percent of participants above 150 percent of poverty were "savers," and they averaged monthly net IDA savings of $18.18, with an IDA savings rate of 0.9 percent. Thus, while the lowest-income poor participants in ADD saved less in IDAs than the highest-income poor participants, they still saved, and their IDA savings rate from income was almost twice as high.

Why was income only weakly linked with IDA savings outcomes in ADD? Possible explanations include censoring at the match cap, measurement error, and institutional factors (Schreiner et al., 2001; Sherraden, Schreiner, and Beverly, 2003).

In terms of censoring, if higher income was strongly linked with IDA savings outcomes but if match caps kept observed net IDA savings below desired net IDA savings, then censoring at the match cap might have obscured the link between income and outcomes. Regressions that control for censoring, however, find only slightly stronger links (Schreiner, 2004d).

In terms of measurement error, income data from ADD were subject to at least six possible biases, most of which tended to mask positive links between income and savings. First, income in most surveys is underreported, and qualitative research by Edin and Lein (1997) finds that very poor people understate their income more than less-poor people. The very poor may have concealed income to maintain eligibility for means-tested public assistance, and they may have received a larger share of income from informal, irregular, or in-kind sources that are more likely to be underreported. Moreover, eligibility for IDAs in ADD had an income test, and participants may have thought that understating income would help their chances of qualifying. Second, the largest program in ADD patched income data together from several sources, and the questions used did not exactly match those in MIS IDA. In general, income data were collected by IDA staff, not trained enumerators, possibly increasing measurement error and attenuating estimated associations. Third, the question about income in MIS IDA asked for "monthly gross income of household by source." Some participants may have interpreted "monthly" as average monthly household income in the past calendar year or as average monthly income in the twelve months before enrollment. Others may have reported their income in the month of enrollment, or in an average month. Fourth, income varies month-to-month, and ADD measured monthly income only at enrollment. Monthly data probably has more variation than annual data, and income variation may be large for the poor (Deaton, 1997). Fifth, income variation through time introduces a subtle bias. Because people have more resources available to save when income is higher, ADD participants were probably more likely to enroll in months when their income was unusually high. If income then regressed to its long-term mean, people with higher reported monthly income at enrollment would appear to have had lower IDA savings rates. In the same way, people who happened to enroll in months when their income was unusually low probably then progressed to their mean, with higher apparent IDA savings rates. Sixth, people may have been more likely to enroll if they expected their future income to increase, as this reduces the expected cost of future saving. Thus, ADD may have caught some poor participants on their way up. In this case, income at enrollment was lower than in subsequent months, so the IDA savings rate in terms of income at enrollment was higher than the IDA savings rate in terms of average income in all months of participation. The economy grew rapidly during most of ADD, so this effect may have mattered. In general, these six sources of bias tend to obscure any positive link that might have been present between income and savings. Thus, the weakly positive link that was estimated might be explained partly (or completely) by these measurement issues.

In terms of institutional features, theory suggests that external variables beyond income mattered and that asset-building resulted in part from "institutionalized mechanisms involving explicit connections, rules, incentives, and subsidies" (Sherraden, 1991, p. 116). In other words, IDA savings outcomes depended not only on participant characteristics (such as income) but also on program characteristics (such as match caps). For example, higher match rates increased the chances of being a "saver," and more hours of required financial education increased monthly net IDA savings (chapter 6). Participants apparently turned match caps into savings targets, tried to reach the targets, and ended up with greater net IDA savings. These institutional-design elements affected IDA savings outcomes beyond the effects of participant characteristics.

In ADD, institutional factors may have swamped censoring and measurement issues. If institutional effects were strongest for the poorest, it could explain the weak links between income (and public assistance) and IDA savings outcomes. For example, turning match caps into savings targets would affect poorer participants more because, without targets, they would be less likely to want to "max out" their IDA. Likewise, poorer participants may have benefited more from financial education, narrowing savings differences that would otherwise have been caused by income differences.

For IDAs in ADD, income was not strongly linked with savings outcomes. This suggests that IDA policy need not target only the "working poor" or "stable poor." Even very poor people saved in ADD, perhaps because IDAs' supportive institutional structure had its greatest effects for the poorest participants.

Liquid Assets in Bank Accounts

Presence

Participants in ADD were asked to report individual assets and liabilities. At enrollment, 38 percent had both passbook and checking accounts, 26 percent had only a checkbook, 12 percent had only a passbook, and 23 percent were "unbanked" with no account (table 7.8).

For three reasons, the presence of a bank account may have been linked with IDA savings outcomes (chapter 6). First, people who already had bank accounts probably also possessed characteristics such as facility with math or comfort with banks that were linked with saving but omitted from the regression. Second, people who already had liquid assets could more easily "reshuffle" assets into IDAs. Third, people who already had bank accounts could more easily make deposits into IDAs, for example by mailing a check, using an ATM or the internet to transfer between accounts, or setting up automatic transfer from an existing account to the IDA.

A passbook requires less management than a checkbook, so passbook ownership should be a weaker marker of omitted characteristics correlated with greater saving. Hogarth and Lee (2000) find that people who own only a

Table 7.8
Associations between Savings Outcomes and Checking and Passbook Savings Accounts of Participants in ADD

Independent variable	Prob.("Saver")			Net IDA savings/month		
	Mean	Δ% pts.	p-value	Mean	Δ$	p-value
Passbook and checking accounts						
Both passbook and checkbook	0.38			0.45		
Checking only	0.26	+4.6	0.23	0.30	+2.44	0.04
Passbook only	0.12	-12.8	0.01	0.10	-2.13	0.16
Unbanked (no passbook, no checking)	0.23	-8.0	0.06	0.15	+0.85	0.58
Passbook savings balance ($)						
0 to $400 (spline)	94	+0.049	0.01	113	+0.0133	0.01
$400 to $3,000 (spline)	134	-0.007	0.03	175	+0.0012	0.19
Checking balance ($)						
0 to $1,500 (spline)	198	+0.012	0.01	260	-0.0007	0.62
$1,500 to $3,000 (spline)	21	-0.010	0.33	29	+0.0016	0.50

Note: All regression estimates were derived from a single "Heckit"-type selection specification with two steps. The first step was a Probit (n=2,350, k=104) for the likelihood of being a "saver." The second step was ordinary least-squares (n=1,232, k=111) for net IDA savings per month for "savers." Means were taken over non-missing observations.

passbook savings account resemble the "unbanked" more than they resemble people who own a checking account.

The regression results from ADD show that participants with checkbooks had better IDA savings outcomes than others and that participants with pass-books had worse outcomes than others (table 7.8). In the first step, participants with only a checkbook were more likely to be "savers" than "unbanked" partici-pants (by about 13 percentage points), passbook-only participants (17 percent-age points), and participants with both a passbook and a checkbook (5 percentage points, p < 0.10 for all pair-wise comparisons). Passbook-only participants were about 5 percentage points less likely to be "savers" than the "unbanked."

This pattern appeared again in the second-step regression on monthly net IDA savings for "savers." Checkbooks were linked with higher IDA savings, while passbooks were linked with lower IDA savings (although not all pair-wise comparisons were statistically significant).

Should IDA programs advise participants to close passbook accounts? Owning a passbook probably does not cause low IDA saving; rather, it prob-ably signals the presence of characteristics omitted from the regression that reduce saving. To make policy recommendations requires identifying the omitted characteristics. The most important omitted factor may be "financial sophistication." A checkbook differs from a passbook in the ability to write checks. This means that a checkbook may be overdrawn, creating a need to track balances. People who struggle with balancing a checkbook and/or who have bounced checks in the past—whether because of math or because inad-vertent overdrafts are more likely for low-balance accounts—may be limited (voluntarily or not) to passbooks. While IDA programs could teach partici-pants how to track balances, this is only one dimension of "financial sophisti-cation," and saving in IDAs does not depend directly on the ability to balance a checkbook. Instead, financial-education requirements might be reduced for more-sophisticated participants with checking accounts, freeing up resources for general financial education for less-sophisticated participants. For example, IDA programs might require everyone to attend three to five hours of class, giving checkbook owners the option of skipping the final class or two.

Being "unbanked" or owning a passbook did not preclude saving in IDAs. Without keeping other factors in the regression constant, about 34 percent of the "unbanked" were "savers," and these "unbanked" participants had monthly net IDA savings of $9.43. Likewise, 42 percent of those participants with only a passbook were "savers," and these passbook-only participants had monthly net IDA savings of $11.29.

Balance

Like the presence of an account, the balance in an account might be linked with IDA saving by providing assets to "reshuffle" and/or by signalling the presence of omitted characteristics linked with saving. To allow for non-linearities, both steps in the regression specify balances in passbooks and checkbooks as two-piece splines.

Passbooks. The average passbook balance was $266 (this exceeds the sum of the average values of the spline segments in table 7.8 because the second segment is capped at $3,000), and the median was 0. For those with passbooks, the average balance was $545. Controlling for other factors in the regression, each $100 of balances from 0 to $400 was linked with an increase in the likelihood of being a "saver" of 4.9 percentage points (p = 0.01). Given that 52 percent of participants were "savers," this is a large effect. For balances in excess of $400, each $100 was linked with a 0.7 percentage-point decrease in the likelihood of being a "saver." Theory does not explain why this might be, but perhaps participants who had high balances were already saving for an asset purchase (such as a house) and left ADD because they did not want to wait to fulfill all program requirements before making a matched purchase.

In the second-step regression for "savers," higher passbook balances were linked with higher monthly net IDA savings. For balances from 0 to $400, each $100 was linked with $1.33 more net IDA savings per month (a large associa-tion), while for higher balances, a $100 increase was linked with a additional 12 cents of monthly net IDA savings. For participants who owned passbooks, higher balances signaled greater financial sophistication and/or a greater abil-ity to "reshuffle."

The presence of a passbook was linked with worse IDA savings outcomes, but higher passbook balances were (for most passbook owners) linked with better outcomes. Which link was stronger? Among ADD participants who owned a passbook, 58 percent were "savers," and monthly net IDA savings per partici-pant with a passbook was $28.83. If these participants did not own a passbook, the share who were "savers" would remain at 58 percent. Net IDA savings per month per participant would decrease by about a dollar, to $27.71.

Checkbooks. The average checkbook balance in ADD was $254 ($391 for those with a positive balance), with a median of $50. As for passbook balances, additional checkbook balances were linked first with an increase in the likeli-hood of being a "saver" (1.2 percentage points per $100 for balances from 0 to $1,500) and then a decrease (p = 0.33, table 7.8). For "savers," checking balances had no statistically significant link with monthly net IDA savings.

After controlling for the presence of the specific type of bank account, a dollar in a passbook was more strongly linked with IDA savings outcomes than a dollar in a checkbook. This may reflect "mental accounting" (Thaler and Shefrin, 1981). Participants may think of passbook balances as "savings" while mentally earmarking checking balances for payment of expenses. If checking balances were "spoken for," they were unavailable—unlike pass-book balances—for "reshuffling" into IDAs. Furthermore, checking balances go up and down much more than passbook balances, and so measured checking balances depended on the day of the month of enrollment. This measurement noise tends to mask links with IDA savings outcomes.

If only passbook balances were available for "reshuffling" and if illiquid assets were not reshuffled at all, then—accounting for match caps—the largest share of net IDA savings in ADD that could have been reshuffled was 20 percent.

Illiquid Assets

The poor hold most of their wealth in illiquid forms, chiefly human capital, homes, and cars. In ADD, 16 percent of participants owned homes, 64 percent owned cars, 2 percent owned land or property, 13 percent owned financial investments (probably mostly illiquid retirement accounts), and 11 percent had small-business assets (table 7.9). On average, total illiquid assets were $12,900 ($19,000 for those with non-zero illiquid assets), with 63 percent of this in housing and 23 percent in cars.

The regression estimates the links between IDA savings outcomes and indicators for the presence of a given type of illiquid asset. While participants may have had difficulty accurately estimating the value of homes, cars, and small businesses (Goodman and Ittner, 1992), they probably could report accurately whether they owned a given type of illiquid asset.

Like the presence of bank accounts, the presence of illiquid assets may serve as a marker for factors omitted from the regression that were linked both with asset ownership and higher savings. For example, people who saved to buy a house or car in the past probably had some traits that improve their saving but that were not recorded in the ADD data.

Few ADD participants sold off illiquid assets and then "reshuffled" the proceeds into IDAs. Still, some may have "reshuffled" out of illiquid assets (Schreiner et al., 2001). For example, participants might have freed up resources for IDAs by putting off repairs to homes or cars. Likewise, they might have contributed less to IRAs than they would have in the absence of ADD, putting the funds instead in IDAs.

Illiquid assets may also reduce expenses and thus free up resources for IDAs (Sherraden, 1991). Cars, for example, may reduce (or increase) on-going cash costs for transportation. Likewise, homeowners may have more (or less) free cash flow, depending on whether installments on home-mortgage debt are smaller than what rent would have been.

Finally, buying an illiquid asset such as a home or car often entails borrowing. Lenders carefully scrutinize applicants to determine whether they are creditworthy. Thus, the presence of mortgage debt signals a lender's belief that the participant is willing and able to pay monthly installments for years or decades. The lender likely bases this judgment of creditworthiness partly on characteristics that are omitted from the regression and that are associated with willingness and ability to save.

Homes

A home is a large, all-or-nothing purchase that requires saving for a down payment and closing costs. Thus, homeowners probably have characteristics that cause greater saving but that were omitted from the regression. Homeownership also decreases expenses (at least for a given level of housing quality in the long term), making more cash available for IDAs. Furthermore, home repair is an "easy" matched use that is relevant at most times for most homeowners.

Keeping other characteristics in the regression constant, homeowners with mortgages were 9.5 percentage points more likely than renters to be "savers" (p = 0.04, table 7.9). This is a huge effect. For free-and-clear homeowners without a mortgage, the likelihood of being a "saver" was statistically the same as for renters.

Among "savers," monthly net IDA savings was slightly higher ($1.55, p = 0.20) for homeowners with mortgages versus renters, and much higher ($6.17, p = 0.01) for free-and-clear homeowners. This is consistent with the idea that homeownership may not increase available resources until after the mortgage is paid-off.

Without other factors constant, renters in ADD saved less than homeowners. In particular, 48 percent of renters were "savers," and monthly net IDA savings per renter was $14.83 (versus versus 76 percent and $26.68 for homeowners). These differences were greater than the regression-based associations, suggesting that homeowners were more likely to have characteristics included in the regression—as well as omitted—that were positively correlated with saving. Still, many renters in ADD did save in IDAs, and homeownership—the most common planned use—was the most salient saving goal for them.

IDA programs may want to target extra attention to renters. They tend to save for homeownership, but this is a particularly "difficult" matched use. Renters have also had less experience with saving, and they tend to possess characteristics linked with worse outcomes.

Cars

About 64 percent of ADD participants owned cars, about two-thirds of them free-and-clear (table 7.9). Buying a car requires saving the full purchase price or saving for a down payment and then borrowing. Thus, cars might be linked with IDA saving via characteristics omitted from the regression that cause saving and that are correlated with creditworthiness and car ownership. Cars may also increase available resources by widening the geographic range over which a participant can search for jobs or by reducing the transport costs associated with making deposits or attending financial education. Finally, cars might

Table 7.9
Associations between Savings Outcomes and Ownership of Homes, Cars, Land or Property, Financial Investments, and Small Businesses by Participants in ADD

Independent variable	Prob.("Saver")			Net IDA savings/month		
	Mean	Δ% pts.	p-value	Mean	Δ$	p-value
Homeownership						
Renter	0.84			0.78		
Owned with mortgage	0.12	+9.5	0.04	0.17	+1.55	0.20
Owned free-and-clear	0.04	+3.4	0.62	0.05	+6.17	0.01
Car ownership						
None	0.36			0.26		
Owned with loan	0.24	+4.0	0.26	0.26	-0.88	0.46
Owned free-and-clear	0.40	+11.3	0.01	0.48	+0.71	0.54
Land or property ownership						
None	0.98			0.97		
Owned with mortgage	0.01	+55.4	0.07	0.01	-3.66	0.57
Owned free-and-clear	0.01	+68.0	0.02	0.02	-6.33	0.40
Financial investments						
No	0.87			0.84		
Yes	0.13	+12.8	0.01	0.16	-0.49	0.69
Small-business ownership						
No	0.89			0.86		
Yes	0.11	-0.6	0.91	0.14	+2.24	0.11

Note: All regression estimates were derived from a single "Heckit"-type selection specification with two steps. The first step was a Probit (n=2,350, k=104) for the likelihood of being a "saver." The second step was ordinary least-squares (n=1,232, k=111) for net IDA savings per month for "savers." Means were taken over non-missing observations.

decrease available resources because—like homes—they entail on-going out-flows for debt repayment, taxes, licenses, insurance, repairs, and fuel.

In the regression, car owners with a loan were 4 percentage points more likely than non-owners to be "savers," but the association was not statistically significant ($p = 0.26$). Free-and-clear car owners, however, were 11 percentage points more likely to be "savers" (a huge effect, with $p = 0.01$). Whatever the links between car ownership and characteristics omitted from the regression, they were apparently overwhelmed by the presence of car payments and their effects on available resources. In the second-step regression for "savers," car ownership was not statistically associated with monthly net IDA savings.

Without controlling for other factors, ADD participants without a car saved less, but this did not preclude their saving in IDAs. About 40 percent of partici-pants without a car were "savers," and participants without a car had monthly net IDA savings of $10.68.

Given that about one-fourth of ADD participants were making car pay-ments, the link between IDA savings outcomes and car loans may be impor-tant. IDA programs might provide one-on-one credit counseling to all enrollees (not just those who plan for home purchase) because paying off car loans or other debts (see below) absorb resources that might otherwise be saved in IDAs. Of course, debts must be repaid even if it precludes saving in IDAs. But until partici-pants can build net worth not only by reducing liabilities but also by increas-ing assets, programs might encourage participants to keep IDAs open and refrain from kicking out participants with low balances or sporadic deposits.

Land or Property

A small share of ADD participants (2 percent) owned land or property apart from their house. Membership in this select group of low-income owners of real estate was strongly and positively linked with factors omitted from the regression that improved IDA savings outcomes. In the first-step regression, land or property owners (with or without mortgage debt) were 55 to 68 per-centage points more likely to be "savers" (table 7.9). In the second step, how-ever, "savers" who owned land or property did not have higher levels of monthly net IDA savings.

Financial Investments

About 13 percent of participants had financial investments apart from pass-book or checking accounts, probably mostly in IRAs or 401(k) plans. While direct reshuffling from these illiquid accounts was probably difficult, their presence might act as a proxy for characteristics (such as financial sophistica-tion or future orientation) omitted from the regression that favor saving. Fur-thermore, owners of financial investments might "reshuffle" into IDAs part of what they would have saved in IRAs, especially if they were eligible for matches for retirement savings.

Owners of financial investments were about 13 percentage points more likely to be "savers" (p = 0.01, table 7.9). This is another massive association between asset ownership and IDA savings outcomes.

Because financial investments were not linked with the level of monthly net IDA savings for "savers," the presence of financial investments probably signals not "reshuffling" but rather financial sophistication. Again, this means that IDA programs might try to target resources for financial education to enrollees who enter with less experience with saving and asset-building.

Small Business

About 11 percent of ADD participants had business assets. About 19 percent were involved with self-employment, as indicated by their reporting business assets, business liabilities, or self-employment income.

Income and expenses are more volatile for the self-employed, providing a precautionary motive to save. (Volatile cash flows may also lead to unmatched withdrawals.) The self-employed also have more reason to save because they can invest in an asset—the small business itself—unavailable to others. Finally, microenterprise is an "easy" matched use, as many poor people do odd jobs (Losby et al., 2002; Edin and Lein, 1997), and almost any self-employment activity (regardless of scale or formality) can use some small durable items suitable for small matched withdrawals. Still, the investments available to small-business owners may increase the opportunity cost of keeping resources tied up in IDAs (Edgcomb and Klein, 2004).

In the regression, small-business ownership was not linked with the likelihood of being a "saver" (table 7.9). Among "savers," monthly net IDA savings was $2.24 greater for business owners (p = 0.11). Given that average monthly net IDA savings among all "savers" was 29.08, this is an 8 percent increase. (Defining "small-business owner" as anyone with any involvement in self-employment wipes out this association.)

In Mills et al. (2004), IDAs seem to improve small-business outcomes for Caucasians but not for African Americans. Adding interactions for race to the regression here indicates no racial differences in the likelihood of a business owner being a "saver," but African-American "savers" (perhaps due to precautionary motives) saved about $5 more per month than Caucasian "savers."

Liabilities

Liabilities (debts) are the opposite of assets. *Net worth* is defined as assets minus liabilities, so decreasing liabilities (paying off debts) increases net worth and is a form of saving.

In ADD, 17 percent of participants had student loans at enrollment, 18 percent had informal debts, 28 percent had overdue household bills, 18 percent had overdue medical bills, and 33 percent had credit-card debt (table 7.10). On average, total liabilities were $9,800 ($13,900 for those with non-zero debt). Of this, 47 percent were home mortgages, 15 percent were car loans, and 15 percent were student loans.

As with illiquid assets, participants probably could report the presence of a given type of liability more accurately than outstanding balances. Thus, the regression includes only indicators for the presence of given types of liabilities.

The presence of debt might be associated with worse IDA savings outcomes simply because debt service reduces the resources available to save. Also, monthly installments on debts (except from family or friends) come first in the financial pecking order. In months with low income and/or high expenses, debts must be paid before making IDA deposits. The presence of debt may also serve as a marker of shortsightedness, impatience, or other factors that are omitted from the regression and that cause low saving.

Debt might also be associated with better IDA savings outcomes. For example, debt could signal creditworthiness and thus the ability to "reshuffle" from loans into IDAs. Beyond this, creditworthiness may be correlated with characteristics that are causes of better savings outcomes but that are omitted from the regression. Finally, participants can use debt to "reshuffle" resources into IDAs by paying household bills late, using credit cards more, or slowing the rate of prepayment of home mortgages or car loans.

Whether debt signals omitted factors that help or harm saving may depend on the debt's source and use. Borrowing from banks for investment in assets (such as homes, cars, or post-secondary education) is expected to be positive, while borrowing for consumption from non-bank lenders (via credit cards or overdue bills) is more likely to be negative.

For example, the previous section showed that owners of homes and cars—with or without loans for these assets—generally had better IDA savings outcomes. Participants who were still paying off loans for a home or car usually had worse IDA savings outcomes than free-and-clear owners, but even indebted owners saved more than non-owners. Thus, "investment" loans for homes or cars were linked with omitted characteristics that improved IDA savings outcomes.

Student loans pay for human-capital assets and thus are "investment" debt. Consistent with this, the presence of student loans in the regression was linked with improved IDA savings outcomes, although the estimates were not statistically significant (table 7.10).

Loans from family and friends, overdue household and medical bills, and credit cards are more likely to be used for consumption. In accord with this, "consumption" debt was linked with a decreased likelihood of being a "saver,"

Table 7.10

Associations between Savings Outcomes and the Presence of Debts for Students Loans, Informal Loans from Family or Friends, Overdue Household Bills, Overdue Medical Bills, and Credit-Card Debts for Participants in ADD

	Prob. ("Saver")			Net IDA savings/month		
Independent variable	Mean	Δ% pts.	p-value	Mean	Δ$	p-value
Student loans						
No	0.83			0.84		
Yes	0.17	+3.4	0.34	0.16	+1.41	0.22
Informal loans from family or friends						
No	0.82			0.82		
Yes	0.18	−3.7	0.27	0.18	+2.24	0.03
Debt as overdue household bills						
No	0.72			0.75		
Yes	0.28	−1.2	0.68	0.25	−1.97	0.03
Debt as overdue medical bills						
No	0.82			0.84		
Yes	0.18	−4.2	0.22	0.16	−1.40	0.21
Credit-card debt						
No	0.67			0.67		
Yes	0.33	−4.7	0.10	0.33	+0.37	0.68

Note: All regression estimates were derived from a single "Heckit"-type selection specification with two steps. The first step was a Probit (n=2,350, k=104) for the likelihood of being a "saver." The second step was ordinary least-squares (n=1,232, k=111) for net IDA savings per month for "savers." Means were taken over non-missing observations.

although only the estimate for credit-card debt was statistically significant (p = 0.10). The one-third of participants who enrolled in ADD with outstanding credit-card debt were about 5 percentage points less likely to be "savers."

In the regression for "savers," overdue household and medical bills were linked with $1.50 to $2 less net IDA savings per month. Credit-card debt was not linked with the level of IDA savings. Unexpectedly, the presence of informal loans from family or friends was linked with $2.24 more monthly net IDA savings. Perhaps informal debts serve as signals of creditworthiness or of strong social networks and thus act as markers of the ability to borrow to "reshuffle" into IDAs. Overall, however, "consumption" debts were usually associated with worse IDA savings outcomes.

In sum, "investment" debt was linked with better IDA savings outcomes. "Consumption" debt impeded saving, but it did not preclude it. In particular, participants with "consumption" debt had net IDA savings per month of $16.66, and 52 percent were "savers." This is about the same as for ADD overall, suggesting that "consumption" debtors were more likely to have characteristics (omitted or included in the regression) that were linked with greater IDA saving. Perhaps the most-disadvantaged participants in ADD could not get "consumption" loans, helping (and perhaps pushing) them to save, while the less-disadvantaged could get "consumption" loans, to the detriment of their saving.

Building assets is easier without the encumbrance of debt, but it is not impossible, and ADD shows that even indebted poor people can save. Simply getting started with IDAs may have social and psychological effects that help participants get back to sea level. While one-on-one credit counseling is probably a good idea for most participants, "credit repair" should not be a prerequisite for participation. Instead, participants should be enrolled and encouraged to save something while paying off their debts. Financial education may also help participants to understand the costs of debt and to reverse its accumulation.

Insurance Coverage

MIS IDA added questions about insurance after ADD started, so there was no data for 62 percent of participants. Among those with data, 61 percent had health insurance (including Medicaid or Medicare), and 39 percent had life insurance (table 7.11).

The link between insurance and saving is ambiguous (chapter 4). First, premiums consume resources. On the other hand, pay-outs increase resources, although pay-outs cannot be planned for and are by definition accompanied by negative events whose effects on saving may negate the pay-outs' effects. Second, insurance coverage may act as a marker of characteristics linked with saving but omitted from the regression. For example, people who buy life insurance may possess unusual foresight and future orientation. On the other

Table 7.11

Associations between Savings Outcomes and Coverage by Life Insurance and Health Insurance for Participants in ADD

Independent variable	Prob.("Saver")			Net IDA savings/month		
	Mean	Δ % pts.	p-value	Mean	Δ $	p-value
Health insurance						
No	0.39			0.33		
Yes	0.61	+6.1	0.18	0.67	+0.09	0.95
Life insurance						
No	0.61			0.59		
Yes	0.39	–8.1	0.08	0.41	+0.81	0.57

Note: All regression estimates were derived from a single "Heckit"-type selection specification with two steps. The first step was a Probit (n=2,350, k=104) for the likelihood of being a "saver." The second step was ordinary least-squares (n=1,232, k=111) for net IDA savings per month for "savers." Means were taken over non-missing observations.

hand, people may buy insurance because they know something (such as an incipient illness, or a switch to a dangerous occupation) that the insurer does not know. These risk factors—and the shortened expected life span that goes with them—may also affect saving. Third and finally, insurance reduces the risk of catastrophic bills and so dampens precautionary motives. On the other hand, life insurance may signal a strong bequest motive, a trait linked with greater saving.

Other factors in the regression constant, ADD participants with health insurance were 6 percentage points more likely to be "savers," although the p-value was 0.18. For "savers," health insurance was not linked with the level of net IDA savings per month.

Life insurance was associated with an 8-percentage-point reduction in the likelihood of being a "saver" (p = 0.08). As with health insurance, life insurance was not linked with monthly net IDA savings for "savers."

Given that the insurance data were missing for most participants, these results may not mean much. As a speculation, perhaps health insurance smoothed shocks to expenses, helping participants avoid unmatched withdrawals from IDAs.

Enrollment Characteristics

The regression includes three controls for omitted characteristics that may be correlated with both saving and the enrollment context (table 7.12).

Previous Relationship with the Host Organization

Participants in ADD were program-selected and self-selected. Because hosts probably invited their most dedicated or successful clients to enroll in IDAs, previous contact was linked with omitted characteristics associated with greater saving. For their part, only participants who had received non-IDA services had previous contact with the host. Receipt of such services might signal omitted characteristics linked with less saving. Thus, the net effect of previous contact could be positive or negative.

In the regression, participants who had a previous relationship with the host were 4 percentage points less likely to be "savers," although the p-value was 0.20. The link with monthly net IDA savings for "savers" was statistically insignificant. This is mild evidence that, compared with other IDA participants, even the most dedicated clients of service organizations had omitted characteristics linked with lower saving.

Referred by a Partner Organization

Like participants with previous contact with the host, participants referred by a partner organization were probably dedicated clients. Nevertheless, they may have differed from non-referred participants in ways that affected saving and were omitted from the regression.

Table 7.12

Associations between Savings Outcomes and the Enrollment Context for Participants in ADD

Independent variable	Prob.("Saver")			Net IDA savings/month		
	Mean	Δ% pts.	p-value	Mean	Δ$	p-value
Previous relationship with IDA host organization						
No	0.70			0.73		
Yes	0.41	–3.8	0.20	0.41	–0.47	0.61
Referred by a partner organization						
No	0.70			0.73		
Yes	0.30	–5.3	0.13	0.27	–0.91	0.42
Enrolled in last six months possible						
No	0.58			0.61		
Yes	0.42	–3.7	0.29	0.39	–2.47	0.04

Note: All regression estimates were derived from a single "Heckit"-type selection specification with two steps. The first step was a Probit (n=2,350, k=104) for the likelihood of being a "saver." The second step was ordinary least-squares (n=1,232, k=111) for net IDA savings per month for "savers." Means were taken over non-missing observations.

Participants referred by partner organizations were less likely to be "savers" (5 percentage points), although the p-value of 0.13 again fell short of statistical significance. The link with monthly net IDA savings for "savers" was again statistically insignificant. As before, this is mild evidence that, vis-à-vis similar participants with no social-service experience, even outstanding social-service clients had omitted characteristics that decrease saving.

Enrolled in Last Six Months Possible

To meet enrollment goals by ADD's deadline, some programs accelerated enrollment in the last six months before December 31, 1999. For example, 300 people enrolled in December 1999. (After the deadline, 102 people enrolled.)

For three reasons, this last cohort might have had omitted characteristics linked with lower saving. First, some programs tightened their income cap after September 1999, reducing it from 200 percent of the poverty line to 150 percent. Second, participants who expected better savings outcomes probably enrolled sooner after learning about IDAs than others, and such expectations were probably positively correlated with characteristics omitted from the regression that affected IDA savings outcomes. Third, programs may have screened participants more in the early stages of ADD than as they rushed to meet targets just before the enrollment deadline.

In the regression, the 42 percent of ADD participants who enrolled in the last six months of 1999 were about 4 percentage points less likely to be "savers" (table 7.12). This estimate was consistent with expectations but not statistically significant (p = 0.29). For "savers," the final cohort had about $2.50 less monthly net IDA savings (p = 0.04). Overall, the final cohort did have characteristics omitted from the regression that reduced saving.

Scorecard for At-Risk Participants

The Probit regression for the likelihood of being a "saver" described above is large (estimating 106 associations) and complex (using the cumulative Normal probability function). It is not a practical tool for IDA staff who, in order to target assistance more effectively, want a quick evaluation of the likelihood than a new enrollee will be a "saver."

An alternative is a simple scorecard based a few easy-to-collect participant characteristics (Schreiner et al., 2004; Schreiner, 2002d). At in-take, program staff could quickly run down a short list of questions with the enrollee, compute the score on paper or in a spreadsheet, and assign the participant to an assistance track. Such a scorecard might allow programs to target more assistance to high-risk participants, reduce assistance to low-risk participants, and thus improve IDA savings outcomes without increasing costs (Schreiner and Sherraden, 2005).

Can a small scorecard accurately identify at-risk participants? Table 7.13 is an example scorecard based on data from ADD. After participants answer the

10 simple questions, program staff add up the points associated with each answer to give a score ranging from 0 (least likely to be a "saver") to 100 (most likely to be a "saver").

As an example of the use of the scorecard, suppose a new enrollee is female (+4 points), not married (0 points), 25-years-old (+6), without a college degree (0), and with only a passbook (+26) with a balance of $250 (0). The participant is a home owner (+11), has other financial investments (+6), has credit-card debt (–5 points), and plans to use the IDA for post-secondary education (0). Adding up the points for each question gives a total score of 48.

The simple scorecard ranks participants by the likelihood of being a "saver." That is, a participant with a score of 48 does *not* have a 48 percent chance of being a "saver." Rather, the participant is more likely to be a "saver" than other participants with scores of less than 48.

Table 7.14 shows the likelihood of being a "saver" for ADD participants by score decile. If the simple scorecard works, then participants with lower scores should have less likelihood of being a "saver," and that is indeed the case. For example, participants in the lowest score decile (scores 0 to 16) had a 22-percent chance of being "savers," while participants in the highest score decile (scores 54 to 100) had an 85-percent chance. Although there is some non-

Table 7.13
Simple Scorecard for Assigning New Enrollees to an Assistance Track
Based on the Likelihood of Being a "Saver"

Question	Points "No"	"Yes"
1. Is the participant female?	0	+4
2. Are you married?	0	+9
3. How old are you?		
a. 18 or younger	0	+12
b. 19 to 22	0	0
c. 23 to 35	0	+6
d. 36 or older	0	+13
4. Do you have a 2-year or 4-year college degree?	0	+9
5. Do you have a checking account or a passbook savings account in a bank?		
a. Both checking and savings	0	+40
b. Only checking	0	+37
c. Only savings	0	+26
d. Neither checking nor saving	0	+20
6. Does your passbook savings account have $500 or more in it?	0	+8
7. Do you own your home?	0	+11
8. Do you have financial investments other than a checking or savings account?	0	+6
9. Do you have any credit-card debt or overdue household or medical bills?	0	–5
10. Do you plan to use your IDA to buy a house?	0	–15

Note: The minimum score, corresponding to the least likelihood of being a "saver," is 0. The maximum score, corresponding to the greatest likelihood of being a "saver," is 100.

Table 7.14
Probability of Being a "Saver" in ADD by Score Decile from a Simple,
10-Question Scorecard

Score	Cases	% of cases	"Savers"	Likelihood "Saver" (%)
0–16	236	10.0	52	22.0
17–22	243	10.3	75	30.9
23–27	242	10.3	100	41.3
28–31	227	9.7	115	50.7
32–35	229	9.7	144	62.9
36–38	225	9.6	119	52.9
39–42	231	9.8	148	64.1
43–47	260	11.1	129	49.6
48–53	226	9.6	165	73.0
54–100	231	9.8	196	84.8
Total	2,350	100.0	1,243	52.9

monotonicity in the middle deciles, the likelihood of being a "saver" generally increases as the score increases.

How might an IDA program use this simple scorecard to target assistance? Suppose a program sets up three assistance tracks: "intensive," "regular," and "low." Supposing participants resemble those in ADD and that the "regular" track resembles the services provided in ADD, then putting enrollees with scores from 0 to 22 (the lowest two deciles) on the "intensive" track would target additional services to a group who would, with "regular" services, have a likelihood of being a "saver" of 27 percent. Putting participants with scores of 48 to 100 (the highest two deciles) on the "low" track would reduce services to a group whose likelihood of being a "saver" with "regular" services would be 79 percent. Participants in the middle six deciles would then take the "regular" track, with a likelihood of being a "saver" of 53 percent, close to the overall ADD average of 52 percent.

This simple, ten-question scorecard shows how IDA programs could quickly and inexpensively assign new enrollees to tailored service tracks. This would focus resources on at-risk participants while reducing resources used on participants likely be "savers" anyway.

Chapter Summary

Participant characteristics did matter for IDA saving in ADD. Still, no single characteristic (or group of characteristics) precluded (or guaranteed) saving. In the regression, for example, groups such as welfare recipients, "not working" people, and very low-income people saved less in IDAs. Looking at group averages without holding other regression factors constant, however, some people in these groups did save in IDAs. So while there is room to target more support to specific groups and/or to adjust IDA design to accommodate specific situations, many poor people—regardless of their characteristics—saved in IDAs. Not giving all groups access to IDAs would exclude some people who, if they had access, would save.

The regression estimates reported here sometimes hint at possible changes to IDA design. For example, participants planning for home purchase (the most "difficult" matched use) were the least likely to be "savers," while participants planning for home repair (an "easy" matched use) were the most likely to be "savers," with other planned uses between these two extremes. IDA programs might target greater assistance to participants planning for "difficult" uses or at least repeatedly tell such participants that they are free to change their plans and make a matched withdrawal for an "easier" use (for example, retirement savings in a Roth IRA).

Along these same lines, the relevance of different types of matched uses varies with age. For example, post-secondary education was the most salient use for youth, while home purchase was the most relevant use for college-age participants. With age, saliency increases for home purchase, post-secondary education, small-business ownership, and retirement savings. For a given participant at a point in time, only one or two matched uses may be meaningful. IDA programs can increase the relevance of IDAs by expanding (in a sensible way, see chapter 5) the types of matched uses and by giving participants as long as possible to save.

The analysis finds no support for restricting IDA eligibility to the "working poor" or to other relatively advantaged groups. For example, while married participants had better IDA savings outcomes than non-married participants, single mothers had better outcomes—other regression factors constant—than non-married men or women. Likewise, women saved more than men, perhaps because they had greater precautionary motives. Furthermore, while "not working" participants saved less in IDAs than "working" participants, the level of income itself was not strongly associated with IDA savings outcomes. Apparently, income was a much weaker cause of savings outcomes—even for the poor—than predicted by economic theory.

Participants had better IDA savings outcomes if they already owned assets when they enrolled in ADD. Not only could they "reshuffle" existing assets into IDAs but they also probably possessed characteristics (such as financial sophistication or future orientation) that caused greater saving but that were omitted from the regression.

For example, participants with more human capital (a college degree versus a high-school diploma, or a high-school diploma versus no diploma) saved more in IDAs. Likewise, participants with checking accounts saved more than those with only passbook savings accounts.

Participants who had illiquid assets (homes, cars, or financial investments) had above-average IDA savings outcomes. Debt also mattered. "Investment" debt for post-secondary education, homes, or cars was linked with greater savings outcomes, but "consumption" debt (from overdue bills and credit cards) was linked with worse savings outcomes. To counter this, IDA programs might target one-on-one counseling soon after enrollment to participants who have "consumption" debt or who do not have illiquid assets or checking accounts.

American society treats people of different races/ethnicities differently, so social capital differs by race/ethnicity. Through the centuries to this day, this has directly and indirectly led to wealth gaps and created a link between race/ethnicity and characteristics—whether or not included in a regression—that affect savings outcomes. While IDAs in ADD reduced the ratio of average Caucasian net worth to average African-American net worth, IDAs increased absolute differences. These linkages were not due to IDA programs' discriminating for or against people of color but rather to past and current discrimination by society as a whole that produced different distributions of characteristics across races.

What does the association between IDA savings outcomes and previous asset ownership mean for policy? IDA programs cannot accelerate aging, play matchmaker for unmarried participants, or alter gender or race/ethnicity. Asset ownership, however, often signals the presence of omitted factors that policy might influence.

For example, IDA programs might increase "financial sophistication" and "future orientation" via financial education. Because some matched uses are more difficult and because some participants start at a disadvantage, programs could offer participants one-on-one counseling, allow participants to save at their own pace (ideally for a lifetime), and remind participants that they can switch planned uses. If married participants save more because their spouses help them persevere, then programs might assign unmarried participants a "saving buddy" to supply the missing encouragement. If Native Americans and African Americans have lower monthly net IDA savings because history teaches them that their assets will be stolen and that their savings will be scammed, then IDA programs must put in extra effort to show that IDAs are safe and that matches are for real (Page-Adams, 2002).

Of course, knowing how participant characteristics were linked with IDA savings outcomes is not the same as knowing how to change participant characteristics. In the case of links with omitted characteristics, even the identity of the characteristics is uncertain. The policy speculations here are based on theory and evidence from ADD, but they cannot say whether any given adjustment (such as targeting more financial education to some groups) will have benefits that exceed costs, nor how a program would deliver the services in practice. Non-experimental, quantitative research can point out links and, using theory, suggest possible responses and the direction of their effects, but it cannot determine the magnitude of benefits nor costs.

Adjusting IDA design to provide more and better service entails higher costs. Whatever the policy being tested, one way to control costs is to use a simple scorecard to target those who would otherwise be most at-risk.

8

Toward Inclusion in Asset-Based Policy

This study of the American Dream Demonstration (ADD) has shown that the poor can save and accumulate assets in Individual Development Accounts (IDAs). For the 2,350 participants in ADD, net IDA savings per month was $16.60. Was this a significant amount of savings? We think it was. Over the life of ADD, the average participant had $558 of net IDA savings (median $302). At enrollment, average balances in passbook savings and checking accounts were $555 (median $125). If much of IDA savings were "new," then ADD participants greatly increased their financial assets. Furthermore, participants reported that they viewed their IDA savings as substantial (Sherraden et al., 2003a and 2003b). Among the 52 percent of participants who were "savers" with net IDA savings of $100 or more, monthly net IDA savings was $29.08, or $997 over the life of ADD. With an average match rate of 1.88:1, "savers" accumulated assets in IDAs at a rate of about $84 per month or $1,000 per year. Many "savers" used these funds to buy homes, pay for post-secondary education, or finance small businesses. These facts suggest that many ADD participants found saving in IDAs to be worthwhile.

ADD suggests that the possibility of saving and asset accumulation by the poor—even the very poor—cannot be dismissed. While savings outcomes were associated with participant characteristics, no single characteristic—such as very low income or welfare receipt—precluded saving. This runs counter to the assumption that the poor—or some segments of the poor—would not save even if they had access to structured, subsidized savings policies. Furthermore, institutional aspects of IDA design were strongly associated with savings outcomes, suggesting that policy has great potential—for good or ill—to affect saving and asset accumulation by the poor. From the perspective of asset building for long-term improvement in the well-being of the poor, it is encouraging to know that the poor can save and that policy has a lot to say about their savings outcomes.

ADD demonstrated both a concept (asset-building by the poor) and a mechanism (matched savings in the form of IDAs). Because these concepts and mechanisms are new and because the ADD data are unique, this study of ADD has enriched empirical knowledge of saving by the poor, shed light on saving theory (for the poor and non-poor), and informed policy.

In this final chapter, we highlight the book's key points and their meaning, with special attention to lessons for the design of inclusive asset-based policy.

Savings Outcomes in ADD

To our knowledge, this is the only data derived from monthly bank statements in a subsidized savings program, whether for the poor or non-poor. The data allow an unusually thorough analysis as well as the development of several new measures of savings outcomes.

"Savers"

About 52 percent of participants in ADD were "savers" with net IDA savings of $100 or more. The vast majority of the other 48 percent of participants saved and held IDA balances for a time, but they ended up with less than $100 of net IDA savings.

Did access to IDAs increase participants' overall saving? The MIS IDA data cannot address this question directly. Research on Individual Retirement Accounts and 401(k) plans, however, consistently finds that contributions from low-income people are more likely than contributions from others to represent "new" saving rather than "reshuffled" assets (Benjamin, 2003; Engelhardt, 2001; Engen and Gale, 2000; Bernheim, 1997; Skinner, 1997; Joines and Manegold, 1991; Venti and Wise, 1986). Sherraden (1991) points out that the poor are less likely to reshuffle simply because they have fewer existing assets.

In ADD, participants made deposits from both "new" savings and "reshuffled" assets. Moore et al. (2001 and 2000) find that most ADD participants surveyed came up with "new" savings by working more in the household (for example, eating out less often or shopping more carefully for food). Also, about a third said that they worked more hours in the labor market to increase income. Many participants also shifted assets: one-third said that IDAs made them less likely to save in other forms, 20 percent said that they used debt to fund IDAs, and 17 percent said that they decreased maintenance of non-IDA assets. In sum, IDA deposits came from some unknown mixture of "new" savings and "reshuffled" assets. In any case, "savers" probably saved more than they would have in the absence of IDAs. At enrollment, average balances in passbook and checking accounts for "savers" was $675 (median $220), while average net IDA savings was $1,004 (median $753).

Participants Who Were Not "Savers"

If 52 percent of ADD participants were "savers," then 48 percent—about half—were not "savers." Does this mean that few poor people can save in

IDAs? It does suggest that saving is difficult for some of the poor, even in the context of the supportive institutional structure of IDAs. Saving is never easy—especially for the poor—and the share of participants who are "savers" can never be 100 percent. Still, policy and IDA design have a lot to say about the likelihood of being a "saver" (chapter 6 and below).

In particular, a policy of permanent and universal access would maximize the likelihood of being a "saver." Given enough time, almost anyone could save and build assets in IDAs. Permanent, universal access would also obviate the need for participants to close out their IDAs with unmatched withdrawals when they move. (The analysis in this book excludes ADD enrollees who were forced to close their IDAs due to moves.)

Also, some unknown share of ADD participants was kicked out involuntarily because they had low balances or irregular deposits and the program wanted to make room for others. Had they had more time, at least some of these "kick-outs" would have become "savers." If the goal of IDAs is long-term improvement in well-being, then it makes little sense to cut off access precisely to those for whom saving is most difficult. Not all people can save the same amount in the same period of time, but this does not mean that those for whom saving is most difficult should not have access to subsidized savings policies. To help those for whom saving is most difficult, programs might use statistical profiling to identify at-risk participants soon after enrollment for targeted assistance (Schreiner and Sherraden, 2005).

Deposit Frequency

Participants in ADD made a deposit in one of every two months in which an IDA was open. "Savers" made deposits in seven of every twelve months. Frequent depositors had better savings outcomes, although the direction of cause and effect was unclear. Furthermore, there are few benchmarks against which to compare these figures. In Individual Retirement Accounts, most contributors make one or two deposits per year. In 401(k) plans, contributors make a deposit in each pay period, but these are always direct deposits made by the employer. In ADD, 6 percent of participants used automatic transfer to their IDA. As argued in chapter 6, many probably lacked access to automatic transfer. Thus, the conscious choice to make deposits "by hand" from cash every other month may have represented a level of commitment not found in (or at least not required of) most participants in subsidized savings policies.

Saving from Tax Refunds

In ADD, deposits increased markedly in tax season, probably because IDA participants saved some of their tax refunds (much of came from the Earned Income Tax Credit). Policy could facilitate this saving from tax refunds by allowing people to specify that refunds be split across a check and automatic transfers to multiple accounts.

Gross Deposits

The average ADD participant had an IDA open for 26.0 months out of 33.6 months eligible for matchable deposits. In months eligible for matchable deposits, gross deposits averaged $34.47 ($44.63 in months with an IDA open). Excluding months without deposits, the average gross deposit per month was $88.59. Gross deposits exceeded net IDA savings because they ignore unmatched withdrawals. As discussed below, policies that reduce unnecessary unmatched withdrawals might shrink the gap between net savings and gross deposits. Overall, 99.4 percent of ADD participants made at least one deposit.

Net IDA Savings

Net IDA savings are defined as gross deposits minus unmatched withdrawals minus gross deposits in excess of the match cap. Net IDA savings is the central measure of savings outcomes in ADD and represent funds that either were matched before the data cut-off date or that may have been matched after that. Net IDA savings per participant were $558 ($1,004 for "savers").

Net IDA savings per month—defined as net IDA savings divided by the months eligible for matchable deposits—was $16.60 ($29.08 for "savers"). With an average match rate (weighted by participant-level net IDA savings) of 1.88:1, the average ADD participant accumulated assets in IDAs at a rate of about $48 per month or $576 per year. These figures suggest that the poor can save and build assets in IDAs.

Use of Match Eligibility

Participants saved about 42 cents for every $1 that could have been matched. Given an average match rate—weighted by participant-level match eligibility—of 1.85:1 and an average match cap of $1,329, net IDA savings for the average participant was $771 under the match cap, leaving $1,426 in matches "on the table". Most unused match eligibility pertained to participants with less than $100 in net IDA savings; among "savers," net IDA savings were 69 percent of the match cap. About one-fifth of ADD participants (and one-third of "savers") had savings at the match cap, "maxing out" their IDA.

Is the glass half-empty or half-full? If half-empty, leaving so many match dollars "on the table" may mean that some poor people cannot save much or do not care to make the effort. If half-full, the use of 42 percent of match dollars may signal that the poor can make extraordinary efforts to save. For comparison, about 5 percent of participants in 401(k) plans (and about 5 percent of eligibles for Individual Retirement Accounts) "maxed out" their eligibility in 1997 (Gale, Iwry, and Orszag, 2004). Thus, nineteen in twenty (95 percent) of non-poor participants leave money (employer matches and tax breaks) from subsidized-savings policies "on the table." In ADD, four in five (80 percent) of participants did so. In this sense, the poor differ from the non-poor only in that the poor are more likely to "max out" their subsidized savings plans.

IDA Saving Rate

Participants converted about 1.1 percent of their monthly household income into net IDA savings. Surprisingly, the IDA saving rate decreased as income increased. Sherraden, Schreiner, and Beverly (2003) argue that the institutional effects of IDAs in ADD may have been stronger than the economic effects of greater income. Furthermore, these institutional effects may have been stronger for poorer participants. While it is undoubtedly more difficult for the poor to save, they may also have more to gain from saving and more to gain from access to institutions that facilitate saving.

Asset Accumulation

In ADD, the matches (actual and potential) that corresponded to net IDA savings were $1,049 per participant. Thus, if all net IDA savings were used in matched withdrawals, total asset accumulation in IDAs (net IDA savings plus matches) would be $1,609 per participant. Among "savers," asset accumulation in IDAs averaged $2,900.

Are these assets enough to make a difference? At enrollment, mean liquid assets in passbook and checking accounts for ADD participants were $555 (median $125). Median illiquid assets (mostly homes and cars) were $1,588, median debt was $1,510, and median net worth was $200. Thus, as a share of assets or net worth at enrollment, asset accumulation in IDAs was large. For the non-poor, a few hundred dollars—or even a few thousand dollars—may not seem like enough to make a difference (Bernstein, 2005). But ADD participants did use IDAs to buy assets that were expected to have high returns and that marked key steps in the life course. They also said that asset accumulation improved their outlooks (Sherraden et al., 2003a and 2003b). Perhaps what matters is not only the amount of accumulation but also simply its existence.

Dollar-Years Moved

If saving is moving resources through time, then the most relevant measure of saving is *dollar-years moved*. In ADD, the average participant moved 1,090 dollar-years through time (1,810 for "savers"), equivalent to 362 dollar-years per year eligible for matchable deposits (597 for "savers"). Unlike other measures of savings outcomes, this new measure shows that even participants who were not "savers" (that is, who had net IDA savings of less than $100) still moved resources through time (296 dollar-years on average).

Unmatched Withdrawals

By design, ADD placed few restrictions on unmatched withdrawals, reducing the risk that participants could harm themselves by saving too much. About 64 percent of participants made unmatched withdrawals from matchable balances, removing about 37 percent of balances that were at one time matchable. For participants who made unmatched withdrawals, the average number was 4.1, and the average amount taken out was $504. With an average match rate of 1.77:1 for these balances, the loss of potential matches for these participants was about $892. Given matching and the supportive institutional context of IDAs, the size and frequency of unmatched withdrawals was surprising and again highlights the difficulty of asset building for the poor.

Many unmatched withdrawals were likely harmless from a developmental perspective. About half were less than $100, perhaps used for paying bills or similar short-term subsistence needs. Furthermore, about half of participants who made matched withdrawals subsequently made unmatched withdrawals, likely "cleaning out" a few "leftover" dollars after buying a matched asset. Finally, 23 percent of participants were "unbanked" at enrollment, so their IDA was probably their only account. These participants probably never intended to use all their IDA deposits in matched withdrawals.

Some other unmatched withdrawals were undoubtedly due to financial pressures. Emergencies are a fact of life for the poor, so strict limits on unmatched withdrawals might deter saving more than they would reduce unmatched withdrawals. Participants may hesitate to make deposits if they fear that then taking them out later in an emergency will be a hassle. At the same time, many participants recognize that mild restrictions may help them to resist temptations to make unwise unmatched withdrawals. The challenge for IDA design is to strike a good balance between commitment and liquidity. While the analysis here has highlighted the trade-offs involved, there is little it can say with certainty about exactly what a good balance might be.

IDA programs might consider providing—alongside the IDA—a second savings account, one explicitly labeled "for emergencies." Participants who anticipate possibly needing an unmatched withdrawal could "meet the IDA halfway," putting some funds in the "emergency" account and some in the IDA. If an emergency happens, then they can take out their funds from the "emergency" account without dealing with whatever withdrawal restrictions are placed on the IDA. If the emergency never happens, then it is a small step to transfer the "emergency" funds into the IDA. Even if participants do not save more in the two accounts together than they would in an IDA alone, the mere existence of the second "emergency" account might help to preserve IDA balances if it helps participants see IDAs as tools for long-term savings and if it encourages them to make a deposit now even if they fear that they may need to take it out later.

In ADD, mild restrictions on unmatched withdrawals seemed to be associated with being a "saver." AFIA sites owned IDAs jointly with participants, so staff had to sign off on any unmatched withdrawal. Staff immediately obliged, but the need to discuss the unmatched withdrawal likely made participants think more carefully about whether the unmatched withdrawal was in their own long-term best interest. Getting staff approval also created a de facto "waiting period." In contrast, IDA participants at non-AFIA sites could enter their depository institutions and walk out a few minutes later with their savings.

Finally, some participants likely found that the available matched uses were not relevant given their stage in the life cycle and their current asset holdings. Unmatched withdrawals would likely decrease if IDAs were to match "roll-overs" for retirement savings in Roth Individual Retirement Accounts or for post-secondary education in 529 College Savings Plans.

Matched Withdrawals

As of the data cut-off date, about 31 percent of ADD participants had made a matched withdrawal. (In most ADD programs, participants could still make matched withdrawals—or unmatched withdrawals—for several months after the data cut-off date). The average match rate per dollar of matched withdrawals was 1.81:1. The average participant with a matched withdrawal had made 2.6 matched withdrawals worth a total of $921. For this group, average total asset accumulation (matched withdrawals plus matches) in IDAs was about $2,600. As of the data cut-off date, about 41 percent of "savers" (about 21 percent of all participants) had yet to make a matched withdrawal. ADD set deadlines for matched withdrawals because of the time-limited nature of its funding. From a developmental perspective, however, it would be better to let participants wait until they are ready to make matched withdrawals.

Matched Uses

The most common use of matched withdrawals was home purchase (27 percent), followed by microenterprise (23 percent), home repair (20 percent), post-secondary education (19 percent), retirement savings (8 percent), and job training (2 percent). Among "savers" yet to make a matched withdrawal, 52 percent planned for home purchase, 21 percent for microenterprise, 4 percent for home repair, 16 percent for post-secondary education, 5 percent for retirement, and 2 percent for job training. Participants saving for home purchase saved for more time and saved larger amounts, probably reflecting the desire to accumulate as large a down payment as possible as well as the length and complexity of the process of home purchase. In contrast, participants made matched withdrawals for home repair rather quickly.

Although 8 percent of all ADD participants made matched withdrawals for retirement savings, only four of the 14 programs offered this matched use. Among participants at these four programs, one in five (20 percent) made matched withdrawals for retirement savings. As might be expected, such matched withdrawals were more common and larger among older participants. Similarly, matched withdrawals for home ownership were more common among renters than existing home owners; matched withdrawals for post-secondary education were more common among younger participants; and matched withdrawals for microenterprise were more common among self-employed participants. In general, the relevance of different matched uses varied with a given participant's stage in the life cycle and existing asset ownership.

For what uses should IDAs provide matches? IDAs differ from means-tested cash transfers (such as Temporary Assistance for Needy Families, Food Stamps, and Medicaid) by focusing on saving and asset accumulation rather than immediate consumption. (For this reason, IDAs are complements for means-tested income support, not substitutes.) One way that IDAs do this is by restricting matched withdrawals to purchases of illiquid, productive assets with high personal and social impacts. If a matched use meets these standards and if it gives the poor access to a savings subsidy previously reserved for the non-poor, then it has a good chance of being perceived as fair and of receiving public support.

By these normative standards, IDAs should provide matches for the three "cornerstone" uses of home purchase for first-time buyers, post-secondary education and job training, and microenterprise. Furthermore, IDAs should also match retirement savings, car purchase, computer purchase, and medical expenses for those without access to group health insurance. The non-poor already have access to subsidies for all of these assets (except for cars and computers). While all 14 programs in ADD provided matches for the three "cornerstone" uses, a subset of programs provided matches for retirement savings, and no programs provided matches for car purchase, computer purchase, or medical expenses. Some programs in ADD provided matches for home repair, but this use scores poorly against the standards set forth here. Debt paydown does not meet the standards of a matched use.

There is a final consideration. If the goal is to promote inclusion in asset-building policy, it might hasten change to limit matches to a few assets unlikely to spark political opposition. In this sense, the best bets are the three "cornerstone" uses of home purchase, post-secondary education, and microenterprise, perhaps along with retirement savings.

Summary: Savings Outcomes

IDA participants in ADD had monthly net IDA savings of $16.60 or $200 per year, equivalent to about one percent of their income. They made a deposit every other month and accumulated a little less than $600 per year. About half of participants were "savers" with net IDA savings of $100 or more. The average match rate was about 2:1, and many "savers" used IDAs to invest in homes, post-secondary education, and small business.

ADD set out to demonstrate that the poor could save and build assets in IDAs, and from this perspective, these savings outcomes are encouraging. Still, many important questions remain unanswered. Did ADD participants save more than they would have in the absence of IDAs? What would happen if IDAs were offered to all people or to all poor people? How would savings outcomes change if IDAs were permanent?

Now that we know that the poor can save and build assets in IDAs, we can start to tackle the next round of questions. ADD also revealed something about how savings outcomes were associated with IDA design and with participant characteristics, topics to which we now turn.

Program Characteristics and Savings Outcomes

The associations between program (institutional) characteristics and savings outcomes matters because IDA design is set by policy. The estimated associations discussed below come from a two-step regression that controls for a wide range of program and participant characteristics. For all participants, the first step looks at the likelihood of being a "saver." For "savers," the second step looks at monthly net IDA savings. Overall, program characteristics were strongly associated with savings outcomes in ADD, suggesting that policy design has a lot to say about how the poor save and build assets.

Match Rates

A central feature of IDAs is the match rate. Qualitative evidence from ADD and elsewhere (Sherraden et al., 2003a and 2003b; Kempson, McKay, and Collard, 2003) suggests that matches attract people to IDAs. The quantitative estimates presented here suggest that higher match rates were associated with a higher likelihood of being a "saver." If this association is more cause than correlation—and we think it is—then one way to increase inclusion in matched-saving policies is to offer a higher match rate.

For "savers," higher match rates were associated with a lower level of monthly net IDA savings. This is consistent with the hypothesis that many ADD participants were saving for fixed goals and that higher match rates allowed them to reach those goals with lower levels of saving. Thus, an increase in the match rate improved inclusion by making more participants "savers," but it also decreased the level of savings per "saver." Accounting for both these effects, higher match rates increased asset accumulation per participant. The policy question is then whether greater inclusion and greater asset accumulation are worth the cost of higher match rates and the consequence of lower savings per "saver."

In terms of research methods, the match-rate estimates illustrate the use of the two-step regression. A one-step regression would have found no association between match rates and monthly net IDA savings for participants. Rather than nuanced policy advice about the various (and sometimes opposing) associations between match rates and different aspects of savings outcomes, a one-step regression would have concluded that match rates did not matter.

Match Caps (Saving Targets)

The match cap limits the amount of IDA savings eligible for matches. Participants in ADD appear to have turned this limit into a goal or saving target, as a $1 increase in the match cap was associated with a 57-cent increase in monthly net IDA savings. This huge association remains even after controlling for the censoring of net IDA savings at the match cap. Apparently, many participants tried to "max out" their IDAs because they believed that the match cap represented the amount that they "should" save. This led to greater saving effort when match caps were higher. If this estimate represents more cause than correlation, then one way to increase savings in subsidized-savings policies is to increase the match cap.

Of course, this estimate applies only to changes in the match cap in the range seen in ADD; it may be that increasing annual caps past $1,000 or so would have diminishing effects. Given a match rate, higher caps also mean higher program costs. In practice, higher match caps are usually combined with lower match rates, and vice versa. For the match-rate/match-cap combinations in ADD, a low match rate with a high match cap produced fewer "savers" but more monthly net IDA savings (per "saver" and per participant). Costs were lower, and monthly asset accumulation per participant was little changed. While the optimal match-rate/match-cap combination is unknown, ADD suggests that for some ranges and combinations, there are trade-offs between costs, the goal of inclusion, and the goals of saving and asset accumulation.

Match-Cap Structure

Because there was little within-program variation in match-cap structure in ADD, the data have little to say about this aspect of IDA design. Theory, however, suggests that a "hybrid" annual/lifetime structure might boost long-term savings outcomes by giving participants annual reasons not to procrastinate while allowing them the flexibility to carry-forward unused match eligibility. Such hybrid structures are not without precedent.

Months Eligible to Make Matchable Deposits

Unlike subsidized-savings policies for the non-poor, ADD set deadlines (time caps) for making matchable deposits and for making matched withdrawals. Theory predicts that longer time caps will lead to more "savers" by giving participants more opportunities to save, and ADD bears this out. For example, a participant might not save anything in the first two years, but then save a lot in the third year. With a two-year time cap, the participant would not qualify as a "saver." Thus, the goal of inclusion is better served by longer periods of eligibility. At the same time (and also as predicted by theory), longer time caps were associated in ADD with lower monthly net IDA savings for "savers," as they had more time over which to spread out their potential to save. We speculate that permanent access would further reduce monthly net IDA savings but also increase lifetime saving and asset accumulation as well as encouraging a social norm of asset building among the poor.

The original IDA proposal called for universal, permanent accounts, opened at birth, with greater subsidies for the poor (Sherraden, 1991). In this sense, IDAs were never meant to be short-term "programs" with ending dates any more than Individual Retirement Accounts or 401(k) plans are. In practice, IDAs have been time-limited because they have been funded as demonstrations (Edwards and Mason, 2003). If, however, the goal is to improve the long-term well-being of the poor, then many practices common in demonstrations—such as setting deadlines for matched withdrawals or kicking out participants with low savings or irregular deposits—are counterproductive. After all, Individual Retirement Accounts, 529 College Savings plans, and 401(k) plans do not kick out participants or suspend their tax benefits if they save small amounts, if they stop making contributions altogether, or if they take decades to open an account and start participating. (This is another example of America's dual asset-building policy that places greater restrictions on the poor than on the non-poor.) From a developmental perspective, a better design would allow participants to save and hold IDA balances for as long as they wish. Some participants would be content to save for years without making a matched withdrawal, sometimes depositing regularly, sometimes not depositing, and sometimes making unmatched withdrawals in emergencies. But everyone would have an account, always available, and periodic statements—regardless of balance—that would act as gentle reminders of the possibility of saving and the potential of building assets.

Use of Automatic Transfer

ADD participants who set up automatic transfer to their IDAs were much more likely to be "savers." This suggests that efforts to facilitate the use of automatic transfer may have large impacts on inclusion in subsidized asset-building policies. For example, the Internal Revenue Service and employers could allow taxpayers and employees to split tax refunds and paychecks across checks and direct deposits to multiple accounts. The technical capability already exists; all the Internal Revenue Service and employers have to do is provide access to it. Because facilitating this type of automatic transfer is simpler and less costly than other IDA features designed to facilitate saving (for example, staff support or financial education), it is a good candidate for initial policy efforts aimed to improve saving and asset accumulation by the poor.

Financial Education

Required financial education was a central feature of IDAs in ADD. Each additional hour up to 10 was linked with large increases in monthly net IDA savings (about $1 per hour), but hours after that were not associated with net IDA savings. For policy, this suggests not only that financial education may matter but also that its costs may be contained—without sharp trade-offs of effectiveness—by limiting the hours required. The content and quality of classes probably also mattered, but the data did not record this information.

Restrictions on Unmatched Withdrawals

Data from the AFIA sites in ADD suggest that restrictions on unmatched withdrawals helped participants become "savers," although the optimal strength and formality for such restrictions are unknown. On the one hand, participants may welcome "silken handcuffs" as a way to deter unwise withdrawals. On the other hand, participants sometimes do need to make unmatched withdrawals, and the prospect of having to go through hoops to do so may deter them from making IDA deposits in the first place. Our opinion is that mild, informal restrictions are likely to balance the two desires. If—as in the AFIA sites— IDAs are jointly owned by the participant and the program, then the program should always immediately sign off on withdrawal requests.

Program Characteristics Overall

Aspects of IDA design were strongly associated with savings outcomes in ADD. This institutional approach is useful because it offers direct lessons for policy. Want more "savers"? Increase match rates, lengthen time caps, facilitate automatic transfer, and mildly restrict unmatched withdrawals. Want to increase monthly net IDA savings? Decrease match rates, raise match caps, and require a few hours of financial education. More broadly, the central lesson is that policy has a lot to say about how the poor save and build assets.

While ADD shows that institutions matter, and while Schreiner et al. (2001) and Beverly and Sherraden (1999) start to develop an institutional theory of saving, informing policy requires knowing not only the associations between institutions and savings outcomes but also the reasons behind these associations. As always, determining causality is the central challenge. Short of randomized experiments, theory (and regressions that control for a wide range of factors) is the best guide to untangling cause from correlation. This book has used theory and regression to discuss how aspects of the institutional structure of IDAs are likely causes of savings outcomes, but the results are still tentative and incomplete. While the research here should help policymakers by pointing out where they should start, it still leaves them most of the hard work.

The impacts of IDA design may vary across participants. For example, financial education may help the financially unsophisticated more than others. With this in mind, we now turn to the associations between savings outcomes and participant characteristics. It is easier to change policies than to change people, but knowing how different people respond to policies may provide some lessons about how to make IDA design more inclusive.

Participant Characteristics and Savings Outcomes

ADD participants were not a random sample of IDA-eligible people; they were both program-selected (they met program-defined eligibility criteria) and self-selected (they voluntarily chose to participate). In other words, programs targeted certain groups, and the people in the targeted groups who expected the greatest net benefits were the most likely to enroll. This means that the savings outcomes described in this book may be extrapolated only to IDA-eligible people who, if they had the choice, would choose to enroll in IDAs.

Compared with the overall low-income U.S. population, IDA participants were more disadvantaged in that they were more likely to be female, African-American, or never-married. IDA participants were less disadvantaged, however, in that they were more educated, more likely to be employed, and more likely to have a bank account. Thus, ADD participants were not generally among the "poorest of the poor" (those without jobs, education, or bank accounts), nor were they among the "richest of the poor" (married Caucasian males). These patterns likely reflect the explicit targeting of the "working poor" by programs in ADD and the nature of the pre-existing client base of the host organizations.

While savings outcomes did vary with participant characteristics (other factors in the regression constant), no characteristic precluded saving. In particular, single mothers, participants who were not employed, welfare recipients, and very low-income participants all saved and built assets in ADD. This suggests that excluding the poor from subsidized savings policies cannot be justified by claiming that they would not save even if they had access.

Gender, Marital Status, and Household Composition

Four in five ADD participants were female. Among females, 85 percent were not married. Among not married females, 79 percent had children. Overall in ADD, 52 percent of participants were single mothers (not-married women with children).

Other factors in the regression constant, women were much more likely than men to be "savers." Looking at marital status and household composition together, married participants (with or without children) were the most likely to be "savers," followed by single mothers. Never-married or divorced participants without children were the least likely to be "savers."

Overall, these estimates suggest that women and single mothers were more likely to be "savers" than men, divorcees, and those without children. From the perspective of inclusion, it is encouraging that women and single mothers—groups that represent a disproportionately large share of the poor—saved in IDAs in ADD. It is an open question whether IDA design could (or should) be tweaked to coax more "savers" from the other groups.

Age

Other factors in the regression constant, the likelihood of being a "saver" (and the level of monthly net IDA savings for "savers") decreased from the ages of 13 to 20 and then increased after that. Apparently, the relevance of saving in IDAs varies across the life cycle, whether because something in IDA design (such as the types of matchable assets) matters differently at different ages and/or because saving in general varies with age. In any case, if IDA policy wants to include more young people, it may need to seek ways to make saving for post-secondary education more relevant to them or provide matches for assets with quicker pay-offs (such as cars or computers). Because children and youth tend to have very low incomes, policy might also provide them with higher matches, or, as in the Saving for Education, Entrepreneurship, and Downpayment program and in the United Kingdom's Child Trust Fund, deposits from third parties that—unlike matches—are not linked to saving by the participant but rather to the accomplishment of milestones, such as being born, passing a grade, or graduating from high school. For older participants, IDA policy could provide matches for retirement savings, as the saliency of that use tends to increase with age.

Race/Ethnicity

About 47 percent of ADD participants were African American, 37 percent were Caucasian, 9 percent were Hispanic, 3 percent were Native American, 2 percent were Asian American, and 3 percent were "Other." Although monthly net IDA savings for all groups was at least $11.76 and the share of "savers" was always at least 44 percent, there were differences across groups. In the regression, Asian Americans were the most likely to be "savers," followed by "Other" ethnicities and then Hispanics. Caucasians, African Americans, and Native Americans were the least likely to be "savers." In terms of monthly net IDA savings, Asian Americans and "Other" ethnicities saved the most, followed by Caucasians and Hispanics, with African Americans and Native Americans saving less than others.

Of course, these differences were not due to race/ethnicity per se but rather to a constellation of socially produced characteristics that are both correlates of race/ethnicity and causes of saving. In a perfect regression with no omitted factors, there would be no association between saving and race/ethnicity.

IDAs narrowed racial gaps in terms of ratios of net worth while widening absolute differences in mean net worth. Racial/ethnic differences in saving outcomes are a concern. Unequal savings outcomes represent disproportionate lost potential for asset building. So far, no one has proposed specific ways to boost IDA savings outcomes for African Americans and Native Americans (see, however, Sherraden, 1999b). Of course, participants in these groups might be offered higher match rates and/or higher match caps, or they might receive additional financial education and/or one-on-one counseling and support from IDA staff. But such explicit targeting by race/ethnicity tends draw controversy—unfairly, in our view—and so is rare in public policy. As Conley (1999) points out, however, any policy that broadly targets the poor—regardless of race/ethnicity—will likely provide disproportionate benefits to African Americans (and Native Americans). Along the lines of Grinstein-Weiss and Sherraden (2004), future work should explore whether and how the institutional characteristics of IDAs interact with race/ethnicity. This might lead to simple changes to IDA design that benefit African Americans and Native Americans disproportionately and thus help to level savings outcomes.

Education

Most ADD participants (61 percent) had attended some college, and 21 percent of participants had a two-year or four-year college degree. Of the 39 percent who had not attended any college, about 38 percent (15 percent of all participants) had not finished high school. Given that they were low-income people, ADD participants were highly educated.

Participants with four-year degrees were much more likely to be "savers." Among "savers," they also had higher monthly net IDA savings. This makes sense; it would be surprising if a four-year degree was not correlated with omitted factors that cause higher saving, both pre-existing characteristics that also caused success in college and characteristics (such as skills, knowledge, and habits) developed in college. This association between education and savings outcomes may highlight the potential benefits of financial education, especially for participants with less educational experience.

Still, participants at all levels of education saved and accumulated assets in ADD. For example, 42 percent of participants who did not finish high school were "savers," and this group had monthly net IDA savings of $12.19. Furthermore, there were no consistent differences in savings outcomes by education among participants without four-year degrees.

Employment

About 89 percent of participants in ADD were employed and/or were students, and 78 percent worked full time or part time. Students who were also employed were the most likely to be "savers," followed by participants who were employed full-time or part-time. Students who were not employed, homemakers (including the retired and disabled), and the unemployed were less likely to be "savers."

In terms of the level of monthly net IDA savings and with other factors in the regression constant, students who were employed saved the most. Homemakers, the unemployed, and—oddly—the full-time employed saved the least. Perhaps students were motivated by having an immediately salient, divisible matched use (post-secondary education), and perhaps employed students—because of their jobs—had more funds available to deposit in IDAs.

While savings outcomes in ADD varied with employment status, the absence of employment did not preclude saving: participants who were not employed had monthly net IDA savings of $12.68, and 48 percent of them were "savers." From the standpoint of targeting policy, this suggests that the focus of many IDA programs in ADD and elsewhere on the "working poor" is superfluous and harms inclusion directly by restricting access to IDAs and indirectly by sending the message that the "non-working" poor cannot or should not save.

Welfare Receipt

About 45 percent of participants in ADD had received some form of means-tested public assistance ("welfare") at or before enrollment. With the exception of lower monthly net IDA savings for participants who received Food Stamps, welfare receipt per se was not associated with savings outcomes.

Welfare receipt was not a proxy for omitted characteristics causing both welfare receipt and low saving. In other words, there was nothing "different" about welfare recipients that caused them to save less, after accounting for income, existing assets, demographics, and other factors in the regression. About 38 percent of participants who received Temporary Assistance for Needy Families at enrollment were "savers," and these participants had monthly net

IDA savings of $10.85. Even welfare recipients saved in ADD. Policy cannot exclude them based on the belief that they would not save in subsidized structures even if they had access.

Income

IDA participants in ADD were poor. Average income was 127 percent of the federal poverty guideline (median 107 percent), and about 20 percent of participants were below 50 percent of the poverty line.

Economic theory suggests that—at least in some range—more income should induce more saving. Furthermore, more should be saved from "intermittent" income than from "recurrent" income (Sherraden, Schreiner, and Beverly, 2003). While more income was sometimes associated with more saving in ADD, the associations were weak. For example, an additional $100 of "intermittent" income in the range from 0 to $2,000 was associated with an increase in the likelihood of being a "saver" of 0.7 percentage points and an increase in monthly net IDA savings for "savers" of eighteen cents. While positive, these associations are small. In fact, the higher the income, the lower the share of income saved in IDAs.

Why was income per se so weakly related with saving? Possible explanations include institutional factors, bias from censoring, and measurement error. We speculate, however, that institutional factors may have mattered most, especially for the poorest. For example, we think that very low-income people were more affected by attending financial education and by changing the match cap into a saving target. Like single mothers, not-employed people, and welfare recipients, people with very low incomes saved in ADD. For example, 48 percent of those below 50 percent of the poverty line were "savers," and these participants had monthly net IDA savings of $14.91. Although some IDA programs to date have targeted the "working poor" or the "stable poor," ADD suggests that asset-based policy can include people across the full range of income, all the way to the bottom.

Asset Ownership

In general, asset ownership was associated with better savings outcomes in ADD. At least three factors lie behind this. First, asset ownership may have served as a proxy for omitted characteristics that caused both greater past saving and greater IDA saving. For example, owners of checking accounts or financial investments likely had greater financial sophistication and thus more fully appreciated the benefits of saving in IDAs. Second, ownership may have signaled greater availability of assets to "reshuffle" into IDAs. Third, asset ownership may have directly facilitated IDA saving. For example, making deposits by mail (or via automatic transfer) was simpler for participants with checking accounts. Likewise, getting to the depository institution to make a deposit was easier for participants who owned cars.

Bank accounts. Participants who owned a checking account—whether or not they also owned a passbook account—were more likely to be "savers" and had higher monthly net IDA savings. For participants with passbook accounts, the converse held. Because checkbooks differ from passbooks mostly in the need to track balances to avoid overdrafts, ownership of checkbooks probably served as a proxy for financial sophistication. For policy, the lesson is that efforts to boost saving by the poor—especially those who do not already have checking accounts or who are "unbanked"—may well want to feature financial education as a core component.

Looking at account value, higher passbook balances (up to $400) were associated with an increased likelihood being a "saver" and with more monthly net IDA savings, although the association was small (and fell sharply above $400). Additional checking balances (up to $1,500) were associated with being a "saver" but not with monthly net IDA savings. In general, the association between liquid assets and net IDA savings for "savers" was weak, suggesting that ADD participants probably reshuffled little into IDAs from their existing accounts.

Overall, account ownership seemed to matter more than account balance. On the one hand, this may be because account ownership was measured more accurately. On the other hand, perhaps the presence of an account was a stronger proxy than account balances for omitted characteristics associated with saving.

Being "unbanked" or owning only a passbook savings account did not preclude saving in IDAs. Among the "unbanked," 34 percent were "savers," and monthly net IDA savings was $9.43. Likewise, 42 percent of those with only a passbook savings account were "savers," and these participants had monthly net IDA savings of $11.29. Although these groups had worse savings outcomes than others, many participants in these groups saved in IDAs.

Non-bank assets. Participants who owned homes, cars, land or property, and/or financial investments were much more likely to be "savers." Furthermore, "savers" who owned cars or small businesses had higher monthly net IDA deposits. Because these assets are illiquid, participants probably did not reshuffle them into IDAs, especially given that they reshuffled little from liquid assets. Instead, these associations reflect in part the indirect effects of owners' greater financial sophistication. Participants who were owners at enrollment must have saved something before enrollment, and they probably had omitted characteristics that both caused past saving and contributed to saving in IDAs. Furthermore, asset ownership probably directly facilitated saving by reducing both cash expenses (making more resources available to save) and transaction costs (making it easier to make deposits, see Sherraden, 1991 and 1989).

About 13 percent of ADD participants reported owning no assets—passbook or checking accounts, homes, cars, land or property, financial investments, or small businesses—at enrollment. Of the "asset-less," 25 percent were "savers," and monthly net IDA savings was $7.05. While these participants had worse average savings outcomes, some still saved, and what they did save was apparently all "new." IDA programs could straightforwardly identify the "asset-less" at enrollment and then provide them additional support.

Debts

In general, debt in ADD was associated with worse savings outcomes. For example, car owners who were "free-and-clear" were more likely to be "savers" than car owners who were still making payments. In the same way, participants with credit-card debt were less likely to be "savers." (Debt-free homeowners were—surprisingly—less likely to be "savers.") The presence of other types of debt was not associated with being a "saver."

Among "savers" and with all else in the regression constant, free-and-clear homeowners and free-and-clear car owners had higher monthly net IDA savings. Likewise, overdue household bills were associated with lower monthly net IDA savings. (The only exception to the pattern was the presence of informal loans, which was associated with higher monthly net IDA savings.)

While debt makes saving more difficult, it did not preclude saving in ADD. The largest estimates were for owners of homes and cars, people who had already shown some ability and willingness to save (or else they could not have made a down payment). Denying access to IDAs until a home or car is paid-off would not likely improve the well-being of the poor. (The non-poor can save in Individual Retirement Accounts and 401(k) plans regardless of their debt, and of course tax deductions for home-mortgage interest and student-loan interest require debt.) While "credit repair" may be necessary in some cases (especially before matched withdrawals for home purchase), saving is possible in spite of debt. Participation in IDAs may also help reduce debt, as financial education exposes the cost of debt and as positive asset accumulation sparks hope and greater ability to see light at the end of the debt tunnel.

Insurance Coverage

About two-thirds of participants in ADD had health insurance, and 42 percent had life insurance. Health insurance was associated with a greater likelihood of being a "saver," and life insurance was associated with a lower likelihood of being a "saver." For "savers," insurance coverage was not associated with net IDA savings. We do not want to make too much of these estimates, as more than half of participants had missing values, and the estimates do not fit neatly into a theoretical framework. If health insurance mitigated shocks due to illness, it may have helped participants to keep savings in IDAs. In this case, universal health coverage may contribute to inclusive asset building. The presence of life insurance should be correlated with omitted characteristics such as "future orientation" that are also causes of better savings outcomes, so it is unclear why life insurance would be associated with a lower likelihood of being a "saver," unless it signals the presence of savings in the form of cash-value life insurance and thus fewer resources available to save in IDAs.

Planned Use

Participants' planned use for future matched withdrawals as reported at enrollment likely indicated something about their expectations for their own saving. In this way, planned use was a proxy for omitted characteristics that were causes of saving.

Participants were most likely to be "savers" if they planned for home repair, followed by retirement savings, post-secondary education, microenterprise, and finally home purchase. The pattern is that matched uses that were divisible, did not require large life changes, and that required less saving were associated with a higher likelihood of being a "saver." In particular, home purchase required the greatest sustained saving (and also the cleanest credit record). Thus, those who started off planning for home purchase may also have been at-risk of discovering that they could not keep up with the pace and length of saving effort required for that goal, perhaps becoming discouraged and ending up with little savings.

In terms of monthly net IDA savings, "savers" who planned for home repair again saved the most, following by those planning for retirement and home purchase, with "savers" planning for post-secondary education and microenterprise saving the least.

From the perspective of inclusion, a possible policy lesson is the value of a menu of matched uses, some of which "work" even without a lot of saving (for example, "roll-overs" into Roth Individual Retirement Accounts or 529 College Savings plans). Furthermore, participants should be allowed to change their plans, as those who begin aiming high may later save less than they planned. Given options, disappointed participants will be less likely to give up entirely.

Summary: Participant Characteristics and Savings Outcomes

The section has made two broad points. The first is that in ADD, many participant characteristics were associated with savings outcomes. The estimated associations show how (other factors in the regression constant) savings outcomes varied *at the margin* with changes in participant characteristics.

The second point is that *on average*, many ADD participants in all groups defined by specific characteristics saved and built assets in IDAs. This includes several groups whose willingness and ability to save have been questioned: single mothers, African Americans and Native Americans, people who did not finish high school, people who were not employed, welfare recipients, people with very low incomes, the "unbanked," and people with debts.

In sum, even though some participant characteristics were associated with worse (or better) savings outcomes (the first point), no single characteristic was the "kiss of death" (or life) for saving in IDAs (the second point). Many participant (and program) characteristics were associated with savings outcomes, and no single characteristic was dominant. Also, most participants had a mix of characteristics that were associated with both better and worse savings outcomes.

The ADD data contradict the presumption that excluding certain groups from subsidized savings policies does them no harm because they would not have saved anyway. In ADD, many participants of all stripes saved. Thus, limiting access by age, employment, welfare receipt, income, or any other participant characteristic would not promote long-term improvement in well-being as well as universal access would. For their part, the poor seem ready to be included; most likely, they have always been ready. The question is whether policy is ready to include them.

ADD shows that IDAs are an asset-building policy that can reach the poorest and most disadvantaged. Still, the program design that would best support saving by the poor—a design that may vary with participants' characteristics—is still unknown. We suspect that two of the simplest, least expensive, and most effective policy directions are automatic sign-up (beyond universal access, this would give everyone an account) and automatic transfer.

Finally, the associations between participant characteristics and savings outcomes do not imply that some groups should be excluded from access to subsidized savings policies. Rather, statistical profiling can take advantage of these associations to identify at-risk participants to receive additional, targeted support (Schreiner and Sherraden, 2005). Also, work is needed to check whether and how various aspects of IDA design interact with participant characteristics to influence savings outcomes. In terms of IDA design, it may be that one size does not fit all.

Policy Topics

We turn next to some topics that often come up in discussions of inclusive asset-based policy. The topics are prompted, in part, by people at two ends of a continuum. People at one end worry that IDAs do not do enough, while people at the other end expect IDAs to do everything. Like any intervention, IDAs—if effective—have positive impacts for some people, but they cannot be everything to everyone.

First, IDAs are not a cure-all. They aim to support saving and asset accumulation by the poor. This is an important goal, but it is not the only goal. Support for subsistence (and medical care, and education, and other dimensions of well-being) is also important. Asset building is important because it promotes development and because it is something that public policy can do comparatively well (Sherraden, 1991). But asset building cannot solve all problems.

Second, voluntary participation and choice are essential. There is a worry that access to IDAs would harm the poorest because, with few resources available to save, their saving could cause hardship. After all, saving does mean postponing consumption, so, at least in the short term, people who save also consume less and, all else constant, are worse off for the time being. Savers choose to make this short-term sacrifice because they expect that it will improve their long-term well-being. Of course, saving can be overdone, and participants could mistakenly overestimate the benefits of saving and/or underestimate the costs. In any case, saving in IDAs is voluntary; no one is forced to participate, and unmatched withdrawals are possible at any time. IDAs offer access, they do not impose obligation.

Third, IDAs are not for everyone. In ADD, about half of participants had less than $100 in net IDA savings. People should decide for themselves whether and how much to save. No one wants very poor people on the edge of subsistence to give up immediate necessities in order to save for long-term purposes. In terms of impacts on those who were not "savers," the MIS IDA data are silent. Most likely, impacts—whether positive or negative—were slight. Perhaps participation made these people more discouraged about saving. Or perhaps they learned something (maybe from financial education) that will improve their future savings outcomes.

Fourth, IDAs *are* for some people. In ADD, participants from all groups—no matter how poor or disadvantaged—did save. No one yet knows how poor is too poor to save in IDAs. In non-industrialized countries, even desperately poor people can and do save (at least for short-term uses) when they have access to supportive institutions (Robinson, 2001; Rutherford, 2000). In this regard, IDAs provide the poor access to supportive savings institutions similar to those enjoyed by the non-poor. IDAs help the poor to save, but they do not force them to save. This fits the idea of "libertarian paternalism" of Sunstein and Thaler (2003), "libertarian" because of the absence of coercion, and "paternalistic" because it tries to help people make choices that they themselves usually would like to make, if only they had greater self-discipline (Benartzi and Thaler, 2004). The point is choice. Given access, some people save in IDAs. Others cannot or will not. But the fact that some do not save is not a reason to restrict access to others who are willing and able.

Fifth, IDAs are for long-term development, and the relevance of different matched uses varies over the life cycle and with existing asset ownership.

Thus, more people would find IDAs more useful more often if there were a range of matched uses rather than just one or two. Within the political constraints that IDAs must be seen as fair and the guidelines in chapter 5, IDAs should provide matches for a range of uses.

Sixth, greatly expanded uses might not be the best way to promote inclusive asset-building policies. Because IDAs appear to be a politically feasible way to transfer resources to the poor, some advocates for the poor sometimes wish to link IDAs to their particular cause. This might be called the *IDAs and x* phenomenon, as in "IDAs and microenterprise," "IDAs and people with disabilities, or "IDAs and the homeless." While there is little political risk in targeting IDAs to specific disadvantaged groups (such as the homeless or disabled, and in contrast to current asset-based policy which mostly targets advantaged groups), there may be political risk in carelessly expanding matchable uses (for example, providing matches for food purchases or for repaying debts). If IDAs go beyond well-reasoned and politically defensible uses, then they run the risk of being seen as giveaways that transfer resources without increasing saving and asset accumulation. Whatever the equity and efficiency reasons for making more transfers to the poor with fewer strings attached, IDAs are probably not the way to do it. Expanding matchable uses might erode political support and might also detract from the fundamental purpose of saving and asset accumulation.

Seventh, IDAs should not replace income support. Some advocates for the poor worry that IDAs could divert funds away from cash subsistence support. (Some worry that even floating the idea that the poor can save is the first step down a slippery slope leading to the abolition of means-tested cash assistance.) Of course, a dollar allocated to IDAs is a dollar not allocated elsewhere. Still, we have no direct evidence that funding for IDAs has displaced funding for traditional welfare. States that fund IDAs from allocations for Temporary Assistance for Needy Families do so only from funds already earmarked for innovative or rainy-day uses. As Sherraden (1991, p. 294) writes, cash assistance is "absolutely essential." Income support aims to maintain people in the short term, while IDAs aim to help people develop over the long term. These purposes are complementary and need not be traded-off against each other.

Toward Inclusive Asset-Based Policy

To escape poverty usually requires asset accumulation. The United States has many policies that subsidize saving, but they often exclude the poor because they leverage existing wealth and operate via tax breaks. Individual Development Accounts are a new policy proposal meant to help the poor build assets without these requirements. Based on the research in this book, the possibility of saving by the poor cannot be dismissed. IDAs may have the potential to boost saving and asset accumulation for at least some poor people.

This research was motivated by our belief that asset-based policy in the United States and elsewhere should be reformulated. Current policies are highly regressive, giving much more to the rich than the poor (and usually excluding the poor). A fairer, more pro-development policy would feature progressive subsidies and include everyone. As a guiding principle, asset-building policy should provide—at minimum—an equal dollar amount to every household (Sherraden, 2001b).

Following Sherraden (1991) and Seidman (2001), the cost to the federal government for these policies in 2003 was estimated by Woo, Schweke, and Buchholz (2004) at about $335 billion. Their analysis of the largest spending categories shows that more than "a third of the benefits go to the wealthiest 1 percent of Americans—those who typically earn over $1 million per year. In contrast, less than 5 percent of the benefits go to the bottom 60 percent of taxpayers" (p. 1). Howard (1997, pp. 8–9) makes a similar point: "There is, still, a misconception that U.S. social programs primarily benefit the poor . . . (Social spending) flows overwhelmingly to citizens with above-average incomes."

As an example, the United States in 2003 provided more than $100 billion in subsidies for home ownership (Woo, Schweke, and Buchholz, 2004). A rich person with a million-dollar mortgage would receive annual subsidies of $20,000 or more, while a poor person would receive nothing unless he or she owns a home, has a mortgage, and has tax liability. The rationale for tying housing subsidies to income, debt, assets, and tax rates seems to be based more on political and administrative expediency than on the principles of efficiency, equity, and inclusive development. The current policy is no different than collecting all taxes with no mortgage-interest deduction and then sending $20,000 checks to some of the wealthiest people and no checks to millions of the poor. Beyond equity considerations, current policy is also inefficient, producing the "McMansion" phenomenon of overinvestment in underused housing. To be sure, promoting home ownership may be a legitimate use of public funds, but that is not primarily what this current policy does. Most housing subsidies go to the richest half of households, precisely those who probably would be homeowners even without subsidies. Thus, rather than raising home-ownership rates, the subsidy mainly supports luxury in housing and increased consumption for the richest half of households. In terms of both equity and efficiency, this is not a wise use of public resources, which are, after all, supposed to promote the public good.

If policy aims to support home ownership, then it would be fairer and more effective to focus almost all subsidies where the likely impact is greatest, that is, on the poorest half of households (or individuals). At the least, the poorest half of households should get half the subsidies. Why should this be the policy guidepost? Besides efficiency, an important principle of good government is *fairness* in public benefits. A healthy democracy requires a reasonable attempt to treat everyone the same (unless there are well-founded reasons not to). Equal subsidies for asset building would be a step in this direction. Such a policy would increase home ownership at the bottom and increase perceptions of fairness in government at all levels. Ultimately, this would strengthen the nation's economy and civic vitality.

Fairness and good government also suggest that asset-building subsidies should be transparent (as they are in IDAs). While there is legitimate debate about the proper extent and progressivity of taxation, the public good would be better served if tax policy were transparent, not just in terms of nominal tax rates, but also in terms of effective tax rates (how much is actually paid by whom). Furthermore, tax benefits such as deductions for home-mortgage interest and deferrals for contributions to Individual Retirement Accounts and 401(k) plans should be presented and discussed as *expenditures* rather than as lower levels of taxation. Unless counted as expenditures, such tax benefits opaquely subvert the intent of the overall tax structure.

Similar examples are possible for other asset-based policies such as retirement, education, and medical care. Again, the minimum standard should be that the poor benefit at least equally in dollar terms. Returning to the housing example, if the government is to provide annual subsidies of $100 billion for home ownership, then those subsidies should be distributed equally, for example, with 100 million households receiving $1,000 each.

How could this be done? After all, many people—especially among the poor—do not own houses, and many do not want to own a house. How then can they receive subsidies for home ownership? Likewise, how can they receive subsidies for post-secondary education when they may never go to college, or subsidies for retirement when they do not have a 401(k)?

One way is a policy of universal, permanent, individual asset-building accounts. This policy might be called IDAs, a universal 401(k) plan, or a universal Thrift Savings Plan; what matters is the universal, permanent structure that would serve as a framework for inclusive asset-based policy. With such a policy in place, each person would have an account to receive the annual $1,000 home-ownership subsidies suggested above (and/or larger unearmarked "asset-building" subsidies). People would receive the subsidies regardless of whether they owned a home, attended college, or had some other retirement account. Balances would build through time and could be used to acquire a few key types of assets, such as those discussed in this book in the context of IDAs. Even if a person never bought a home or attended college, the balance would be available for other asset-building purposes.

Asset-based policy has a long way to go before it includes everyone and treats them all at least equally, and further still before it achieves progressivity through greater subsidies for the poorest. While ADD did not model permanence or universality, it did model progressivity. ADD also showed that the poor—whatever their characteristics—can save and accumulate assets in IDAs. Finally, ADD offers lessons for the design of an inclusive asset-based policy by showing how aspects of the institutional structure of IDAs were associated with savings outcomes.

References

Aaron, H.J. (2000) "Seeing Through the Fog—Policymaking with Uncertain Forecasts," *Journal of Policy Analysis and Management*, Vol. 19, No. 2, pp. 193–206.

Ackerman, B.; and Alstott, A. (1999) *The Stakeholder Society*. New Haven, CT: Yale University Press, ISBN 0–300–07826–9.

Adams, D.W. (1995) "Transaction Costs in Decentralized Rural Financial Markets," pp. 249–265 in D.U. Deininger and C. Maguire (eds.) *Agriculture in Liberalizing Economies: Changing Roles for Governments*, Washington, DC: World Bank, ISBN 0–8213–3354–2.

Adams, D.W. (1978) "Mobilizing Household Savings through Rural Financial Markets," *Economic Development and Cultural Change*, Vol. 26, No. 3, pp. 547–560.

Adams, D.W.; and Fitchett, D.A. (1992) *Informal Finance in Low-Income Countries*, Boulder, CO: Westview Press, ISBN 0–8133–1504–2.

Adams, D.W.; and Von Pischke, J.D. (1992) "Microenterprise Credit Programs: Déjà Vu," *World Development*, Vol. 20, No. 10, pp. 1463–1470.

Agarwal, S.; Liu, C.; and Mielnicki, L. (2003) "Exemption Laws, Consumer Delinquency, and Bankruptcy Behavior: An Empirical Analysis of Credit-Card Data," *Quarterly Review of Economics and Finance*, Vol. 43, pp. 273–289.

Ainslie, G. (1984) "Behavioural Economics II: Motivated, Involuntary Behavior," *Social Science Information*, Vol. 23, No. 1, pp. 47–78.

Altonji, J.G.; and Doraszelski, U. (2001) "The Role of Permanent Income and Demographics in Black/White Differences in Wealth," National Bureau of Economic Research Working Paper No. 8473, http://www.nber/org/papers/w8473.

Ameriks, J.; Caplin, A.; and Leahy, J. (2002) "Wealth Accumulation and the Propensity to Plan," NBER Working Paper No. 8920, http://www.nber.org/papers/w8920.

Anderson, S.; and Baland, J.-M. (2002) "The Economics of RoSCAs and Intrahousehold Resource Allocation," *Quarterly Journal of Economics*, Vol. 117, No. 3, pp. 963–995.

Andrews, E.S. (1992) "The Growth and Distribution of 401(k) Plans," pp. 149–176 in John A. Turner and Daniel J. Beller (eds.) *Trends in Pensions 1992*, Pension and Welfare Benefits Administration: U.S. Department of Labor, ISBN 0–16–035936–8.

Angeletos, G.-M.; Laibson, D.; Repetto, A.; Tobacman, J.; and Weinberg, S. (2001) "The Hyperbolic Consumption Model: Calibration, Simulation, and Empirical Evaluation," *Journal of Economic Perspectives*, Vol. 15, No. 3, pp. 47–68.

Ardener, S.; and Burman, S. (1995) *Money-Go-Rounds: The Importance of Rotating Savings and Credit Associations For Women*, Oxford: Berg, ISBN 1–85973–170–8.

Aronson, R.L. (1991) *Self-Employment: A Labor-Market Perspective*, Ithaca, NY: ILR Press, ISBN 0–87546–175–1.

Arrow, K.J. (1998) "What Has Economics to Say About Racial Discrimination?" *Journal of Economic Perspectives*, Vol. 12, No. 2, pp. 91–100.

Ashraf, N.; Gons, N.; Karlan, D.S.; and W. Yin. (2003) "A Review of Commitment Savings Products in Developing Countries," Manila: Asian Development Bank, http://www.adb.org/Documents/ERD/Working_Papers/wp045.pdf.

Åstebro, T.; and Bernhardt, I. (2003) "Start-Up Financing, Owner Characteristics, and Survival," *Journal of Economics and Business*, Vol. 55, pp. 303–319.

Atkinson, A.B. (1992) "Measuring Inequality and Differing Social Judgements," *Research on Economic Inequality*, Vol. 3, pp. 29–56.

Attanasio, O.P.; and DeLeire, T. (2002) "The Effect of Individual Retirement Accounts on Household Consumption and National Saving," *Economic Journal*, Vol. 112, pp. 504–538.

Attanasio, O.P.; and Székely, M. (1999) "An Asset-Based Approach to the Analysis of Poverty in Latin America," Washington, DC: Inter-American Development Bank, http://www.iadb.org/res/publications/pubfiles/pubR-376.pdf.

Ayres, I.; and Siegelman, P. (1995) "Race and Gender Discrimination in Bargaining for a New Car," *American Economic Review*, Vol. 85, pp. 304–321.

Badu, Y.A.; Daniels, K.N.; and Salandro, D.P. (1999) "An Empirical Analysis of Differences in Black and White Asset and Liability Combinations," *Financial Services Review*, Vol. 8, pp. 129–147.

Bailey, J.; Curley, J.; Grinstein-Weiss, M.; and Edwards, K. (2004) "Individual Development Account Initiatives in Rural Areas: Challenges and Opportunities for Policy Development and Implementation," Center for Social Development, Washington University in St. Louis.

Bailey, J.M.; and Preston, K. (2003) *Swept Away: Chronic Hardship and Fresh Promise on the Rural Great Plains*, Lyons, NE: Center for Rural Affairs, http://www.cfra.org/pdf/Swept_Away.pdf.

Balkin, S. (1989) *Self-Employment and Low-Income People*, New York: Praeger, ISBN 0–275–92807–1.

Bardach, E. (2002) "Educating the Client: An Introduction," *Journal of Policy Analysis and Management*, Vol. 21, No. 1, pp. 115–117.

Barrow, L.; and McGranahan, L. (2000) "The Effects of the Earned Income Credit on the Seasonality of Household Expenditures," *National Tax Journal*, Vol. 53, No. 4, Part 2, pp. 1211–1243.

Bassett, W.F.; Fleming, M.J.; and Rodrigues, A.P. (1998) "How Workers Use 401(k) Plans: The Participation, Contribution, and Withdrawal Decisions," *National Tax Journal*, Vol. 51, No. 2, pp. 263–289.

Bates, T. (1997) *Race, Self-Employment, and Upward Mobility: An Illusive American Dream,* Baltimore, MD: Johns Hopkins University Press, ISBN 0–8018–5798–8.

Bates, T. (1996) "The Financial Needs of Black-Owned Businesses," *Journal of Developmental Entrepreneurship*, Vol. 1, No. 1, pp. 1–15.

Bayer, P. J.; Bernheim, B.D.; and Scholz, J. K. (1996) "The Effects of Financial Education in the Workplace: Evidence from a Survey of Employers," National Bureau of Economic Research Working Paper No. 5655, http://www.nber.org/papers/w5655.

Becker, G.S. (1995) "Habits, Addictions, and Traditions," pp. 218–237 in Ramon Febrero and Pedro S. Schwartz (eds.) *The Essence of Becker*, Stanford, CA: Hoover Institution Press, ISBN 0–817–99342–8.

Becker, G.S.; and Mulligan, C.B. (1997) "The Endogenous Determination of Time Preference," *Quarterly Journal of Economics*, Vol. 112, No. 3, pp. 729–758.

Benartzi, S.; and Thaler, R. (2002) "How Much Is Investor Autonomy Worth?" *Journal of Finance*, Vol. 57, No. 4, pp. 1593–1616.

Benartzi, S.; and Thaler, R. (2004) "Save More Tomorrow™: Using Behavioral Economics to Increase Employee Saving," *Journal of Political Economy*, Vol. 112, No. S1, pp. S164–S187.

Benjamin, D.J. (2003) "Does 401(k) Eligibility Increase Saving? Evidence from Propensity-Score Sub-Classification," *Journal of Public Economics*, Vol. 87, pp. 1259–1290.

Berger, A.N.; and G.F. Udell. (1998) "The Economics of Small-Business Finance: The Roles of Private Equity and Debt Markets in the Financial-Growth Cycle," *Journal of Banking and Finance*, Vol. 22, pp. 613–673.

Bernheim, B.D. (1994) "Personal Saving, Information, and Economic Literacy: New Directions for Public Policy," pp. 53–78 in *Tax Policy for Economic Growth in the 1990s*, Washington, DC: American Council for Capital Formation, ISBN 1–884–03201–X.

Bernheim, B.D. (1995) "Do Households Appreciate Their Financial Vulnerabilities? An Analysis of Actions, Perceptions, and Public Policy," pp. 3–46 in *Tax Policy and Economic Growth,* Washington, DC: American Council for Capital Formation, ISBN 1–884032–03–6.

Bernheim, B.D. (1997) "Rethinking Savings Incentives," pp. 259–311 in A.J. Auerbach (ed.) *Fiscal Policy: Lessons from Economic Research*, Cambridge, MA: MIT Press, ISBN 0–262–01160–3.

Bernheim, B.D. (1998) "Financial Illiteracy, Education, and Retirement Saving," pp. 38–68 in O.S. Mitchell and S.J. Schieber (eds.) *Living with Defined-Contribution Pensions: Remaking Responsibility for Retirement*, Philadelphia: University of Pennsylvania Press, ISBN 0–8122–3439–1.

Bernheim, B.D. (2002) "Taxation and Saving," pp. 1173–1249 in A. Auerback and M. Feldstein (eds.) *Handbook of Public Economics*, Volume 3, North-Holland, ISBN 0–444–82314–X.

Bernheim, B.D.; and Garrett, D.M. (2003) "The Effects of Financial Education in the Workplace: Evidence from a Survey of Households," *Journal of Public Economics*, Vol. 87, pp. 1487–1519.

Bernheim, B.D.; Garrett, D.M.; and Maki, D.M. (2001) "Education and Saving: The Long-Term Effects of High-School Financial-Curriculum Mandates," *Journal of Public Economics*, Vol. 80, pp. 435–465.

Bernheim, B.D.; and Scholz, J.K. (1993) "Private Saving and Public Policy," *Tax Policy and the Economy*, Vol. 7, pp. 73–110.

Bernstein, J. (2003) "Savings Incentives for the Poor: Why the Scale Doesn't Match the Promise," *American Prospect*, Vol. 14, No. 5, pp. A14–A15.

Bernstein, J. (2005). "Critical Questions in Asset-Based Policy," pp. 351-359 in M. Sherraden (ed.) *Inclusion in the American Dream: Assets, Poverty, and Public Policy*, New York: Oxford University Press, ISBN 0-19-516819-4

Bertrand, M.; and Mullainathan, S. (2003) "Are Emily and Greg More Employable than Lakisha and Jamal? A Field Experiment on Labor Market Discrimination," National Bureau of Economic Research Working Paper No. 9873, http://www.nber.org/papers/w9873.

Berube, Alan; Kim, Anne; Forman, Benjamin; and Megan Burns. (2002) "The Price of Paying Taxes: How Tax Preparation and Refund-Loan Fees Erode the Benefits of the EITC," Survey Series, Center on Urban and Metropolitan Policy, The Brookings Institution and the Progressive Policy Institute, www.brookings.edu/dybdocroot/es/urban/publications/berubekimeitc.pdf.

Besley, T. (1992) "Savings, Credit, and Insurance," pp. 2125–2207 in T.N. Srinivasan and J. Behrman (eds.), *Handbook of Development Economics, Volume III A*, Amsterdam: Elsevier, ISBN 0–444–88481–5.

Besley, T., and Kanbur, M.R. (1993) "The Principles of Targeting," pp. 67–90 in Michael Lipton and Jacques Van der Gaag (eds.), *Including the Poor,* Washington, DC: World Bank, ISBN 0–8213–2674–0.

Beverly, S.G. (2004) "Best Practices in Financial Education: Implementation and Performance Measurement," manuscript, University of Kansas School of Social Welfare, sbeverly@ku.edu.

Beverly, S.G. (1999) "Automobile Ownership and Labor Market Outcomes for Welfare Recipients," Center for Social Development, Washington University in Saint Louis, sbeverly@ku.edu.

Beverly, S.G. (1997) "How Can the Poor Save? Theory and Evidence on Saving in Low-Income Households," Center for Social Development Working Paper 97–3, Washington University in Saint Louis, http://gwbweb.wustl.edu/csd/Publications/1997/wp97-3.pdf.

Beverly, S.G.; and Burkhalter, E. (2004) "Improving the Financial Literacy and Practices of Youth," manuscript, University of Kansas Social of Social Welfare, sbeverly@ku.edu.

Beverly, S.G.; McBride, A.M.; and Schreiner, M. (2003) "A Framework of Asset-Accumulation Strategies," *Journal of Family and Economic Issues*, Vol. 24, No. 2, pp. 143–156.

Beverly, S.G.; Romich, J.L.; and Tescher, J. (2003) "Linking Tax Refunds and Low-Cost Bank Accounts: A Social Development Strategy for Low-Income Families?" *Social Development Issues*, Vol. 25, No. 1–2, pp. 235–246.

Beverly, S.G.; and Sherraden, M. (1999) "Institutional Determinants of Savings: Implications for Low-Income Households and Public Policy," *Journal of Socio-Economics*, Vol. 28, No. 4, pp. 457–473.

Beverly, S.G.; Tescher, J.; and Marzahl, D. (2000) "Low-Cost Bank Accounts and the EITC: How Financial Institutions Can Reach the Unbanked and Facilitate Saving," Center for Social Development, Washington University in Saint Louis, http://gwbweb.wustl.edu/csd/Publications/2000/wp00-19.pdf.

Birch, D.L. (1979) "The Job Generation Process," MIT Program on Neighborhood and Regional Change.

Bird, E.J.; Hagstrom, P.A.; and Wild, R. (1997) "Credit Cards and the Poor," Institute for Research on Poverty Discussion Paper No. 1148–97, http://www.ssc.wisc.edu/irp/pubs/dp114897.pdf.

Black, H.; Schweitzer, R.L.; and Mandell, L. (1978) "Discrimination in Mortgage Lending," *American Economic Review*, Vol. 68, No. 2, pp. 186–191.

Black, S.; and Morgan, D.P. (1998) "Risk and the Democratization of Credit Cards," manuscript, Federal Reserve Bank of New York, www.ny.frb.org/rmaghome/rsch_pap/9815.htm.

Blanchflower, D.G. (2000) "Self-employment in OECD countries," *Labour Economics*, Vol. 7, pp. 471–505.

Blanchflower, D.G.; Levine, P.B.; and Zimmerman, D.J. (1998) "Discrimination in the Small-business Credit Market," National Bureau of Economic Research Working Paper No. 6840, http://www.nber.org/papers/w6840.

Blanchflower, D.G.; and Oswald, A.J. (1998) "What Makes an Entrepreneur?" *Journal of Labor Economics*, Vol. 16, No. 1, pp. 26–68.

Blau, F.D.; and Graham, J.W. (1990) "Black-White Differences in Wealth and Asset Composition," *Quarterly Journal of Economics*, Vol. 105, No. 2, pp. 321–339.

Blinder, A.S. (1973) "Wage Discrimination: Reduced Form and Structural Estimates," *Journal of Human Resources*, Vol. 8, No. 3, pp. 436–455.

Bonnen, J.T.; and Schweikhardt, D.B. (1999) "Getting from Economic Analysis to Policy Advice," *Review of Agricultural Economics*, Vol. 20, No. 2, pp. 584–600.

Borleis, M.W.; and Wedell, K.K. (1994) "How to Spark Employee Interest with Employer Matching Contributions: A Sure-Fire Way to Increase 401(k) Participation," *Profit Sharing*, Vol. 42, No. 1, pp. 7–10, 16.

Boshara, R.; Scanlon, E.; and Page-Adams, D. (1998) *Building Assets for Stronger Families, Better Neighborhoods, and Realizing the American Dream*, Washington, DC: Corporation for Enterprise Development.

Boshara, R.; and Sherraden, M. (2004) "Status of Asset Building Worldwide," New American Foundation, http://www.assetbuilding.org/AssetBuilding/Download_Docs/Doc_File_891_1.pdf.

Bowles, S.; and Gintis, H. (2002) "The Inheritance of Inequality," *Journal of Economic Perspectives*, Vol. 16, No. 3, pp. 3–30.

Brieman, L. (2001) "Statistical Modeling: Two Cultures," *Statistical Science*, Vol. 16, No. 3, pp. 199–231.

Browning, M.; and Collado, M.D. (2001) "The Response of Expenditures to Anticipated Income Changes: Panel Data Estimates," *American Economic Review*, Vol. 91, No. 3, pp. 681–692.

Browning, M.; and Lusardi, A. (1996) "Household Saving: Micro Theories and Micro Facts," *Journal of Economic Literature*, Vol. 34, pp. 1797–1855.

Burtless, G. (1995) "The Case of Randomized Field Trials in Economic and Policy Research," *Journal of Economic Perspectives*, Vol. 9, No. 2, pp. 63–84.

Bush, G.W. (2000) "New Prosperity Initiative," speech in Cleveland, Ohio, April 11, http://www.georgewbush.com/speeches/newprosperity.asp.

Caner, A. (2003) "Savings of Entrepreneurs," Working Paper No. 390, The Levy Economics Institute, Bard College, http://www.levy.org/pubs/wp/390.pdf.

Carney, S.; and Gale, W.G. (2001) "Asset Accumulation in Low-Income Households," pp. 165–205 in T.M. Shapiro and E.N. Wolff (eds.) *Assets for the Poor: The Benefits of Spreading Asset Ownership*, New York, NY: Russell Sage Foundation, ISBN 0–87154–949–2.

Carroll, C.D.; and Samwick, A.A. (1998) "How Important Is Precautionary Saving?" *Review of Economics and Statistics*, Vol. 80, No. 3, pp. 410–419.

Carroll, C.D.; and Samwick, A.A. (1997) "The Nature of Precautionary Wealth," *Journal of Monetary Economics*, Vol. 40, No. 1, pp. 41–71.

Caskey, J.P. (2002) "Bringing Unbanked Households into the Banking System," *Capital Xchange*, Center on Urban and Metropolitan Policy, The Brookings Institution, http://www.brookings.edu/es/urban/CapitalXchange/caskey.pdf.

Caskey, J.P. (2001) "Can Lower-Income Households Increase Savings with Financial-Management Education?" *Cascade*, Federal Reserve Bank of Philadelphia, No. 46.

Caskey, J.P. (1997) "Beyond Cash-and-Carry: Financial Savings, Financial Services, and Low-Income Households in Two Communities," report to the Consumer Federation of America.

Caskey, J.P. (1994) *Fringe Banking: Check-Cashing Outlets, Pawnshops, and the Poor*, New York: Russell Sage Foundation, ISBN 0–87154–180–7.

Cavalluzzo, J.S.; and L.C. Cavalluzzo. (1998) "Market Structure and Discrimination: The Case of Small Business," *Journal of Money, Credit, and Banking*, Vol. 30, No. 4, pp. 771–792.

Chang, A.E. (1996) "Tax Policy, Lump-Sum Distributions, and Household Saving," *National Tax Journal*, Vol. 49, No. 2, pp. 235–252.

Cheng, L.-C. (2003) "Developing Family Development Accounts in Taipei: Policy Innovation from Income to Assets," Center for Social Development Working Paper No. 03–09, Washington University in Saint Louis, http://gwbweb.wustl.edu/csd/.

Chiteji, N.S.; and Hamilton, D. (2002) "Family Connections and the Black-White Wealth Gap among the Middle Class," *Review of Black Political Economy*, Vol. 30, No. 1, pp. 9–28.

Chiteji, N.S.; and Hamilton, D. (2000) "Family Matters: Kin Networks and Asset Accumulation," manuscript, Skidmore College, nchiteji@skidmore.edu.

Choi, J.J.; Laibson, D.; and Madrian, B.C. (2004) "Plan Design and 401(k) Savings Outcomes," National Bureau of Economic Research Working Paper No. 1086, http://www.nber.org/papers/w10486.

Choi, J.J.; Laibson, D.; Madrian, B.C.; and Metrick, A. (2003) "Optimal Defaults," *American Economic Review*, Vol. 93, No. 2, pp. 180–185.

Clancy, M.M. (2003) "College Savings Plans and Individual Development Accounts: Potential for Partnership," Center for Social Development, Washington University in Saint Louis, http://gwbweb.wustl.edu/csd/.

Clancy, M.M. (1996) "IDA Education and Communication," manuscript, George Warren Brown School of Social Work, Washington University in Saint Louis.

Clancy, M.M. (1995) "Low-Wage Employees' Participation and Saving in 401(k) Plans," manuscript, George Warren Brown School of Social Work, Washington University in Saint Louis.

Clancy, M.M.; Orszag, P.; and Sherraden, M. (2004) "State College Savings Plans: A Platform for Inclusive Policy?" Center for Social Development, Washington University in Saint Louis, http://gwbweb.wustl.edu/csd/.

Clancy, M.M.; and Sherraden, M. (2003) "The Potential for Inclusion in 529 Savings Plans: Report on a Survey of States," Research Report, Center for Social Development, Washington University in Saint Louis, http://gwbweb.wustl.edu/csd/.

Clark, P.; Kays, A.; Zandniapour, L.; Soto, E.; and Doyle, K. (1999) *Microenterprise and the Poor: Findings from the Self-Employment Learning Project Five-Year Study of Microentrepreneurs*, Washington, DC: Aspen Institute, ISBN 0–89843–260–X.

Clark, R.L.; Goodfellow, G.P.; Schieber, S.J.; and Warwick, D. (2000) "Making the Most of 401(k) Plans: Who's Choosing What and Why?" pp. 95–138 in O.S. Mitchell, P.B. Hammond, and A.M. Rappaport (eds.) *Forecasting Retirement Needs and Retirement Wealth*, Philadelphia: University of Pennsylvania Press, ISBN 0–8122–3529–0.

Clark, R.L.; and Schieber, S.J. (1998) "Factors Affecting Participation Rates and Contribution Levels in 401(k) Plans," pp. 69–97 in O.S. Mitchell and S.J. Schieber (eds.) *Living with Defined Contribution Pensions: Remaking Responsibility for Retirement*, Philadelphia: University of Pennsylvania Press, ISBN 0–8122–3439–1.

Clinton, W.J. (1999) "State of the Union Address," Washington, DC: U.S. Executive Office of the President.

Conley, D. (1999) *Being Black, Living in the Red: Race, Wealth, and Social Policy in America*, Berkeley, CA: University of California Press, ISBN 0–520–21672–5.

Cowger, C.D. (1984) "Statistical Significance Tests: Scientific Ritualism or Scientific Method?" *Social Service Review*, Vol. 58, pp. 358–372.

Cunningham, C.R.; and Engelhardt, G.V. (2002) "Federal Tax Policy, Employer Matching, and 401(k) Saving: Evidence from HRS W-2 Records," *National Tax Journal*, Vol. 55, No. 3, pp. 617–645.

Curley, J.; and M. Grinstein-Weiss. (2003) "A Comparative Analysis of Rural and Urban Saving Performance in Individual Development Accounts," *Social Development Issues*, Vol. 25, Nos. 1–2, pp. 89–105.

Curley, J., and Sherraden, M. (2000) "Policy Lessons from Children's Allowances for Children's Savings Accounts," *Child Welfare*, Vol. 79, No. 6, pp. 661–687.

Darity, W.A., Jr.; and Mason, P.L. (1998) "Evidence on Discrimination in Employment: Codes of Color, Codes of Gender," *Journal of Economic Perspectives*, Vol. 12, No. 2, pp. 63–90.

Dawes, R.M. (1979) "The Robust Beauty of Improper Linear Models in Decision Making," *American Psychologist*, Vol. 34, No. 7, pp. 571–582.

Deaton, A. (1992a) "Household Saving in LDCs: Credit Markets, Insurance and Welfare," *Scandinavian Journal of Economics*, Vol. 94, No. 2, pp. 253–273.

Deaton, A. (1992b) *Understanding Consumption,* Oxford: Clarendon Press, ISBN 0–19–828824–7.

Deaton, A. (1997) *The Analysis of Household Surveys: A Microeconometric Approach to Development Policy,* Baltimore, MD: Johns Hopkins University Press, ISBN 0–8018–5254–4.

Dercon, S. (1998) "Wealth, Risk and Activity Choice: Cattle in Western Tanzania," *Journal of Development Economics*, Vol. 55, pp. 1–42.

Dercon, S. (1996) "Risk, Crop Choice and Savings: Evidence from Tanzania," *Economic Development and Cultural Change*, Vol. 44, No. 3, pp. 487–513.

Dewald, W.G.; Thursby, J.G.; and Anderson, R.G. (1986) "Replication in Empirical Economics: The Journal of Money, Credit and Banking Project," *American Economic Review*, Vol. 76, No. 4, pp. 587–602.

Dietrich, J. (2003) "Under-Specified Models and Detection of Discrimination in Mortgage Lending," Economic and Policy Analysis Working Paper No. 2003–2, Office of the Comptroller of the Currency, http://www.occ.treas.gov/ftp/workpaper/wp2003-2.pdf.

Dowla, A.; and Alamgir, D. (2003) "From Microcredit to Microfinance: Evolution of Savings Products by MFIs in Bangladesh," *Journal of International Development*, Vol. 15, No. 8, pp. 969–988.

DuBois, W.E.B. (1970) *The Souls of Black Folk*, Greenwich, CT: Fawcett Publications (originally published in 1903).

Dunham, C. (2000) "Financial Service Usage Patterns of the Poor: Financial Cost Considerations," manuscript, Washington, DC: Office of the Comptroller of the Currency.

Dynarski, S. (2002) "The Behavioral and Distribution Implications of Aid for College," *American Economic Review*, Vol. 92, No. 2, pp. 279–285.

Easterly, W. (2003) "Can Foreign Aid Buy Growth?" *Journal of Economic Perspectives*, Vol. 17, No. 3, pp. 23–48.

Eberts, R.W. (2001) "Targeting Welfare-to-Work Services Using Statistical Tools," *Employment Research*, Vol. 8, No. 4, pp. 1–3.

Edgcomb, E.; and Klein, J. (2004) "Opening Opportunities, Building Ownership: Fulfilling the Promise of Microenterprise in the United States," manuscript, Aspen Institute.

Edgcomb, E.; and Thetford, T. (2004) "The Informal Economy: Making It in Rural America," Washington, DC: Aspen Institute, ISBN 0–89843–401-7.

Edgcomb, E.; and Armington, M.M. (2003) "The Informal Economy: Latino Enterprises at the Margins," Washington, DC: Aspen Institute, ISBN 0-89843-383-5.

Edin, K. (2001) "More Than Money: The Role of Assets in the Survival Strategies and Material Well-Being of the Poor," pp. 206–231 in T.M. Shapiro and E.N. Wolff (eds.) *Assets and the Poor: The Benefits of Spreading Asset Ownership*, New York, NY: Russell Sage, ISBN 0–87154–949–2.

Edin, K.; and Lein, L. (1997) *Making Ends Meet: How Single Mothers Survive Welfare and Low-Wage Work*, New York, NY: Russell Sage, ISBN 0–8175–4229–3.

Edwards, K.; and Mason, L.M. (2003) "State Policy Trends for Individual Development Accounts in the United States: 1993–2003," *Social Development Issues*, Vol. 25, No. 1–2, pp. 118–129.

Emshoff, J.G.; Courtenay-Quirk, C.; Broomfield, K.; and Jones, C. (2002) "Atlanta Individual Development Account (IDA) Pilot Program, Final Report," report to the United Way of Metropolitan Atlanta.

Engelhardt, G.V. (2001) "Have 401(k)s Raised Household Saving? Evidence from the Health and Retirement Study," Aging Studies Program Paper No. 24, Center for Policy Research, Syracuse University, http://www-cpr.maxwell.syr.edu/agpapser/pdf/age24.pdf.

Engelhardt, G.V. (1996) "Tax Subsidies and Household Saving: Evidence from Canada," *Quarterly Journal of Economics*, Vol. 111, pp. 1237–68.

Engelhardt, G.V. (1993) *Down Payments, Tax Policy, and Household Saving*, unpublished Ph.D. dissertation, Massachusetts Institute of Technology.

Engelhardt, G.V.; and Kumar, A. (2003) "Understanding the Impact of Employer Matching on 401(k) Saving," Research Dialogue No. 76, TIAA-CREF Institute.

Engen, E.M.; and Gale, W.G. (2000) "The Effects of 401(k) Plans on Household Wealth: Differences across Earnings Groups," National Bureau of Economic Research Working Paper No. 8032, http://www.nber.org/papers/w8032.

Engen, E.M.; Gale, W.G.; and Scholz, J.K. (1996) "The Illusory Effects of Saving Incentives on Saving," *Journal of Economic Perspectives*, Vol. 10, No. 4, pp. 113–138.

Esser, H. (1993) "The Rationality of Everyday Behavior: A Rational Choice Reconstruction of the Theory of Action by Alfred Schütz," *Rationality and Society*, Vol. 5, No. 1, pp. 7–31.

Evans, D.S.; and Jovanovic, B. (1989) "An Estimated Model of Entrepreneurial Choice under Liquidity Constraints," *Journal of Political Economy*, Vol. 97, No. 4, pp. 808–827.

Evans, D.S.; and Leighton, L.S. (1989) "Some Empirical Aspects of Entrepreneurship," *American Economic Review*, Vol. 79, No. 3, pp. 519–535.

Even, W.E.; and Macpherson, D.A. (2003) "Determinants and Effects of Employer Matching Contributions in 401(k) Plans," http://econwpa.wustl.edu:8089/eps/lab/papers/0405/0405001.pdf.

Even, W.E.; and Macpherson, D.A. (1997) "Factors Influencing Participation and Contribution Levels in 401(k) Plans," Economics Working Paper No. 98–05–01, Florida State University.

Even, W.E.; and MacPherson, D.A. (1994) "Why Did Male Pension Coverage Decline in the 1980s?" *Industrial and Labor Relations Review*, Vol. 47, No. 3, pp. 439–453.

Feagan, J.R. (2000) "Documenting the Costs of Slavery, Segregation, and Contemporary Discrimination: Are Compensation and Reparations in Order for African Americans?" paper presented at the Inclusion in Asset Building: Research and Policy Symposium, Center for Social Development, Washington University in Saint Louis, Sept. 21–23, gwbweb.wustl.edu/csd/Publications/2000/wp00-10.pdf.

Feenberg, D.; and Skinner, J. (1989) "Sources of IRA Saving," pp. 25–46 in L. H. Summers (ed.) *Tax Policy and the Economy*, Vol. 3, ISBN 0–262–06126–0.

Feldstein, M. (1995) "College Scholarship Rules and Private Saving," *American Economic Review*, Vol. 85, No. 3, pp. 552–556.

Finlayson, J.; and Peacock, K. (2003) "Gauging the Economic Contribution of Large and Small Businesses: A Reassessment," *Policy Perspectives*, Business Council of British Columbia, Vol. 10, No. 4, http://www.bcbc.com/archive/ppv10n4.pdf.

Fitzgerald, F.S. (1925) *The Great Gatsby*, New York, NY: Charles Scribner's Sons.

Frank, R.H. (1999) *Luxury Fever: Why Money Fails to Satisfy in an Era of Excess*, New York, NY: Free Press, ISBN 0–684–84234–3.

Frederick, S.; Loewenstein, G.; and O'Donoghue, T. (2002) "Time Discounting and Time Preference: A Critical Review," *Journal of Economic Literature*, Vol. XL, pp. 351–401.

Friedman, J.H. (1991) "Multivariate Adaptive Regression Splines," *Annals of Statistics*, Vol. 19, March, pp. 1–141.

Friedman, R. (1988) *The Safety Net as Ladder: Transfer Payments and Economic Development*, Washington, DC: Council of State Policy and Planning Agencies, ISBN 0–934842–42–6.

Gale, W.G; Iwry, J.M.; and Orszag, P.R. (2004) "The Saver's Credit: Issues and Options," The Brookings Institution, http://www.brookings.edu/dybdocroot/views/papers/gale/20040419.pdf.

Gale, W.G.; and Scholz, J.K. (1994) "IRAs and Household Saving," *American Economic Review*, Vol. 84, No. 5, pp. 1233–1260.

Galenson, M. (1972) "Do Blacks Save More?" *American Economic Review*, Vol. 62, No. 1/2, pp. 211–216.

Galster, G.C. (1990) "Racial Discrimination in Housing Markets during the 1980s: A Review of the Audit Evidence," *Journal of Planning and Education Research*, Vol. 9, No. 3, pp. 165–175.

Garfinkle, I.; Manski, C.F.; and Michalopoulos, C. (1992) "Micro Experiments and Macro Effects," pp. 253–273 in C.F. Manski and I. Garfinkle (eds.) *Evaluating Welfare and Training Programs*, Cambridge, MA: Harvard University Press, ISBN 0–674–27017–7.

Gates, J. (1998) *The Ownership Solution: Toward a Shared Capitalism for the Twenty-First Century.* Reading, MA: Addison-Wesley, ISBN 0–738–20131–6.

General Accounting Office. (1997) "401(k) Pension Plans: Loan Provision Enhance Participation But May Affect Income Security for Some," GAO/HEHS–98–5.

Gersovitz, M. (1988) "Saving and Development," pp. 382–424 in H. Chenery and T.N. Srinivasan (eds.), *Handbook of Development Economics*, Amsterdam: Elsevier, ISBN 0–444–70337–3.

Gokhale, J.; Kotlikoff, L.J.; and Warshawsky, M.J. (2001) "Life-Cycle Saving, Limits on Contributions to DC Pension Plans, and Lifetime Tax Benefits," National Bureau of Economic Research Working Paper No. 8170, http://www.nber.org/papers/w8170.

Goldberg, F.; and Cohen, J. (2000) "The Universal Piggy Bank: Designing and Implementing a System of Savings Accounts for Children," Paper presented at the Inclusion in Asset Building: Research and Policy Symposium, Center for Social Development, Washington University in Saint Louis, Sept. 21–23, http://gwbweb.wustl.edu/csd/Publications/2000/PolicyReport-Goldberg.pdf.

Goodman, J.L.; and Ittner, J.B. (1992) "The Accuracy of Home Owner's Estimates of House Value," *Journal of Housing Economics*, Vol. 2, pp. 339–357.

Green, R.K.; and White, M.J. (1997) "Measuring the Benefits of Homeowning: Effects on Children," *Journal of Urban Economics*, Vol. 41, pp. 441–461.

Greenberg, M. (1999) "Developing Policies to Support Microenterprise in the TANF Structure: A Guide to the Law," Washington, DC: Aspen Institute, ISBN 0–89843–273–1.

Greene, W.H. (1993) *Econometric Analysis: Second Edition.* New York, NY: Macmillan, ISBN 0–02–346391–0.

Grinstein-Weiss, M.; and Sherraden, M. (2004) "Racial Differences in Savings Outcomes in Individual Development Accounts," Center for Social Development Working Paper No. 04-04, Washington University in Saint Louis, http://gwbweb.wustl.edu/csd/Publications/2004/WP04-04.pdf.

Grinstein-Weiss, M.; Zhan, M.; and Sherraden, M. (2004) "Saving Performance in Individual Development Accounts: Does Marital Status Matter?" Center for Social Development Working Paper No. 04–01, Washington University in Saint Louis, http://gwbweb.wustl.edu/csd/Publications/2004/WP04-01.pdf.

Grinstein-Weiss, M.; and Curley, J. (2002) "Individual Development Accounts in Rural Communities: Implications for Research," pp. 328–340 in T.L. Scales and C.L. Streeter (eds.) *Rural Social Work: Building and Sustaining Community Assets*, Pacific Grove, CA: Brooks/Cole, ISBN 0–534–62163–5.

Gruber, J.; and Yelowitz, A. (1999) "Public Health Insurance and Private Savings," *Journal of Political Economy*, Vol. 107, No. 6, Part 1, pp. 1249–1274.

Gugerty, M.K. (2003) "You Can't Save Alone: Testing Theories of Rotating Savings and Credit Associations in Kenya," University of Washington, http://www.international.ucla.edu/CMS/files/gugerty_roscas.doc.

Hamermesh, D.S.; and Biddle, J.E. (1993) "Beauty and the Labor Markets," National Bureau of Economic Research Working Paper No. 4518, Cambridge, MA.

Hand, D.J.; and Adams, N.M. (2000) "Defining attributes for scorecard construction in credit scoring," *Journal of Applied Statistics*, Vol. 27, No. 5, pp. 527–540.

Hand, D.J.; Blunt, G.; Kelly, M.G.; and Adams, N.M. (2000) "Data Mining for Fun and Profit," *Statistical Science*, Vol. 15, No. 2, pp. 111–131.

Haruf, K. (1999) *Plainsong*, New York: Vintage Books, ISBN 0–375–705–856.

Haveman, R. (1988) *Starting Even: An Equal Opportunity Program to Combat the Nation's New Poverty*, New York, NY: Simon and Schuster, ISBN 0–671–66762–9.

Heckman, J.J. (1976) "The common structure of statistical models of truncation, sample selection and limited dependent variables and a simple estimator for such models," *Annals of Economic and Social Measurement*, Vol. 5, No. 4, pp. 475–492.

Heckman, J.J. (1979) "Sample-selection bias as a specification error," *Econometrica*, Vol. 47, No. 1, pp. 153–161.

Heckman, J.J. (1998) "Detecting Discrimination," *Journal of Economic Perspectives*, Vol. 12, No. 2, pp. 101–116.

Hinterlong, J.; and Johnson, E. (2000) "Integrating Best Practice Guidelines with Technology: Shaping Policies for Family Economic Development," paper presented at the Annual Meeting of the Council on Social Work Education.

Hirad, A.; and Zorn, P.M. (2001) "A Little Knowledge is a Good Thing: Empirical Evidence of the Effectiveness of Pre-Purchase Homeownership Counseling," Freddie Mac, http://www.freddiemac.com/corporate/reports/pdf/homebuyers_study.pdf.

H.M. Treasury. (2003) "Detailed Proposals for the Child Trust Fund," London, http://www.hm-treasury.gov.uk/media/C7914/child_trust_fund_proposals_284.pdf.

H.M. Treasury. (2001) "Savings and Assets for All," The Modernisation of Britain's Tax and Benefit System, No. 8, London.

Hoch, S.J.; and Loewenstein, G.F. (1991) "Time-inconsistent Preferences and Consumer Self-Control," *Journal of Consumer Research*, Vol. 17, pp. 492–507.

Hogarth, J.M., and Lee, J. (2000) "Banking Relationships of Low-to-Moderate Income Households: Evidence from the 1995 and 1998 Surveys of Consumer Finances," Paper presented at the Inclusion in Asset Building: Research and Policy Symposium, Center for Social Development, Washington University in Saint Louis, Sept. 21–23, http://gwbweb.wustl.edu/csd/Publications/2000/wp00-13.pdf.

Hogarth, J.M.; and O'Donnell, K.H. (1999) "Banking Relationships of Lower-Income Families and the Government Trend toward Electronic Payment," *Federal Reserve Bulletin*, July, pp. 459–473.

Hogarth, J.M.; and Swanson, J. (1995) "Using Adult-Education Principles in Financial Education for Low-Income Audiences," *Family Economics and Resource Management Biennial*, pp. 139–146.

Holden, S.; and VanDerhei, J. (2001) "401(k) Plan Asset Allocation, Account Balances, and Loan Activity in 2000," *Investment Company Institute Perspective*, Vol. 7, No. 5, pp. 1–27, http://www.ici.org/pdf/per07-05.pdf.

Holtz-Eakin, D.; Joulfaian, D.; and Rosen, H.S. (1994) "Sticking It Out: Entrepreneurial Survival and Liquidity Constraints," *Journal of Political Economy*, Vol. 102, No. 1, pp. 53–75.

Howard, C. (1997) *The Hidden Welfare State: Tax Expenditures and Social Policy in the United States*. Princeton, NJ: Princeton University Press, ISBN 0–691–02646–7.

Hubbard, R.G.; and Skinner, J.S. (1996) "Assessing the Effectiveness of Saving Incentives," *Journal of Economic Perspectives*, Vol. 10, No. 4, pp. 73–90.

Hubbard, R.G.; Skinner, J.S.; and Zeldes, S.P. (1995) "Precautionary Savings and Social Insurance," *Journal of Political Economy*, Vol. 103, No. 2, pp. 360–399.

Hubbard, R.G.; Skinner, J.S.; and Zeldes, S.P. (1994) "Expanding the Life-Cycle Model: Precautionary Saving and Public Policy," *American Economic Review*, Vol. 84, No. 2, pp. 174–179.

Huberman, G.; Iyengar, S.; and Jiang, W. (2003) "Defined-Contribution Pension Plans: Determinants of Participation and Contribution Rates," Columbia Business School.

Hurley, J.F. (2002) *The Best Way to Save for College: A Complete Guide to 529 Plans*, Pittsford, NY: BonaCom, ISBN 0–9670322–6–1.

Hurst, E.; and Ziliak, J.P. (2004) "Do Welfare Asset Limits Affect Household Saving? Evidence from Welfare Reform," National Bureau of Economic Research Working Paper No. 10487, http://www.nber.org/w10487.

Ippolito, R. (1997) *Pension Plans and Employee Performance: Evidence, Analysis, and Policy*, Chicago: University of Chicago Press, ISBN 0–226–384551.

Iskander, M. (2003) "Evaluating Your IDA Investment: Three Tough Questions to Ask Grant Recipients," manuscript, Yale Law School.

Jacob, K.; Hudson, S.; and Bush, M. (2000) *Tools for Survival: An Analysis of Financial-Literacy Programs for Lower-Income Families*, Chicago, IL: Woodstock Institute, http://woodstockinst.org/document/toolsforsurvival.pdf.

Johnson, C. (2000) "Welfare Reform and Asset Accumulation: First We Need a Bed and a Car," *Wisconsin Law Review*, Vol. 6, pp. 1221–1290.

Johnson, E.; Hinterlong, J.; and M. Sherraden. (2001) "Strategies for Creating MIS Technology to Improve Social Work Practice and Research," *Journal of Technology for the Human Services*, Vol. 18, No. 3/4, pp. 5–22.

Johnson, E.; Ssewamala, F.; Sherraden, Ma.; and McBride, A.M. (2003) "Programs that Promote Asset-Accumulation and Economic Justice: Implications for Social Work," paper presented at the Council on Social Work Education Annual Conference, February 27 to March 3.

Joines, D.H.; and Manegold, J.H. (1991) "IRAs and Saving: Evidence from a Panel of Taxpayers," Research Working Paper No. 91–05, Federal Reserve Bank of Kansas City.

Joulfaian, D.; and Richardson, D. (2001) "Who Takes Advantage of Tax-Deferred Savings Programs? Evidence from Federal Income-Tax Data," *National Tax Journal*, Vol. 54, No. 3, pp. 669–688.

Kafer, K. (2004) "Refocusing Higher Education Aid on Those Who Need It," Backgrounder No. 1753, Washington, DC: Heritage Foundation, http://www.heritage.org/research/education/bg1753.cfm.

Kahneman, D.; and Tversky, A. (1979) "Prospect Theory: An Analysis of Decision under Risk," *Econometrica*, Vol. 47, No. 2, pp. 263–291.

Kasarda, J.D. (1995) "Industrial Restructuring and the Changing Location of Jobs"; pp. 215–267 in R. Farley (ed.) *State of the Union: America in the 1990s, Volume One: Economic Issues*. New York, NY: Russell Sage Foundation, ISBN 0–87154–240–4.

Katz Reid, C. (2004) "Achieving the American Dream? A Longitudinal Analysis of Homeownership Experiences of Low-Income Households," Center for Studies in Demography and Ecology Working Paper 04–04, University of Washington.

Kempson, E.; McKay, S.; and Collard, S. (2003) "Evaluation of the CFLI and Saving Gateway Pilot Projects," Personal Finance Research Centre, University of Bristol, http://www.ggy.bris.ac.uk/research/pfrc/publications/SG_report_Oct03.pdf.

Kennedy, P. (1998) *A Guide to Econometrics, Fourth Edition*. Cambridge, MA: MIT Press, ISBN 0–262–11235–3.

Kessler, G. (2000) "Gore to detail retirement savings plan," *Washington Post*, June 19, p. A01.

Kim, A.S. (2002) "Taken for a Ride: Subprime Lenders, Automobiles, and the Working Poor," Policy Report, Washington, DC: Progressive Policy Institute, www.ppionline.org/ppi_ci.cfm?knlgAreaID=114&subsecID=143 &contentID=251014.

King, G. (1986) "How Not to Lie with Statistics: Avoiding Common Mistakes in Quantitative Political Science," *American Journal of Political Science*, Vol. 30, pp. 666–687.

King, M. (1985) "The Economics of Saving: A Survey of Recent Contributions," pp. 227–295 in K.J. Arrow and S. Honkapohja (eds.) *Frontiers of Economics*, Oxford: Basil Blackwell, ISBN 0-63-1134-085.

Kingston, P.W. (1994) "Having a Stake in the System: The Sociopolitical Ramifications of Business and Home Ownership," *Social Science Quarterly*, Vol. 75, No. 3, pp. 679–686.

Kosanovich, W.T.; and Fleck, H. (2001) "Final Report: Comprehensive Assessment of Self-Employment Assistance Programs," DTI Associates, Inc. and Madonna Yost Opinion Research for the U.S. Department of Labor.

Ladd, H.F. (1998) "Evidence on Discrimination in Mortgage Lending," *Journal of Economic Perspectives*, Vol. 12, No. 2, pp. 41–62.

Lazear, D. (1999) "Implementation and Outcomes of an Individual Development Account Project," Center for Social Development, Washington University in Saint Louis, http://gwbweb.wustl.edu/csd/Publications/1999/researchreportlazear.pdf.

Levenson, A.R.; and Maloney, W.F. (1996) "The Informal Sector, Firm Dynamics, and Institutional Participation," Milken Institute for Job and Capital Formation Working Paper 96-3.

Lewis, E.M. (1990) *An Introduction to Credit Scoring*, San Rafael: Athena Press, ISBN 99-956-4223-9.

Lewis, O. (1966) *La Vida: A Puerto Rican Family in the Culture of Poverty—San Juan and New York,* New York, NY: Random House, ISBN 0-39-4450-469.

Lindley, J.T.; Selby, E.B., Jr.; and Jackson, J.D. (1984) "Racial Discrimination in the Provision of Financial Services," *American Economic Review*, Vol. 74, No. 4, pp. 735–741.

Lipton, M.; and Ravallion, M. (1995) "Poverty and Policy," pp. 2553–2657 in J. Behrman and T.N. Srinivasan (eds.) *Handbook of Development Economics, Volume IIIB*, Amsterdam: Elsevier, ISBN 0-444-82302-6.

Littlefield, E.; Morduch, J.; and Hashemi, S. (2003) "Is Microfinance an Effective Strategy to Reach the Millennium Development Goals?" Focus Note No. 24, Washington, DC; Consultative Group to Assist the Poorest, http://www.cgap.org/assets/images/FOCUS24_MDGs.pdf.

Long, M. (2003) "The impact of asset-tested college financial aid on household savings," *Journal of Public Economics*, Vol. 88, pp. 63–88.

Losby, J.L.; Kingslow, M.E.; and Else, J.F. (2003) "The Informal Economy: Experiences of African Americans," Washington, DC: Aspen Institute, ISBN 0-89843-384-3.

Losby, J.L.; Else, J.F.; Kingslow, M.E.; Edgcomb, E.L.; Malm, E.T.; and Kao, V. (2002) "Informal Economy Literature Review," Washington, DC: Aspen Institute, http://fieldus.org/li/pdf/InformalEconomy.pdf.

Loury, G.C. (1998) "Discrimination in the Post-Civil Rights Era: Beyond Market Interactions," *Journal of Economic Perspectives*, Vol. 12, No. 2, pp. 117–126.

Lovie, A.D.; and Lovie, P. (1986) "The Flat Maximum Effect and Linear Scoring Models for Prediction," *Journal of Forecasting*, Vol. 5, pp. 159–168.

Lusardi, A. (2000) "Explaining Why So Many Households Do Not Save," manuscript. University of Chicago, http://harrisschool.uchicago.edu/pdf/wp_00_1.pdf.

Madrian, B.C.; and Shea, D.F. (2001) "The Power of Suggestion: Inertia in 401(k) Participation and Savings Behavior," *Quarterly Journal of Economics*, Vol. 116, No. 4, pp. 1149–1187.

Maital, S. (1986) "Prometheus Rebound: On Welfare-Improving Constraints," *Eastern Economic Journal*, Vol. 12, No. 3, pp. 337–344.

Maital, S.; and Maital, S.L. (1994) "Is the Future What It Used To Be? A Behavioral Theory of the Decline of Saving in the West," *Journal of Socio-Economics*, Vol. 23, No. 1/2, pp. 1–32.

Manski, C.F. (1995) "Learning about Social Programs from Experiments with Random Assignment of Treatments," Institute for Research on Poverty Discussion Paper No. 1061–95, http://www.ssc.wisc.edu/irp/pubs/dp106195.pdf.

Massey, D.S.; and Denton, N.A. (1994) *American Apartheid: Segregation and the Making of the Underclass*, Cambridge, MA: Harvard University Press, ISBN 0–67–401821–4.

Massey, D.S.; and Lundy, G. (1998) "Use of Black English and Racial Discrimination in Urban Housing Markets: New Methods and Findings," Population Studies Center, University of Pennsylvania, http://www.ksg.harvard.edu/inequality/Seminar/Papers/Massey.PDF.

McBride, A.M.; Sherraden, M.S.; Johnson, E. and Ssewamala, F. (2003) "How Do Poor People Save Money? Implications for Social Work," poster presented at Society for Social Work and Research Annual Conference, Washington, DC, January 16.

McBride, A.M.; Lombe, M.; and Beverly, S.G. (2003) "The Effects of Individual Development Account Programs: Perceptions of Participants," *Social Development Issues*, Vol. 25, Nos. 1–2, pp. 59–73.

McCloskey, D.N. (1985) "The Loss Function Has Been Mislaid: The Rhetoric of Significance Tests," *American Economic Review*, Vol. 75, No. 2, pp. 201–205.

McCullough, B.D.; and Vinod, H.D. (2003) "Verifying the Solution from a Nonlinear Solver: A Case Study," *American Economic Review*, Vol. 93, No. 3, pp. 873–892.

Meyer, R.L.; and Nagarajan, G. (1992) "An Assessment of the Role of Informal Finance in the Development Process," pp. 644–654 in G.H. Peters and B.F. Stanton (eds.) *Sustainable Agricultural Development: The Role of International Cooperation*, Dartmouth, ISBN 1–855–21272–2.

Miller, D.J. (2003) "Everything You Own Belongs to the Land: Land, Community, and History in Tillery, North Carolina," Center for Social Development Working Paper No. 03–22, Washington University in Saint Louis, http://gwbweb.wustl.edu/csd/Publications/2003/WP03-22.pdf.

Milligan, K. (2002) "Tax Preferences for Education Saving: Are RESPs Effective?" Commentary No. 174, C.D. Howe Institute.

Milligan, K. (2003) "How Do Contribution Limits Affect Contributions to Tax-Preferred Savings Accounts?" *Journal of Public Economics*, Vol. 87, pp. 253–281.

Mills, G.; Patterson, R.; Orr, L.; and DeMarco, D. (2004) "Evaluation of the American Dream Demonstration: Final Evaluation Report," Cambridge, MA: Abt Associates.

Miranda, M.J.; and Fackler, P.L. (2002) *Applied Computational Economics and Finance*, Cambridge, MA: MIT Press, ISBN 0-262-13420-9.

Mischel, W. (1977) "The Interaction of Person and Situation," pp. 333–352 in D. Magnusson and N. S. Endler (eds.) *Personality at the Crossroads: Current Issues in Interactional Psychology*, Hillsdale, NJ: Lawrence Erlbaum Associates, ISBN 0–470–99135–6.

Moffitt, R. (1986) "Work Incentives in the AFDC System: An Analysis of the 1981 Reforms," *American Economic Review*, Vol. 76, No. 2, pp. 219–223.

Moffitt, R. (1990) "The Econometrics of Kinked Budget Constraints," *Journal of Economic Perspectives*, Vol. 4, No. 2, pp. 119–139.

Moffitt, R. (1991) "Program Evaluation with Non-Experimental Data," *Evaluation Review*, Vol. 15, No. 3, pp. 291–314.

Montgomery, M.; Johnson, T.; and S. Faisal. (2000) "Who Succeeds at Starting a Business? Evidence from the Washington Self-Employment Demonstration," Grinnell College, http://web.grinnell.edu/individuals/montgome/Start%20Business.PDF.

Moore, A.; Beverly, S.; Sherraden, M.; Sherraden, M.; Johnson, L.; and Schreiner, M. (2000) "How Do Low-Income Individuals Save, Deposit, and Maintain Financial Assets?" Paper presented at the Inclusion in Asset Building: Research and Policy Symposium, Center for Social Development, Washington University in Saint Louis, Sept. 21–23.

Moore, A.; Beverly, S.; Schreiner, M.; Sherraden, M.; Lombe, M.; Cho, E. Y.; Johnson, L.; and Vonderlack, R. (2001) "Saving, IDA Programs, and the Effects of IDAs: A Survey of Participants," Center for Social Development, Washington University in Saint Louis, http://gwbweb.wustl.edu/csd/Publications/2001/shortsurveyreport.pdf.

Morris, G.A.; and Meyer, R.L. (1993) "Women and Financial Services in Developing Countries: A Review of the Literature," Economics and Sociology Occasional Paper No. 2056, The Ohio State University.

Mullainathan, S.; and Thaler, R.H. (2000) "Behavioral Economics," National Bureau of Economic Research Working Paper No. 7948, http://www.nber.org/papers/w7948.

Munnell, A.H.; Sundén, A.; and Taylor, C. (2002) "What Determines 401(k) Participation and Contributions?" *Social Security Bulletin*, Vol. 64, No. 3, pp. 64–75.

Munnell, A.H.; Tootell, G.M.B.; Browne, L.E.; and McEneaney, J. (1996) "Mortgage Lending in Boston: Interpreting HMDA Data," *American Economic Review*, Vol. 86, No. 1, pp. 25–53.

Neumark, D.; and Powers, E. (1998). "The Effect of Means-Tested Income Support for the Elderly on Pre-Retirement Saving: Evidence from the SSI Program in the United States," *Journal of Public Economics*, Vol. 68, No. 2, pp. 181–206.

Ng, G.T. (2001) "Costs of IDAs and Other Capital-Development Programs," Center for Social Development Working Paper No. 01–8, Washington University in Saint Louis, http://gwbweb.wustl.edu/csd/Publications/2001/wp01-8.pdf.

Oaxaca, R. (1973) "Male-Female Wage Differentials in Urban Labor Markets," *International Economic Review*, Vol. 14, No. 3, pp. 693–709.

Oliver, M.L.; and Shapiro, T.M. (1995) *Black Wealth/White Wealth: A New Perspective on Racial Inequality*, New York: Routledge, ISBN 0–415–91375–6.

Olney, M.L. (1998) "When Your Word Is Not Enough: Race, Collateral, and Household Credit," *Journal of Economic History*, Vol. 58, No. 2, pp. 408–431.

Ong, P.M. (1996) "Work and Automobile Ownership among Welfare Recipients," *Social Work Research*, Vol. 20, No. 4, pp. 255–262.

Orme, J.G.; and Reis, J. (1991) "Multiple Regression with Missing Data," *Journal of Social Service Research*, Vol. 15, No. 1/2, pp. 61–91.

Orr, L.L. (1999) *Social Experiments: Evaluating Public Programs with Experimental Methods*, Thousand Oaks, CA: Sage, ISBN 0-7619-1294-0.

Orszag, P.R. (2001) "Asset Tests and Low Saving Rates among Lower-Income Families," Center on Budget and Policy Priorities, http://www.cbpp.org/4-13-01wel.pdf.

Orszag, P.R.; and Hall, M.G. (2003) "The Saver's Credit," Tax Policy Center, The Brookings Institution, http://www.taxpolicycenter.org/taxfacts.

Orszag, P.R.; and Greenstein, R. (2004) "Progressivity and Government Incentives to Save," Building Assets, Building Credit Working Paper No. 04–16, Joint Center for Housing Studies, Harvard University, http://www.jchs.harvard.edu/publications/finance/babc/babc_04-16.pdf.

Owens, J.V.; and Wisniwiski, S.B. (1999) "Microsavings: What We Can Learn from Informal Savings Schemes," manuscript.

Page-Adams, D. (2002) "Design, Implementation, and Administration of Individual Development Account Programs," Research Report, Center for Social Development, Washington University in Saint Louis, http://gwbweb.wustl.edu/csd/Publications/2002/PageAdamsResearchReport2002.pdf.

Papke, L.E. (1995) "Participation in and Contributions to 401(k) Pension Plans," *Journal of Human Resources*, Vol. 30, pp. 311–325.

Papke, L.E.; and Poterba, J.M. (1995) "Survey Evidence on Employer Match Rates and Employee Saving Behavior in 401(k) Plans," *Economics Letters*, Vol. 49, pp. 313–317.

Plotnick, R.D.; and Deppman, L. (1999) "Using Benefit-Cost Analysis to Assess Child-Abuse Prevention and Intervention Programs," *Child Welfare*, Vol. 78, No. 3, pp. 381–407.

Poterba, J.M.; Venti, S.F.; and Wise, D.A. (1995) "Lump-Sum Distributions from Retirement Savings Plans: Receipt and Utilization," National Bureau of Economic Research Working Paper No. 5298, http://www.nber.org/papers/w5298.

Poterba, J.M.; Venti, S.F.; and Wise, D.A. (1996) "How Retirement Saving Programs Increase Saving," *Journal of Economic Perspectives*, Vol. 10, No. 4, pp. 91–112.

Powers, E. T. (1998) "Does Means-Testing Welfare Discourage Saving? Evidence from a Change in AFDC Policy in the United States," *Journal of Public Economics*, Vol. 68, pp. 33–53.

Prelec, D.; and Loewenstein, G. (1998) "The Red and the Black: Mental Accounting of Savings and Debt," *Marketing Science*, Vol. 17, No. 1, pp. 4–28.

Pritchett, L. (2002) "It Pays to be Ignorant: A Simple Political Economy of Rigorous Program Evaluation," *Journal of Policy Reform*, Vol. 5, No. 4, pp. 251–269.

Pudney, S. (1989) *Modeling Individual Choice: The Econometrics of Corners, Kinks, and Holes*, Cambridge, MA: Basil Blackwell, ISBN 0-631-14589-3.

Pyle, D. (1999) *Data Preparation for Data Mining*, San Francisco: Morgan Kaufmann, ISBN 1–55860–529–0.

Ramsey, F.P. (1929) "A Mathematical Theory of Saving," *Economic Journal*, *38*(152), pp. 543–559.

Ravaillon, M. (2001) "The Mystery of the Vanishing Benefits: An Introduction to Impact Evaluation," *World Bank Economic Review*, Vol. 15, No. 1, pp. 115–140.

Richardson, P. (1995) "401(k) Education Coming of Age," *Institutional Investor*, Vol. 29, No. 9, pp. 2–13.

Robinson, M.S. (2001) *The Microfinance Revolution: Sustainable Finance for the Poor*, Washington, DC: World Bank, ISBN 0–8213–4524–9.

Robinson, M.S. (1994) "Savings Mobilization and Microenterprise Finance: The Indonesian Experience," pp. 27–54 in María Otero and Elisabeth Rhyne (eds.) *The New World of Microenterprise Finance*, West Hartford: Kumarian, ISBN 1–56549–031–2.

Romich, J.L.; and Weisner, T. (1999) "How Families View and Use the EITC: Advance-Payment Versus Lump-Sum Delivery," *National Tax Journal*, Vol. 53, No. 4, Part 2, pp. 1245–1264.

Rossi, P.H. (1987) "The Iron Law of Evaluation and Other Metallic Rules," pp. 3–20 in J.L. Miller and M. Lewis (eds.) *Research in Social Problems and Social Policy*, Vol. 4, ISBN 0–89232–560–7.

Royse, D. (1991) *Research Methods in Social Work*, Chicago: Nelson-Hall, ISBN 0–8304–1210–7.

Rutherford, S. (2000) *The Poor and Their Money.* Delhi: Oxford University Press, ISBN 0–195–65255–X.

Sawhill, I.V. (1988) "Poverty in the U.S.: Why is it so Persistent?" *Journal of Economic Literature*, Vol. 26, pp. 1073–1119.

Scanlon, E. (1996) "Homeownership and its Impacts: Implications for Housing Policy For Low-Income Families," Center for Social Development Working Paper No. 96–2, Washington University in Saint Louis.

Schreiner, M. (1999a) "Self-Employment, Microenterprise, and the Poorest Americans," *Social Service Review*, Vol. 73, No. 4, pp. 496–523.

Schreiner, M. (1999b) "Lessons for Microenterprise Programs from a Fresh Look at the Unemployment Insurance Self-employment Demonstration," *Evaluation Review*, Vol. 23, No. 5, pp. 503–526.

Schreiner, M. (2000a) "A Framework for Financial Benefit-Cost Analysis of Individual Development Accounts at the Experimental Site of the American Dream Demonstration," Center for Social Development, Washington University in Saint Louis, http://gwbweb.wustl.edu/csd/Publications/2000/researchdesignschreiner.pdf.

Schreiner, M. (2000b) "Resources Used in 1998 and 1999 to Produce Individual Development Accounts in the Experimental Program of the American Dream Demonstration at the Community Action Project of Tulsa County," Center for Social Development, Washington University in Saint Louis, http://gwbweb.wustl.edu/csd/Publications/2000/researchreportschreiner.pdf.

Schreiner, M. (2002a) "What Do Individual Development Accounts Cost? The First Three Years at CAPTC," Center for Social Development, Washington University in Saint Louis.

Schreiner, M. (2002b) "Data from the American Dream Demonstration Collected by the Management Information System for Individual Development Accounts Through December 31, 2001," Data Documentation, Center for Social Development, Washington University in Saint Louis.

Schreiner, M. (2002c) "Evaluation and Microenterprise Programs," *Journal of Microfinance*, Vol. 4, No. 2, pp. 67–91.

Schreiner, M. (2002d) "Scoring: The Next Breakthrough in Microfinance?" Occasional Paper No. 7, Washington, DC Consultative Group to Assist the Poorest, http://www.cgap.org/html/p-occasional-papers07.html.

Schreiner, M. (2004a) "Program Costs for Individual Development Accounts: Final Figures from CAPTC in Tulsa," Center for Social Development, Washington University in Saint Louis, http://www.microfinance.com/English/Papers/IDA_Costs_98_03.pdf.

Schreiner, M. (2004b) "Support for Microenterprise as Asset-Building: Concepts, Good Practices, and Measurement," Center for Social Development, Washington University in Saint Louis, http://www.microfinance.com/English/Papers/Microenterprise_as_Asset_Building.pdf.

Schreiner, M. (2004c) "Measuring Saving," Center for Social Development, Washington University in Saint Louis, http://www.microfinance.com/English/Papers/Measuring_Saving.pdf.

Schreiner, M. (2004d) "Match Rates, Individual Development Accounts, and Savings by the Poor," Center for Social Development, Washington University in St. Louis, http://www.microfinance.com/English/Papers/Match Rates.pdf..

Schreiner, M.; Sherraden, M.; Clancy, M.; Johnson, L.; Curley, J.; Zhan, M.; Beverly, S.; and Grinstein-Weiss, M. (2005) "Assets and the Poor: Evidence from Individual Development Accounts" pp. 185-215 in M. Sherraden (ed.) *Inclusion in the American Dream: Assets, Poverty, and Public Policy*, New York, NY: Oxford University Press, ISBN 0-19-516819-4.

Schreiner, M.; Matul, M.; Pawlak, E.; and Kline, S. (2004) "The Power of Prizma's Poverty Scorecard: Lessons for Microfinance," Saint Louis, MO: Microfinance Risk Management.

Schreiner, M.; and Sherraden, M. (2005) "Drop-Out from Individual Development Accounts: Prediction and Prevention," *Financial Services Review*, Vol. 14, No. 1, pp. 37-54.

Schreiner, M.; Ng, G.T.; and M. Sherraden. (2003) "Cost-Effectiveness in Social Work Practice: A Framework with Application to Individual Development Accounts," Center for Social Development, Washington University in Saint Louis.

Schreiner, M.; and G. Woller. (2003) "Microenterprise in the First and Third Worlds," *World Development*, Vol. 31, No. 9, pp. 1567–1580.

Schreiner, M.; Clancy, M.; and M. Sherraden. (2002) *Saving Performance in the American Dream Demonstration: Final Report*, Center for Social Development, Washington University in Saint Louis, http://gwbweb.wustl.edu/csd/Publications/2002/ADDreport2002.pdf.

Schreiner, M.; and J. Morduch. (2002) "Opportunities and Challenges for Microfinance in the United States," pp. 19–61 in J. Carr and Z.-Y. Tong (eds.) *Replicating Microfinance in the United States*, Washington, DC: Woodrow Wilson Center Press, ISBN 1–930365–10–1.

Schreiner, M.; Sherraden, M.; Clancy, M.; Johnson, L.; Curley, J.; Grinstein-Weiss, M.; Zhan, M.; and S. Beverly. (2001) *Savings and Asset Accumulation in Individual Development Accounts*, Center for Social Development, Washington University in Saint Louis, http://gwbweb.wustl.edu/csd/Publications/2001/ADDreport2001/index.htm.

Schwartz, S. (2001) "'A Feather in the Scales of Our Difficulties': The Problems and Prospects of IDAs," manuscript, Carleton University.

Seidman, L.S. (2001) "Assets and the Tax Code," pp. 324–356 in T.M. Shapiro and E.N. Wolff (eds.) *Assets and the Poor: The Benefits of Spreading Asset Ownership*, New York, NY: Russell Sage, ISBN 0–87154–949–2.

Sen, A.K. (1999) *Commodities and Capabilities*, Oxford: Oxford University Press, ISBN 0–1956–50–387.

Sen, A.K. (1985) *Commodities and Capabilities*, Amsterdam: North-Holland, ISBN 0–444–877–304

Servon, L.J.; and Bates, T. (1998) "Microenterprise as an Exit Route from Poverty: Recommendations for Programs and Policy Makers," *Journal of Urban Affairs*, Vol. 20, No. 4, pp. 419–441.

Shapiro, T.M; and E.N. Wolff. (2001) *Assets for the Poor: The Benefits of Spreading Asset Ownership*, New York, NY: Russell Sage Foundation, ISBN 0–87154–949–2.

Shefrin, H.M.; and Thaler, R.H. (1988) "The Behavioral Life-Cycle Hypothesis," *Economic Journal*, Vol. 26, pp. 609–643.

Sherraden, M. S.; McBride, A.M.; Hanson, S.; and Johnson, L. (2004) "The Meaning of Savings in Low-Income Households: Evidence from Individual Development Accounts," Center for Social Development, Washington University in Saint Louis.

Sherraden, M. S.; Williams, T; McBride, A.M.; Ssewamala, F. (2003a) "Creating Hope for the Future: Building Assets in Low-Income Households," presented at Society for Social Work and Research Annual Conference, Washington, DC, January 17.

Sherraden, M. S.; Williams, T; McBride, A.M.; Ssewamala, F. (2003b) "Overcoming Poverty: Supported Savings as a Household Development Strategy," Center for Social Development Working Paper No. 04–13, Washington University in Saint Louis, http://gwbweb.wustl.edu/csd/Publications/2004/WP04-13.pdf.

Sherraden, M.S.; Moore, A.; and Hong, P. (2000) "Savers Speak: Case Studies of IDA Participants," presentation at Society for Social Work Research, Charleston, South Carolina, January 31.

Sherraden, M. (1988) "Rethinking Social Welfare: Toward Assets," *Social Policy*, Vol. 18, No. 3, pp. 37–43.

Sherraden, M. (1989) "Poverty and Transaction Costs," manuscript, Washington University in Saint Louis, sherrad@wustl.edu.

Sherraden, M. (1991) *Assets and the Poor: A New American Welfare Policy*. Armonk, NY: M.E. Sharpe, ISBN 0–87332–618–0.

Sherraden, M. (1997) "Social Security in the 21st Century," pp. 121–140 in J. Midgley and M. Sherraden (eds.) *Alternatives to Social Security in the 21st Century: An International Inquiry*, Westport, CT: Auburn House, ISBN 0-865-6924-59.

Sherraden, M. (1999a) "Key Questions in Asset-Building Research, Revised," Center for Social Development, Washington University in Saint Louis.

Sherraden, M. (1999b) "Building Assets among African-American Males," pp. 315–331 in L.E. Davis (ed.), *Working with African-American Males: A Guide to Practice*, Thousand Oaks, CA: Sage, ISBN 0–7619–0471–9.

Sherraden, M. (2000) "On Costs and the Future of Individual Development Accounts," Center for Social Development, Washington University in Saint Louis, http://gwbweb.wustl.edu/csd/Publications/2000/perspectivesherradenoct2000.pdf.

Sherraden, M. (2001a) "Asset-Building Policy and Programs for the Poor," pp. 302–323 in T.M. Shapiro and E.N. Wolff (eds.) *Assets for the Poor: The Benefits of Spreading Asset Ownership*, New York, NY: Russell Sage Foundation, ISBN 0–87154–949–2.

Sherraden, M. (2001b) "Assets and the Poor: Implications for Individual Accounts and Social Security," Testimony to the President's Commission on Social Security, Washington, DC, October 18, http://gwbweb.wustl.edu/csd/Publications/2001/Sherraden_testimony.pdf.

Sherraden, M. (2003). "Individual Accounts in Social Security: Can They Be Progressive?" *International Journal of Social Welfare*, Vol. 12, No. 2, pp. 97–107.

Sherraden, M. (2005) *Inclusion in the American Dream: Assets, Poverty, and Public Policy*, New York, NY: Oxford University Press, ISBN 0-19-516819-4.

Sherraden, M.; and Barr, M.S. (2004) "Institutions and Inclusion in Saving Policy," Building Assets, Building Credit Working Paper No. 04–15, Joint Center for Housing Studies, Harvard University, http://www.jchs.harvard.edu/publications/finance/babc/babc_04-15.pdf.

Sherraden, M; Schreiner, M.; and S. Beverly. (2003) "Income and Saving Performance in Individual Development Accounts," *Economic Development Quarterly*, Vol. 17, No. 1, pp. 95–112.

Sherraden, M.; Johnson, L.; Clancy, M.; Beverly, S.; Schreiner, M.; Zhan, M.; and Curley, J. (2000) *Savings Patterns in IDA programs—Down Payments on the American Dream Policy Demonstration*. Center for Social Development, Washington University in Saint Louis, http://gwbweb.wustl.edu/csd/Publications/2000/ADDreport2000/index.htm.

Sherraden, M.; Page-Adams, D.; Johnson, L.; Scanlon, E.; Curley, J.; Zhan, M.; Bady, F.; and Hinterlong, J. (1999) *Down Payments on the American Dream Policy Demonstration*, Start-Up Evaluation Report, Center for Social Development, Washington University in Saint Louis, http://gwbweb.wustl.edu/csd/Publications/1999/Startup_ADDreport/index.htm.

Sherraden, M.; Page-Adams, D.; Emerson, S.; Beverly, S.; Scanlon, E.; Cheng, L.-C.; Sherraden, M. S.; and Edwards, K. (1995) *IDA Evaluation Handbook: A Practical Guide and Tools for Evaluation of Pioneering IDA Projects*, Center for Social Development, Washington University in Saint Louis, http://gwbweb.wustl.edu/csd/Publications/1995/IDA_Evaluation_Handbook.pdf.

Skinner, J.S. (1997) "Comment," pp. 331–338 in Alan J. Auerbach (ed.) *Fiscal Policy: Lessons from Economic Research*, Cambridge, MA: MIT Press, ISBN 0–262–01160–3.

Slemrod, J. (2003) "Thanatology and Economics: The Behavioral Economics of Death," *American Economic Review*, Vol. 93, No. 2, pp. 371–375.

Smeeding, T.M. (2000) "The EITC and USAs/IDAs: Maybe a Marriage Made in Heaven?" Center for Social Development Working Paper 00–18, Washington University in Saint Louis, http://gwbweb.wustl.edu/csd/Publications/2000/wp00-18.pdf.

Smeeding, T.M.; Phillips, K.R.; and O'Conner, M. (2000) "The EITC: Expectation, Knowledge, Use, and Economic and Social Mobility," *National Tax Journal*, Vol. 53, pp. 1187–1209.

Smith, P. (1979) "Splines as a Useful and Convenient Statistical Tool," *American Statistician*, Vol. 33, No. 2, pp. 57–62.

Smyth, D.J. (1993) "Toward a Theory of Saving," pp. 47–107 in J.H. Gapenski (ed.) *The Economics of Saving*, Boston: Kluwer, ISBN 0–7923–9256–6.

Souleles, N.S. (1999) "The Response of Household Consumption to Income-Tax Refunds," *American Economic Review*, Vol. 89, No. 4, pp. 947–958.

Spalter-Roth, R.M.; Hartmann, H.I.; and Shaw, L.B. (1993) "Exploring the Characteristics of Self-Employment and Part-Time Work among Women," Washington, DC: Institute For Women's Policy Research.

Ssewamala, F.M. (2003) *Savings for Microenterprise in Individual Development Accounts: Factors Related to Performance*, unpublished Ph.D. dissertation, Washington University in Saint Louis.

Ssewamala, F.M.; and Sherraden, M. (2004). "Integrating Savings Into Microenterprise Programs for the Poor: Do Institutions Matter?" Center for Social Development Working Paper No. 04–05, Washington University in Saint Louis, http://gwbweb.wustl.edu/csd/Publications/2004/WP04-05.pdf.

Stoesz, D.; and Saunders, D. (1999) "Welfare Capitalism: A New Approach to Poverty Policy?" *Social Service Review*, Vol. 73, No. 3, pp. 380–400.

Suits, D.B.; Mason, A.; and Chan, L. (1978) "Spline Functions Fitted by Standard Regression Methods," *Review of Economics and Statistics*, Vol. 60, No. 1, pp. 132–139.

Taylor, M. (1999) "Survival of the Fittest? An Analysis of Self-Employment Duration in Britain," *Economic Journal*, Vol. 109, pp. C140–C155.

Thaler, R.H. (1990) "Saving, Fungibility, and Mental Accounts," *Journal of Economic Perspectives*, Vol. 4, No. 1, pp. 193–205.

Thaler, R.H. (1992) "How to Get Real People to Save," pp. 143–159 in M.H. Kosters (ed.) *Personal Saving, Consumption, and Tax Policy*, Washington, DC: American Enterprise Institute, ISBN 0–8447–7015–9.

Thaler, R.H. (1994) "Psychology and Savings Policies," *American Economic Review*, Vol. 84, No. 2, pp. 186–192.

Thaler, R.H. (2000) "From *Homo Economicus* to *Homo Sapiens*," *Journal of Economic Perspectives*, Vol. 14, No. 1, pp. 133–141.

Thaler, R.H.; and Shefrin, H.M. (1981) "An Economic Theory of Self-Control," *Journal of Political Economy*, Vol. 89, No. 2, pp. 392–406.

Thaler, R.H.; and Sunstein, C.R. (2003) "Libertarian Paternalism," *American Economic Review*, Vol. 93, No. 2, pp. 175–179.

VanDerhei, J.; and Copeland, C. (2001) "A Behavioral Model for Predicting Employee Contributions to 401(k) Plans: Preliminary Results," *North American Actuarial Journal*, Vol. 5, No. 1, pp. 80–94.

Varian, H.R. (2004) "Analyzing the Marriage Gap," *New York Times*, July 29, p. C2.

Venti, S.F.; and Wise, D.A. (1986) "Tax-Deferred Accounts, Constrained Choice, and Estimation of Individual Saving," *Review of Economic Studies*, Vol. 53, No. 4, pp. 579–601.

Vonderlack, R.M.; and Schreiner, M. (2002) "Women, Microfinance, and Savings: Lessons and Proposals," *Development in Practice*, Vol. 12, No. 5, pp. 602–612.

Wainer, H. (1976) "Estimating Coefficients in Linear Models: It Don't Make No Nevermind," *Psychological Bulletin*, Vol. 83, pp. 213–217.

Wayne, L. (1999) "U.S.A. Accounts Are New Volley in Retirement Savings Debate," *New York Times*, Jan. 24, p. 4.

Williams, T.R. (2003) "Asset-Building Policy as a Response to Wealth Inequality: Drawing Implications from the Homestead Act," *Social Development Issues*, Vol. 25, No. 1–2, pp. 47–58.

Wolff, E.N. (2004) "Changes in Household Wealth in the 1980s and 1990s in the United States," Levy Economics Institute Working Paper No. 407, http://www.levy.org/2/bin/datastore/pubs/files/wp/407.pdf.

Wolff, E.N. (1998) "Recent Trends in the Size Distribution of Household Wealth," *Journal of Economic Perspectives*, Vol. 12, No. 3, pp. 131–150.

Woo, L.G.; Schweke, F.W.; and Buchholz, D.E. (2004) "Hidden in Plan Sight: A Look at the $335 Billion Federal Asset-Building Budget," Washington, DC: Corporation for Enterprise Development, http://content.knowledgeplex.org/kp2/cache/kp/24095.pdf.

Yinger, J. (1998) "Evidence on Discrimination in Consumer Markets," *Journal of Economic Perspectives*, Vol. 12, No. 2, pp. 23–40.

Yinger, J. (1986) "Measuring Racial Discrimination with Fair Housing Audits: Caught in the Act," *American Economic Review*, Vol. 76, pp. 881–893.

Zhan, M. (2003) "Savings Outcomes of Single Mothers in Individual Development Accounts," *Social Development Issues*, Vol. 25, Nos. 1–2, pp. 74–88.

Zhan, M.; Sherraden, M.; and Schreiner, M. (2004) "Welfare Recipiency and Savings Outcomes in Individual Development Accounts," *Social Work Research*, Vol. 28, No. 3, pp. 165-181.

Zhan, M.; and Schreiner, M. (2004) "Saving for Post-Secondary Education in Individual Development Accounts," Center for Social Development Working Paper No. 01–11, Wasington University in Saint Louis, http://gwbweb.wustl.edu/csd/Publications/2004/WP04-11.pdf.

Ziliak, J.P. (2003) "Income Transfers and Assets of the Poor," *Review of Economics and Statistics*, Vol. 85, No. 1, pp. 63–76.

Index